ON THE COVER
Autumn Leaves by Martin Storey
Photographer Gisella Torres
Stylist Emma Freemantle
Hair & Make-up Jeni Dodson
Model Alexsandra
Editor in Chief Kate Buller
Deputy Editor Marie Wallin
Magazine Coordinator Sarah Hatton
Publication Manager Lee Wills
Design Layout Simon Wagstaff

With special thanks to the following handknitters:
Joan Pavey, Barbara Wiltshire, Violet Ellis, Elsie Eland, Teresa
Gogay, Judith Chamberlain, Joan Broadbent, Arna Ronan,
Janet Oakey, Pat Garden, Janet Mann, Glennis Garnett, Maisie
Laing, Yvonne Rawlinson, Susan Grimes, Patricia Odea,
Yvonne Morgan, Carol Bayliss, Audrey Kidd, Wendy
Shipman, Ann Newton, Betty Lumley, Ann Banks, Irene
Vickers, Betty Falconer, Joyce Coop, Mrs Pickering, Andrea
Mc Hugh, Joyce Limon, Elaine Hart, Jenny Cooper, Clare Landi, Angela Lomax, Joyce Sledmore, Ella
Taylor, Mrs Wilmott, Helen Dawson, Joyce Buzza, Susan Cresswell, Jean Mitchel, Elizabeth Jones, Margaret
Goddard, Jean Fletcher, Paula Dukes, Marie Donachy, Wendy Stevens, Sandra Richardson, Diane Messenger
and Jenny Shore.

First published in Great Britain in 2006 by Rowan Yarns Ltd, Green Lane Mill, Holmfirth, West Yorkshire,
England, HD9 2DX E-mail: mag40@knitrowan.com
British Library Cataloguing in Publication Data
Rowan Yarns. Rowan Knitting & Crochet Magazine Number 40 ISSN 1365 5264
Copyright Rowan 2006 Printed in Singapore

REGULAR FEATURES

Dear Knitter

Welcome to Rowan Magazine 40 which is packed with patterns and new features. This season has come round so quickly, it seems only yesterday we were planning our yarns and colours for autumn 2006, but it was nearly 18 months ago. Find out all the steps we go through, from selecting the yarn to our photo shoots, to bring you our latest collection in our feature, **Design Diary**.

EDITOR'S LETTER

For Autumn Winter 2006 we have 3 different collections for you inspired by an eclectic mix of simplicity, adornment, nature and fantasy; **Fade To Grey** uses delicate blends of black and grey tones in the stunningly stark surroundings of Dungeness in Kent; **Kindred Spirit** takes the colour and texture of the countryside in the Autumn as its main inspiration and the combination of rural tones and folk design creates a story with a magical, handcrafted feel; and finally **Legend,** which is a wonderful and theatrical story with lots of adornment dramatically photographed at Birtsmorten Court in Worcestershire. Crochet has become such an important look that we show you the simple crochet techniques needed to complete some of the designs in the magazine.

We have introduced 2 new and exciting yarns this season which are a joy to knit and create some ravishing effects; **Tapestry** is a self striping Wool and Soya Bean blend which has a wonderful sheen and drape; and **Romance**, a light and airy chunky yarn with a subtle sparkle.

In **The New Generation** we introduce you to an inspirational group of new designers who will delight you with their specially commissioned collection of accessories from hats to muffs and braces to socks. Rowan is proud to support such exciting emerging talents who are clearly going to go far.

Marie Wallin is Rowan's Senior Designer and she gives you an insight into what makes her tick and **Sabrina Gschwandter** has her finger on the pulse of the latest American trends which she shares with us.

Finally in this issue you will notice that we have altered our sizing to bring the Rowan size chart in line with the High Street template. We have the full size charts explained for you, complete with measuring instructions so you can be sure your Rowan garment will fit you beautifully.

At Rowan we have worked very hard to bring you a magazine with something for everyone and we all wish you a happy season of knitting.

Kate Buller
Editor in Chief, Rowan Knitting & Crochet Magazine

PS I would love to see your feedback or any pictures of garments that you have knitted from this magazine so please do feel free to email me. editors@knitrowan.com

FADE TO
GREY

ANYA
in Kid Classic,
Kidsilk Haze
& Kidsilk Night
by Marie Wallin
pattern page 160.

8

This page
VIKTOR
in Tapestry & Kid Classic,
by Marie Wallin,
pattern page 166.
Opposite
SORREL
in Tapestry,
by Sarah Hatton,
pattern page 122.

This page
NAKITA
in Kidsilk Haze
by Marie Wallin,
pattern page 120.
Opposite
OLGA
in Kid Classic, Kidsilk Night,
Kidsilk Haze & Lurex Shimmer
by Antoni & Alison,
pattern page 118.

This page
ANNA SOCKS
in 4 Ply Soft, by Nina Chakkour,
pattern page 119.
Opposite
CELTIC in Felted Tweed & Kid Classic
by Martin Storey, pattern page 152.

This page
SADIE
in Wool Cotton,
by Sarah Hatton,
pattern page 170.
Opposite
RUFFLE SCARF
in Kid Classic,
by Nikki Ryan,
pattern page 151.

This page
ANYA
in Kid Classic,
Kidsilk Haze
& Kidsilk Night
by Marie Wallin
pattern page 160.
Opposite
SERGE
in Tapestry,
by Sarah Hatton,
pattern page 112.

19

This page
WRAPAROUND
in 4 Ply Soft
by Sarah Dallas,
pattern page 103.
Opposite
GRANTIS SCARF
in Kidsilk Night, Kid Classic
& Lurex Shimmer
by Julia Neill,
pattern page 111.

This page
SASHA
in Big Wool
& Big Wool Fusion
by Marie Wallin,
pattern page 150.
Opposite
KAY
in Big Wool
& Kidsilk Spray,
by Leah Sutton,
pattern page 157.

Photographer: Chris Bracewell
Stylist: Louise Sykes
Hair & Makeup: Jonathon Malone
Models: Jenny Richards, Ruben Quesada
Many thanks to Nougat & Toast for clothing
Shot on location in Dungeness, Kent
Location van by JJ Locations

Clothing, Sculpture, Graffiti or Gift:
THE POSSIBILITIES OF KNITTING

By Sabrina Gschwandtner

Work by Dave Cole

I started knitting to stop thinking. It began as a way to make things without over-deliberating their artistic value or semiotic meaning, which is what I did during most of my college classes. Back then, I would knit quietly for as long as I could before I had to turn on my computer to write a paper. When I wore knit vests and sweaters to the film class for which I was a teaching assistant, a couple of students asked me to make them clothes. I started selling hats, scarves, and mittens first to my students, then to boutiques in New York City like TG-170, Steven Alan, and Bird, and finally to large department stores like Henri Bendel.

During the years after college that I focused on making clothing, I wondered if handcraft could accommodate my training and continued passion for making fine art. As this question became a dilemma, I came to see work made by friends who were using knitting in their fine art projects. These were people who had come to knitting, like me, from other pursuits. Riding my bike home from a park one day in the fall of 2002, I thought, *I'm going to interview Jim Drain and Jamie Peterson, and make a 'zine about handcraft and conceptual art.* As I was riding, pushing down on each pedal, I thought, *"knit," "knit," "knit," "knit."* "KnitKnit" became the name for my 'zine, my art project, and my way out of having to choose either knitting or fine art. KnitKnit continues to express my interest in the ways in which handcraft can express the unconventional, the philosophical, the obsessive, the political, the inventive, and the extreme. Published bi-annually for three years, KnitKnit has showcased people who have knit the unpredictable.

Since the time I started KnitKnit, knitting has so permeated US culture that I no longer feel a minority in my welcoming of the knitted extreme. A very popular recent exhibition at the Massachusetts Museum of Contemporary Art featured a performance by sculptor Dave Cole, known for creating complicated knit pieces using unusual materials like fiberglass, lead, and steel. For the Mass MoCA show, Cole used two John Deere construction vehicles to knit a gigantic American flag of acrylic felt, using twenty-five foot poles as needles. "I always want to see what's possible," Cole has stated, "and I haven't found impossible yet."

During the recent launch event for KnitKnit issue #6 at the New Museum of Contemporary Art in New York, Laure Drogoul's "Orchestral Apparatus for Knitting" caused a commotion. Drogoul attached contact microphones to pairs of knitting needles and ran the amplified sound of knitting through a mixing board, adding effects to different sets of needles. The sound was alternately clunky, ethereal, noisy, and calming. The audience was captivated by both what they heard and the way her apparatus looked, and they stood in lines to try out her musical needles.

Further evidence that Americans have embraced the art of extreme knitting is the lauded work of "Knitta," graffiti knitter Moms in Texas who tag trees, lampposts, and car antennas with knitted cozies at nighttime before returning home to put their kids into bed.

Not just something Americans appreciate in its extreme forms, knitting is also a response to disaster. Altruistic knit projects have sprung up in the wake of hurricane Katrina, in response to widespread psychological and socioeconomic anxiety. "Knit for Katrina," a project started by a woman from upstate New York, collects donated knit and crochet squares to make blankets for children displaced by the 2005 hurricane. "Squares for Survivors," a similar project run by a longtime resident of central Louisiana, received over 2,000 squares in just three months. People have embraced knitting as one way to help restore a sense of their own—and someone else's—security.

Capable of producing clothing, sculpture, graffiti or gift, knitting is a resilient and mobile medium. You can take your knitting needles anywhere (they're even welcome on airplanes again), and you can do anything with them. As knitting continues to move out of the home and into the public, we'll see more examples of it in its extreme; people trying the impossible.

Graffiti knitting by Moms

Dave Cole crew

Knit Knit covers

marie wallin

Marie Wallin is Senior Designer and part of Rowan's in-house team, responsible for such beautiful designs as 'Nakita' and 'Sasha' in **Fade To Grey**, 'Glade' and 'Furrow' in **Kindred Spirit** and 'Arwen' and 'Mystic' in **Legend**. But she nearly didn't make it into design. Her brother is a scientist of global renown and Marie herself studied Science at A-level. After switching degree courses at the last minute and opting for a degree in textiles from DeMontfort University, Marie then went on to design commercial knitwear for all the major high street chains and even run her own business designing and manufacturing handknits, mainly for Japan and the US. Marie is a prolific and highly creative designer, and in this article we find out what makes her tick, what inspires her and what really goes on behind that calm and professional exterior?

Who do you most admire?
From the world of design it would have to be Paul Smith but also from the world of science, Watson and Crick, who first discovered DNA and my brother Phil Mullineaux who is a Professor of Plant Genetics.

Knitting or crochet?
My mum taught me to knit when I was about 6 or 7 and I taught myself to crochet later. I really like both but I would probably say crochet. I find it more fluid and more relaxing.

Where would you most like to live?
I love rugged landscapes such as Swaledale in the Yorkshire Dales, but I also would like to live by the sea.

What is your favourite place on earth?
There is an elephant orphanage at Pinnawela in Sri Lanka where the elephants are allowed to live as naturally as possible as a herd. Going there is a very moving experience.

What is your favourite Rowan Yarn?
That's really hard. I like Felted Tweed because it is classic Rowan and Tapestry because of its subtle blend of colours and the fantastic handle.

What is your favourite film?
The Matrix

And film star?
Johnny Depp

Which was the last film that made you cry?
I tend to avoid soppy movies because I know I will cry. Forrest Gump gets me every time!

What's your favourite smell?
Fresh ginger and basil

Is there a phrase that inspires you?
'It is better to have loved and lost than never to have loved at all.' I think you can apply this to so many things.

Who is the greatest influence in your life?
Without a doubt my husband – we do everything together.

If you hadn't been a designer what would you be?
Before I joined Rowan I was thinking about retraining as a gardener. To work in horticulture at a National Trust property must be amazing.

Handbags or shoes?
Shoes

What's the most unusual thing you've eaten?
The worm at the bottom of a Tequila bottle – yuk!

What's the most romantic thing you've done?
My honeymoon in Florence was magical.

Which is your favourite design in this magazine?
That's really hard but I think I would have to choose Antoni & Alison's 'Olga' and Martin Storey's 'Celtic', both in **Fade To Grey**.

In a fire what would you save?
My dogs and cat.

THE NEW GENERATION

Words by Juliet Bernard.

For almost 30 years Rowan has been encouraging young handknit designers throughout the UK, supporting them with yarn for their final collections, giving them the opportunity to contribute to Rowan's magazine and even commissioning books from them through Rowan's publishing arm. All of this means that each season you are offered versatile and vibrant patterns to complement the high quality of our established designers.

This season the design team in the Rowan Studio are delighted to be able to show case some of this talent as we introduce 5 new Rowan designers to you, each of whom was briefed to create exciting new accessories to fit into the 3 collections for Autumn Winter 2006. The patterns that were submitted were as varied as the designers themselves; from 4ply to chunky; from lace knits to felting. We give you the class of 06

Below:
Bronwen with Organic Bag

Bronwen Harlow is a full time student in Textile Design at Bradford University. A mother of two teenagers, Bronwen decided on a complete career change three years ago – she once worked as a buyer for Harrods. "I had never really thought about studying fashion as an option but with the encouragement of my tutor I started my degree course," Bronwen explains. When it came to work placements, she was very clear that there was only one place she wanted to work - at Rowan. "I was absolutely terrified when I turned up at the mill but I was soon made to feel welcome." During her first week Bronwen was encouraged to experiment with felting before she was given the New Designers brief. Her beautiful bag, called Organic, uses new yarn, Tapestry, which has been felted and adorned with felted crocheted chains and balls in Kid Classic. The combination is very striking.

In June 2005 **Gabrielle Carter** graduated from Kingston University having gained a degree in Fashion specialising in knitting and she now freelances. "Knitting is an extremely versatile medium," she enthuses. "I feel I am in control and can translate what's in my head to what my hands are doing." Gabrielle's fascination with cut and construction together with her love of geometry have translated into some unusual yet very wearable items including arm warmers, a cape, braces, a cable hat and fingerless mittens. Gabrielle's designs featured are the lovely 'St Brides Bay Cape' in Felted Tweed and Wool Cotton, the fun 'Marloes Sand Hat' in Ribbon Twist and 'Skomer Island Armwarmers' in Felted Tweed, Kid Classic and Wool Cotton, the original 'Murmansk Braces' and 'Ana Fingerless Mittens', both in Kid Classic and Wool Cotton.

*Gabrielle wearing
St. Brides Bay Cape,
Marloes Sand Hat,
Skomer Island Armwarmers,
Murmansk Braces
& Ana Fingerless Mittens.*

> Gabrielle's fascination with cut and construction together with her love of geometry have translated into some unusual yet very wearable items...

Julia Neill is studying for an MA at the Royal College of Art having graduated in 2005 from Brighton University. While at Brighton Julia gained an amazing amount of experience on a work placement with John Rocha, designing his knitwear collection. She worked very closely with John himself and her time there left a great impression on her and the way she designs. "He encouraged me to be instinctive and not to follow a set thought. I would just start knitting and let my ideas develop organically," she says. Julia believes that accessories can be frivolous and fun, "I prefer to crochet to achieve this because it can be more instant and dynamic than knitting.

Rowan chose two amazing accessories from Julia; 'Grantis' a scarf woven from crocheted strips, embellished with cascades of floral droplets in Kidsilk Night, Kid Classic and Lurex Shimmer and 'Bella Rose' a high waisted corset in Scottish Tweed 4 Ply and Felted Tweed.

Julia wearing her Bella Rose Corset
and Below left Grantis Scarf.

"He encouraged me to
be instinctive and not to
follow a set thought.

31

Nikki Ryan's freelance career has kicked off to a flying start since graduating from Brighton. She sells her swatches extensively and has already contributed designs to Knitting magazine – she won their student award last year. "I was thrilled to win the award from Knitting and it has led to more and more contacts," she explains. Although her work is varied Nikki feels her signature is one of tactile cosiness. 'Proper winter woolly snugness' as she describes it.

Rowan is showcasing a purple muffler 'Cozy Muffler' in Big Wool and Kid Classic, 'Square Wrap' a gorgeous wrap in Big Wool and Ribbon Twist and also 'Ruffle Scarf' a lovely piece from Nikki in Kid Classic.

Nikki wearing Square Wrap,
Ruffle Scarf & Cozy Muffler.

Although her work is varied
Nikki feels her signature is one
of tactile cosiness.

For our interview and photo shoot **Nina Chakkour** flew in from Max Mara in Italy via Sweden. Having completed an MA at the Royal College of Art, she is now knitwear designer for Max & Co, Max Mara's diffusion range. Nina learned to knit when she was young: "My mum always knitted and I remember learning when I was at Kindergarten in Sweden. Knitting as a tradition is an important inspiration to me". It is a fascination with the sense of history you get from knitting and the passing on of skills that is keenly reflected in Nina's accessories – 2 pairs of beautiful vintage long socks called Anna in 4 ply soft.

Nina wearing Anna Socks.

"My mum always knitted and I remember learning when I was at Kindergarten in Sweden."

Feature Photography: Gisella Torres
Stylist: Emma Freemantle
Hair & Makeup: Jenni Dodson
Shot on location at Portland Place, London.

KINDRED SPIRIT

ROAM
in Big Wool, by Sarah Hatton,
pattern page 110
& ANA FINGERLESS MITTENS
in Kid Classic & Wool Cotton,
by Gabrielle Carter, pattern page 115.

This page
DOTTY in Felted Tweed & Tapestry,
by Kaffe Fassett, pattern page 134
& RUSTIC
in 4 Ply Soft & Scottish Tweed 4 Ply,
by Jenny Atkinson, pattern page 130.
Opposite
DOTTY

This page
ORGANIC BAG in Tapestry & Kid Classic,
by Bronwen Harlowe, pattern page 134.
Opposite
JUNO in Wool Cotton,
by Amanda Crawford, pattern page 145.

This page & opposite
GLADE
in Tapestry & Kidsilk Haze,
by Marie Wallin, pattern page 106.

This page & opposite
ST BRIDES BAY CAPE
in Felted Tweed & Wool Cotton,
by Gabrielle Carter, pattern page 116.

This page
FURROW in Tapestry, Wool Cotton & Kid Classic,
by Marie Wallin, pattern page 128.
Opposite
HICKORY in Felted Tweed,
by Marie Wallin, pattern page 174.

This page & opposite
LICHEN in Kid Classic,
by Lisa Richardson, pattern page 104.
& MARLOES SAND HAT in Ribbon Twist,
by Gabrielle Carter, pattern page 123.
Opposite
FURROW in Tapestry, Wool Cotton & Kid Classic,
by Marie Wallin, pattern page 128.

This page
SHADED FLOWER in Felted Tweed,
by Kaffe Fassett, pattern page 136.
Opposite
PAMPAS in Big Wool,
by Marie Wallin, pattern page 132.

ROAM
in Big Wool, by Sarah Hatton,
pattern page 110
& ANA FINGERLESS MITTENS
in Kid Classic & Wool Cotton,
by Gabrielle Carter, pattern page 115.

This page
Autumn Leaves in Felted Tweed, Kid Classic, 4 Ply Soft
& Lurex Shimmer, by Martin Storey, pattern page 163.
Opposite
Marloes Sand Hat in Ribbon Twist by Gabrielle Carter,
pattern page 123
& Square Wrap
in Big Wool & Ribbon Twist, by Nikki Ryan, pattern page 127.

LORELEI
in Felted Tweed & Wool Cotton,
by Amanda Crawford,
pattern page 138.

Photographer: Gisella Torres
Stylist: Emma Freemantle
Hair & Makeup: Jonathon Malone, Jeni Dodson
Models: Alexsandra, Aaron
Shot on location at Birtmorton Court, Worcestershire

It's a reaction we all recognise. You scan a fashion spread in a magazine of a gorgeous girl with endless legs wearing great clothes and think "Well, that looks marvellous – but maybe not for me".

It's usually a case of the clothes appearing to be destined only to be worn by the under 25's. Occasionally it may be the other way round where a twenty something might think "a bit too classic for me".

I COULD WEAR THAT

Words by Kathryn Samuel

Flicking through a magazine and imagining how you yourself, whatever your age, might look wearing a key piece is never easy. And when that magazine spread is showing knitting pattern ideas, the leap of faith has to be even greater – after all you can't go to a shop and try it on first. Plus it will involve you in hours of work and financial outlay on yarn, so you want to be pretty sure that you're actually going to like and wear the results of your efforts.

The Rowan team love to produce inspirational sweater designs, and the cutting edge pictures of their work that appear in the magazines. But they also listen – and they have heard, loud and clear that in their quest for original chic design some of you feel nervous about attempting some of the newer styles.

And so this story was born.

Introducing from left to right:
Lily Stevens representing the **40's,**
Hayley Smith representing the **20's**
and **Maureen Freemantle** representing the **60's.**

Top to Bottom
Lily wears Juno,
Maureen wears wraparound and
Hayley wears Pampas,
Maureen wearing Sorrel.

Opposite (from left to right)
Lily Stevens wears Sorrel,
Hayley Smith wears Wraparound
& Maureen Freemantle wears Mystic.

Top to Bottom
Hayley wears Juno,
Lily wears Wraparound & Maureen wears Eva
& Maureen wears Pampas.

Opposite
Maureen wears Eva.

THE PLAN

TAKE six sweaters which appear in various stories in the new magazine and show just how different age groups might wear them.

Choose some of the more challenging styles – don't play it safe with obvious classics. Show them worn for day and night-time situations both the relaxed and the slightly more formal.

Use real women as models – all beautiful, certainly, but with busy demanding lives and their own distinctive style.

ACTION

The team scoured their address books for friends and relations who fitted the bill and the cast for this exercise was finalised.

In the 60's corner is Maureen Freemantle. She recently retired from a busy and successful career as a film and theatre make-up artist working on jobs as disparate as Worzel Gummidge to Chariots of Fire. She's done the easy jobs, making the beautiful look even more so but also the tricky, gory jobs of blood, guts and scars. Her daughter, Emma Freemantle, was the stylist on these photographs, which could have been tricky, but this mother and daughter have a mutual respect. Maureen is adventurous and stylish and Emma is caring and creative – what better combination?

Representing the 40 plus generation is Lily Stevens. She's had a jack-of-all trades career which has covered production, advertising and also children's theatre. This eventually led her to a new career teaching Pilates, and she is a shining example of the benefits of the regime. She exudes a brilliant, healthy bloom and has a confident almost balletic grace. "I've never been as confident about clothes as I have been in my 40's," she says "I use them to get me in the mood, to have fun in whatever I happen to be doing."

Last but not least, there is Hayley Smith, who has just hit her twenties and hopes to have her first R&B/soul album out before the end of this year. "I love dressing-up – but sometimes I'm not as adventurous as I'd like to be. It has been fun trying out new things and putting together unexpected combinations for this project."

Top to Bottom
Hayley wears Eva,
Hayley wears Sorrel with Maureen wearing Juno,
Maureen wears mystic and Lily wears Sorrel.

Opposite
Lily wears Pampas.

Top to Bottom
Lily wears Mystic,
Maureen wears Eva with Hayley wearing mystic
& Maureen wears Wraparound.

Opposite
Hayley wears Juno with Maureen wearing Pampas.

Photographer: Gisella Torres
Stylist: Emma Freemantle
Hair & Makeup: Jeni Dodson

CONCLUSION

If there was any link between the three candidates it was that, regardless of age, they all have an enthusiasm to embrace the new; to try something out even if it wasn't immediately the sort of sweater they would ear-mark as just their kind of look.

If you track through the pictures, you can see the different visions of how each sweater can be worn, and we hope you will also feel inspired to perhaps attempt something beyond the safe. As you can see from these photographs, one sweater will work with a pair of jeans or a more formal skirt or even in some instances over a very fluid dress.

There are no rules in fashion today. You can wear cashmere with chiffon or silk with denim. It is all there to be experimented with.

Be brave!

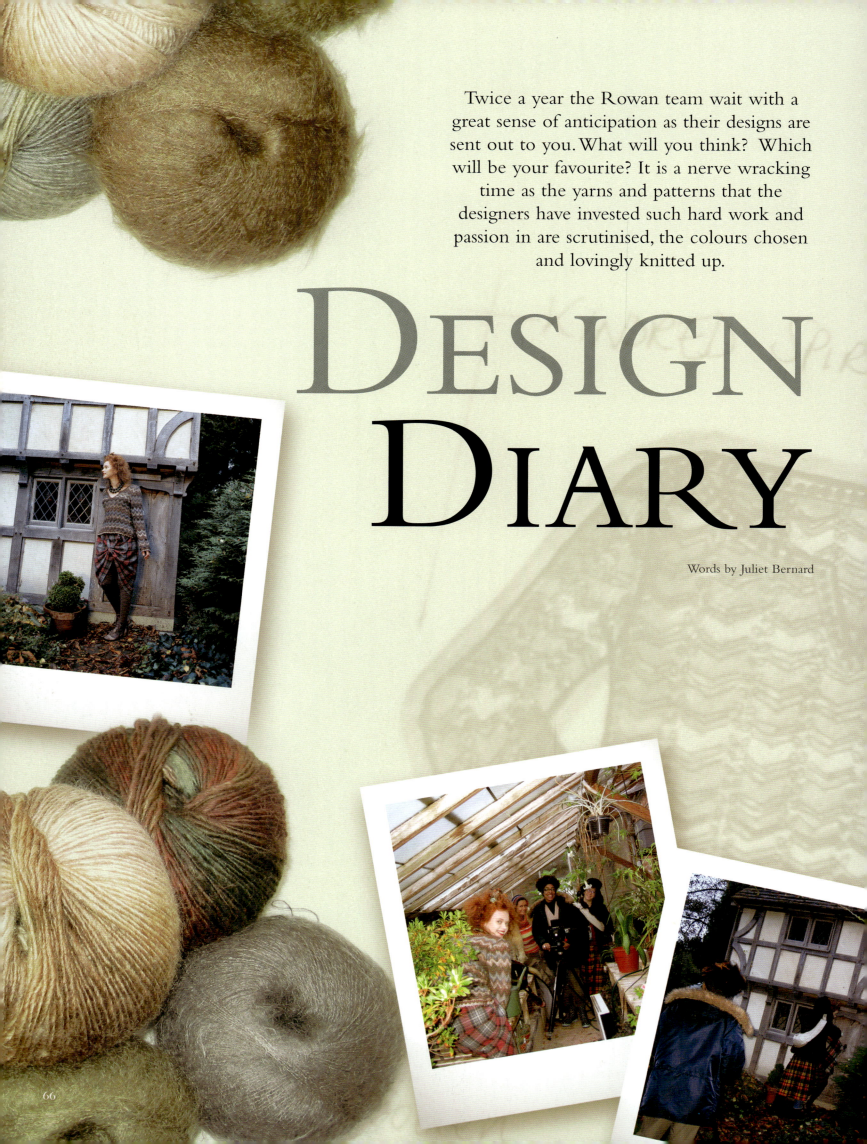

Twice a year the Rowan team wait with a great sense of anticipation as their designs are sent out to you. What will you think? Which will be your favourite? It is a nerve wracking time as the yarns and patterns that the designers have invested such hard work and passion in are scrutinised, the colours chosen and lovingly knitted up.

DESIGN
DIARY

Words by Juliet Bernard

There is a huge amount of work that goes into each and every magazine and brochure from Rowan. The team calls on nearly 30 years of experience and there are a myriad of steps along the way. Magazine 40 showcases the Autumn Winter 2006 collection but the work actually started up at the Rowan mill in Holmfirth way back in May 2005.

May 2005, Rowan works very closely with its suppliers sourcing yarns from all over the world and their spinners develop new yarn samples for the team to look at well over a year in advance. By looking at global yarn trends from prediction companies, the Rowan team are able to pinpoint the key new yarns that want to add to the collection. These are the yarns they believe you will enjoy knitting the most. This season there are 4 new yarns Romance, Country, Tapestry and Little Big Wool.

Rowan selects new yarns based on several key points. All yarns must have great ball appeal, a soft handle, good knitability and wash and wear well. The yarns must perform to all these criteria before they become a part of the Rowan yarn range.

As soon as the new yarns are chosen to go with the existing Rowan range, it is time to decide on the colours and the moods for the entire collection. The Rowan design team draw on their wealth of experience as well as trend information and images from the catwalks of London, Paris, Milan and New York to interpret the key looks shapes and colours that will keep Rowan patterns and Magazine at the forefront of hand knitting.

July 2005 was a very intense time in the Holmfirth Studio as the mood boards began to take shape into 3 distinct stories Legend, Kindred Spirit and Fade to Grey.

By August Rowan was briefing its creative bank of designers from classic and well-known names, to emerging new talents – nearly 20 in all including 3 in-house. Each received an inspiration pack containing samples of the new yarns and mood boards for winter 2006, just about the time the 2005 collection was launching in the stores.

While Rowan waits for the range to be designed, there is no time to sit back and relax. Photo shoots will begin in November so locations need to be found and the photographers and stylists briefed.

At the end of September 2005 each designer has submitted their interpretations and designs complete with knitted swatches. That's a total of nearly 80 designs that Rowan needs to edit down to under 50 which is an enormous task. The designs not only need to convey the story they are designed for, use the key shapes and textures but must also fit together as a collection and convey that unique quality that is Rowan. That's quite some jigsaw puzzle. The design you see here, Glade by Rowan's own Marie Wallin was chosen to fit into the Kindred Spirit story because it has a country feel to it in its use of colour with a magical twist in the way the new yarn Tapestry has been used together with perennial favourite Kid Silk Haze. The use of a chevron stitch gives a look inspired by Missoni and the body skimming shape is very flattering to wear.

After 5 months in development the final collection was selected. The pattern for each design was then written and by the end of October the samples are being knitted by Rowan's team of dedicated knitters. . By November Rowan are well into their photo shoots. Even this article is being written 7 months before you will read it.

From start to finish, from choosing new yarns to the finished garment you see here takes an intricate blend of experience, organisation, and inspiration so that Rowan can deliver another design packed magazine to you.

lace stripe

KINDRED SPIRIT...

shell lace stripe

wooden beading

GLADE

67

LEGEND

ROSA
in Kidsilk Haze,
by Lois Daykin,
pattern page 125.

This page
EVA in Kid Classic
by Amanda Crawford, pattern page 107.
Opposite
COBWEB in Kidsilk Night & Lurex Shimmer,
by Marie Wallin, pattern page 158.

AELF
in Kid Classic
by Leah Sutton,
pattern page 140.

This page
DEW in Wool Cotton,
by Amanda Crawford,
pattern page 168.
Opposite
EVELEEN in 4 Ply Soft, Kidsilk Haze
& Lurex Shimmer, by Lois Daykin,
pattern page 148.

BELLA ROSE CORSET
in Felted Tweed & Scottish 4 Ply,
by Julia Neill,
pattern page 109.

This page
ROSA in Kidsilk Haze,
by Lois Daykin, pattern page 125.
Opposite
PARKER in Tapestry,
by Sarah Hatton, pattern page 113.

This page
MYSTIC
in Romance,
by Marie Wallin,
pattern page 176.
Opposite
TITANIA
in Romance,
Kid Classic,
Kidsilk Haze
& Lurex Shimmer,
by Marie Wallin,
pattern page 141.

This page
TINTAGEL in Romance,
Kidsilk Haze & Soft Baby,
by Sarah Hatton, pattern page 144.
Opposite
WONDER in Romance,
by Marie Wallin, pattern page 126.

ARWEN BALL GOWN
in Kidsilk Night & Kidsilk Haze,
by Marie Wallin, pattern page 172.

This page
PAISLEY
in Kid Classic,
by Martin Storey,
pattern page 154.

Opposite
ARWEN
in Kidsilk Night
& Kidsilk Haze,
by Marie Wallin,
pattern page 172
& COZY MUFFLER
in Big Wool
& Kid Classic,
by Nikki Ryan,
pattern page 147.

ARWEN BALL GOWN
in Kidsilk Night & Kidsilk Haze,
by Marie Wallin, pattern page 172
& COZY MUFFLER
in Big Wool & Kid Classic,
by Nikki Ryan, pattern page 147.

Photographer: Gisella Torres
Stylist: Emma Freemantle
Hair & Makeup: Jeni Dodson
Model: Miriam
Shot on location
at Birtsmorton Court, Worcestershire

89

SIMPLY CROCHET

Crochet is once again set to create a big impact in fashion with heavily crochet tops and dresses, strongly predicted for Spring Summer 2007 and Autumn Winter 2007/2008. You will have noticed that the trend for crochet has been building slowly over last few seasons, and this Autumn Winter you will see more garments embellished with crochet trims.

To highlight this growing trend, we have included in the collections six designs which have crochet edgings; 'Nakita' in **Fade To Grey,** 'Glade' and 'Pampas' in **Kindred Spirit** and 'Arwen', 'Titania' and 'Cobweb' in **Legend.** We also have 'Hickory' in **Kindred Spirit**, which is a beautiful multi coloured crochet belted cardigan and five crochet accessories; 'Cozy Muffler', 'Ruffle Scarf', 'Square wrap', 'Grantis' and the very feminine 'Bella Rose' corset.

SIMPLY CROCHET

Although the crochet effects used within these designs may seem daunting to the beginner, they are actually very simple and use the very basic crochet stitches.

We hope this article will explain the basic stitches needed to complete the designs within the magazine, and encourage everyone to pick up a crochet hook and 'have a go'. You will be surprised how easy it is and once you have mastered the basics, you can then go onto create some beautiful effects.

MAKING A CHAIN STITCH (CH) AND FOUNDATION CHAIN.

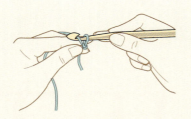
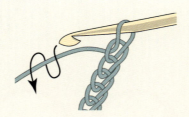
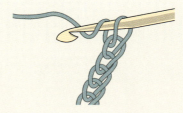

1. All crochet is started by making a slip knot in exactly the same way as you would begin knitting. Slip this knot onto the crochet hook and you're ready to make your first foundation chain. As when knitting, this slip knot is your first stitch.

2. Hold the crochet hook in your right hand and grip the base of the slip knot between

the thumb and first finger of the left hand. Wind the ball end of the yarn (working) around the fingers of your left hand to control the tension – exactly as you would when knitting but on the other hand. To make the first **chain**, twist the hook back and under the working strand of yarn so that it loops around the hook. Pull this new loop of yarn through the loop already on

the hook and you have made another chain.

3. Continue in this way, drawing new loops of yarn through the loop on the hook, until you have made the required number of chains.

MAKING A SLIP STITCH (SS).

1. A **slip stitch** is the very shortest and easiest of the basic stitches. To work a slip stitch, insert the hook into the work and take the yarn over the hook in the same

way as if you were going to make a chain stitch. Pull this new loop of yarn through both the work and the loop on the hook – this completes the slip stitch.

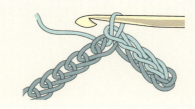

MAKING A DOUBLE CROCHET (DC) AMERICAN SINGLE CROCHET (SC)

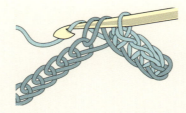
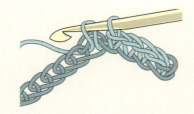

1. The next tallest stitch, the **double crochet** is one of the two most commonly used crochet stitches. This is worked in a similar way to a slip stitch. Start by inserting the hook into the work, and taking the yarn over the hook.

2. Draw this new loop through just the work, leaving two loops on the hook.

3. Take the yarn over the hook again. Draw this new loop through both the loops on the hook thereby completing the double crochet stitch.

MAKING A TREBLE (TR) AMERICAN DOUBLE CROCHET (DC)

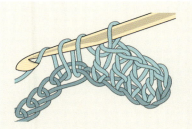   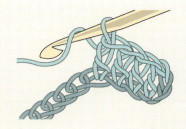

1. The other most commonly used crochet stitch is the **treble**. To make a treble start by taking the yarn over the hook BEFORE inserting into the work.

2. Then insert the hook into the work, take

the yarn over the hook again and draw this new loop through. There are now three loops on the hook.

3. Take the yarn over the hook and draw this new loop through the first two loops only

on the hook. There are now two loops on the hook.

4. Take the yarn over the hook, and draw this through the remaining two loops on the hook to complete the treble stitch.

MAKING A DOUBLE TREBLE (DTR) AMERICAN TREBLE (TR)

1. The taller **double treble** is worked as for the treble, except that the yarn is wrapped around the hook twice before it is inserted into the work. To begin take the yarn twice round the hook. Insert the hook into the work, take the yarn over the hook and draw through the work. There are now four loops on the hook. Take the yarn over

the hook and draw through the first two loops only on the hook. There are now three loops on the hook. Continue taking the yarn over the hook and drawing through two loops at a time until just one loop remains. The double treble is now complete.

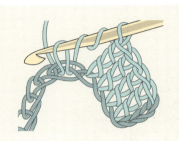

WORKING IN ROUNDS.

1. To start a piece of circular crochet, begin by making the foundation chain. Now secure the ends of this chain to each other by working a slip stitch into the first chain to form a loop.

2. Make sure you don't twist the chain before you join the ends as this could make the

work twisted or the stitches uneven. The first 'round' of crochet is worked into the ring. The instructions in the pattern will tell you which stitches and how many need to be worked.

3. At the end of each round you will need to secure the last stitch to the first stitch to

close the round. Do this by working a slip stitch into the top of the first stitch. Also in following rounds the stitches need to be raised, this is done by working twice into the same stitch were instructed. The work is not turned at the end of a round, so the right side is always facing you.

FASTENING OFF.

To fasten off your crochet work, cut the yarn about 8cm from the work. Pass this loose end through the one remaining loop on the hook and pull tight. Darn the loose ends into the back of the work, using a blunt ended needle.

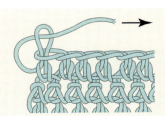

The new Autumn/Winter 2006 CLASSIC Collection ...

For autumn/winter 2006, Martin Storey has designed a further series of the popular RYC brochures with the style conscious knitter in mind. Whether you are looking for that simple little sweater or something more complicated, you can be sure there will be something to meet your knitting needs.

The new RYC range caters for every autumn and winter occasion, from classic winter DK knits and chunky knits, to more feminine, soft and pretty knits. The designs range from easy to knit accessories to more complicated cables, lace, fairisle and beaded garments.

The new collection features a DK brochure, **CLASSIC Alpaca**, photographed in South Africa on an Alpaca farm. The range includes a unisex 'Cambridge' cable slipover, a traditional 'Gansey' knit and the 'Oxford' stripe sweater for men. A second DK brochure, **CLASSIC Style,** contains fashionable knits in new yarn Silk & Wool DK, and **CLASSIC Spirit** features home and accessory designs in all your favourite RYC winter yarns such as Soft Tweed, Soft Lux and Cashsoft Aran. The fourth and final brochure is **CLASSIC Landscapes**, which was shot along the coastline of the Cape Peninsula. This brochure features the new Alpaca Soft, and contains chunky knits such as unisex cable knits, cosy coats and wraps, plus accessories.

All brochures are designed by Martin Storey, and include personal introductions – his ideas and inspiration for the season - original sketches and swatches for the designs.

To accompany our autumn/winter 2006 brochures are three **new** luxurious winter yarns:

Alpaca Baby DK – a wonderfully soft & pure, 100% baby alpaca yarn knitted on 4 mm needles and in a 'Natural' inspired range of colours including 'Jacob' cream, 'Southdown' grey, 'Cheviot' brown, 'Chambray' blue, 'Blossom' pink, 'Thistle', 'Kashmir' and 'Zinc'

Alpaca Soft – a cosy, textured, alpaca/cotton chunky blend knitted on 6 mm needles and in a 'Landscape' inspired range of colours including 'Whitewash' cream, 'Shingle' grey, 'Delft' blue, 'Tuscan' green, 'Lichen', 'Old Rose' and 'Ebony'

Silk & Wool DK – a silky and soft, silk/wool blend knitted on 4 mm needles and in a cool 'Winter' inspired range of colours including 'Limewash' cream, 'Porcelain' green, 'Scallop' pink, 'Clay' grey, 'Velvet', 'Cord' and 'Milk'

The **RYC CLASSIC RANGE** is designed with your pleasure in mind – designs that are a joy to knit, yarns that are a joy to wear. If you want to boost your wardrobe with those key handknits that complement every outfit and occasion, then RYC is for you.

Top: **Cosy Coat** [Man] in Alpaca Soft, Shingle & **Duvet** in Alpaca Soft, Tuscan. *Above left:* **Berry Sweater** in Cashsoft Aran, Oat. *Right:* **Peace** in Silk & Wool DK, Scallop. *Opposite:* **Cambridge** [Woman] in Baby Alpaca DK, Southdown

... a joy to knit,
a pleasure
to wear

CLASSIC

What's New

A whole season's worth of knitting books, magazines, exhibitions and websites covering all aspects of knitting and textile design.

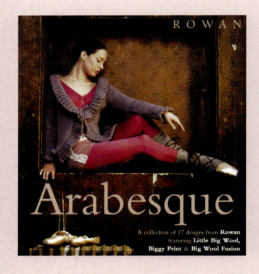

ARABESQUE

Arabesque is a graceful dance inspired collection debuting another of Rowan's new yarns for Winter 2006. Photographed using real ballet dancers, Little Big Wool is complemented with designs in Biggy Print and Big Wool Fusion and the brochure features 17 stunning, elegant designs by Marie Wallin and Martin Storey. Little Big Wool is a soft, cocoon like yarn which is finer and more versatile than Big Wool. This lovely yarn is available in 50g balls in ten beautiful chalky colours, ranging from the pretty, pastel tones of Quartz, Onyx, Pearl, Moonstone and Aquamarine to the stronger, more vibrant tones of Garnet, Amethyst, Topaz, Jasper and Amber. Little Big Wool knits on 9mm needles so it will be satisfyingly quick to knit the lovely designs in Arabesque.

Arabesque is available from Rowan Stockists
or online at www.knitrowan.com
ISBN 1-904485-73-1

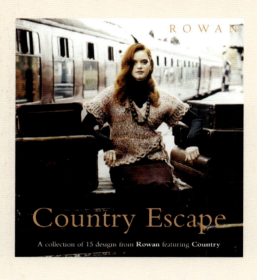

COUNTRY ESCAPE

Beautifully photographed at the atmospheric Great Central Steam Railway in Loughborough, Country Escape features one of Rowan's new exciting yarns for Winter 2006. Country is a lovely, soft multi-coloured tweed effect yarn in 100% Wool and will be available in eight stunning tweedy colours, ranging from the rustic tones of Heather, Cedarwood and Ash to the pretty, brighter tones of Rose, Clover and Damson. The brochure features a collection of fifteen delightful easy to wear designs by Marie Wallin and Antoni & Alison. Country knits on 9mm needles and is available at your Rowan stockist in 50g balls.

Country Escape is available from Rowan Stockist
or online at www.knitrowan.com
ISBN 1-904485-72-3

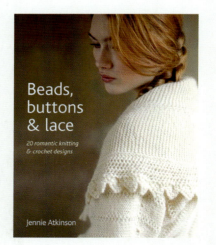

BEADS, BUTTONS & LACE

If you like beautiful and delicate knitting and crochet, then this book is a must! In *Beads, Buttons and Lace*, Jennie Atkinson has created a wonderful collection of garments and accessories, full of magic and romance, in ice-cream colours, with the help of some of Rowan's favourite designers: Kim Hargreaves, Martin Storey, Lois Daykin and Sharon Miller. Drawing on some classic designs of the '30s but with a contemporary twist, Jennie's collection is a sophisticated combination of designs that will appeal to intermediate and experienced knitters while providing an introduction to crochet for those new to this increasingly popular technique.

THE NUREYEV STYLE

A very special display of costumes, personal clothes and textiles which belonged to the world famous ballet dancer Rudolf Nureyev is on show at the Museum of Costume in Bath until February 2007. This exhibition will give visitors a unique chance to see for themselves some of the most magnificent ballet costumes worn throughout a long and illustrious career in which he danced on the world's most famous stages. In addition people will also see some of his personal clothes and some textiles he collected all of which played a part in creating his own particular and iconic style. A highlight of the display is a blue and silver silk brocade costume worn by Nureyev when he danced the role of the Prince Siegfried in the 1964 Vienna State Opera Ballet's of Swan Lake. There will also be two stunning costumes from Nureyev's own production of Romeo and Juliet (shown on the left) first staged by the London Festival Ballet in 1977.

Museum of Costume, Bath
Tel: 01225 477789 • www.museumofcostume.co.uk
Until February 2007

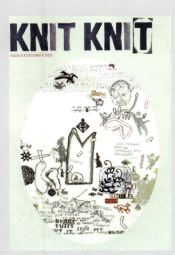

ELABORATE SIMPLICITY

It's all about contrasts this season. Minimalism – meets – old English heritage as Kim Hargreaves designs relaxed slouchy pieces that contrast with tailored classic styles. For autumn the palette mixes shades of oatmeal, camel, putty and slate, while winter's somber, moody greys are cut through with a splash of scarlet red and deepest plum. Designs include both garments and accessories that are all available in kit form from Kim's web site. Pictured is Cherish knitted in Rowan Big Wool, from the Evergreen collection. Photography Graham Watts

For further information visit www.kimhargreaves.co.uk

KNIT KNIT

KnitKnit is an artist's publication dedicated to the intersection of traditional craft and contemporary art. Conceived, curated and produced by artist Sabrina Gschwandtner, KnitKnit reflects a growing cultural interest in traditional crafts informed by a contemporary, critical perspective. KnitKnit is published twice per year and includes interviews, profiles, articles, reviews and drawings. Each issue comes either with or without a limited edition, handmade cover created by a fine artist. KnitKnit has been included in art exhibitions across the US and can be purchased at bookstores, yarn shops, boutiques and art galleries America, Canada, England, Ireland and France.

Sabrina is the author of our 'A Letter from America' feature within the magazine.
Available in the UK & Ireland:
Loop. 41 Cross Street, Islington, London N1 2BB • Tel: 020 7288 1160
Anthology Books Ltd. The Studio Building, Meeting House Square, Temple Bar, Dublin 2, Ireland.
Tel: 353 1 635 1422

For other stockists please visit www.knitknit.net

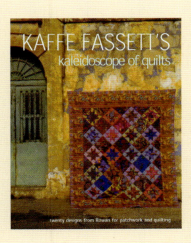

KAFFE FASSETT'S KALEIDOSCOPE OF QUILTS

Edited and styled by Kaffe Fassett, this book features 20 sumptuous quilts by Kaffe and other renowned designers, photographed on location in historic Malta. The quilts showcase the range of new Rowan patchwork fabrics from Martha Negley, Carla Miller and David Wolverson, among others. To help readers put different colour combinations together successfully, Kaffe shows how to create a completely different look and mood by making the same quilt in two very different colourways.
A feast of colour and design, Kaleidoscope of Quilts is a wonderful showcase of what Rowan Patchwork and Quilting has to offer.

EmmaKing.co.uk

Inspired by the beautiful colours and textures of Rowan yarns I started to design my own collection of hand knitted bags whilst working as a Design Consultant. My love of accessories encouraged me to expand my collection to include hand warmers, scarves, hats and even cushions!

Log on to the website where you can browse the collection and also read about up coming workshops, events and publications. My current book '25 Bags to Knit' is available in the shops now and my new book 'Fun and Funky Knitting' will be available in May 2006.

Website: emmaking.co.uk
'25 Bags to Knit' by Emma King published by Collins and Brown
'Fun and Funky Knitting' by Emma King published by Collins and Brown

Rowan International

Why not join the Rowan International Club, and become part of the world's largest knitting circle? Membership includes exclusive access to the Rowan Discussion Forums, where you can swap knitting tips and techniques with Members worldwide, as well as find knitting groups in your area. You will also receive a free gift on joining or renewing, which is currently Dolly, a cute cabled bag in Handknit Cotton, which is available in four colourways.

To join, visit www.knitrowan.com, or contact Rowan on 01484 681881.

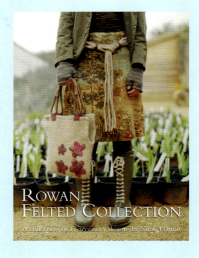

Rowan Felted Collection

From small purse bags to large buckets bags, and hot water bottle covers to bracelets, this new brochure from Rowan will inspire and excite all knitters who wish to try felting.

Rowan Felts introduces 16 lovely designs by Sarah Hatton, using Tapestry, Big Wool, Big Wool Fusion, Kid Classic, Little Big Wool and Scottish Tweed. Photographed at the beautiful Petersham Nurseries in Surrey, Sarah has created a collection of felting projects that will appeal to knitters of all experience, including the novice. Using soft, subtle colours many of the designs are embellished with beads, ribbons and embroidery.

Rowan Felts is available from Rowan Stockists or online at www.knitrowan.com

ISBN 1-904485-78-2

Kids Learn to Knit

Lucinda Guy and Francois Hall have applied their unique style (so successful in their previous books, Designs for Kids and And So to Bed,) to a new book showing small children how to knit. With the help of two cartoon mice and a friendly wolf, children learn everything they need to know about knitting, with a wonderful selection of bright projects that demonstrate each new lesson. From the simplest project of garter stitch bunting to cute little toy dogs or owls, Lucinda's charming ideas and clear lessons will captivate, and encourage, a whole new generation of young knitters.

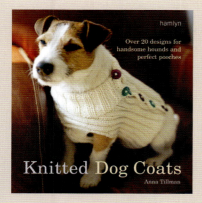

KNITTED DOG COATS

Knitted Dog Coats has 20 great projects for dogs of all sizes and knitters of all abilities, with full measuring instructions plus step-by-step knitting guidance. The book includes patterns for classic coats for discerning dogs, funky knits for cool canines and pretty coats for the perfect pooch.
Anna Tillman was knitting scarves for her teddy bears by the time she was 6 years old, and began her knitting career at Rowan. Anna's knitwear designs have appeared in a number of Rowan magazines. This is her first book.

Available from August 2006, you can find this book at your Rowan Stockist
or at www.knitrowan.com priced £14.99

ISBN 0600614336

CUTE CROCHET FOR TINY TOTS

From the tiniest bootees for a newborn baby to colourful cushions to delight the most discerning toddler, you'll be spoilt for choice with 25 adorable crochet designs for clothes, accessories and toys every child will love.
Helen Ardley studied Textiles at Huddersfield University before becoming a full-time crochet and knitwear designer. She has worked for a number of international companies, and was the crochet designer for Patons until the birth of her daughter. Helen now works as a freelance crochet and knitwear designer.
This is the sequel to Helen Ardley's successful book Adorable Knits for Tiny Tots.

Available from June 2006 from your Rowan Stockist at £14.99
or online at www.knitrowan.com

ISBN 0600614255

SELVEDGE

Selvedge is the first independent magazine to cover every facet of fine textiles – interiors, fashion, fine art, travel and shopping – in an intelligent, stylish and contemporary way. The aim of Selvedge is to put textiles in an international context, breaking down barriers between textile arts and its mainstream counterparts in fine art, fashion and interior design.
Selvedge is thought provoking, providing a catalyst for change and a focus point for the energy and enthusiasm of makers, academics and consumers.

Retail Price: £7.50 List of stockists available on www.selvedge.org

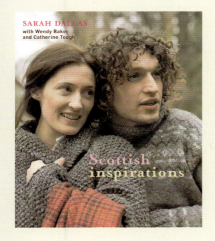

SCOTTISH INSPIRATIONS

Renowned knitwear designer Sarah Dallas, joins forces with Royal College of Art colleague, Wendy Baker, and former student, Catherine Tough, to create a singularly beautiful, contemporary collection of garments and accessories inspired by the soft colours and traditional patterns and texture of the Outer Hebrides. All the designs have been designed in a celebration of Rowan Scottish Tweed – an extraordinarily beautiful pure wool yarn from a stunningly rugged landscape.

THE DESIGN GALLERY

FADE TO GREY

ANYA
Kid Classic, Kidsilk Haze &
Kidsilk Night
Marie Wallin
Pattern page 160
Main image page 9 & 19

SORREL
Tapestry
Sarah Hatton
Pattern page 122
Main image page 10

VIKTOR ★
Tapestry & Kid Classic
Marie Wallin
Pattern page 166
Main image page 11

NAKITA
Kidsilk Haze
Marie Wallin
Pattern page 120
Main image page 12

OLGA ●
Kid Classic, Kidsilk Night,
Kidsilk Haze & Lurex Shimmer
Antoni & Alison
Pattern page 118
Main image page 13

ANNA SOCKS ✚
4 Ply Soft
Nina Chakkour
Pattern page 119
Main image page 14

CELTIC ●
Felted Tweed & Kid Classic
Martin Storey
Pattern page 152
Main image page 15

SADIE
Wool Cotton
Sarah Hatton
Pattern page 170
Main image page 16

KINDRED SPIRIT

SASHA ★
Big Wool & Big Wool Fusion
Marie Wallin
Pattern page 150
Main image page 25

ROAM ▲
Big Wool
Sarah Hatton
Pattern page 110
Main image page 35, 52 & 53

ANA FINGERLESS MITTENS ✚
Kid Classic & Wool Cotton
Gabrielle Carter
Pattern page 115
Main image page 35, 52 & 53

DOTTY ★
Felted Tweed & Tapestry
Kaffe Fassett
Pattern page 134
Main image page 36 & 37

RUSTIC ●
4 Ply Soft
& Scottish Tweed 4 Ply
Jenny Atkinson
Pattern page 130
Main image page 36

JUNO ■
Wool Cotton
Amanda Crawford
Pattern page 145
Main image page 38

ORGANIC BAG ✚
Tapestry & Kid Classic
Bronwen Harlowe
Pattern page 134
Main image page 39

MURMANSK BRACES ✚
Kid Classic & Wool Cotton
Gabrielle Carter
Pattern page 133
Main image page 50 & 51

SKOMER ISLAND ARMWARMERS ✚
Felted Tweed, Kid Classic &
Wool Cotton, Gabrielle Carter
Pattern page 124
Main image page 50 & 51

AUTUMN LEAVES ▲
Felted Tweed, Kid Classic,
4 Ply Soft & Lurex Shimmer
Martin Storey
Pattern page 163
Main image page 54

SQUARE WRAP ✚
Big Wool & Ribbon Twist
Nikki Ryan
Pattern page 127
Main image page 55

LORELEI ■
Felted Tweed & Wool Cotton
Amanda Crawford
Pattern page 138
Main image page 56

LEGEND

ROSA ●
Kidsilk Haze
Lois Daykin
Pattern page 125
Main image page 69 & 79

EVA ▲
Kid Classic
Amanda Crawford
Pattern page 107
Main image page 70

WONDER ▲
Romance
Marie Wallin
Pattern page 126
Main image page 82

TINTAGEL ■
Romance, Kidsilk Haze &
Soft Baby
Sarah Hatton
Pattern page 144
Main image page 83

ARWEN GOWN ◆
Kidsilk Night & Kidsilk Haze
Marie Wallin
Pattern page 172
Main image page 84, 85, 87 & 88

PAISLEY ▲
Kid Classic
Martin Storey
Pattern page 154
Main image page 86

COZY MUFFLER ✚
Big Wool & Kid Classic
Nikki Ryan
Pattern page 147
Main image page 87 & 88

SIZE KEY

- ■ SIZE 8 – 18
- ● SIZE 8 – 22
- ▲ SIZE S – XL
- ◆ SIZE S – L
- ★ SIZE S – XXL (MENS)
- ✚ ACCESSORY
  (Refer to pattern page)

Our easy reference guide to the designs featured in this magazine, plus a handy yarn & size table.

Row 1

…FLE SCARF
…Classic
…Ryan
…page 151
…image page 17

★ **SERGE**
Tapestry
Sarah Hatton
Pattern page 112
Main image page 18

● **RICH**
Kidsilk Haze, Kidsilk Night & Wool Cotton
Carol Meldrum
Pattern page 162
Main image page 20

✚ **ANA FINGERLESS MITTENS**
Kid Classic & Wool Cotton
Gabrielle Carter
Pattern page 115
Main image page 21

✚ **MURMANSK BRACES**
Kid Classic & Wool Cotton
Gabrielle Carter
Pattern page 133
Main image page 21

✚ **GRANTIS SCARF**
Kidsilk Night, Kid Classic & Lurex Shimmer
Julia Neill
Pattern page 111
Main image page 22

▲ **WRAPAROUND**
4 Ply Soft
Sarah Dallas
Pattern page 103
Main image page 23

▲ **KAY**
Big Wool & Kidsilk Spray
Leah Sutton
Pattern page 157
Main image page 24

Row 2

…DE
…ry & Kidsilk Haze
…Wallin
…page 106
…image page 40 & 41

✚ **ST. BRIDES BAY CAPE**
Felted Tweed & Wool Cotton
Gabrielle Carter
Pattern page 116
Main image page 42 & 43

★ **FURROW**
Tapestry, Wool Cotton & Kid Classic
Marie Wallin
Pattern page 128
Main image page 44 & 46

▲ **HICKORY**
Felted Tweed
Marie Wallin
Pattern page 174
Main image page 45

● **LICHEN**
Kid Classic
Lisa Richardson
Pattern page 104
Main image page 46 & 47

✚ **MARLOES SAND HAT**
Ribbon Twist
Gabrielle Carter
Pattern page 123
Main image page 46, 47 & 55

▲ **PAMPAS**
Big Wool
Marie Wallin
Pattern page 132
Main image page 48

● **SHADED FLOWER**
Felted Tweed
Kaffe Fassett
Pattern page 136
Main image page 49

Row 3

…WEB
…k Night
…ex Shimmer
…Wallin
…page 158
…image page 71

■ **AELF**
Kid Classic
Leah Sutton
Pattern page 140
Main image page 72 & 73

● **DEW**
Wool Cotton
Amanda Crawford
Pattern page 168
Main image page 74

■ **EVELEEN**
4 Ply Soft, Kidsilk Haze & Lurex Shimmer
Lois Daykin
Pattern page 148
Main image page 75

✚ **BELLA ROSE CORSET**
Felted Tweed & Scottish Tweed 4 Ply
Julia Neill
Pattern page 109
Main image page 76 & 77

● **PARKER**
Tapestry
Sarah Hatton
Pattern page 113
Main image page 78

▲ **TITANIA**
Romance, Kid Classic, Kidsilk Haze & Lurex Shimmer
Marie Wallin
Pattern page 141
Main image page 80

● **MYSTIC**
Romance
Marie Wallin
Pattern page 176
Main image page 81

THE YARNS

WOOL COTTON
Skomer Island Armwarmers
Lorelei
Sadie
Juno
Rich*
Ana Fingerless Mittens*
Murmansk Braces*
Furrow*
Dew
St. Brides Bay Cape

BIG WOOL FUSION
Tintagel*

KID CLASSIC
Anya*
Olga*
Celtic*
Viktor*
Ruffle Scarf*
Grantis Scarf*
Ana Fingerless Mittens*
Murmansk Braces*
Skoner Island Armwarmers*
Autumn Leaves*
Organic Bag*
Aelf
Furrow*
Lichen
Cozy Muffler*
Titania*

PAISLEY
Eva

KIDSILK NIGHT
Anya*
Olga*
Rich*
Grantis Scarf*
Arwen Gown*
Cobweb*

KIDSILK SPRAY
Kay*

SCOTTISH TWEED 4 PLY
Rustic*
Bella Rose Corset*

TAPESTRY
Sorrel
Serge
Viktor*
Organic Bag*
Dotty*
Furrow*
Glade*
Parker

BIG WOOL
Sasha*
Kay*
Roam
Square Wrap*
Pampas
Cozy Muffler*

ROMANCE
Square Wrap
Wonder
Tintagel*
Mystic
Titania*

FELTED TWEED
Celtic*
Skomer Island Armwarmers*
Dotty*
Lorelei*
Bella Rose Corset*
Shaded Flower
St. Brides Bay Cape*
Hickory
Autumn Leaves

4 PLY SOFT
Wraparound
Anna Socks
Autumn Leaves*
Rustic*
Eveleen*

BIG WOOL FUSION
Sasha*

LUREX SHIMMER
Olga*
Grantis*
Autumn Leaves*
Cobweb*
Titania*
Eveleen*

KIDSILK HAZE
Anya*
Nakita
Olga*
Rich*
Glade*
Tintagel*
Arwen Gown*
Eveleen*
Titania*
Rosa

RIBBON TWIST
Marloes Sand Hat
Square Wrap*

SOFT BABY
Tintagel*

* A design which uses more than one yarn

101

ROWAN SIZING GUIDE

When you knit and wear a Rowan design we want you to look and feel fabulous. This all starts with the size and fit of the design you choose. To help you to achieve a great knitting experience we have looked at the sizing of our womens and menswear patterns. This has resulted in the introduction of our new sizing guide which includes the following exciting features:

Our sizing now conforms to standard clothing sizes. Therefore if you buy a standard size 12 in clothing, then our size 12 or Medium patterns will fit you perfectly.

We have extended the size range of our patterns, with over half of the designs shown being available to knit from size 8 to 22, or Small through to Xlarge.

The menswear designs are now available to knit in menswear sizes Small through to XXlarge ie. 40" to 48" chest.

Dimensions in the charts below are body measurements, not garment dimensions, therefore please refer to the measuring guide to help you to determine which is the best size for you to knit.

STANDARD SIZING GUIDE FOR WOMEN

UK SIZE	8	10	12	14	16	18	20	22	
USA Size	6	8	10	12	14	16	18	20	
EUR Size	34	36	38	40	42	44	46	48	
To fit bust	32	34	36	38	40	42	44	46	inches
	82	87	92	97	102	107	112	117	cm
To fit waist	24	26	28	30	32	34	36	38	inches
	61	66	71	76	81	86	91	96	cm
To fit hips	34	36	38	40	42	44	46	48	inches
	87	92	97	102	107	112	117	122	cm

CASUAL SIZING GUIDE FOR WOMEN

As there are some designs that are intended to fit more generously, we have introduced our casual sizing guide. The designs that fall into this group can be recognised by the size range: Small, Medium, Large & Xlarge. Each of these sizes cover two sizes from the standard sizing guide, ie. Size S will fit sizes 8/10, size M will fit sizes 12/14 and so on.

The sizing within this chart is also based on the larger size within the range, ie. M will be based on size 14.

UK SIZE	S	M	L	XL	
DUAL SIZE	8/10	12/14	16/18	20/22	
To fit bust	32 – 34	36 – 38	40 – 42	44 – 46	inches
	82 – 87	92 – 97	102 – 107	112 – 117	cm
To fit waist	24 – 26	28 – 30	32 – 34	36 – 38	inches
	61 – 66	71 – 76	81 – 86	91 – 96	cm
To fit hips	34 – 36	38 – 40	42 – 44	46 – 48	inches
	87 – 92	97 – 102	107 – 112	117 – 122	cm

STANDARD SIZING GUIDE FOR MEN

UK SIZE	S	M	L	XL	XXL	
EUR Size	50	52	54	56	58	
To fit chest	40	42	44	46	48	inches
	102	107	112	117	122	cm
To fit waist	32	34	36	38	40	inches
	81	86	91	96	101	cm

MEASURING GUIDE

For maximum comfort and to ensure the correct fit when choosing a size to knit, please follow the tips below when checking your size.

Measure yourself close to your body, over your underwear and don't pull the tape measure too tight!

Bust/chest – measure around the fullest part of the bust/chest and across the shoulder blades.

Waist – measure around the natural waistline, just above the hip bone.

Hips – measure around the fullest part of the bottom.

If you don't wish to measure yourself, note the size of a favourite jumper that you like the fit of. Our sizes are now comparable to the clothing sizes from the major high street retailers, so if your favourite jumper is a size Medium or size 12, then our casual size Medium and standard size 12 should be approximately the same fit.

To be extra sure, measure your favourite jumper and then compare these measurements with the Rowan size diagram given at the end of the individual instructions.

Finally, once you have decided which size is best for you, please ensure that you achieve the tension required for the design you wish to knit.

Remember if your tension is too loose, your garment will be bigger than the pattern size and you may use more yarn. If your tension is too tight, your garment could be smaller than the pattern size and you will have yarn left over.

Furthermore if your tension is incorrect, the handle of your fabric will be too stiff or floppy and will not fit properly. It really does make sense to check your tension before starting every project.

Main image page 23

SIZE

	S	M	L	XL	
	8/10	12/14	16/18	20/22	
To fit bust
	82-87	92-97	102-107	112-117	cm
	32-34	36-38	40-42	44-46	in

YARN

Rowan 4 ply Soft

3 colour version

A	Sooty 372

	4	4	4	5	x 50gm

B Black 383

	8	8	8	9	x 50gm

C Rain Cloud 387

	4	4	4	4	x 50gm

2 colour version

A Sooty 372

	1	1	1	1	x 50gm

B Rain Cloud 387

	15	16	17	18	x 50gm

NEEDLES

1 pair 3¼ mm (no 10) (US 3) needles
Fastener: 1 x Kilt pin 000414 or 000412

TENSION

28 sts and 36 rows to 10 cm measured over stocking stitch using 3¼ mm (US 3) needles.

3 colour version

BODY (worked sideways in one piece beg at right front opening edge)
Using 3¼ mm (US 3) needles and yarn A cast on 185 [191: 197: 203] sts.
Break off yarn A and join in yarn C.
***Row 1 (RS): K1, *P1, K1, rep from * to end.
Row 2: P1, *K1, P1, rep from * to end.
These 2 rows form rib.
Cont in rib for a further 4 rows, ending with RS facing for next row.
Row 7 (RS): (K1, P1) 4 times, K to last 8 sts, (P1, K1) 4 times.
Row 8: (P1, K1) 4 times, P to last 8 sts, (K1, P1) 4 times.
These 2 rows set the sts.
Cont as set until work meas 21 cm, ending with RS facing for next row.
Break off C and join in A.
Cont straight until work meas 40 cm **from cast-on edge**, ending with RS facing for next row.
Break off A and join in B.
Cont straight until work meas 51 cm **from cast-on edge**, ending with RS facing for next row.
Shape right armhole
**Next row (RS): Patt 50 sts and turn, leaving rem sts on a holder.
Work a further 12 rows on these 50 sts only, ending with **WS** facing for next row.
Break yarn and leave these sts on a second holder.
Return to sts left on first holder, rejoin yarn

with RS facing, cast off 59 [63: 67: 71] sts, patt to end.
76 [78: 80: 82] sts.
Dec 1 st at end of next row and at same edge on foll 3 rows. 72 [74: 76: 78] sts.
Work 2 rows, ending with **WS** facing for next row.******
Break off yarn B and join in yarn C.
Work 2 rows.
Inc 1 st at end of next row and at same edge on foll 3 rows.
76 [78: 80: 82] sts.
Next row (WS): Patt 76 [78: 80: 82] sts of lower section, turn and cast on 59 [63: 67: 71] sts, turn and patt across 50 sts left on second holder.
185 [191: 197: 203] sts.
Cont straight until work meas 13 [14: 16: 17] cm **from armhole cast-on edge**, ending with RS facing for next row.
Break off yarn C and join in yarn A.
Cont straight until work meas 32 [34: 37: 40] cm **from armhole cast-on edge**, ending with RS facing for next row.
Shape left armhole
Work as given for right armhole from ****** to ******.
Break off yarn A and join in yarn B.
Work 2 rows.
Inc 1 st at end of next row and at same edge on foll 3 rows. 76 [78: 80: 82] sts.
Next row (WS): Patt 76 [78: 80: 82] sts of lower section, turn and cast on 59 [63: 67: 71] sts, turn and patt across 50 sts left on second holder.
185 [191: 197: 203] sts.
Cont straight until work meas 51 cm **from left armhole cast-on edge**, ending with RS facing for next row.
Work in rib for 6 rows, ending with RS facing for next row.*******
Break off yarn B and join in yarn A.
Cast off in rib.

SLEEVES
Using 3¼ mm (US 3) needles and yarn A cast on 67 [71: 75: 79] sts.
Break off yarn A and join in yarn B.
Work in rib as given for body for 20 rows, ending with RS facing for next row.
Beg with a K row, work in st st, shaping sides by inc 1 st at each end of 3rd and every foll 4th row to 109 [115: 121: 131] sts, then on every foll 6th row until there are 123 [129: 135: 141] sts.
Cont straight until sleeve meas 45 [46: 47: 47] cm, ending with RS facing for next row.
Shape top
Dec 1 st at each end of next 4 rows, ending with RS facing for next row.
115 [121: 127: 133] sts.
Cast off 12 sts at beg of next 2 rows.
Cast off rem 91 [97: 103: 109] sts.

2 colour version

BODY (worked sideways in one piece beg at right front opening edge)
Using 3¼ mm (US 3) needles and yarn A cast on 185 [191: 197: 203] sts.
Break off yarn A and join in yarn B.
Work as given for 3 colour version from ******* to *******, using yarn B throughout.
Break off yarn B and join in yarn A.
Cast off in rib.

SLEEVES
Work as given for sleeves of 3 colour version.

Both versions

MAKING UP
Press as described on the information page.
Join sleeve seams using back stitch, or mattress stitch if preferred. Matching top of sleeve seam to base of armhole and centre of sleeve cast-off edge to centre of armhole top row-end edge, sew sleeves into armholes.

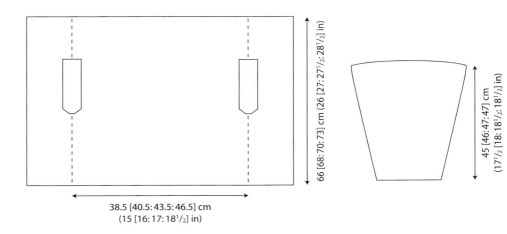

66 [68:70:73] cm (26 [27:27½:28½] in)

38.5 [40.5:43.5:46.5] cm
(15 [16:17:18½] in)

45 [46:47:47] cm
(17½ [18:18½:18½] in)

Main image page 46 & 47

LICHEN BY LISA RICHARDSON

SIZE
8 10 12 14 16 18 20 22
To fit bust
82 87 92 97 102 107 112 117 cm
32 34 36 38 40 42 44 46 in

YARN
Rowan Kid Classic
9 9 9 10 10 11 12 12 x 50gm
(photographed in Straw 851)

NEEDLES
1 pair 4mm (no 8) (US 6) needles
1 pair 5mm (no 6) (US 8) needles
4mm (no 8) (US 6) circular needle
Cable needle

BUTTONS – 4 x 00322

TENSION
27½ sts and 23 rows to 10 cm measured over
pattern using 5mm (US 8) needles.

SPECIAL ABBREVIATIONS
C4B = slip next 2 sts onto cable needle and
leave at back of work, K2, then K2 from cable
needle; **C4F** = slip next 2 sts onto cable needle
and leave at front of work, K2, then K2 from
cable needle; **C5B** = slip next 3 sts onto cable
needle and leave at back of work, K2, then K3
from cable needle; **C5F** = slip next 2 sts onto
cable needle and leave at front of work, K3,
then K2 from cable needle; **Cr3R** = slip next st
onto cable needle and leave at back of work,
K2, then P1 from cable needle; **Cr3L** = slip
next 2 sts onto cable needle and leave at front
of work, P1, then K2 from cable needle.

BACK
Using 4mm (US 6) needles cast on 85 [89: 93:
99: 103: 109: 115: 121] sts.
Row 1 (RS): K1, *P1, K1, rep from * to end.
Row 2: As row 1.
These 2 rows form moss st.
Work in moss st for a further 17 rows, ending
with **WS** facing for next row.
Row 20 (inc) (WS): Moss st 12 [12: 14:
15: 13: 14: 15: 16] sts, M1, (moss st 2 sts, M1)
30 [32: 32: 34: 38: 40: 42: 44] times, moss st
to end.
116 [122: 126: 134: 142: 150: 158: 166] sts.
Change to 5mm (US 8) needles.
Beg and ending rows as indicated and repeating
the 16 row patt rep throughout, now work in
patt from chart as folls:
Work 10 rows.
Keeping patt correct, dec 1 st at each end of
next and every foll 4th row until 106 [112:
116: 124: 132: 140: 148: 156] sts rem.
Work 9 rows, ending with RS facing for
next row.
Inc 1 st at each end of next and every foll 6th
row until there are 116 [122: 126: 134: 142:
150: 158: 166] sts, taking inc sts into patt.
Cont straight until back meas 39 [39: 38: 41:
40: 42: 41: 43] cm, ending with RS facing for

next row.
Shape armholes
Keeping patt correct, cast off 5 [6: 6: 7: 7:
8: 8: 9] sts at beg of next 2 rows.
106 [110: 114: 120: 128: 134: 142: 148] sts.
Dec 1 st at each end of next 3 [3: 5: 5: 7:
7: 9: 9] rows, then on foll 1 [2: 1: 2: 1: 2: 2: 3]
alt rows.
98 [100: 102: 106: 112: 116: 120: 124] sts.
Cont straight until armhole meas 19 [19: 20:
20: 21: 21: 22: 22] cm, ending with RS facing
for next row.
Shape back neck
Next row (RS): Patt 28 [29: 30: 32: 34: 36: 38:
40] sts and turn, leaving rem sts on a holder.
Work each side of neck separately.
Dec 1 st at neck edge of next 3 rows, ending
with RS facing for next row.
Shape shoulder
Cast off rem 25 [26: 27: 29: 31: 33: 35: 37] sts.
With RS facing, rejoin yarn to rem sts, cast
off centre 42 [42: 42: 42: 44: 44: 44: 44] sts,
patt to end.
Complete to match first side, reversing
shapings.

LEFT FRONT
Using 4mm (US 6) needles cast on 41 [43: 45:
47: 51: 53: 57: 59] sts.
Work in moss st as given for back for 19 rows,
ending with **WS** facing for next row.
Row 20 (inc) (WS): Moss st 6 [6: 7: 6: 8:
7: 9: 8] sts, M1, (moss st 2 sts, M1) 14 [15: 15:
17: 17: 19: 19: 21] times, moss st to end.
56 [59: 61: 65: 69: 73: 77: 81] sts.
Change to 5mm (US 8) needles.
Beg and ending rows as indicated, now work in
patt from chart as folls:
Work 10 rows.
Keeping patt correct, dec 1 st at beg of next
and every foll 4th row until 51 [54: 56: 60:
64: 68: 72: 76] sts rem.
Work 9 rows, ending with RS facing for
next row.
Inc 1 st at beg of next and every foll 6th row
until there are 56 [59: 61: 65: 69: 73: 77: 81] sts,
taking inc sts into patt.
Cont straight until 4 rows less have been
worked than on back to beg of armhole
shaping, ending with RS facing for next row.
Shape front slope
Keeping patt correct, dec 1 st at end of next
and foll alt row.
54 [57: 59: 63: 67: 71: 75: 79] sts.
Work 1 row.
Shape armhole
Keeping patt correct, cast off 5 [6: 6: 7: 7:
8: 8: 9] sts at beg and dec 1 st at end of next
row. 48 [50: 52: 55: 59: 62: 66: 69] sts.
Work 1 row.
Dec 1 st at armhole edge of next 3 [3: 5: 5: 7:
7: 9: 9] rows, then on foll 1 [2: 1: 2: 1: 2: 2: 3]
alt rows **and at same time** dec 1 st at front
slope edge of next and every foll alt row.
41 [41: 42: 43: 46: 47: 48: 49] sts.

Dec 1 st at front slope edge **only** of 2nd and
foll 14 [13: 12: 11: 12: 11: 8: 7] alt rows, then
on every foll 4th row until 25 [26: 27: 29: 31:
33: 35: 37] sts rem.
Cont straight until left front matches back to
shoulder cast-off, ending with RS facing for
next row.
Shape shoulder
Cast off rem 25 [26: 27: 29: 31: 33: 35: 37] sts.

RIGHT FRONT
Using 4mm (US 6) needles cast on 41 [43: 45:
47: 51: 53: 57: 59] sts.
Work in moss st as given for back for 19 rows,
ending with **WS** facing for next row.
Row 20 (inc) (WS): Moss st 6 [6: 7: 6: 8:
7: 9: 8] sts, M1, (moss st 2 sts, M1) 14 [15: 15:
17: 17: 19: 19: 21] times, moss st to end.
56 [59: 61: 65: 69: 73: 77: 81] sts.
Change to 5mm (US 8) needles.
Beg and ending rows as indicated, now work in
patt from chart as folls:
Work 10 rows.
Keeping patt correct, dec 1 st at end of next
and every foll 4th row until 51 [54: 56: 60:
64: 68: 72: 76] sts rem.
Complete to match left front, reversing
shapings.

SLEEVES
Using 4mm (US 6) needles cast on 45 [45: 47:
47: 49: 49: 51: 51] sts.
Work in moss st as given for back for 13 rows,
ending with **WS** facing for next row.
Row 14 (inc) (WS): Moss st 8 [8: 9: 9: 10:
10: 11: 11] sts, M1, (moss st 2 sts, M1) 14 times,
moss st to end.
60 [60: 62: 62: 64: 64: 66: 66] sts.
Change to 5mm (US 8) needles.
Beg and ending rows as indicated, now work in
patt from chart, shaping sides by inc 1 st at
each end of 3rd and every foll alt row to
66 [70: 70: 74: 74: 78: 82: 86] sts, then on every
foll 4th row until there are 102 [104: 106: 108:
110: 112: 114: 116] sts, taking inc sts into patt.
Cont straight until sleeve meas 43 [43: 44: 44:
45: 45: 44: 44] cm, ending with RS facing for
next row.
Shape top
Keeping patt correct, cast off 5 [6: 6: 7: 7:
8: 8: 9] sts at beg of next 2 rows.
92 [92: 94: 94: 96: 96: 98: 98] sts.
Dec 1 st at each end of next 9 rows, then on
every foll alt row until 64 sts rem, then on foll
11 rows, ending with RS facing for next row.
42 sts.
Cast off 5 sts at beg of next 2 rows.
Cast off rem 32 sts.

MAKING UP
Press as described on the information page.
Join shoulder seams using back stitch, or
mattress stitch if preferred.
Front bands and collar
With RS facing and using 4mm (US 6) circular

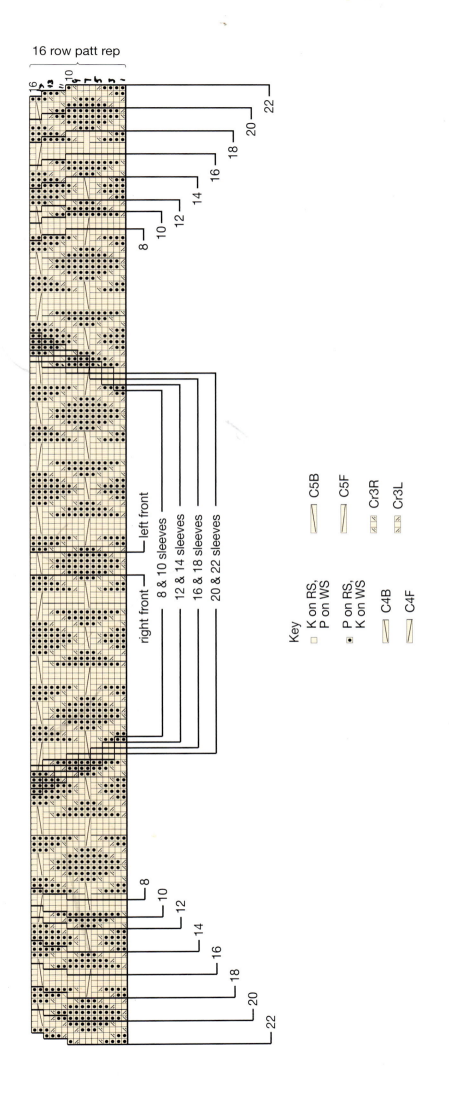

16 row patt rep

left front

right front

8 & 10 sleeves
12 & 14 sleeves
16 & 18 sleeves
20 & 22 sleeves

Key

| ☐ | K on RS, P on WS |
| ■ | P on RS, K on WS |

| ╲ | C4B |
| ╱ | C4F |

| ╲ | C5B |
| ╱ | C5F |

| ▨ | Cr3R |
| ▨ | Cr3L |

needle, beg and ending at cast-on edges, pick up and knit 63 [63: 61: 65: 63: 67: 65: 69] sts up right front opening edge to beg of front slope shaping, 50 [50: 52: 52: 54: 54: 56: 56] sts up right front slope, 53 [53: 53: 53: 55: 55: 55: 55] sts from back, 50 [50: 52: 52: 54: 54: 56: 56] sts down left front slope to beg of front slope shaping, then 63 [63: 61: 65: 63: 67: 65: 69] sts down left front opening edge.
279 [279: 279: 287: 289: 297: 297: 305] sts.
Work in moss st as given for back for 1 row, ending with RS facing for next row.

Shape for collar
Row 1: Moss st 169 [169: 169: 173: 175: 179: 179: 183] sts, wrap next st (by slipping next st onto right needle, taking yarn to opposite side of work between needles and then slipping same st back onto left needle) and turn.
Row 2: Moss st 59 [59: 59: 59: 61: 61: 61: 61] sts, wrap next st and turn.
Row 3: Moss st 62 [62: 62: 62: 64: 64: 64: 64] sts, wrap next st and turn.
Row 4: Moss st 65 [65: 65: 65: 67: 67: 67: 67] sts, wrap next st and turn.
Cont in this way, working 3 more sts before wrapping next st and turning, until the foll row has been worked:
Next row: Moss st 125 [125: 131: 131: 139: 139: 145: 145] sts, wrap next st and turn.
Work 4 rows across all sts, ending with RS facing for next row.
Next row (RS): Moss st 28 [28: 26: 30: 28: 32: 30: 34] sts, (cast off 2 sts, moss st until there are 9 sts on right needle after cast-off) 3 times, cast off 2 sts, moss st to end.
Next row: Moss st to end, casting on 2 sts over those cast off on previous row.
Work a further 6 rows, ending with RS facing for next row.
Cast off in moss st.
See information page for finishing instructions, setting in sleeves using the set-in method.

60 [60: 60: 63: 63: 65: 65: 67] cm
(23½ [23½: 23½: 25: 25: 25½: 25½: 26½] in)

42 [44.5: 46: 48.5: 51.5: 54.5: 57.5: 60.5] cm
(16½ [17½: 18: 19: 20½: 21½: 22½: 24] in)

43 [43: 44: 44: 45: 45: 44: 44] cm
(17 [17: 17½: 17½: 17½: 17½: 17½: 17½] in)

Main image page 40 & 41

GLADE BY MARIE WALLIN

SIZE

8	10	12	14	16	18	
To fit bust						
82	87	92	97	102	107	cm
32	34	36	38	40	42	in

YARN
Rowan Tapestry and Kidsilk Haze

A	Tapestry Rustic 174						
	2	2	2	2	2	3	x 50gm
B	Kidsilk Haze Drab 588						
	1	1	1	1	1	1	x 25gm
C	Kidsilk Haze Jacob				631		
	1	1	1	2	2	2	x 25gm
D	Tapestry Country 170						
	4	4	4	5	5	5	x 50gm
E	Kidsilk Haze Smoke 605						
	1	1	1	1	1	1	x 25gm
F	Tapestry Moorland 175						
	2	2	2	3	3	3	x 50gm

NEEDLES
1 pair 4mm (no 8) (US 6) needles
4.00mm (no 8) (US G6) crochet hook

BEADS – approx 420 [430: 440: 460: 470: 490] wooden beads *Ref Wooden Bead WB5 col 2 Brown from Creative Bead Craft Ltd.

TENSION
27½ sts and 32 rows to 10 cm measured over pattern using 4mm (US 6) needles.

UK CROCHET ABBREVIATIONS
ch = chain; **dc** = double crochet;
ss = slip stitch; **tr(s)** = treble(s).

US CROCHET ABBREVIATIONS
ch = chain; **dc** = single crochet;
ss = slip stitch; **tr(s)** = double crochet(s).

BACK
Using 4mm (US 6) needles and yarn A cast on 147 [153: 159: 167: 175: 183] sts.
Row 1 (RS): Using yarn A, K3 [6: 2: 2: 6: 3], (K2tog, K3, yfwd, K2) 0 [0: 1: 0: 0: 1] times, *yfwd, K3, K3tog, K3, yfwd, K2, rep from * to last 1 [4: 7: 0: 4: 8] sts, (yfwd, K3, K2tog) 0 [0: 1: 0: 0: 1] times, K1 [4: 2: 0: 4: 3].
Row 2: Using yarn A, knit.
These 2 rows form patt.
Keeping patt correct, now work in stripe sequence as folls:
Rows 3 to 6: Using yarn A.
Rows 7 and 8: Using yarn B.
Rows 9 and 10: Using yarn C, dec 1 st at each end of first of these rows.
145 [151: 157: 165: 173: 181] sts.
Rows 11 to 16: Using yarn D, dec 1 st at each end of 3rd of these rows.
143 [149: 155: 163: 171: 179] sts.
Rows 17 and 18: Using yarn C, dec 1 st at each end of first of these rows.
141 [147: 153: 161: 169: 177] sts.
Rows 19 and 20: Using yarn E.
Rows 21 to 26: Using yarn F, dec 1 st at each

end of first and 5th of these rows.
137 [143: 149: 157: 165: 173] sts.
Rows 27 and 28: Using yarn E.
Rows 29 and 30: Using yarn B, dec 1 st at each end of first of these rows.
135 [141: 147: 155: 163: 171] sts.
These 30 rows form stripe sequence.
Keeping stripes and patt correct, dec 1 st at each end of 3rd and every foll 4th row until 117 [123: 129: 137: 145: 153] sts rem.
Cont straight until back meas 32 [32: 31: 34: 33: 35] cm, ending with RS facing for next row.
Shape armholes
Keeping stripes and patt correct, cast off 5 [6: 6: 7: 7: 8] sts at beg of next 2 rows.
107 [111: 117: 123: 131: 137] sts.
Dec 1 st at each end of next 5 [5: 7: 7: 9: 9] rows, then on foll 3 [4: 4: 5: 5: 6] alt rows.
91 [93: 95: 99: 103: 107] sts.
Cont straight until armhole meas 19 [19: 20: 20: 21: 21] cm, ending with RS facing for next row.
Shape back neck
Next row (RS): Patt 22 [23: 24: 26: 27: 29] sts and turn, leaving rem sts on a holder.
Work each side of neck separately.
Dec 1 st at neck edge of next 4 rows.
18 [19: 20: 22: 23: 25] sts.
Work 2 rows, ending with **WS** facing for next row.
Shape shoulder
Cast off (on **WS**).
With RS facing, rejoin yarn to rem sts, cast off centre 47 [47: 47: 47: 49: 49] sts, patt to end.
Complete to match first side, reversing shapings.

FRONT
Work as given for back until 4 rows less have been worked than on back to beg of armhole shaping.
Divide for front opening
Next row (RS): Patt 57 [60: 63: 67: 71: 75] sts and turn, leaving rem sts on a holder.
Work each side of neck separately.
Keeping stripes and patt correct, work 3 rows, dec 1 st at neck edge of 2nd of these rows and ending with RS facing for next row.
56 [59: 62: 66: 70: 74] sts.
Shape armhole
Keeping stripes and patt correct, cast off 5 [6: 6: 7: 7: 8] sts at beg of next row.
51 [53: 56: 59: 63: 66] sts.
Work 1 row.
Dec 1 st at armhole edge of next 5 [5: 7: 7: 9: 9] rows, then on foll 3 [4: 4: 5: 5: 6] alt rows **and at same time** dec 1 st at neck edge of next and 5 foll 4th rows.
37 [38: 39: 41: 43: 45] sts.
Cont straight until 38 [38: 38: 40: 40: 40] rows less have been worked than on back to shoulder cast-off, ending with **WS** facing for next row.
Shape neck
Keeping stripes and patt correct, cast off 6 [6: 6:

5: 6: 6] sts at beg of next row.
31 [32: 33: 36: 37: 39] sts.
Dec 1 st at neck edge of next 7 rows, then on foll 6 [6: 6: 7: 7: 7] alt rows.
18 [19: 20: 22: 23: 25] sts.
Work 18 rows, ending with **WS** facing for next row.
Shape shoulder
Cast off (on **WS**).
With RS facing, rejoin yarn to rem sts, cast off centre 3 sts, patt to end.
Complete to match first side, reversing shapings.

SLEEVES
Using 4mm (US 6) needles and yarn A cast on 79 [79: 81: 81: 83: 83] sts.
Row 1 (RS): Using yarn A, K2 [2: 3: 3: 4: 4], *yfwd, K3, K3tog, K3, yfwd, K2, rep from * to last 0 [0: 1: 1: 2: 2] sts, K0 [0: 1: 1: 2: 2].
Row 2: Using yarn A, knit.
These 2 rows form patt.
Keeping patt correct, now work in stripe sequence as given for back, beg with a further 4 rows using yarn A and shaping sides by dec 1 st at each end of 5th and every foll 4th row until 69 [69: 71: 71: 73: 73] sts rem.
Work 17 rows, ending with RS facing for next row.
Keeping stripes and patt correct, inc 1 st at each end of next and every foll 4th row to 81 [87: 87: 93: 91: 97] sts, then on every foll 6th row until there are 99 [101: 103: 105: 107: 109] sts, taking inc sts into patt.
Cont straight until sleeve meas 43 [43: 44: 44: 45: 45] cm, ending with RS facing for next row.
Shape top
Keeping stripes and patt correct, cast off 5 [6: 6: 7: 7: 8] sts at beg of next 2 rows.
89 [89: 91: 91: 93: 93] sts.
Dec 1 st at each end of next 9 rows, then on every foll alt row to 59 sts, then on foll 19 rows, ending with RS facing for next row.
21 sts.
Cast off 4 sts at beg of next 2 rows.
Cast off rem 13 sts.

MAKING UP
Press as described on the information page.
Join both shoulder seams using back stitch, or mattress stitch if preferred.
Neck edging
With RS facing and using 4.00mm (US G6) crochet hook, attach yarn A to neck edge at one shoulder seam, 1 ch (does NOT count as st), work 1 round of dc evenly around entire neck and front opening edge, ending with ss to first dc, turn.
Round 1 (WS): 1 ch (does NOT count as st), 1 dc into each dc to end, missing dc and working extra dc into corner points as required to ensure edging lays flat, ss to first dc, turn.
Rounds 2 and 3: As round 1.
Fasten off.

See information page for finishing instructions, setting in sleeves using the set-in method.

Hem edging

Work as given for neck edging to end of round 3, attaching yarn at base of one side seam and ensuring number of sts worked in round 3 is divisible by 4.

Round 4 (RS): 3 ch (counts as 1 tr), miss first 3 dc, ★1 tr into next dc, 3 ch★★, 4 tr around stem of tr just worked, miss 3 dc, rep from ★ to end, ending last rep at ★★, 3 tr around stem of tr just worked, ss to top of 3 ch at beg of round.

Fasten off.

Cuff edging

Work as given for hem edging, attaching yarn at base of sleeve seam.

Using photograph as a guide, attach beads around neck, hem and cuff edges – place beads on every other st of round 2. Attach beads to points of round 4 of cuff and hem edgings as in photograph.

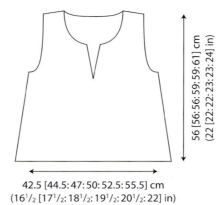

56 [56: 56: 59: 59: 61] cm
(22 [22: 22: 23: 23: 24] in)

42.5 [44.5: 47: 50: 52.5: 55.5] cm
(16½ [17½: 18½: 19½: 20½: 22] in)

46 [46: 47: 47: 48: 48] cm
(18 [18: 18½: 18½: 19: 19] in)

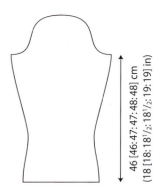

Main image page 70

EVA BY AMANDA CRAWFORD

SIZE

	S	M	L	XL
	8/10	12/14	16/18	20/22

To fit bust

82–87	92–97	102–107	112–117	cm
32–34	36–38	40–42	44–46	in

YARN

Rowan Kid Classic

7	7	8	8	x 50gm

(photographed in Sherbet Dip 850 and Feather 828)

NEEDLES

1 pair 4mm (no 8) (US 6) needles
1 pair 4½mm (no 7) (US 7) needles

RIBBON – 3 m of 3-4 cm wide organza ribbon

TENSION

22 sts and 28 rows to 10 cm measured over stocking stitch using 4½ mm (US 7) needles.

SPECIAL ABBREVIATIONS

MB = (K1, P1, K1, P1, K1, P1, K1) all into next st, lift 2nd, 3rd, 4th, 5th, 6th and 7th sts on right needle over first st and off right needle.

BACK

Using 4½ mm (US 7) needles cast on 96 [106:
120: 134] sts.
Beg with a K row, work in st st for 48 rows, ending with RS facing for next row.
(Back should meas 17 cm.)

Shape armholes

Cast off 4 sts at beg of next 2 rows.
88 [98: 112: 126] sts.
Dec 1 st at each end of next and foll alt row.
84 [94: 108: 122] sts.
Cont straight until armhole meas 19 [20: 21: 22] cm, ending with RS facing for next row.

Shape back neck

Next row (RS): K30 [32: 34: 36] and turn, leaving rem sts on a holder.
Work each side of neck separately.
Cast off 4 sts at beg of next row.
26 [28: 30: 32] sts.
Work 2 rows, ending with RS facing for next row.

Shape shoulder

Cast off rem 26 [28: 30: 32] sts.
With RS facing, rejoin yarn to rem sts, cast off centre 24 [30: 40: 50] sts, K to end.
Complete to match first side, reversing shapings.

LEFT FRONT

Using 4½ mm (US 7) needles cast on 9 [14: 21: 28] sts.

Beg with a K row, work in st st as folls:
Work 1 row, ending with **WS** facing for next row.
Inc 1 st at beg of next row and at same edge on foll 20 rows.
30 [35: 42: 49] sts.
Place marker at beg of last row.
Work 2 rows, ending with RS facing for next row.
Dec 1 st at end of next and foll 11 [11: 9: 4] alt rows, then at same edge on foll 0 [0: 5: 15] rows.
18 [23: 27: 29] sts.
Work 1 [1: 0: 0] row, ending with RS facing for next row. (Left front should match back to beg of armhole shaping.)

Shape armhole

Cast off 4 sts at beg and dec 1 st at end of next row.
13 [18: 22: 24] sts.
Work 1 row, dec 0 [0: 1: 1] st at beg of row.
13 [18: 21: 23] sts.
Dec 1 st at armhole edge of next and foll alt row **and at same time** dec 1 st at front slope edge of next and foll 0 [0: 2: 2] rows, then on foll 1 [1: 0: 0] alt row.
9 [14: 16: 18] sts.
Dec 1 st at front slope edge **only** of 2nd [next: next: next] and foll 2 [0: 0: 0] alt rows, then on foll 4 [11: 13: 15] rows, ending with **WS** facing

for next row.
2 sts.
Next row (WS): P2tog and fasten off.

RIGHT FRONT
Using 4½ mm (US 7) needles cast on 9 [14: 21: 28] sts.
Beg with a K row, work in st st as folls:
Work 1 row, ending with **WS** facing for next row.
Inc 1 st at end of next row and at same edge on foll 20 rows.
30 [35: 42: 49] sts.
Place marker at end of last row.
Complete to match left front, reversing shapings.

SLEEVES
Using 4½ mm (US 7) needles cast on 48 [50: 52: 52] sts.
Beg with a K row, work in st st, shaping sides by inc 1 st at each end of 3rd and every foll 4th row to 68 [74: 78: 90] sts, then on every foll 6th row until there are 80 [84: 88: 92] sts.
Cont straight until sleeve meas 32 [33: 34: 34] cm, ending with RS facing for next row.
Shape top
Cast off 4 sts at beg of next 2 rows.
72 [76: 80: 84] sts.
Dec 1 st at each end of next and foll alt row.
68 [72: 76: 80] sts.
Work 1 row, ending with RS facing for next row.
Cast off 21 [22: 24: 25] sts at beg of next 2 rows.
Cast off rem 26 [28: 28: 30] sts.

MAKING UP
Press as described on the information page.
Join side seams using back stitch, or mattress stitch if preferred.
Left front neck and right hem trim
Using 4½ mm (US 7) needles cast on 29 sts.
Row 1 and every foll alt row (WS): K1, P4, K1, P to last 6 sts, K1, P4, K1.
Row 2: K1, K2tog, (yfwd) twice, sl 1, K1, psso, P1, K5, K2tog, (yfwd, K1) 3 times, yfwd, sl 1, K1, psso, K5, P1, K2tog, (yfwd) twice, sl 1, K1, psso, K1.
31 sts.
Row 4: K1, K2tog, (yfwd) twice, sl 1, K1, psso, P1, K4, K2tog, K7, sl 1, K1, psso, K4, P1, K2tog, (yfwd) twice, sl 1, K1, psso, K1.
29 sts.
Row 6: K1, K2tog, (yfwd) twice, sl 1, K1, psso, P1, K3, K2tog, K1, yfwd, K1, yfwd, K3, (yfwd,

K1) twice, sl 1, K1, psso, K3, P1, K2tog, (yfwd) twice, sl 1, K1, psso, K1.
31 sts.
Row 8: K1, K2tog, (yfwd) twice, sl 1, K1, psso, P1, K2, K2tog, K5, MB, K5, sl 1, K1, psso, K2, P1, K2tog, (yfwd) twice, sl 1, K1, psso, K1.
29 sts.
Row 10: K1, K2tog, (yfwd) twice, sl 1, K1, psso, P1, K1, K2tog, K2, yfwd, K1, yfwd, K5, yfwd, K1, yfwd, K2, sl 1, K1, psso, K1, P1, K2tog, (yfwd) twice, sl 1, K1, psso, K1.
31 sts.
Row 12: K1, K2tog, (yfwd) twice, sl 1, K1, psso, P1, K2tog, K6, MB, K1, MB, K6, sl 1, K1, psso, P1, K2tog, (yfwd) twice, sl 1, K1, psso, K1.
29 sts.
These 12 rows form patt.
Cont in patt until trim meas 14 [15: 15: 15] cm, ending with RS facing for next row.
Place marker at beg of last row – this marker matches to fasten-off point of left front.
Cont in patt until trim **from marker** fits down left front slope, from fasten-off point to left front marker, ending with RS facing for next row.
Slip stitch trim in place to left front slope.
Cont in patt until trim meas 12 cm from marker on left front, ending with RS facing for next row.
Place marker at end of last row – this matches to marker on **right** front.
Cont in patt until trim fits down lower edge of right front, and across cast-on edge of right front and back to centre back, ending with RS facing for next row.
Cast off.
Right front neck and left hem trim
Work to match left front neck and right hem trim, reversing position of markers.
Join cast-off ends of trims, then slip stitch trims to lower edges of fronts and back, overlapping trims at centre front.
Back neck band
With RS facing and using 4mm (US 6) needles, pick up and knit 7 sts down right side of back neck, 24 [30: 40: 50] sts from back, then 7 sts up left side of back neck.
38 [44: 54: 64] sts.
Work in g st for 2 rows, ending with **WS** facing for next row.
Cast off knitwise (on **WS**).
Join shoulder seams by sewing cast-on edge of trims to back shoulder edges, positioning edge of trim against cast-off edge of back neck band – row-end edge of trim forms part of armhole edge.

Cuff trims (both alike)
Using 4½ mm (US 7) needles cast on 29 sts.
Work in patt as given for left front neck and right hem trim until strip fits across cast-on edge of sleeve, ending with RS facing for next row.
Cast off.
Slip stitch one edge of cuff trim to cast-on edge of sleeve.
See information page for finishing instructions, setting in sleeves using the shallow set-in method.
Cut ribbon into 2 equal lengths. Using photograph as a guide, thread ribbon through eyelet holes along side of trim, and tie ends in a bow at centre back hem edge.

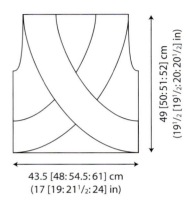

49 [50: 51: 52] cm (19½ [19½: 20: 20½] in)

43.5 [48: 54.5: 61] cm (17 [19: 21½: 24] in)

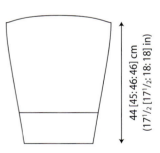

44 [45: 46: 46] cm (17½ [17½: 18: 18] in)

Main image page 76 & 77

BELLA ROSE CORSET BY JULIA NEILL

SIZE

	S	L	
To fit waist	61-66	71-76	cm
	24-26	28-30	in

YARN
Rowan Scottish Tweed DK and Felted Tweed

A Scot Porridge 024	3	4	x 50gm
B F Twd Sigh 148	2	3	x 50gm
C F Twd Melody 142	1	1	x 50gm

CROCHET HOOK
3.00mm (no 11) (US D3) crochet hook

RIBBON – 2 m of 15mm wide satin ribbon

TENSION
25½ sts and 10 rows to 10 cm measured over pattern using 3.00mm (US D3) crochet hook.

UK CROCHET ABBREVIATIONS
ch = chain; **ss** = slip stitch; **dc** = double crochet; **htr** = half treble; **tr** = treble; **dtr** = double treble; **sp(s)** = space(s).

US CROCHET ABBREVIATIONS
ch = chain; **ss** = slip stitch; **dc** = single crochet; **htr** = half double; **tr** = double crochet; **dtr** = treble; **sp(s)** = space(s).

FINISHED SIZE
Completed corset measures 26 cm (10¼ in) wide and 79 [93] cm (31 [36½] in) long.

MAIN SECTION
Using 3.00mm (US D3) crochet hook and yarn A make 206 [242] ch.
Row 1 (RS): 1 tr into 8th ch from hook, *2 ch, miss 2 ch, 1 tr into next ch, rep from * to end, turn. 202 [238] sts, 67 [79] ch sps.
Row 2: 5 ch (counts as 1 tr and 2 ch), miss (tr at base of 5 ch and 2 ch), (1 tr into next tr, 2 ch, miss 2 ch) 3 times, *1 tr into next tr, 4 ch, miss 2 ch, 1 dtr into next tr, (miss 2 ch, 1 dtr into next tr) 3 times, 4 ch, miss 2 ch, 1 tr into next tr, 2 ch, miss 2 ch, rep from * to last 3 ch sps, (1 tr into next tr, 2 ch, miss 2 ch) 3 times, 1 tr into 3rd of 5 ch at beg of previous row, turn. 10 [12] patt reps plus edge sts.
Row 3: 5 ch (counts as 1 tr and 2 ch), miss (tr at base of 5 ch and 2 ch), (1 tr into next tr, 2 ch, miss 2 ch) 3 times, *1 tr into next tr, 4 ch, miss 4 ch, 1 dc into each of next 4 dtr, 4 ch, miss 4 ch, 1 tr into next tr, 2 ch, miss 2 ch, rep from * to last 3 ch sps, (1 tr into next tr, 2 ch, miss 2 ch) 3 times, 1 tr into 3rd of 5 ch at beg of previous row, turn.
Row 4: 5 ch (counts as 1 tr and 2 ch), miss (tr at base of 5 ch and 2 ch), (1 tr into next tr, 2 ch, miss 2 ch) 3 times, *1 tr into next tr,

4 ch, miss 4 ch, 1 dc into each of next 4 dc, 4 ch, miss 4 ch, 1 tr into next tr, 2 ch, miss 2 ch, rep from * to last 3 ch sps, (1 tr into next tr, 2 ch, miss 2 ch) 3 times, 1 tr into 3rd of 5 ch at beg of previous row, turn.
Row 5: As row 4.
Row 6: 5 ch (counts as 1 tr and 2 ch), miss (tr at base of 5 ch and 2 ch), (1 tr into next tr, 2 ch, miss 2 ch) 3 times, *1 tr into next tr, 2 ch, miss 4 ch, 1 dtr into next dc, (2 ch, 1 dtr into next dc) 3 times, 2 ch, miss 4 ch, 1 tr into next tr, 2 ch, miss 2 ch, rep from * to last 3 ch sps, (1 tr into next tr, 2 ch, miss 2 ch) 3 times, 1 tr into 3rd of 5 ch at beg of previous row, turn.
Row 7: 5 ch (counts as 1 tr and 2 ch), miss (tr at base of 5 ch and 2 ch), 1 tr into next tr, *2 ch, miss 2 ch, 1 tr into next st, rep from * to end, working last tr into 3rd of 5 ch at beg of previous row, turn.
Rows 8 to 19: As row 2 to 7, twice.
Fasten off.

SCALLOP EDGING
Divide long edges of main section into 9 [11] equal sized sections – each of these sections will have a scallop worked along it. Place red markers at edges of each division. Now place a further 8 markers evenly spaced within each division.
With RS facing, using 3.00mm (US D3) crochet hook and yarn B, attach yarn to one long edge of main section at one end (this is first red marker) and work scallops as folls: *ss along and into 4th marker, 4 ch, ss to 5th marker, 3 ch, ss to 6th marker, turn, miss 3 ch, 10 tr into next 4 ch sp, ss to 3rd marker, 3 ch, ss to 2nd marker, turn, (2 tr into next tr, 1 tr into next tr) 5 times, ss to 7th marker, 3 ch, ss to 8th marker, turn, 1 tr into next tr, (1 ch, miss 1 tr, 1 tr into next tr) 7 times, ss to first marker, 3 ch, ss to red marker at beg of scallop division, turn, 1 tr into first tr, (2 tr into next ch sp, 1 tr into next tr) 7 times, ss to next red marker at end of this (and beg of next) scallop division, rep from * to end.
Fasten off.
Work scallop edging along other long edge in same way.

MAKING UP
Press as described on the information page.
Flowers (make 5 [6])
Using 3.00mm (US D3) crochet hook and yarn B make 8 ch and join with a ss to form a ring.
Round 1 (RS): 1 ch (does NOT count as st), 16 dc into ring, ss to first dc. 16 sts.
Round 2: 5 ch (counts as first tr and 2 ch), miss dc at base of 5 ch and next dc, (1 tr into

next dc, 2 ch, miss 1 dc) 7 times, ss to 3rd of 5 ch at beg of round.
8 ch sps.
Round 3: Ss across and into first ch sp, 1 ch (does NOT count as st), (1 dc, 1 htr, 1 tr, 1 htr and 1 dc) into each ch sp to end, ss to first dc. 8 petals.
Round 4: Working behind petals of previous round, ss across and into base of tr at centre of first petal, 1 ch (does NOT count as st), 1 dc into same place as last ss, *3 ch, 1 dc into base of tr at centre of next petal, rep from * to end, replacing dc at end of last rep with ss to first dc.
8 ch sps.
Round 5: Ss across and into first ch sp, 1 ch (does NOT count as st), (1 dc, 1 htr, 3 tr, 1 htr and 1 dc) into each ch sp to end, ss to first dc. 8 petals.
Round 6: Working behind petals of previous round, ss across and into base of tr at centre of first petal, 1 ch (does NOT count as st), 1 dc into same place as last ss, *5 ch, 1 dc into base of tr at centre of next petal, rep from * to end, replacing dc at end of last rep with ss to first dc.
8 ch sps.
Round 7: Ss across and into first ch sp, 1 ch (does NOT count as st), (1 dc, 1 htr, 5 tr, 1 htr and 1 dc) into each ch sp to end, ss to first dc. 8 petals.
Round 8: Working behind petals of previous round, ss across and into base of tr at centre of first petal, 1 ch (does NOT count as st), 1 dc into same place as last ss, *7 ch, 1 dc into base of tr at centre of next petal, rep from * to end, replacing dc at end of last rep with ss to first dc. 8 ch sps.
Round 9: Ss across and into first ch sp, 1 ch (does NOT count as st), (1 dc, 1 htr, 7 tr, 1 htr and 1 dc) into each ch sp to end, ss to first dc. 8 petals.
Fasten off.
Leaves (make 20 [24] in total)
Using 3.00mm (US D3) crochet hook and yarn B make 6 ch.
Round 1 (RS): 1 ss into first ch, 1 dc into next ch, 1 htr into next ch, 1 tr into next ch, 1 htr into next ch, 2 dc into last ch, now working back along other side of foundation ch: 1 htr into next ch, 1 tr into next ch, 1 htr into next ch, 1 dc into next ch, 1 ss into last ch (this is same ch as used for ss at beg of round).
Fasten off.
Make a further 9 [11] leaves using yarn B, and 10 [12] leaves using yarn C.
Using photograph as a guide, sew flowers and leaves evenly spaced along centre of main section. Thread ribbon through row end edges as in photograph.

Main image page 35, 52 & 53

ROAM BY SARAH HATTON

SIZE

	S	M	L	XL
	8/10	12/14	16/18	20/22

To fit bust

82-87	92-97	102-107	112-117	cm
32-34	36-38	40-42	44-46	in

YARN

Rowan Big Wool

9	10	11	13	x 100gm

(photographed in Sandstone 040)

NEEDLES

1 pair 9mm (no 00) (US 13) needles
1 pair 10mm (no 000) (US 15) needles
Cable needle

TENSION

9 sts and 12½ rows to 10 cm measured over reverse stocking stitch using 10mm (US 15) needles. Cable panel (34 sts) measures 27 cm.

SPECIAL ABBREVIATIONS

Cr3R = slip next st onto cable needle and leave at back of work, K2, then P1 (or K1 depending on point in patt) from cable needle;
Cr3L = slip next 2 sts onto cable needle and leave at front of work, P1 (or K1 depending on point in patt), then K2 from cable needle;
C4B = slip next 2 sts onto cable needle and leave at back of work, K2, then K2 from cable needle; **C4F** = slip next 2 sts onto cable needle and leave at front of work, K2, then K2 from cable needle.

BACK

Using 10mm (US 15) needles cast on 36 [40: 44: 48] sts.
Beg and ending rows as indicated and repeating the 28 row patt rep throughout, cont in patt from chart as folls:
Work 2 rows, ending with RS facing for next row.
Inc 1 st at each end of next and foll 4 alt rows. 46 [50: 54: 58] sts.
Cont straight until back meas 60 [62: 64: 66] cm, ending with RS facing for next row.
Shape back neck
Next row (RS): Patt 18 [20: 21: 23] sts and turn, leaving rem sts on a holder.
Work each side of neck separately.
Cast off 3 sts at beg of next row.
15 [17: 18: 20] sts.
Shape shoulder
Cast off 7 [8: 9: 10] sts at beg of next row.
Work 1 row.
Cast off rem 8 [9: 9: 10] sts.
With RS facing, rejoin yarn to rem sts, cast off centre 10 [10: 12: 12] sts, patt to end.
Complete to match first side, reversing shapings.
FRONT
Work as given for back until 6 rows less have been worked than on back to start of **shoulder** shaping, ending with RS facing for next row.
Shape front neck
Next row (RS): Patt 18 [20: 21: 23] sts and turn, leaving rem sts on a holder.

Work each side of neck separately.
Dec 1 st at neck edge of next 3 rows.
15 [17: 18: 20] sts.
Work 2 rows, ending with RS facing for next row.
Shape shoulder
Cast off 7 [8: 9: 10] sts at beg of next row.
Work 1 row.
Cast off rem 8 [9: 9: 10] sts.
With RS facing, rejoin yarn to rem sts, cast off centre 10 [10: 12: 12] sts, patt to end.
Complete to match first side, reversing shapings.

MAKING UP

Press as described on the information page. Join shoulder seams using back stitch, or mattress stitch if preferred.
Hood
With RS facing and using 10mm (US 15) needles, cast on 12 [12: 13: 13] sts, pick up and knit 19 [19: 21: 21] sts from back, turn and cast on 12 [12: 13: 13] sts.
43 [43: 47: 47] sts.
Beg with a K row, work in rev st st until hood meas 26 [27: 28: 29] cm from pick up row, ending with RS facing for next row.
Shape top
Next row (RS): Cast off 14 [14: 15: 15] sts, P until there are 15 [15: 17: 17] sts on right needle, cast off rem 14 [14: 15: 15] sts.
Break yarn.
With **WS** facing, rejoin yarn to centre 15 [15:

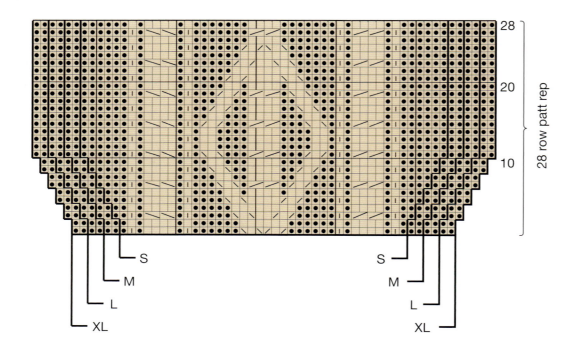

Key

- ☐ K on RS, P on WS
- ⊡ P on RS, K on WS
- ⊡ sl 1
- ◢◣ Cr3R
- ◤◥ Cr3L
- ◢◢ C4B
- ◣◣ C4F

110

17: 17] sts, K to end.
Cont straight until hood meas 16 [16: 17: 17] cm from cast-off sts, ending with RS facing for next row.
Cast off.
Join top seams of hood.

Hood edging
With RS facing and using 9mm (US 13) needles, pick up and knit 70 [72: 76: 78] sts evenly along entire front edge of hood.
Cast off knitwise (on **WS**).
Positioning cast-off edges of hood edging at centre front neck, sew hood to front neck, easing in fullness.

Edging
Using 9mm (US 13) needles cast on 8 sts.
Row 1 (RS): K8.

Row 2: K2, P4, K2.
Row 3: K2, C4B, K2.
Row 4: As row 2.
These 4 rows form patt.
Cont in patt until edging fits neatly around entire outer edge of front and back, beg and ending at centre of back cast-on edge, ending after patt row 4 and with RS facing for next row.
Cast off.
Join ends of edging, then slip stitch in place.

Belt
Work as given for edging until belt meas 143 cm, ending after patt row 4 and with RS facing for next row.
Cast off.
See information page for finishing instructions.

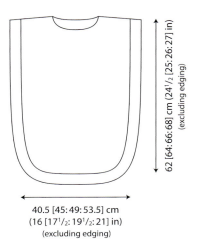

62 [64: 66: 68] cm (24½ [25: 26: 27] in) (excluding edging)

40.5 [45: 49: 53.5] cm
(16 [17½: 19½: 21] in)
(excluding edging)

Main image page 22

GRANTIS SCARF BY JULIA NEILL

YARN
Rowan Kidsilk Night, Kid Classic and Lurex Shimmer

A Night Oberon 613	1	x 25gm
B Night Starry Night 610	1	x 25gm
C Classic Crystal 840	1	x 50gm
D Classic Smoke 831	1	x 50gm
E Lurex Black 334	1	x 25gm
F Lurex Pewter 333	1	x 25gm

CROCHET HOOK
2.50mm (no 12) (US C2) crochet hook

TENSION
Strip A measures 2.5 cm (1 in) wide using 2.50mm (US C2) crochet hook.

UK CROCHET ABBREVIATIONS
ch = chain; **ss** = slip stitch; **dc** = double crochet;
tr = treble; **dtr** = double treble;
sp = space.

US CROCHET ABBREVIATIONS
ch = chain; **ss** = slip stitch; **dc** = single crochet;
tr = double crochet; **dtr** = treble;
sp = space.

STRIP A
Using 2.50mm (US C2) hook and yarn A make a ch approx 160 cm long.
Row 1 (RS): 1 tr into 4th ch from hook, 1 tr into each ch to end, turn.
Row 2: 3 ch (counts as first tr), miss tr at base of 3 ch, 1 tr into each tr to end, working last tr into top of 3 ch at beg of previous row, turn.

Row 3: As row 2.
Fasten off.
Make a second strip using yarn B.

STRIP B
Using 2.50mm (US C2) hook and yarn C make a ch approx 160 cm long, ensuring total number of ch worked is an odd number.
Row 1 (RS): 1 tr into 4th ch from hook, 1 tr into each ch to end, turn.
Row 2: 4 ch (counts as first tr and 1 ch), miss tr at base of 3 ch and next tr, *1 tr into next tr, 1 ch, miss 1 tr, rep from * to last st, 1 tr into top of 3 ch at beg of previous row, turn.
Row 3: 3 ch (counts as first tr), miss tr at base of 3 ch, 1 tr into each tr and ch sp to end, working last tr into 3rd of 4 ch at beg of previous row.
Fasten off.

STRIP C
Using 2.50mm (US C2) hook and yarn D make a ch approx 160 cm long.
Row 1 (RS): 1 tr into 4th ch from hook, 1 tr into each ch to end.
Fasten off.
Make a second strip using yarn E.

STRIP D
Using 2.50mm (US C2) hook and yarn F make a ch approx 160 cm long.
Row 1 (RS): 1 dc into 2nd ch from hook, 1 dc into each ch to end.
Fasten off.

DROPLETS
Using 2.50mm (US C2) hook and yarn A

make 6 ch and join with a ss to form a ring.
Round 1 (RS): 5 ch (counts as first tr and 2 ch), (1 tr into ring, 2 ch) 11 times, ss to 3rd of 5 ch at beg of round.
Round 2: 6 ch (counts as first tr and 3 ch), miss st at base of 6 ch and next 2 ch, *1 dtr into next tr, 3 ch, miss 2 ch, 1 tr into next tr, 3 ch, miss 2 ch, 1 dc into next tr, 3 ch, miss 2 ch**, 1 tr into next tr, 3 ch, miss 2 ch, rep from * to end, ending last rep at **, ss to 3rd of 6 ch at beg of round.
Round 3: 1 ch (does NOT count as st), 1 dc into st at base of 1 ch, *3 dc into next ch sp, 1 dc into next st, rep from * to end, replacing dc at end of last rep with ss to first dc.
Round 4: *5 ch, miss 4 dc, 1 dtr into next dc, 5 ch, miss 4 dc, 1 ss into each of next 7 dc, rep from * to end, ss to base of 5 ch at beg of round.
Round 5: 1 ch (does NOT count as st), *5 dc into next ch sp, 1 dc into next dtr, 5 dc into next ch sp, 1 dc into each of next 7 ss, rep from * to end, ss to first dc.
Fasten off.
Make a further 11 droplets in this way – 1 more using yarn A, and 2 in each of yarns B, C, D, E and F.

MAKING UP
Press as described on the information page.
Lay strips next to each other and plait all 6 strips together, beg and ending approx 10–15 cm from ends. Secure strips together near ends and as required along length. Attach a droplet to each end of every strip, using same colour droplet as strip.

Main image page 18

SERGE BY SARAH HATTON

SIZE

S	M	L	XL	XXL	
To fit chest					
102	107	112	117	122	cm
40	42	44	46	48	in

YARN

Rowan Tapestry

11	12	12	13	14	x 50gm

(photographed in Leadmine 177)

NEEDLES

1 pair 3¼ mm (no 10) (US 3) needles
1 pair 4mm (no 8) (US 6) needles

BUTTONS – 4 x 00406

TENSION

22 sts and 30 rows to 10 cm measured over stocking stitch using 4mm (US 6) needles.

BACK

Using 3¼ mm (US 3) needles cast on 122 [126: 134: 138: 146] sts.
Row 1 (RS): K2, *P2, K2, rep from * to end.
Row 2: P2, *K2, P2, rep from * to end.
These 2 rows form rib.
Work in rib for a further 16 rows, inc 0 [1: 0: 1: 1] st at each end of last row and ending with RS facing for next row.
122 [128: 134: 140: 148] sts.
Change to 4mm (US 6) needles.
Beg with a K row, work in st st until back meas 40 [41: 40: 41: 40] cm, ending with RS facing for next row.
Shape armholes
Cast off 6 sts at beg of next 2 rows.
110 [116: 122: 128: 136] sts.
Dec 1 st at each end of next 7 [7: 7: 5: 5] rows, then on foll 3 [2: 1: 1: 1] alt rows.
90 [98: 106: 116: 124] sts.
Cont straight until armhole meas 23 [24: 25: 26: 27] cm, ending with RS facing for next row.
Shape shoulders and back neck
Next row (RS): Cast off 12 [14: 15: 18: 19] sts, K until there are 16 [18: 20: 22: 24] sts on right needle and turn, leaving rem sts on a holder.
Work each side of neck separately.
Cast off 4 sts at beg of next row.
Cast off rem 12 [14: 16: 18: 20] sts.
With RS facing, rejoin yarn to rem sts, cast off centre 34 [34: 36: 36: 38] sts, K to end.
Complete to match first side, reversing shapings.

FRONT

Work as given for back until 18 [18: 22: 22: 24] rows less have been worked than on back to beg of shoulder shaping, ending with RS facing for next row.
Shape neck
Next row (RS): K31 [35: 40: 45: 49] and turn, leaving rem sts on a holder.
Work each side of neck separately.

Dec 1 st at neck edge of next 6 rows, then on foll 1 [1: 3: 3: 4] alt rows.
24 [28: 31: 36: 39] sts.
Work 9 rows, ending with RS facing for next row.
Shape shoulder
Cast off 12 [14: 15: 18: 19] sts at beg of next row.
Work 1 row.
Cast off rem 12 [14: 16: 18: 20] sts.
With RS facing, rejoin yarn to rem sts, cast off centre 28 [28: 26: 26: 26] sts, K to end.
Complete to match first side, reversing shapings.

SLEEVES

Using 3¼ mm (US 3) needles cast on 50 [54: 54: 58: 58] sts.
Work in rib as given for back, inc 1 st at each end of 13th and foll 4th row.
54 [58: 58: 62: 62] sts.
Work 1 row, ending with RS facing for next row.
Change to 4mm (US 6) needles.
Beg with a K row, work in st st, shaping sides by inc 1 st at each end of 3rd and every foll 4th row to 88 [80: 80: 72: 72] sts, then on every foll 6th row until there are 104 [106: 108: 110: 112] sts.
Cont straight until sleeve meas 49 [51: 53: 55: 57] cm, ending with RS facing for next row.
Shape top
Cast off 6 sts at beg of next 2 rows.
92 [94: 96: 98: 100] sts.
Dec 1 st at each end of next 11 rows, then on every foll alt row to 44 sts, then on foll 7 rows, ending with RS facing for next row.
30 sts.
Cast off 4 sts at beg of next 2 rows.
Cast off rem 22 sts.

MAKING UP

Press as described on the information page.
Join right shoulder seam using back stitch, or mattress stitch if preferred.
Shoulder patch
Using 4mm (US 6) needles cast on 31 [35: 39: 43: 47] sts.
Row 1 (RS): *K1, P1, rep from * to last st, K1.
Row 2: P1, *K1, P1, rep from * to end.
Row 3: *P1, K1, rep from * to last st, inc in last st.
Row 4: *P1, K1, rep from * to end.
These 4 rows form patt and beg shaping.
Cont in patt, inc 1 st at end of next and every foll alt row until there are 39 [43: 47: 51: 55] sts, taking inc sts into patt.
Cont straight until patch meas 17 [18: 18: 19: 19] cm, ending with **WS** facing for next row.
Shape neck
Cast off 8 [8: 7: 6: 6] sts at beg of next row.
31 [35: 40: 45: 49] sts.
Dec 1 st at neck edge of next 5 rows, then on

foll 2 [2: 4: 4: 5] alt rows.
24 [28: 31: 36: 39] sts.
Work 9 rows, ending with RS facing for next row.
Shape shoulder
Cast off 12 [14: 15: 18: 19] sts at beg of next row.
Work 1 row.
Cast off rem 12 [14: 16: 18: 20] sts.
Lay patch over left shoulder area of front and sew in place along armhole, shoulder and side neck edge.
Neckband
With RS facing and using 3¼ mm (US 3) needles, pick up and knit 16 [16: 20: 20: 21] sts down left side of neck through both layers, 28 [28: 26: 26: 26] sts from front, 16 [16: 20: 20: 21] sts up right side of neck, then 42 [42: 44: 44: 46] sts from back.
102 [102: 110: 110: 114] sts.
Beg with row 2, work in rib as given for back for 17 rows, ending with RS facing for next row.
Cast off in rib.
Neck trim
Using 4mm (US 6) needles cast on 13 sts.
Row 1 (RS): *K1, P1, rep from * to last st, K1.
Row 2: Inc in first st, *K1, P1, rep from * to end. 14 sts.
Row 3: *P1, K1, rep from * to last 2 sts, P1, inc in last st. 15 sts.
Row 4: K1, *P1, K1, rep from * to end.
These 4 rows form patt and beg shaping.
Cont in patt, inc 1 st at end of next and foll alt row, taking inc sts into patt. 17 sts.
Work 1 row, ending with RS facing for next row.
Dec 1 st at end of next and foll 2 alt rows, then at same edge on foll row, ending with RS facing for next row.
Cast off rem 13 sts.
Sew straight row-end edge of neck trim to front row-end edge of neckband.

Cuff trim
Using 4mm (US 6) needles cast on 33 sts.
Row 1 (RS): *K1, P1, rep from * to last st, K1.
Row 2: Inc in first st, *K1, P1, rep from * to end.
34 sts.
Row 3: *P1, K1, rep from * to last 2 sts, P1, inc in last st.
35 sts.
Row 4: K1, *P1, K1, rep from * to end.
These 4 rows form patt and beg shaping.
Cont in patt, inc 1 st at end of next and foll alt row, taking inc sts into patt.
37 sts.
Work 1 row, ending with RS facing for next row.
Dec 1 st at end of next and foll 2 alt rows, then at same edge on foll row, ending with RS facing for next row.
Cast off rem 33 sts.

Sew straight row-end edge of cuff trim to row-end edge of left sleeve approx 3 cm above rib.

Hem trim

Using 4mm (US 6) needles cast on 49 sts.

Row 1 (WS): ★K1, P1, rep from ★ to last st, K1.

Row 2: Inc in first st, ★K1, P1, rep from ★ to end.
50 sts.

Row 3: ★P1, K1, rep from ★ to last 2 sts, P1, inc in last st. 51 sts.

Row 4: K1, ★P1, K1, rep from ★ to end.
These 4 rows form patt and beg shaping.
Cont in patt, inc 1 st at end of next and foll alt row, taking inc sts into patt.
53 sts.
Work 1 row, ending with **WS** facing for next row.
Dec 1 st at end of next and foll 2 alt rows, then at same edge on foll row, ending with **WS** facing for next row.
Cast off rem 49 sts.
Sew straight row-end edge of hem trim to row-end edge of right front just above cast-on edge.
See information page for finishing instructions, setting in sleeves using the set-in method and

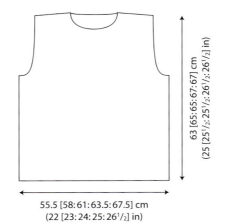

enclosing patch and trims in seams. Using photograph as a guide, attach buttons to both layers to secure patch and shaped ends of trims.

Main image page 78

PARKER BY SARAH HATTON

SIZE

8   10   12   14   16   18   20   22

To fit bust

82   87   92   97   102   107   112   117   cm
32   34   36   38   40   42   44   46   in

YARN

Rowan Tapestry

8   9   9   10   10   11   11   12   x 50gm
(photographed in Pot Pourri 172)

NEEDLES

1 pair 3¼mm (no 10) (US 3) needles
1 pair 4mm (no 8) (US 6) needles
3¼mm (no 10) (US 3) circular needle

BUTTONS - 9 x 00409

TENSION

22 sts and 30 rows to 10 cm measured over stocking stitch using 4mm (US 6) needles.

BACK

Using 3¼mm (US 3) needles cast on 108 [112: 116: 122: 132: 138: 146: 154] sts.

Row 1 (RS): K0 [0: 0: 3: 0: 3: 0: 3], P0 [2: 4: 4: 4: 4: 3: 4], ★K4, P4, rep from ★ to last 4 [6: 0: 3: 0: 3: 7: 3] sts, K4 [4: 0: 3: 0: 3: 4: 3], P0 [2: 0: 0: 0: 0: 3: 0].

Row 2: P0 [0: 0: 3: 0: 3: 0: 3], K0 [2: 4: 4: 4: 4: 3: 4], ★P4, K4, rep from ★ to last 4 [6: 0: 3: 0: 3: 7: 3] sts, P4 [4: 0: 3: 0: 3: 4: 3], K0 [2: 0: 0: 0: 0: 3: 0].

These 2 rows form rib.
Cont in rib for a further 7 rows, ending with **WS** facing for next row.

Row 10 (WS): Rib 3 [5: 7: 10: 6: 9: 4: 8], work 2 tog, ★rib 7, work 2 tog, rep from ★ to last 4 [6: 8: 11: 7: 10: 5: 9] sts, rib to end.
96 [100: 104: 110: 118: 124: 130: 138] sts.
Change to 4mm (US 8) needles.
Beg with a K row, work in st st, shaping side seams by dec 1 st at each end of 11th and every foll 8th row to 90 [94: 98: 104: 112: 118: 124: 132] sts, then on every foll 6th row until 84 [88: 92: 98: 106: 112: 118: 126] sts rem.
Work 13 rows, ending with RS facing for next row.
Inc 1 st at each end of next and every foll 8th row until there are 92 [96: 100: 106: 114: 120: 126: 134] sts.
Cont straight until back meas 39 [39: 38: 41: 40: 42: 41: 43] cm, ending with RS facing for next row.

Shape armholes

Cast off 4 [5: 5: 6: 6: 7: 7: 8] sts at beg of next 2 rows.
84 [86: 90: 94: 102: 106: 112: 118] sts.
Dec 1 st at each end of next 3 [3: 3: 3: 5: 5:

7: 7] rows, then on foll 2 [2: 3: 3: 4: 4: 3: 5] alt rows.
74 [76: 78: 82: 84: 88: 92: 94] sts.
Cont straight until armhole meas 20 [20: 21: 21: 22: 22: 23: 23] cm, ending with RS facing for next row.

Shape back neck

Next row (RS): K25 [26: 27: 29: 29: 31: 33: 34] and turn, leaving rem sts on a holder.
Work each side of neck separately.
Cast off 4 sts at beg of next row.

Shape shoulder

Cast off 8 [9: 9: 10: 10: 11: 12: 13] sts at beg of next row, then 4 sts at beg of foll row.
Cast off rem 9 [9: 10: 11: 11: 12: 13: 13] sts.
With RS facing, rejoin yarn to rem sts, cast off centre 24 [24: 24: 24: 26: 26: 26: 26] sts, K to end.
Complete to match first side, reversing shapings.

LEFT FRONT

Using 3¼mm (US 3) needles cast on 51 [53: 55: 58: 63: 66: 70: 74] sts.

Row 1 (RS): K0 [0: 0: 3: 0: 3: 0: 3], P0 [2: 4: 4: 4: 4: 3: 4], ★K4, P4, rep from ★ to last 3 sts, K3.

Row 2: P3, K4, ★P4, K4, rep from ★ to last 4 [6: 0: 3: 0: 3: 7: 3] sts, P4 [4: 0: 3: 0: 3: 4: 3],

113

K0 [2: 0: 0: 0: 0: 3: 0].

These 2 rows form rib.

Cont in rib for a further 7 rows, ending with **WS** facing for next row.

Row 10 (WS): Rib 2 [3: 4: 5: 3: 5: 2: 4], work 2 tog, *rib 7, work 2 tog, rep from * to last 2 [3: 4: 6: 4: 5: 3: 5] sts, rib to end.

45 [47: 49: 52: 56: 59: 62: 66] sts.

Change to 4mm (US 8) needles.

Beg with a K row, work in st st, shaping side seams by dec 1 st at beg of 11th and every foll 8th row to 42 [44: 46: 49: 53: 56: 59: 63] sts, then on every foll 6th row until 39 [41: 43: 46: 50: 53: 56: 60] sts rem.

Work 13 rows, ending with RS facing for next row.

Inc 1 st at beg of next and every foll 8th row until there are 43 [45: 47: 50: 54: 57: 60: 64] sts.

Cont straight until left front matches back to beg of armhole shaping, ending with RS facing for next row.

Shape armhole

Cast off 4 [5: 5: 6: 6: 7: 7: 8] sts at beg of next row. 39 [40: 42: 44: 48: 50: 53: 56] sts.

Work 1 row.

Shape front slope

Dec 1 st at armhole edge of next 3 [3: 3: 3: 5: 5: 7: 7] rows, then on foll 2 [2: 3: 3: 4: 4: 3: 5] alt rows **and at same time** dec 1 st at front slope edge of next and foll 3 [3: 4: 4: 6: 6: 5: 5] alt rows, then on foll 0 [0: 0: 0: 0: 0: 0: 4th] row. 30 [31: 31: 33: 32: 34: 37: 37] sts.

Dec 1 st at front slope edge **only** of 2nd and foll 4 [4: 1: 1: 0: 0: 0: 0] alt rows, then on every foll 4th row until 17 [18: 19: 21: 21: 23: 25: 26] sts rem.

Cont straight until left front matches back to beg of shoulder shaping, ending with RS facing for next row.

Shape shoulder

Cast off 8 [9: 9: 10: 10: 11: 12: 13] sts at beg of next row.

Work 1 row.

Cast off rem 9 [9: 10: 11: 11: 12: 13: 13] sts.

RIGHT FRONT

Using 3¼mm (US 3) needles cast on 51 [53: 55: 58: 63: 66: 70: 74] sts.

Row 1 (RS): K3, P4, *K4, P4, rep from * to last 4 [6: 0: 3: 0: 3: 7: 3] sts, K4 [4: 0: 3: 0: 3: 4: 3], P0 [2: 0: 0: 0: 0: 3: 0].

Row 2: P0 [0: 0: 3: 0: 3: 0: 3], K0 [2: 4: 4: 4: 4: 3: 4], *P4, K4, rep from * to last 3 sts, P3.

These 2 rows form rib.

Cont in rib for a further 7 rows, ending with **WS** facing for next row.

Row 10 (WS): Rib 2 [3: 4: 5: 3: 5: 2: 4], work 2 tog, *rib 7, work 2 tog, rep from * to last 2 [3: 4: 6: 4: 5: 3: 5] sts, rib to end.

45 [47: 49: 52: 56: 59: 62: 66] sts.

Change to 4mm (US 8) needles.

Beg with a K row, work in st st, shaping side seams by dec 1 st at end of 11th and every foll 8th row to 42 [44: 46: 49: 53: 56: 59: 63] sts, then on every foll 6th row until 39 [41: 43: 46: 50: 53: 56: 60] sts rem.

Complete to match left front, reversing shapings.

SLEEVES

Using 3¼mm (US 3) needles cast on 56 [56: 58: 58: 60: 60: 62: 62] sts.

Row 1 (RS): K2 [2: 3: 3: 0: 0: 0: 0], P4 [4: 4: 4: 0: 0: 1: 1], *K4, P4, rep from * to last 2 [2: 3: 3: 4: 4: 5: 5] sts, K2 [2: 3: 3: 4: 4: 4: 4], P0 [0: 0: 0: 0: 0: 1: 1].

Row 2: P2 [2: 3: 3: 0: 0: 0: 0], K4 [4: 4: 4: 0: 0: 1: 1], *P4, K4, rep from * to last 2 [2: 3: 3: 4: 4: 5: 5] sts, P2 [2: 3: 3: 4: 4: 4: 4], K0 [0: 0: 0: 0: 0: 1: 1].

These 2 rows form rib.

Cont in rib for a further 7 rows, ending with **WS** facing for next row.

Row 10 (WS): Rib 2 [2: 3: 3: 4: 4: 5: 5], work 2 tog, *rib 5, work 2 tog, rep from * to last 3 [3: 4: 4: 5: 5: 6: 6] sts, rib to end.

48 [48: 50: 50: 52: 52: 54: 54] sts.

Change to 4mm (US 8) needles.

Beg with a K row, work in st st, shaping sides by inc 1 st at each end of 5th [3rd: 5th: 3rd: 3rd: 3rd: 3rd: 3rd] and every foll 6th [4th: 6th: 4th: 4th: 4th: 4th: 4th] row to 80 [52: 86: 56: 56: 62: 66: 72] sts, then on every foll 8th [6th: –: 6th: 6th: 6th: 6th: 6th] row until there are 82 [84: –: 88: 90: 92: 94: 96] sts.

Cont straight until sleeve meas 43 [43: 44: 44: 45: 45: 44: 44] cm, ending with RS facing for next row.

Shape top

Cast off 4 [5: 5: 6: 6: 7: 7: 8] sts at beg of next 2 rows.

74 [74: 76: 76: 78: 78: 80: 80] sts.

Dec 1 st at each end of next 7 rows, then on every foll alt row to 34 sts, then on foll 5 rows, ending with RS facing for next row.

24 sts.

Cast off 4 sts at beg of next 2 rows.

Cast off rem 16 sts.

MAKING UP

Press as described on the information page.

Scarf strips (make 2)

Using 4mm (US 6) needles cast on 28 sts.

Beg with row 2, work in rib as given for front band until scarf strip meas 62 [62: 62: 65: 65: 67: 67: 69] cm, ending with RS facing for next row.

Cast off in rib.

Lay cast-on end of scarf strip along front shoulder edge, gathering in slight fullness. Join both shoulder seams using back stitch, or mattress stitch if preferred, enclosing ends of scarf strips in seams.

Front band

With RS facing and using 3¼mm (US 3) circular needle, beg and ending at cast-on edges, pick up and knit 100 [100: 98: 104: 102: 106: 104: 108] sts up right front opening edge to beg of front slope shaping, 51 [51: 53: 55: 56: 56: 58: 58] sts up right front slope, 38 [38: 38: 38: 40: 40: 40: 40] sts from back, 51 [51: 53: 55: 56: 56: 58: 58] sts down left front slope to beg of front slope shaping, then 100 [100: 98: 104: 102: 106: 104: 108] sts down left front opening edge.

340 [340: 340: 356: 356: 364: 364: 372] sts.

Row 1 (WS): P4, *K4, P4, rep from * to end.

Row 2: K4, *P4, K4, rep from * to end.

These 2 rows form rib.

Work in rib for 1 row more, ending with RS facing for next row.

Row 4 (RS): Rib 2 [2: 4: 4: 2: 4: 4], *yrn (to make a buttonhole), work 2 tog, rib 15 [15: 14: 15: 15: 16: 15: 16], rep from * 5 times more, yrn (to make 7th buttonhole), work 2 tog, rib to end.

Work in rib for a further 4 rows, ending with **WS** facing for next row.

Cast off in rib (on **WS**).

See information page for finishing instructions, setting in sleeves using the set-in method.

Scarf strip button loops (make 2)

Using 4mm (US 6) needles cast on 18 sts.

Cast off knitwise.

Sew ends of button loops to front edge of cast-off ends of scarf strips. Attach buttons to side seams 9 cm up from cast-on edge to fasten button loops.

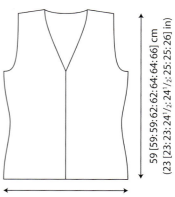

42 [43.5: 45.5: 48: 52: 54.5: 57.5: 61] cm
(16½ [17: 18: 19: 20½: 21½: 22½: 24] in)

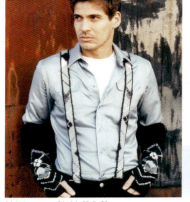

Main image page 21, 34, 52 & 53

ANA FINGERLESS MITTENS
BY GABRIELLE CARTER

YARN
Rowan Kid Classic and Wool Cotton

	1st colourway	2nd colourway	
A	Kid Classic Smoke 831	Bear 817	2 x 50gm
B	Kid Classic Crystal 840	Battle 845	1 x 50gm
C	Kid Classic Feather 828	Straw 851	1 x 50gm
E	Wool Cotton Misty 903	D'st Olive 907	1 x 50gm

NEEDLES
1 pair 4mm (no 8) (US 6) needles

TENSION
23 sts and 28 rows to 10 cm measured over patterned stocking stitch using 4mm (US 6) needles.

GAUNTLET (make 2)
Using 4mm (US 6) needles and yarn A cast on 69 sts.
Row 1 (RS): K1, *P1, K1, rep from * to end.
Row 2: P1, *K1, P1, rep from * to end.
These 2 rows form rib.
Work in rib for a further 24 rows, ending with RS facing for next row.
Beg with a K row, work in st st, dec 1 st at each end of 11th and foll 6th row.
65 sts.
Work 5 rows, ending with RS facing for next row.
Using the **intarsia** technique as described on the information page, cont in patt from chart, which is worked entirely in st st, as folls:
Dec 1 st at each end of next and every foll 6th row to 55 sts, then on every foll 8th row until 47 sts rem.
Work 6 rows, ending with chart row 63 and with **WS** facing for next row.
Right gauntlet only
Next row (WS): Patt 12 sts, cast off next 8 sts, patt to end.
Left gauntlet only
Next row (WS): Patt 27 sts, cast off next 8 sts, patt to end.
Both gauntlets
Next row (RS): K2tog, patt to last 2 sts, casting on 8 sts over those cast off on previous row, K2tog. 45 sts.
Work 5 rows, ending with chart row 70 and with RS facing for next row.
Break off contrasts and cont using yarn A only.
Work 2 rows, ending with RS facing for next row.
Work in rib for 4 rows, ending with RS facing for next row.
Cast off in rib.

MAKING UP
Press as described on the information page.
Join row-end edges to form a tube using back stitch, or mattress stitch if preferred.

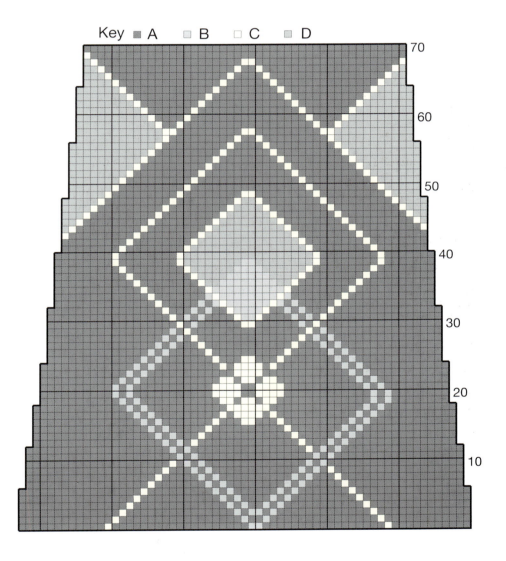

Main image page 42 & 43

SIZE

	S	M	L	
To fit bust				
	82–87	92–97	102–107	cm
	32–34	36–38	40–42	in

YARN

Rowan Wool Cotton and Felted Tweed

A W Cott Coffee Rich 956				
	6	7	8	x 50gm
B F Twd Pickle 155				
	1	1	1	x 50gm
C F Twd Herb 146				
	1	1	1	x 50gm
D F Twd Camel 157				
	1	1	1	x 50gm
E F Twd Ginger 154				
	1	1	1	x 50gm
F F Twd Dragon 147				
	1	1	1	x 50gm
G F Twd Wheat 156				
	1	1	1	x 50gm

Use ALL yarns DOUBLE throughout.

NEEDLES

1 pair 5mm (no 6) (US 8) needles
1 pair 6mm (no 4) (US 10) needles
Cable needle

BUTTONS – 1 x 00339

TENSION

15 sts and 20 rows to 10 cm measured over stocking stitch using yarn DOUBLE and 6mm (US 10) needles.

SPECIAL ABBREVIATIONS

C4B = slip next 2 sts onto cable needle and leave at back of work, K2, then K2 from cable needle; **C4F** = slip next 2 sts onto cable needle and leave at front of work, K2, then K2 from cable needle; **Cr3R** = slip next st onto cable needle and leave at back of work, K2, then P1 from cable needle; **Cr3L** = slip next 2 sts onto cable needle and leave at front of work, P1, then K2 from cable needle.

BACK

Using 5mm (US 8) needles and yarn A DOUBLE cast on 81 [89: 99] sts.
Row 1 (RS): K1, *P1, K1, rep from * to end.
Row 2: As row 1.
These 2 rows form moss st.
Work in moss st for a further 3 rows, ending with **WS** facing for next row.
Row 6 (WS): Purl.
Change to 6mm (US 10) needles.
Beg and ending rows as indicated, using the **intarsia** technique as described on the information page, work in patt from chart for back, which is worked entirely in st st beg with a K row, as folls:
Work 2 rows.
Dec 1 st at each end of next and every foll 8th row until 75 [83: 93] sts rem.
Work 3 rows, ending with chart row 22 and

with RS facing for next row.
Break off contrasts and beg with a K row, cont in st st using yarn A DOUBLE as folls:
Dec 1 st at each end of 3rd and 1 [1: 0] foll 6th rows, then on 3 [2: 2] foll 4th rows, then on every foll alt row until 59 [63: 67] sts rem.
Work 1 row, ending with RS facing for next row.

Shape shoulders and back neck

Cast off 5 [5: 6] sts at beg of next 2 rows.
49 [53: 55] sts.
Next row (RS): Cast off 5 [5: 6] sts, K until there are 8 [10: 9] sts on right needle and turn, leaving rem sts on a holder.
Work each side of neck separately.
Cast off 4 sts at beg of next row.
Cast off rem 4 [6: 5] sts.
With RS facing, rejoin yarn to rem sts, cast off centre 23 [23: 25] sts, K to end.
Complete to match first side, reversing shapings.

LEFT FRONT

Using 5mm (US 8) needles and yarn A DOUBLE cast on 39 [43: 49] sts.
Work in moss st as given for back for 5 rows, dec 0 [0: 1] st at beg of last row and ending with **WS** facing for next row.
39 [43: 48] sts.
Row 6 (WS): Purl.
Change to 6mm (US 10) needles.
Beg with a K row, work in st st, shaping side edge by dec 1 st at beg of 3rd and every foll 8th row to 36 [40: 45] sts, then on 2 [2: 1] foll 6th rows, then on 3 [2: 2] foll 4th rows, then on foll 0 [3: 6] alt rows, ending with **WS** facing for next row.
31 [33: 36] sts.

Shape neck

Cast off 10 sts at beg of next row.
21 [23: 26] sts.
Dec 1 st at neck edge of next 3 rows, then on foll 1 [1: 2] alt rows **and at same time** dec 1 st at side edge of next and every foll alt row.
14 [16: 17] sts.
Work 1 row, ending with RS facing for next row.

Shape shoulder

Cast off 5 [5: 6] sts at beg of next and foll alt row.
Work 1 row.
Cast off rem 4 [6: 5] sts.

RIGHT FRONT

Using 5mm (US 8) needles and yarn A DOUBLE cast on 39 [43: 49] sts.
Work in moss st as given for back for 4 rows.
Row 5 (RS): Moss st 3 sts, M1, (moss st 2 sts, M1) twice, moss st 1 st, M1, moss st 2 sts, M1, moss st 1 st, (M1, moss st 2 sts) twice, M1, moss st to last 0 [0: 2] sts, (work 2 tog) 0 [0: 1] times.
47 [51: 56] sts.
Joining in colours as required, cont as folls:
Row 6: Using yarn A P to last 27 sts, K3, using yarn G P2, using yarn F P2, using yarn A

K4, using yarn E P2, using yarn D P2, using yarn A K4, using yarn C P2, using yarn B P2, using yarn A K4.
Change to 6mm (US 10) needles.

Place chart

Row 1 (RS): Work first 27 sts as row 1 of chart for cable, using yarn A K to end.
Row 2: Using yarn A P to last 27 sts, work last 27 sts as row 2 of chart for cable.
These 2 rows set position of cable chart with st st using yarn A at side edge.
Cont in patt, shaping side edge by dec 1 st at end of next and every foll 8th row to 44 [48: 53] sts, then on 2 [2: 1] foll 6th rows, then on 3 [2: 2] foll 4th rows, then on foll 0 [3: 6] alt rows. 39 [41: 44] sts.
Work 1 row, ending with RS facing for next row.

Shape neck

Keeping chart correct, cast off 14 sts at beg (dec 4 sts evenly across these sts) and dec 1 st at end of next row.
24 [26: 29] sts.
Dec 1 st at neck edge of next 3 rows, then on foll 1 [1: 2] alt rows **and at same time** dec 1 st at side edge of 2nd and every foll alt row.
18 [20: 21] sts.
Work 1 row, ending with **WS** facing for next row.

Shape shoulder

Cast off 5 [5: 6] sts at beg of next and foll alt row.
Work 1 row.
Cast off rem 8 [10: 9] sts, dec 4 sts evenly.

MAKING UP

Press as described on the information page.
Join side/shoulder seams using back stitch, or mattress stitch if preferred.

Left front band

With RS facing, using 5mm (US 8) needles and yarn A DOUBLE, pick up and knit 43 [45: 47] sts down left front opening edge, from neck shaping to cast-on edge.
Work in moss st as given for back for 5 rows, ending with RS facing for next row.

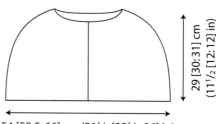

54 [59.5: 66] cm (21½ [23½: 26] in)

29 [30: 31] cm (11½ [12: 12] in)

Cast off in moss st.

Right front band

With RS facing, using 5mm (US 8) needles and yarn A DOUBLE, pick up and knit 43 [45: 47] sts up right front opening edge, from cast-on edge to neck shaping.

Work in moss st as given for back for 1 row, ending with RS facing for next row.

Row 2 (RS): Moss st to last 4 sts, yrn, work 2 tog, moss st 2 sts.

Work in moss st for a further 3 rows, ending with RS facing for next row.

Cast off in moss st.

Collar

With RS facing, using 5mm (US 8) needles and yarn A DOUBLE, beg and ending halfway across top of front bands, pick up and knit 20 [20: 23] sts up right side of neck, 30 [30: 32] sts from back, then 20 [20: 23] sts down left side of neck.

70 [70: 78] sts.

Row 1 (RS of collar, WS of body): P2,

*K2, P2, rep from * to end.

Row 2: K2, *P2, K2, rep from * to end.

These 2 rows form rib.

Cont in rib until collar meas 12 cm.

Cast off in rib.

See information page for finishing instructions. Using 9 strands of different coloured yarn for each strand of plait, make 8 plaits, each 9 cm long. Knot ends and trim ends to form 12 cm long tassel. Using photograph as a guide, attach plaits to inside of cast-on edges.

Key ■ A □ D ■ E

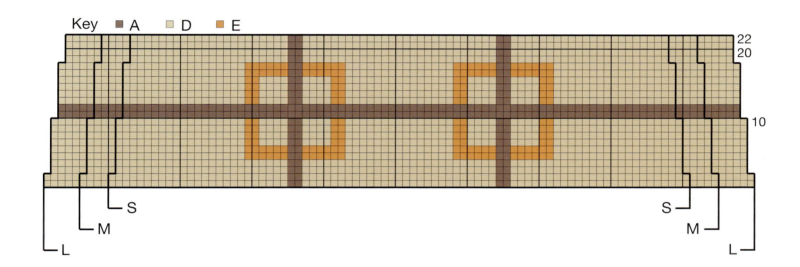

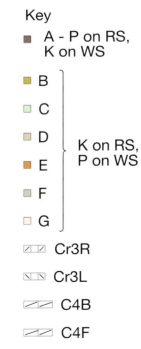

Key

■ A - P on RS, K on WS

■ B ⎫
□ C ⎪
□ D ⎬ K on RS, P on WS
■ E ⎪
■ F ⎪
□ G ⎭

▨▨ Cr3R

◨◨ Cr3L

▱▱ C4B

▱▱ C4F

Cable chart

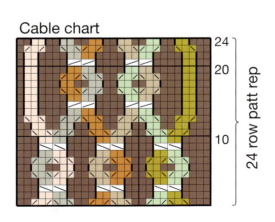

24 row patt rep

Main image page 13

SIZE

	S	M	L	XL	
	8/10	12/14	16/18	20/22	
To fit bust					
	82-87	92-97	102-107	112-117	cm
	32-34	36-38	40-42	44-46	in

YARN

Rowan Kid Classic, Lurex Shimmer, Kidsilk Haze and Kidsilk Night

A	Class Smoke 831				
	10	11	11	12	x 50gm
B	Lurex Black 334				
	4	4	5	5	x 25gm
C	Haze Wicked 599				
	5	5	5	6	x 25gm
D	Night Starry Night 610				
	5	5	5	6	x 25gm
E	Lurex Pewter 333				
	2	2	2	3	x 25gm
F	Haze Smoke 605				
	1	1	1	1	x 25gm
G	Night Moonlight 608				
	1	1	1	2	x 25gm

NEEDLES

1 pair 6mm (no 4) (US 10) needles
1 pair 7mm (no 2) (US 10½) needles

FASTENER – 1 x large Kilt pin 00414 or 00412

TENSION

15½ sts and 21 rows to 10 cm measured over stocking stitch using one strand each of yarns A, B, C and D held together and 6mm (US 10) needles.

BACK

Using 6mm (US 10) needles and one strand each of yarns A, B, C and D held together cast on 71 [79: 85: 95] sts.
Work in g st for 4 rows, ending with RS facing for next row.
Beg with a K row, work in st st until back meas 28 [29: 30: 31] cm, ending with RS facing for next row.
Shape raglan armholes
Cast off 4 sts at beg of next 2 rows.
63 [71: 77: 87] sts.
Dec 1 st at each end of next 3 [9: 11: 19] rows, then on foll 12 [10: 10: 7] alt rows, then on foll row, ending with RS facing for next row.
Cast off rem 31 [31: 33: 33] sts.

LEFT FRONT

Using 6mm (US 10) needles and one strand each of yarns A, B, C and D held together cast on 35 [39: 42: 47] sts.
Work in g st for 4 rows, ending with RS facing for next row.
Beg with a K row, work in st st until left front matches back to beg of raglan armhole shaping, ending with RS facing for next row.
Shape raglan armhole
Cast off 4 sts at beg of next row.

31 [35: 38: 43] sts.
Work 1 row.
Dec 1 st at raglan armhole edge of next 2 rows, ending with RS facing for next row.
Shape front slope
Dec 1 st at end of next row and at same edge on foll 4 [2: 2: 0] rows, then on foll 9 [11: 12: 14] alt rows **and at same time** dec 1 st at raglan armhole edge of next 1 [7: 9: 17] rows, then on foll 12 [10: 10: 7] alt rows, ending with **WS** facing for next row.
Next row (WS): P2tog and fasten off.

RIGHT FRONT

Work to match left front, reversing shapings.

SLEEVES

Using 6mm (US 10) needles and one strand each of yarns A, B, C and D held together cast on 2 sts.
Work in g st, inc 1 st at each end of 2nd and foll 13 [15: 17: 17] rows, then on foll 2 [1: 0: 0] alt rows. 34 [36: 38: 38] sts.
Work 1 row, ending with RS facing for next row.
Place markers at both ends of last row to denote base of sleeve seam.
Beg with a K row, work in st st, shaping sides by inc 1 st at each end of 5th [7th: 7th: 5th] and every foll 8th [8th: 8th: 6th] row to 56 [58: 58: 44] sts, then on every foll – [–: 10th: 8th] row until there are – [–: 60: 62] sts.
Cont straight until sleeve meas 46 [47: 48: 48] cm **from markers**, ending with RS facing for next row.
Shape raglan
Cast off 4 sts at beg of next 2 rows.
48 [50: 52: 54] sts.
Dec 1 st at each end of next 3 rows, then on every foll alt row until 18 sts rem.
Work 1 row, ending with RS facing for next row.
Cast off rem 18 sts.

MAKING UP

Press as described on the information page.
Join raglan seams using back stitch, or mattress stitch if preferred.
Pockets (make 2)
Using 6mm (US 10) needles and one strand each of yarns A, B, C and D held together cast on 34 [36: 40: 46] sts.
Beg with a K row, work in st st for 13 cm, ending with RS facing for next row.
Work in g st, dec 0 [2: 2: 2] sts at each end of next 0 [1: 3: 6] rows, then 1 st at each end of foll 16 [15: 13: 10] rows, ending with RS facing for next row.
Cast off rem 2 sts.
Place pockets onto fronts, matching cast-on edge of pocket to top of g st section of front, and sew in place along side and lower edges.
Fold g st section to RS and secure in place.
Left front band, collar and scarf
Using 7mm (US 10½) needles and one strand

each of yarns A, E, F and G held together cast on 6 sts.
Using one strand each of yarns A, E, F and G held together, work in g st for 6 rows.
Join in one strand each of yarns A, B, C and D held together.
Using one strand each of yarns A, B, C and D held together, work in g st for 6 rows.
These 12 rows form striped g st.
Cont in striped g st until band, when slightly stretched, fits up left front opening edge to beg of front slope shaping, ending with RS facing for next row.
Shape for collar
Beg again with same stripe row as just worked (to reverse RS of work), cont in striped g st, inc 1 st at end of 3rd and every foll alt row to 18 [19: 20: 21] sts, then at same edge of every row until there are 28 [29: 30: 31] sts.
Cont straight until collar, unstretched, fits up front slope and across to centre of sleeve cast-off edge, ending with RS of collar (WS of body) facing for next row.

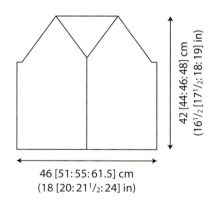

42 [44: 46: 48] cm
(16½ [17½: 18: 19] in)

46 [51: 55: 61.5] cm
(18 [20: 21½: 24] in)

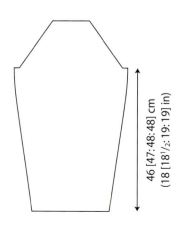

46 [47: 48: 48] cm
(18 [18½: 19: 19] in)

Shape for scarf
Cast on 46 sts at beg of next row.
74 [75: 76: 77] sts.
Cont straight until scarf section fits across to centre back neck, ending with RS of scarf (WS of body) facing for next row.
Cast off.

Right front band, collar and scarf
Work to match left front band, collar and scarf, reversing shaping.
Slip st bands, collars and scarf sections in place – cast-off edges of collar should meet at centre back neck but are NOT joined.
See information page for finishing instructions.

Cut 72 lengths of yarn A and 36 lengths of each of yarns B, C, D, E, F and G, each 30 cm long. Using 6 lengths of yarn A and 3 lengths of each of yarns B, C, D, E, F and G for each knot, knot these lengths of yarn through row-end edges of scarf sections to form fringe, placing 6 knots evenly spaced along each edge.

Main image page 14

ANNA SOCKS BY NINA CHAKKOUR

YARN
One size only.
Rowan 4 ply Soft
    4   x 50gm
(photographed in Teak 397, Clover 396 and Sooty 372)

NEEDLES
4 double-pointed 3¼ mm (no 10) (US 3) needles

RIBBON – 100 cm of 1 cm wide velvet ribbon

TENSION
28 sts and 36 rows to 10 cm measured over pattern using 3¼ mm (US 3) needles.

SOCK (make 2)
Using 3¼ mm (US 3) needles cast on 60 sts and distribute these sts evenly over 3 of the 4 needles (20 sts on each needle).
Round 1 (RS): ★K2, P2, rep from ★ to end.
This round forms rib.
Work in rib for a further 10 rounds.
Round 12 (RS): (rib 15, M1) 4 times. 64 sts.
Re-distribute sts on needles so there are 24 sts on first and third needle, and 16 sts on second needle.
Now work in lace patt as folls:
Round 1: ★K1, (K2tog, yfwd) 3 times, K1, rep from ★ to end.
Round 2: Knit.
Round 3: ★K2, (K2tog, yfwd) twice, K2, rep from ★ to end.
Round 4: Knit.
These 4 rounds form patt.
Cont in patt until sock meas 41 cm, ending after patt row 2.

Shape heel
Next row (RS): K14, inc once in each of next 2 sts, turn.
Slip next 32 sts of last complete round worked onto a holder for instep and now work on rem 34 sts in **rows**, not rounds, for heel as folls:
Row 1 (WS): K1 tbl, P to last st, sl 1 purlwise with yarn at front of work.
Row 2: K1 tbl, K to last st, sl 1 purlwise with yarn at front of work.
Rep last 2 rows 8 times more.
Row 19 (WS): K1 tbl, P to last 3 sts, P2tog, sl 1 purlwise with yarn at front of work. 33 sts.
Row 20: K1 tbl, K16, K2tog tbl, K1 and turn.
Row 21: sl 1 purlwise, P2, P2tog, P1 and turn.
Row 22: sl 1 purlwise, K to within 1 st of turning gap, K2tog tbl, K1 and turn.
Row 23: sl 1 purlwise, P to within 1 st of turning gap, P2tog, P1 and turn.
Rep last 2 rows 5 times more, ending with RS facing for next row.
19 sts.
Row 34 (RS): sl 1 purlwise, K to last 2 sts, K2tog tbl.
Row 35: sl 1 purlwise, P to last 2 sts, P2tog.
17 sts.
Break yarn and leave sts on a holder.
Shape instep
Next round (RS): Using first needle sl 1 purlwise, K16 heel sts, pick up and knit 16 sts down row-end edge of heel, using 2nd needle M1, patt 32 sts, M1, using 3rd needle pick up and knit 16 sts up row-end edge of heel, then K first 9 sts of heel. 83 sts (24 sts on first needle, 34 sts on 2nd needle, and 25 sts on 3rd needle).
Now working in rounds (beg and ending rounds at this new centre back point), cont as folls:

Round 1 (RS): K to last 3 sts on first needle, K2tog, K1, work across sts on 2nd needle as folls: P2tog, patt to last 2 sts, P2tog, work across sts on 3rd needle as folls: K1, sl 1, K1, psso, K to end.
Round 2: K sts on first needle, patt sts on 2nd needle, K sts on 3rd needle.
Round 3: K to last 3 sts on first needle, K2tog, K1, patt sts on 2nd needle, work across sts on 3rd needle as folls: K1, sl 1, K1, psso, K to end.
Round 4: As round 2.
Rounds 5 to 14: As rounds 3 and 4, 5 times.
Rounds 15 and 16: As round 3, twice.
63 sts (15 sts on first needle, 32 sts on 2nd needle, and 16 sts on 3rd needle).
Round 17: K sts on first needle, patt sts on 2nd needle, K sts on 3rd needle.
Rep round 17 until sock meas 19 cm from back of heel.
Shape toe
Round 1 (RS): K to last 3 sts on first needle, K2tog, K1, work across sts on 2nd needle as folls: K1, sl 1, K1, psso, K to last 3 sts, K2tog, K1, work across sts on 3rd needle as folls: K1, sl 1, K1, psso, K to end.
Round 2: Knit.
Rounds 3 to 18: As rounds 1 and 2, 8 times.
27 sts.
Rounds 19 to 23: As round 1, 5 times.
Break yarn and thread through rem 7 sts. Pull up tight and fasten off securely.

MAKING UP
Press as described on the information page.
Cut ribbon into 2 equal lengths and thread through eyelet holes of first round of patt, beg and ending on side of leg. Tie ends in a bow.

Main image page 12

SIZE

8	10	12	14	16	18	
To fit bust						
82	87	92	97	102	107	cm
32	34	36	38	40	42	in

YARN

Rowan Kidsilk Haze

A Wicked 599

9	9	10	10	11	12	x 25gm

B Smoke 605

1	1	1	1	1	1	x 25gm

NEEDLES

1 pair 3¼mm (no 10) (US 3) needles
1 pair 4mm (no 8) (US 6) needles
2.50mm (no 12) (US C2) crochet hook

BUTTONS – 2 x 00319

TENSION

24 sts and 28 rows to 10 cm measured over stocking stitch using yarn DOUBLE and 4mm (US 6) needles.

UK CROCHET ABBREVIATIONS

ch = chain; **dc** = double crochet;
sp(s) = space(es); **ss** = slip stitch;
tr(s) = treble(s); **dtr** = double treble.

US CROCHET ABBREVIATIONS

ch = chain; **dc** = single crochet;
sp(s) = space(es); **ss** = slip stitch;
tr(s) = double crochet; **dtr** = treble.

BACK

Using 4mm (US 6) needles and yarn A DOUBLE cast on 102 [106: 110: 118: 126: 134] sts.
Beg with a K row, work in st st, shaping side seams by dec 1 st at each end of 5th and every foll 4th row until 92 [96: 100: 108: 116: 124] sts rem.
Work 9 rows, ending with RS facing for next row.
Inc 1 st at each end of next and every foll 6th row until there are 102 [106: 110: 118: 126: 134] sts.
Cont straight until back meas 36 [36: 35: 38: 37: 39] cm, ending with RS facing for next row.

Shape armholes

Cast off 4 [5: 5: 6: 6: 7] sts at beg of next 2 rows.
94 [96: 100: 106: 114: 120] sts.
Dec 1 st at each end of next 5 rows, then on foll 2 [2: 3: 4: 6: 7] alt rows.
80 [82: 84: 88: 92: 96] sts.★★
Cont straight until armhole meas 12 [12: 13: 13: 14: 14] cm, ending with RS facing for next row.

Divide for back opening

Next row (RS): K40 [41: 42: 44: 46: 48] and turn, leaving rem sts on a holder.
Work each side of neck separately.
Cont straight until armhole meas 19 [19: 20:

20: 21: 21] cm, ending with **WS** facing for next row.

Shape back neck

Cast off 14 [14: 14: 14: 15: 15] sts at beg of next row, then 3 sts at beg of foll alt row, ending with RS facing for next row.
23 [24: 25: 27: 28: 30] sts.

Shape shoulder

Cast off 10 [10: 11: 12: 12: 13] sts at beg of next row, then 3 sts at beg of foll row.
Cast off rem 10 [11: 11: 12: 13: 14] sts.
With RS facing, rejoin yarn to rem sts, K to end.
Complete to match first side, reversing shapings.

FRONT

Work as given for Back to ★★.
Cont straight until 12 [12: 12: 14: 14: 14] rows less have been worked than on back to beg of shoulder shaping, ending with RS facing for next row.

Shape neck

Next row (RS): K28 [29: 30: 33: 34: 36] and turn, leaving rem sts on a holder.
Work each side of neck separately.
Dec 1 st at neck edge of next 7 rows, then on foll 1 [1: 1: 2: 2: 2] alt rows.
20 [21: 22: 24: 25: 27] sts.
Work 2 rows, ending with RS facing for next row.

Shape shoulder

Cast off 10 [10: 11: 12: 12: 13] sts at beg of next row.
Work 1 row.
Cast off rem 10 [11: 11: 12: 13: 14] sts.
With RS facing, rejoin yarn to rem sts, cast off centre 24 [24: 24: 22: 24: 24] sts, K to end.
Complete to match first side, reversing shapings.

SLEEVES

Using 4mm (US 6) needles and yarn A DOUBLE cast on 55 [55: 57: 57: 59: 59] sts.
Beg with a K row, work in st st, shaping sides by inc 1 st at each end of 3rd and every foll 4th row to 75 [81: 81: 87: 87: 93] sts, then on every foll 6th row until there are 89 [91: 93: 95: 97: 99] sts.
Cont straight until sleeve meas 34 [34: 35: 35: 36: 36] cm, ending with RS facing for next row.

Shape top

Cast off 4 [5: 5: 6: 6: 7] sts at beg of next 2 rows.
81 [81: 83: 83: 85: 85] sts.
Dec 1 st at each end of next 9 rows, then on every foll alt row to 49 sts, then on foll 9 rows, ending with RS facing for next row.
31 sts.
Cast off 4 sts at beg of next 4 rows.
Cast off rem 15 sts.

MAKING UP

Press as described on the information page.

Join both shoulder seams using back stitch, or mattress stitch if preferred.

Neckband

With **WS** facing and using 2.50mm (US C2) crochet hook, attach yarn A DOUBLE to right back neck edge at top of back opening, 1 ch (does NOT count as st), work 1 row of dc evenly around entire neck edge, ensuring number of sts worked is divisible by 8 plus 1, turn.
Row 1 (RS): 6 ch (counts as first tr and 3 ch), miss first 4 sts, ★1 tr into next dc, 3 ch, miss 3 dc, rep from ★ to last dc, 1 tr into last dc, turn.
Row 2: 5 ch (counts as first tr and 2 ch), miss tr at base of 5 ch, ★1 dc into next ch sp, 2 ch★★, 1 tr into next tr, 2 ch, rep from ★ to end, ending last rep at ★★, 1 tr into 3rd of 6 ch at beg of previous row, turn.
Row 3: 6 ch (counts as first tr and 3 ch), miss (tr at base of 6 ch, 2 ch, 1 dc and 2 ch), ★1 tr into next tr, 3 ch, miss (2 ch, 1 dc and 2 ch), rep from ★ to last st, 1 tr into 3rd of 5 ch at beg of previous row, turn.

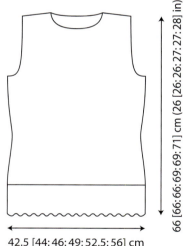

66 [66: 66: 69: 69: 71] cm (26 [26: 26: 27: 27: 28] in)

42.5 [44: 46: 49: 52.5: 56] cm
(16½ [17½: 18: 19½: 20½: 22] in)

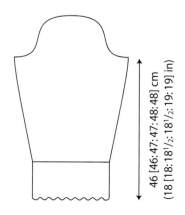

46 [46: 47: 47: 48: 48] cm (18 [18: 18½: 18½: 19: 19] in)

Rows 4 and 5: As rows 2 and 3.

Row 6: 1 ch (does NOT count as st), 1 dc into tr at end of previous row, *3 dc into next ch sp, 1 dc into next tr, 3 dc into next ch sp, turn, 7 ch, miss 6 dc, 1 dc into next dc, turn, (6 dc, 5 ch and 6 dc) into ch sp just formed, 1 dc into next tr, rep from * to end, working dc at end of last rep into 3rd of 6 ch at beg of previous row, turn.

Row 7: 4 ch (counts as first dtr), miss dc at end of previous row, *(1 tr, 3 ch, ss to 3rd ch from hook) 4 times into next 5-ch loop, 1 tr into same loop, miss 6 dc, 1 dtr into next dc, rep from * to end.
Fasten off.

See information page for finishing instructions, setting in sleeves using the set-in method.

Cuff edging

With RS facing and using 2.50mm (US C2) crochet hook, attach yarn A DOUBLE to cast-on edge of sleeve at base of sleeve seam, 1 ch (does NOT count as st), work 1 round of dc evenly around cast-on edge, ensuring number of sts worked is divisible by 8 and ending with ss to first dc.

Round 1 (RS): 6 ch (counts as first tr and 3 ch), miss first 4 sts, *1 tr into next dc, 3 ch, miss 3 dc, rep from * to end, ss to 3rd of 6 ch at beg of round, turn.

Round 2: 5 ch (counts as first tr and 2 ch), miss st at base of 5 ch, *1 dc into next ch sp, 2 ch, 1 tr into next tr, 2 ch, rep from * to end, ss to 3rd of 5 ch at beg of round, turn.

Round 3: 6 ch (counts as first tr and 3 ch), miss (st at base of 6 ch, 2 ch, 1 dc and 2 ch), *1 tr into next tr, 3 ch, miss (2 ch, 1 dc and 2 ch), rep from * to end, ss to 3rd of 6 ch at beg of round, turn.

Rounds 4 to 7: As rounds 2 and 3, twice.

Round 8: 1 ch (does NOT count as st), 1 dc into st at base of 1 ch, *3 dc into next ch sp, 1 dc into next tr, 3 dc into next ch sp, turn, 7 ch, miss 6 dc, 1 dc into next dc, turn, (6 dc, 5 ch and 6 dc) into ch sp just formed, 1 dc into next tr, rep from * to end, replacing dc at end of last rep with ss to first dc, turn.

Round 9: 4 ch (counts as first dtr), miss ss at end of previous round, *(1 tr, 3 ch, ss to 3rd ch from hook) 4 times into next 5-ch loop, 1 tr into same loop, miss 6 dc, 1 dtr into next dc, rep from * to end, replacing dtr at end of last rep with ss to top of 4 ch at beg of round.
Fasten off.

Hem edging

With RS facing and using 2.50mm (US C2) crochet hook, attach yarn A DOUBLE to cast-on edge of back and front at base of one side seam, 1 ch (does NOT count as st), work 1 round of dc evenly around entire lower edge, ensuring number of sts worked is divisible by 8 and ending with ss to first dc.

Work rounds 1 to 5 as given for cuff edging. Complete by working rounds 8 and 9 as given for cuff edging.
Fasten off.

Back opening band

With RS facing, using 3¼ mm (US 3) needles and yarn A DOUBLE, beg and ending at top of neckband, pick up and knit 50 sts down right side of opening, then 50 sts up left side of opening.
100 sts.

Row 1 (WS): Knit.

Row 2: K2, cast off 2 sts, K until there are 19 sts on right needle after cast-off, cast off 2 sts, K to end.

Row 3: K to end, casting on 2 sts over those cast off on previous row.
Cast off.

Sew on buttons to correspond with buttonholes.

Embroidery

Following diagrams and using yarn B SINGLE, embroider design onto sleeves and front.

Chain Stitch

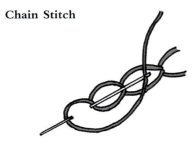

Lazy Daisy Stitch

Starlight Stitch

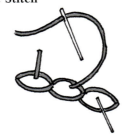

Main image page 10

SORREL BY SARAH HATTON

SIZE

	8	10	12	14	16	18	
To fit bust	82	87	92	97	102	107	cm
	32	34	36	38	40	42	in

YARN
Rowan Tapestry

9 9 10 11 11 12 x 50gm

(photographed in Leadmine 177 and Antique 173)

NEEDLES
1 pair 3¼ mm (no 10) (US 3) needles
1 pair 4mm (no 8) (US 6) needles

TENSION
22 sts and 30 rows to 10 cm measured over stocking stitch using 4mm (US 6) needles.

BACK
Using 3¼ mm (US 3) needles cast on 98 [102: 106: 112: 120: 126] sts.
Row 1 (RS): Purl.
Rows 2 and 3: Knit.
Row 4: Purl.
Row 5: Knit.
Row 6: Purl.
These 6 rows form ridge patt.
Change to 4mm (US 8) needles.
Cont in ridge patt, dec 1 st at end of 11th and 2 foll 4th rows.
92 [96: 100: 106: 114: 120] sts.
Work 1 row, ending after patt row 2 and with RS facing for next row.
Beg with a K row, work in st st, dec 1 st at each end of 3rd and every foll 4th row until 84 [88: 92: 98: 106: 112] sts rem.
Cont straight until back meas 17 [17: 16: 19: 18: 20] cm, ending with RS facing for next row.★★
Inc 1 st at each end of next and every foll 6th row until there are 94 [98: 102: 108: 116: 122] sts.
Work 25 rows, ending with RS facing for next row. (Back should meas 34 [34: 33: 36: 35: 37] cm.)
Shape armholes
Cast off 4 [5: 5: 6: 6: 7] sts at beg of next 2 rows.
86 [88: 92: 108: 104: 108] sts.
Dec 1 st at each end of next 3 [3: 5: 5: 7: 7] rows, then on foll 3 [3: 2: 2: 3: 3] alt rows.
74 [76: 78: 82: 84: 88] sts.
Cont straight until armhole meas 17 [17: 18: 18: 19: 19] cm, ending with RS facing for next row.
Shape back neck
Next row (RS): K31 [32: 33: 34: 35: 37] and turn, leaving rem sts on a holder.
Work each side of neck separately.
Cast off 3 sts at beg of next and foll 3 alt rows, ending with RS facing for next row.
19 [20: 21: 22: 23: 25] sts.
Shape shoulder
Cast off 8 [8: 9: 9: 10: 11] sts at beg of next row, then 3 sts at beg of foll row.

Cast off rem 8 [9: 9: 10: 10: 11] sts.
With RS facing, rejoin yarn to rem sts, cast off centre 12 [12: 12: 14: 14: 14] sts, K to end.
Complete to match first side, reversing shapings.

FRONT
Work as given for back to ★★.
Inc 1 st at each end of next and foll 6th row.
88 [92: 96: 102: 110: 116] sts.
Work 3 rows, ending with RS facing for next row.
Shape front neck
Next row (RS): K38 [40: 42: 45: 49: 52] and turn, leaving rem sts on a holder.
Work each side of neck separately.
Dec 1 st at neck edge of 2nd and foll 2 alt rows, then on 6 [6: 5: 8: 6: 6] foll 4th rows, then on 1 [1: 2: 0: 1: 1] foll 6th row **and at same time** inc 1 st at side seam edge of 2nd and 2 foll 6th rows. 31 [33: 35: 37: 42: 45] sts.
Work 3 [3: 1: 1: 3: 3] rows, ending with RS facing for next row.
Shape armhole
Cast off 4 [5: 5: 6: 6: 7] sts at beg of next row.
27 [28: 30: 31: 36: 38] sts.
Work 1 row.
Dec 1 st at armhole edge of next 3 [3: 5: 5: 7: 7] rows, then on foll 3 [3: 2: 2: 3: 3] alt rows **and at same time** dec 1 st at neck edge of next [next: 3rd: 3rd: next: next] and every foll 6th row. 19 [20: 21: 22: 23: 25] sts.
Dec 1 st at neck edge **only** of 4th [4th: 6th: 6th: 6th: 6th] and every foll 6th row until 16 [17: 18: 19: 20: 22] sts rem.
Cont straight until front matches back to beg of shoulder shaping, ending with RS facing for next row.
Shape shoulder
Cast off 8 [8: 9: 9: 10: 11] sts at beg of next row.
Work 1 row.
Cast off rem 8 [9: 9: 10: 10: 11] sts.
With RS facing, rejoin yarn to rem sts, cast off centre 12 sts, K to end.
Complete to match first side, reversing shapings.

SLEEVES
Using 3¼ mm (US 3) needles cast on 53 [53: 55: 55: 57: 57] sts.
Work in ridge patt as given for back for 6 rows, ending with RS facing for next row.
Change to 4mm (US 8) needles.
Cont in ridge patt, shaping sides by inc 1 st at each end of 3rd [3rd: 3rd: next: next: next] and every foll 10th [10th: 10th: 8th: 8th: 8th] row to 67 [79: 79: 63: 61: 71] sts, then on every foll 12th [-: 12th: 10th: 10th: 10th] row until there are 77 [-: 81: 83: 85: 87] sts.
Cont straight until sleeve meas 43 [43: 44: 44: 45: 45] cm, ending with RS facing for next row.
Shape top
Keeping patt correct, cast off 4 [5: 5: 6: 6: 7] sts

at beg of next 2 rows.
69 [69: 71: 71: 73: 73] sts.
Dec 1 st at each end of next 5 rows, then on every foll alt row to 21 sts, then on foll 3 rows, ending with RS facing for next row.
Cast off rem 15 sts.

MAKING UP
Press as described on the information page.
Join right shoulder seam using back stitch, or mattress stitch if preferred.
Collar
With RS facing and using 3¼ mm (US 3) needles, pick up and knit 88 [88: 90: 90: 92: 92] sts down left side of front neck, 12 sts from front, 88 [88: 90: 90: 92: 92] sts up right side of front neck, 13 sts down right side of back neck, 12 [12: 12: 14: 14: 14] sts from back, then 13 sts up left side of back neck.
226 [226: 230: 232: 236: 236] sts.
Beg with row 3, work in ridge patt as given for back for 6 rows, ending with RS of collar (WS of body) facing for next row.
Change to 4mm (US 6) needles.
Work in ridge patt for a further 42 rows, ending with RS of collar facing for next row.
Cast off in patt.

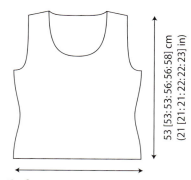

42.5 [44.5: 46.5: 49: 52.5: 55.5] cm
(16½ [17½: 18½: 19½: 20½: 22] in)

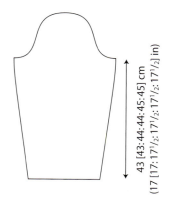

Neck insert
Using 4mm (US 6) needles cast on 14 sts.
Beg with a K row, work in st st, inc 1 st at each
end of 3rd and foll 2 alt rows, then on 6 [6: 5:
8: 6: 6] foll 4th rows, then on 2 [2: 2: 0: 2: 2]
foll 6th rows. 36 [36: 34: 36: 36: 36] sts.

Work 1 [1: 5: 5: 1: 1] rows, ending with RS
facing for next row.
Beg with row 1, work in ridge patt for 8 rows,
inc 1 st at each end of 5th [5th: next: next:
5th: 5th] row.
38 [38: 36: 38: 38: 38] sts.

Cast off in patt.
See information page for finishing instructions,
setting in sleeves using the set-in method and
reversing collar seam for turn-back. Lay neck
insert under base of neck shaping and slip
stitch in place.

Main image page 46, 47 & 55

YARN
Rowan Ribbon Twist
2 x 100gm
(photographed in 124 and 125)

NEEDLES
1 pair 8mm (no 0) (US 11) needles
1 pair 10mm (no 000) (US 15) needles
Cable needle

TENSION
10 sts and 14 rows to 10 cm measured over
stocking stitch using 10mm (US 15) needles.

SPECIAL ABBREVIATIONS
C4B = slip next 2 sts onto cable needle and
leave at back of work, K2, then K2 from cable
needle; **C4F** = slip next 2 sts onto cable needle
and leave at front of work, K2, then K2 from
cable needle; **Cr4R** = slip next 2 sts onto cable
needle and leave at back of work, K2, then P2
from cable needle; **Cr4L** = slip next 2 sts onto
cable needle and leave at front of work, P2,
then K2 from cable needle.

HAT
Using 8mm (US 11) needles cast on 55 sts.
Row 1 (RS): K1, ★P2, K1, rep from ★ to end.
Row 2: P1, ★K2, P1, rep from ★ to end.
These 2 rows form rib.

MARLOES SAND HAT BY GABRIELLE CARTER

Work in rib for a further 3 rows, ending with
WS facing for next row.
Row 6 (WS): Rib 6, (M1, rib 7) 7 times.
62 sts.
Change to 10mm (US 15) needles.
Work in cable patt as folls:
Row 1 (RS): K22, P3, C4B, P4, C4B,
P3, K22.
Row 2: P22, K3, P4, K4, P4, K3, P22.
Row 3: K22, P1, (Cr4R, Cr4L) twice,
P1, K22.
Row 4: P22, K1, P2, K4, P4, K4, P2, K1, P22.
Row 5: K22, P1, K2, P4, C4F, P4, K2, P1,
K22.
Row 6: As row 4.
Row 7: K22, P1, (Cr4L, Cr4R) twice, P1,
K22.
Row 8: As row 2.
These 8 rows form cable patt.
Cont in cable patt until hat meas 15 cm, dec
1 st at centre of last row and ending with RS
facing for next row. 61 sts.
Shape crown
Row 1 (RS): (Patt 7 sts, work 3 tog) 6 times,
K1. 49 sts.
Work 1 row.
Row 3: (Patt 5 sts, work 3 tog) 6 times, K1.
37 sts.
Row 4: P1, (work 3 tog, patt 3 sts) 6 times.
25 sts.

Row 5: (Patt 1 st, work 3 tog) 6 times, K1. 13 sts.
Row 6: P1, (P2tog) 6 times.
Break yarn and thread through rem 7 sts. Pull
up tight and fasten off securely.

EARFLAPS (make 2)
Using 10mm (US 15) needles cast on 11 sts.
Row 1 (RS): K1, ★P1, K1, rep from ★ to end.
Row 2: As row 1.
These 2 rows form moss st.
Work in moss st for a further 4 rows, ending
with RS facing for next row.
Keeping moss st correct, dec 1 st at each end
of next and foll 3 alt rows. 3 sts.
Work 1 row, ending with RS facing for next
row.
Next row (RS): sl 1, K2tog, psso and fasten
off.

MAKING UP
Press as described on the information page.
Join back seam using back stitch, or mattress
stitch if preferred. Attach cast-on edges of
earflaps to cast-on edge of hat, positioning
earflaps 6 cm either side of back seam. Make a
32 cm long plait and knot ends to form a 10-
12 cm long tassel. Attach plaits to fasten-off
points of earflaps. Make a 5 cm diameter
pompon and a 7 cm diameter pompon and
attach pompons to top of hat.

Main image page 50 & 51

YARN

Rowan Felted Tweed, Kid Classic and Wool Cotton

A	F Twd Ginger 154	1	x 50gm
B	Kid Clas Battle 845	1	x 50gm
C	F Twd Phantom 153	1	x 50gm
D	Kid Clas Cherry Red 847	1	x 50gm
E	Wool Cott Pumpkin 962	1	x 50gm
F	Wool Cott Antique 900	1	x 50gm
G	Kid Clas Bear 817	1	x 50gm
H	F Twd Herb 146	1	x 50gm
I	Wool Cott Still 964	1	x 50gm
J	F Twd Dragon 147	1	x 50gm

NEEDLES

1 pair 3¼ mm (no 10) (US 3) needles
1 pair 4mm (no 8) (US 6) needles

TENSION

24 sts and 32 rows to 10 cm measured over stocking stitch using 4mm (US 6) needles.
ARMWARMER (make 2)
Using 3¼ mm (US 3) needles and yarn A cast on 59 sts.
Row 1 (RS): K1, *P1, K1, rep from * to end.
Row 2: P1, *K1, P1, rep from * to end.
These 2 rows form rib.
Work in rib for a further 24 rows, inc 1 st at each end of 15th of these rows and ending with RS facing for next row.
61 sts.
Change to 4mm (US 6) needles.
Using a combination of the **intarsia** and **fairisle** techniques as described on the information page, work in patt from chart as folls:
Work 4 rows.
Inc 1 st at each end of next and every foll 14th row until there are 73 sts.
Work 18 rows, ending with chart row 93 and with **WS** facing for next row.
Break off contrasts and cont using yarn A **only**.
Change to 3¼ mm (US 3) needles.
Beg with row 2, work in rib for 3 rows, ending with RS facing for next row.
Left armwarmer only
Next row (RS): Cast off 22 sts, rib until there are 7 sts on right needle, cast off rem 44 sts.
Right armwarmer only
Next row (RS): Cast off 44 sts, rib until there are 7 sts on right needle, cast off rem 22 sts.
Both armwarmers
Rejoin yarn to rem 7 sts with **WS** facing and work in rib as set for a further 7 cm.
Cast off.

MAKING UP

Press as described on the information page.
Join row-end edges to form a tube using back stitch, or mattress stitch if preferred. Positioning seam centrally along tube, sew cast-off edge of thumb strip to cast-off edge.

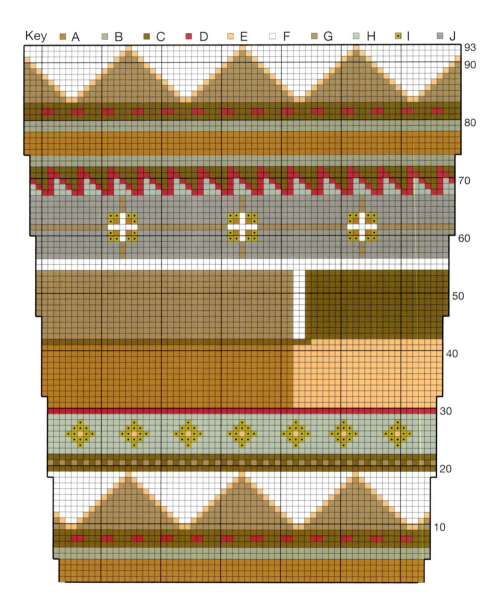

Main image page 69 & 79

SIZE

8   10   12   14   16   18   20   22

To fit bust

82   87   92   97   102   107   112   117   cm
32   34   36   38   40   42   44   46   in

YARN

Rowan Kidsilk Haze

4   4   5   5   5   5   6   6   x 25gm

(photographed in Hurricane 632)

NEEDLES

1 pair 3¾ mm (no 9) (US 5) needles

TENSION

22 sts and 30 rows to 10 cm measured over stocking stitch using 3¾ mm (US 5) needles.

BACK

Using 3¾ mm (US 5) needles cast on 97 [101: 105: 111: 119: 125: 131: 139] sts.

Beg with a K row, work in st st, shaping side seams by dec 1 st at each end of 13th and every foll 6th row until 85 [89: 93: 99: 107: 113: 119: 127] sts rem.

Work 7 rows, ending with RS facing for next row.

Inc 1 st at each end of next and every foll 6th row until there are 93 [97: 101: 107: 115: 121: 127: 135] sts.

Cont straight until back meas 32 [32: 31: 34: 33: 35: 34: 36] cm, ending with RS facing for next row.

Shape armholes

Cast off 4 [5: 5: 6: 6: 7: 7: 8] sts at beg of next 2 rows.

85 [87: 91: 95: 103: 107: 113: 119] sts.★★

Dec 1 st at each end of next 3 [3: 5: 5: 7: 7: 9: 9] rows, then on foll 3 [3: 2: 2: 3: 3: 2: 4] alt rows.

73 [75: 77: 81: 83: 87: 91: 93] sts.

Cont straight until armhole meas 18 [18: 19: 19: 20: 20: 21: 21] cm, ending with RS facing for next row.

Shape back neck

Next row (RS): K21 [22: 23: 25: 25: 27: 29: 30] and turn, leaving rem sts on a holder.

Work each side of neck separately.

Dec 1 st at neck edge of next 4 rows.

17 [18: 19: 21: 21: 23: 25: 26] sts.

Work 1 row, ending with RS facing for next row.

Shape shoulder

Cast off.

With RS facing, rejoin yarn to rem sts, cast off centre 31 [31: 31: 31: 33: 33: 33: 33] sts, K to end.

Complete to match first side, reversing shapings.

FRONT

Work as given for back to ★★.

Divide for neck

Next row (RS): K2tog, K40 [41: 43: 45:

49: 51: 54: 57] and turn, leaving rem sts on a holder.

Work each side of neck separately.

Dec 1 st at armhole edge of next 2 [2: 4: 4: 6: 6: 8: 8] rows, then on foll 3 [3: 2: 2: 3: 3: 2: 4] alt rows **and at same time** dec 1 st at neck edge of 2nd and every foll alt row.

32 [33: 34: 36: 35: 37: 39: 38] sts.

Dec 1 st at neck edge **only** of 2nd and foll 9 [9: 7: 7: 6: 6: 4: 2] alt rows, then on every foll 4th row until 17 [18: 19: 21: 21: 23: 25: 26] sts rem.

Cont straight until front matches back to shoulder cast-off, ending with RS facing for next row.

Shape shoulder

Cast off.

With RS facing, rejoin yarn to rem sts, K2tog, K to last 2 sts, K2tog.

Complete to match first side, reversing shapings.

SLEEVES

Using 3¾ mm (US 5) needles cast on 53 [53: 55: 55: 57: 57: 59: 59] sts.

Beg with a K row, work in st st, shaping sides by inc 1 st at each end of 7th [7th: 7th: 7th: 7th: 7th: 5th: 5th] and every foll 8th [8th: 8th: 8th: 8th: 8th: 8th: 6th] row to 59 [69: 67: 77: 77: 87: 89: 69] sts, then on every foll 10th [10th: 10th: 10th: 10th: –: –: 8th] row until there are 77 [79: 81: 83: 85: –: –: 91] sts.

Cont straight until sleeve meas 43 [43: 44: 44: 45: 45: 44: 44] cm, ending with RS facing for next row.

Shape top

Cast off 4 [5: 5: 6: 6: 7: 7: 8] sts at beg of next 2 rows.

69 [69: 71: 71: 73: 73: 75: 75] sts.

Dec 1 st at each end of next 5 rows, then on every foll alt row to 29 sts, then on foll 3 rows, ending with RS facing for next row.

23 sts.

Cast off 4 sts at beg of next 2 rows.

Cast off rem 15 sts.

MAKING UP

Press as described on the information page.

Join both shoulder seams using back stitch, or mattress stitch if preferred.

Lace trim

Using 3¾ mm (US 5) needles cast on 20 sts.

Row 1 (RS): sl 1, K3, (yfwd, K2tog) 7 times, yfwd, K2.

21 sts.

Row 2: Knit.

Row 3: sl 1, K6, (yfwd, K2tog) 6 times, yfwd, K2.

22 sts.

Row 4: Knit.

Row 5: sl 1, K9, (yfwd, K2tog) 5 times, yfwd, K2.

23 sts.

Row 6: Knit.

Row 7: sl 1, K12, (yfwd, K2tog) 4 times, yfwd, K2.

24 sts.

Row 8: Knit.

Row 9: sl 1, K23.

Row 10: cast off 4 sts, K to end.

20 sts.

These 10 rows form patt.

Cont in patt until trim, when slightly gathered, is long enough to fit up centre front, from cast-on edge to base of V neck, and around entire neck edge, ending after patt row 10 and with RS facing for next row.

Cast off.

Using photograph as a guide, sew lace trim in place.

See information page for finishing instructions, setting in sleeves using the set-in method.

42.5 [44: 46: 48.5: 52.5: 55: 57.5: 61.5] cm
(16½ [17½: 18: 19: 20½: 21½: 22½: 24] in)

52 [52: 52: 55: 55: 57: 57: 59] cm
(20½ [20½: 20½: 21½: 21½: 22½: 22½: 24] in)

43 [43: 44: 44: 45: 45: 44: 44] cm
(17 [17: 17½: 17½: 17½: 17½: 17½: 17½] in)

Main image page 82

SIZE

	S	M	L	XL	
	8/10	12/14	16/18	20/22	
To fit bust					
	82-87	92-97	102-107	112-117	cm
	32-34	36-38	40-42	44-46	in

YARN
Rowan Romance

	13	14	16	18	x 50gm

(photographed in Starlight 094)

NEEDLES
1 pair 6mm (no 4) (US 10) needles
1 pair 7mm (no 2) (US 10½) needles

FASTENER– 1 x Large Kilt pin 00412
or a Brooch

TENSION
11½ sts and 15 rows to 10 cm measured over stocking stitch using 7mm (US 10½) needles.

BACK
Using 6mm (US 10) needles cast on 64 [70: 76: 84] sts.
Row 1 (RS): P0 [0: 1: 1], K1 [0: 2: 2], ★P2, K2, rep from ★ to last 3 [2: 1: 1] sts, P2 [2: 1: 1], K1 [0: 0: 0].
Rows 2 and 3: K0 [0: 1: 1], P1 [0: 2: 2], ★K2, P2, rep from ★ to last 3 [2: 1: 1] sts, K2 [2: 1: 1], P1 [0: 0: 0].
Row 4: As row 1.
These 4 rows form patt.
Cont in patt for a further 22 rows, ending with RS facing for next row.
Change to 7mm (US 10½) needles.
Beg with a K row, work in st st until back meas 42 [43: 44: 45] cm, ending with RS facing for next row.
Shape armholes
Cast off 6 sts at beg of next 2 rows.
52 [58: 64: 72] sts.
Dec 1 st at each end of next 5 [7: 7: 9] rows, then on foll 1 [1: 2: 2] alt rows.
40 [42: 46: 50] sts.
Cont straight until armhole meas 20 [21: 22: 23] cm, ending with RS facing for next row.
Shape back neck
Next row (RS): K13 [14: 15: 17] and turn, leaving rem sts on a holder.
Work each side of neck separately.
Cast off 3 sts at beg of next row.
Shape shoulder
Cast off rem 10 [11: 12: 14] sts.
With RS facing, rejoin yarn to rem sts, cast off centre 14 [14: 16: 16] sts, K to end.
Complete to match first side, reversing shapings.

LEFT FRONT
Using 6mm (US 10) needles cast on 39 [42: 45: 49] sts.
Row 1 (RS): P0 [0: 1: 1], K1 [0: 2: 2], ★P2, K2, rep from ★ to last 2 sts, P2.

Row 2: ★K2, P2, rep from ★ to last 3 [2: 1: 1] sts, K2 [2: 1: 1], P1 [0: 0: 0].
Row 3: K0 [0: 1: 1], P1 [0: 2: 2], ★K2, P2, rep from ★ to last 2 sts, K2.
Row 4: ★P2, K2, rep from ★ to last 3 [2: 1: 1] sts, P2 [2: 1: 1], K1 [0: 0: 0].
These 4 rows form patt.
Cont in patt for a further 21 rows, ending with WS facing for next row.
Row 26 (WS): Patt 15 sts and slip these 15 sts onto a holder, M1, patt to end.
25 [28: 31: 35] sts.
Change to 7mm (US 10½) needles.
Beg with a K row, work in st st until left front matches back to beg of armhole shaping, ending with RS facing for next row.
Shape armhole
Cast off 6 sts at beg of next row.
19 [22: 25: 29] sts.
Work 1 row.
Shape front slope
Dec 1 st at armhole edge of next 5 [7: 7: 9] rows, then on foll 1 [1: 2: 2] alt rows **and at same time** dec 1 st at front slope edge of next and every foll 4th row.
11 [11: 13: 14] sts.
Dec 1 st at front slope edge **only** of 2nd [0: 2nd: 0] row.
10 [11: 12: 14] sts.
Cont straight until left front matches back to shoulder cast-off, ending with RS facing for next row.
Shape shoulder
Cast off rem 10 [11: 12: 14] sts.

RIGHT FRONT
Using 6mm (US 10) needles cast on 39 [42: 45: 49] sts.
Row 1 (RS): ★P2, K2, rep from ★ to last 3 [2: 1: 1] sts, P2 [2: 1: 1], K1 [0: 0: 0].
Row 2: K0 [0: 1: 1], P1 [0: 2: 2], ★K2, P2, rep from ★ to last 2 sts, K2.

Row 3: ★K2, P2, rep from ★ to last 3 [2: 1: 1] sts, K2 [2: 1: 1], P1 [0: 0: 0].
Row 4: P0 [0: 1: 1], K1 [0: 2: 2], ★P2, K2, rep from ★ to last 2 sts, P2.
These 4 rows form patt.
Cont in patt for a further 21 rows, ending with WS facing for next row.
Row 26 (WS): Patt to last 15 sts, M1 and turn, leaving rem 15 sts on a holder.
25 [28: 31: 35] sts.
Complete to match left front, reversing shapings.

SLEEVES
Using 6mm (US 10) needles cast on 30 [32: 32: 32] sts.
Row 1 (RS): K0 [1: 1: 1], P2, ★K2, P2, rep from ★ to last 0 [1: 1: 1] sts, K0 [1: 1: 1].
Rows 2 and 3: P0 [1: 1: 1], K2, ★P2, K2, rep from ★ to last 0 [1: 1: 1] st, P0 [1: 1: 1].
Row 4: As row 1.
These 4 rows form patt.
Cont in patt, shaping sides by inc 1 st at each end of 7th and foll 6th row, taking inc sts into patt.
34 [36: 36: 36] sts.
Work 1 row, ending with RS facing for next row.
Change to 7mm (US 10½) needles.
Beg with a K row, work in st st, shaping sides by inc 1 st at each end of 5th and every foll 6th [8th: 6th: 6th] row to 38 [48: 44: 52] sts, then on every foll 8th [-: 8th: -] row until there are 46 [-: 50: -] sts.
Cont straight until sleeve meas 45 [46: 47: 47] cm, ending with RS facing for next row.
Shape top
Cast off 6 sts at beg of next 2 rows.
34 [36: 38: 40] sts.
Dec 1 st at each end of next 3 rows, then on every foll alt row to 16 sts, then on foll 3 rows, ending with RS facing for next row.

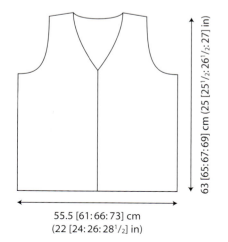

63 [65: 67: 69] cm (25 [25½: 26½: 27] in)

55.5 [61: 66: 73] cm
(22 [24: 26: 28½] in)

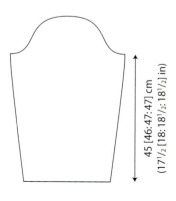

45 [46: 47: 47] cm
(17½ [18: 18½: 18½] in)

Cast off rem 10 sts.

MAKING UP
Press as described on the information page.
Join shoulder seams using back stitch, or
mattress stitch if preferred.

Left front band and collar
With RS facing and using 6mm (US 10)
needles, rejoin yarn to 15 sts on left front
holder, patt to end.
Cont in patt as set until band, when slightly
stretched, fits up left front opening edge to beg
of front slope shaping, ending with RS facing
for next row.

Shape for collar
Inc 1 st at beg of next and foll 4 alt rows, then
on every foll 4th row until there are 23 sts,
taking inc sts into patt.
Cont straight until collar, unstretched, fits up
front slope and across to centre back neck,
ending with RS facing for next row.
Cast off.

Right front band and collar
With **WS** facing and using 6mm (US 10)
needles, rejoin yarn to 15 sts on right front
holder, patt to end.
Cont in patt as set until band, when slightly
stretched, fits up right front opening edge to
beg of front slope shaping, ending with RS
facing for next row.

Shape for collar
Inc 1 st at end of next and foll 4 alt rows, then
on every foll 4th row until there are 23 sts,
taking inc sts into patt.
Cont straight until collar, unstretched, fits up
front slope and across to centre back neck,
ending with RS facing for next row.
Cast off.
Join cast-off edges of collar sections, then slip
stitch bands and collar in place.
See information page for finishing instructions,
setting in sleeves using the set-in method.

Main image page 55

YARN
Rowan Big Wool and Ribbon Twist
A Big Wool
Camouflage 023   2 x 100gm
B Ribbon Twist
Rustic 121   1 x 100gm

NEEDLES
1 pair 10mm (no 000) (US 15) needles
10mm (no 000) (US N15) crochet hook

TENSION
9 sts and 12½ rows to 10 cm measured over
stocking stitch using 10mm (US 15) needles
and yarn A. Crochet motifs measure 22 cm
(8½ in) square.

UK CROCHET ABBREVIATIONS
ch = chain; **ss** = slip stitch; **dc** = double
crochet; **dtr** = double treble.

SQUARE WRAP BY NIKKI RYAN

US CROCHET ABBREVIATIONS
ch = chain; **ss** = slip stitch; **dc** = single
crochet; **dtr** = treble.

MAIN SECTION
Using 10mm (US 15) needles and yarn A cast
on 50 sts.
Beg with a K row, work in st st, dec 1 st at each
end of 3rd and every foll alt row until 26 sts rem.
Work 1 row, ending with RS facing for next row.
Cast off.

MOTIFS (make 2)
Using 10mm (US N15) crochet hook and yarn
B make 10 ch and join with a ss to form a ring.
Round 1 (RS): 11 ch (counts as 1 dtr and
7 ch), (4 dtr into ring, 7 ch) 3 times, 3 dtr into
ring, ss to 4th of 11 ch at beg of round.
Round 2: 1 ch (does NOT count as st),
1 dc into each dtr and ch to end, ss to first dc.

Break off yarn B and join in yarn A.
Round 3: 4 ch (counts as first dtr), 1 dtr into
each of next 4 dc, (7 ch, 1 dtr into each of
next 11 dc) 3 times, 7 ch, 1 dtr into each of
next 6 dc, ss to top of 4 ch at beg of round.
Round 4: As round 2.
Break off yarn A and join in yarn B.
Round 5: As round 2 **but** working dc along
one edge of motif through both sts of round
4 **and** sloping edge of main section.
Fasten off.

MAKING UP
Press as described on the information page.
Ties (both alike)
Attach yarn B to corner st of motif at neck
edge (neck edge is shorter edge) and using
10mm (US N15) crochet hook make a ch
approx 26 cm long.
Fasten off.

Main image page 44 & 46

SIZE

	S	M	L	XL	XXL	
To fit chest						
	102	107	112	117	122	cm
	40	42	44	46	48	in

YARN

Rowan Tapestry, Wool Cotton and Kid Classic

A Tapestry Country 170						
	4	5	5	5	5	x 50gm
B Wool Cotton Deepest Olive 907						
	3	3	3	3	4	x 50gm
C Tapestry Rustic 174						
	4	5	5	5	6	x 50gm
D Wool Cotton Coffee Rich 956						
	2	3	3	3	3	x 50gm
E Kid Classic Bear 817						
	2	2	2	2	2	x 50gm
F Kid Classic Battle 845						
	2	2	2	2	2	x 50gm

NEEDLES

1 pair 3¾ mm (no 9) (US 5) needles
1 pair 4mm (no 8) (US 6) needles

TENSION

24 sts and 42 rows to 10 cm measured over pattern using 4mm (US 6) needles.

Pattern note: Whilst working patt from chart, all slipped sts should be slipped purlwise with yarn at WS of work.

BACK

Using 3¾ mm (US 5) needles and yarn A cast on 131 [140: 146: 155: 161] sts.
Row 1 (RS): K2, *P1, K2, rep from * to end.
Join in yarn B.
Row 2: Using yarn B, P2, *K1, P2, rep from * to end.
These 2 rows form rib.
Cont in rib as set in stripes as folls:
Row 3: Using yarn B.
Rows 4 and 5: Using yarn C.
Rows 6 and 7: Using yarn D.
Rows 8 and 9: Using yarn A.
Rows 10 and 11: Using yarn B.
Rows 12 and 13: Using yarn C.
Rows 14 and 15: Using yarn D.
Rows 16 and 17: Using yarn A.
Using yarn A, P one row, inc [0: 0: dec: dec] 1 st at end of row and ending with RS facing for next row.
132 [140: 146: 154: 160] sts.
Change to 4mm (US 6) needles.
Beg and ending rows as indicated and repeating the 72 row patt repeat throughout, work from chart as folls:
Cont straight until back meas 40 [41: 40: 41: 40] cm, ending with RS facing for next row.

Shape armholes
Keeping patt correct, cast off 6 sts at beg of next 2 rows.
120 [128: 134: 142: 148] sts.

Dec 1 st at each end of next 5 rows.
110 [118: 124: 132: 138] sts.
Cont straight until armhole meas 24 [25: 26: 27: 28] cm, ending with RS facing for next row.

Shape shoulders and back neck
Cast off 11 [12: 13: 14: 15] sts at beg of next 2 rows.
88 [94: 98: 104: 108] sts.
Next row (RS): Cast off 11 [12: 13: 14: 15] sts, patt until there are 15 [17: 17: 19: 19] sts on right needle and turn, leaving rem sts on a holder.
Work each side of neck separately.
Cast off 4 sts at beg of next row.
Cast off rem 11 [13: 13: 15: 15] sts.
With RS facing, rejoin yarns to rem sts, cast off centre 36 [36: 38: 38: 40] sts, patt to end.
Complete to match first side, reversing shapings.

FRONT

Work as given for back until 28 [28: 32: 32: 36] rows less have been worked than on back to beg of shoulder shaping, ending with RS facing for next row.

Shape neck
Next row (RS): Patt 48 [52: 55: 59: 62] sts and turn, leaving rem sts on a holder.
Work each side of neck separately.
Cast off 5 sts at beg of next row.
43 [47: 50: 54: 57] sts.
Dec 1 st at neck edge of next 5 rows, then on foll 3 alt rows, then on every foll 4th row until 33 [37: 39: 43: 45] sts rem.
Work 7 rows, ending with RS facing for next row.

Shape shoulder
Cast off 11 [12: 13: 14: 15] sts at beg of next and foll alt row.
Work 1 row.
Cast off rem 11 [13: 13: 15: 15] sts.
With RS facing, rejoin yarns to rem sts, cast off centre 14 sts, patt to end.
Complete to match first side, reversing shapings.

SLEEVES

Using 3¾ mm (US 5) needles and yarn A cast on 59 [62: 65: 65: 68] sts.
Work in striped rib as given for back for 17 rows, ending with **WS** facing for next row.
Using yarn A, P one row, inc [0: dec: inc: 0] 1 st at end of row and ending with RS facing for next row.
60 [62: 64: 66: 68] sts.
Change to 4mm (US 6) needles.
Beg and ending rows as indicated, work from chart, shaping sides by inc 1 st at each end of 3rd and every foll 4th row to 72 [72: 72: 78: 76] sts, then on every foll 6th row until there are 116 [120: 124: 130: 134] sts, taking inc sts into patt.
Cont straight until sleeve meas 47 [49: 51: 53: 55] cm, ending with RS facing for

next row.

Shape top
Cast off 6 sts at beg of next 2 rows.
104 [108: 112: 118: 122] sts.
Dec 1 st at each end of next and foll 4 alt rows, then on foll row, ending with RS facing for next row.
Cast off rem 92 [96: 100: 106: 110] sts.

MAKING UP

Press as described on the information page.
Join right shoulder seam using back stitch, or mattress stitch if preferred.

Neckband
With RS facing, using 3¾ mm (US 5) needles and yarn D, pick up and knit 31 [31: 33: 33: 35] sts down left side of neck, 14 sts from front, 31 [31: 33: 33: 35] sts up right side of neck, then 43 [45: 45: 45: 47] sts from back.
119 [119: 125: 125: 131] sts.
Beg with row 2, work in rib as given for back using colours as folls:
Row 1 (WS): Using yarn D.
Rows 2 and 3: Using yarn C.
Rows 4 and 5: Using yarn B.
Rows 6 and 7: Using yarn A.
Rows 8 and 9: Using yarn D.
Rows 10 and 11: Using yarn C.
Rows 12 and 13: Using yarn B.
Row 14: Using yarn A.
Cast off in rib (on **WS**).
See information page for finishing instructions, setting in sleeves using the shallow set-in method.

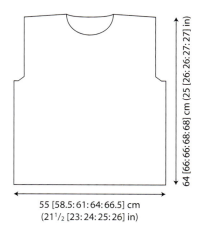

64 [66: 66: 68: 68] cm (25 [26: 26: 27: 27] in)

55 [58.5: 61: 64: 66.5] cm
(21½ [23: 24: 25: 26] in)

47 [49: 51: 53: 55] cm
(18½ [19½: 20: 21: 21½] in)

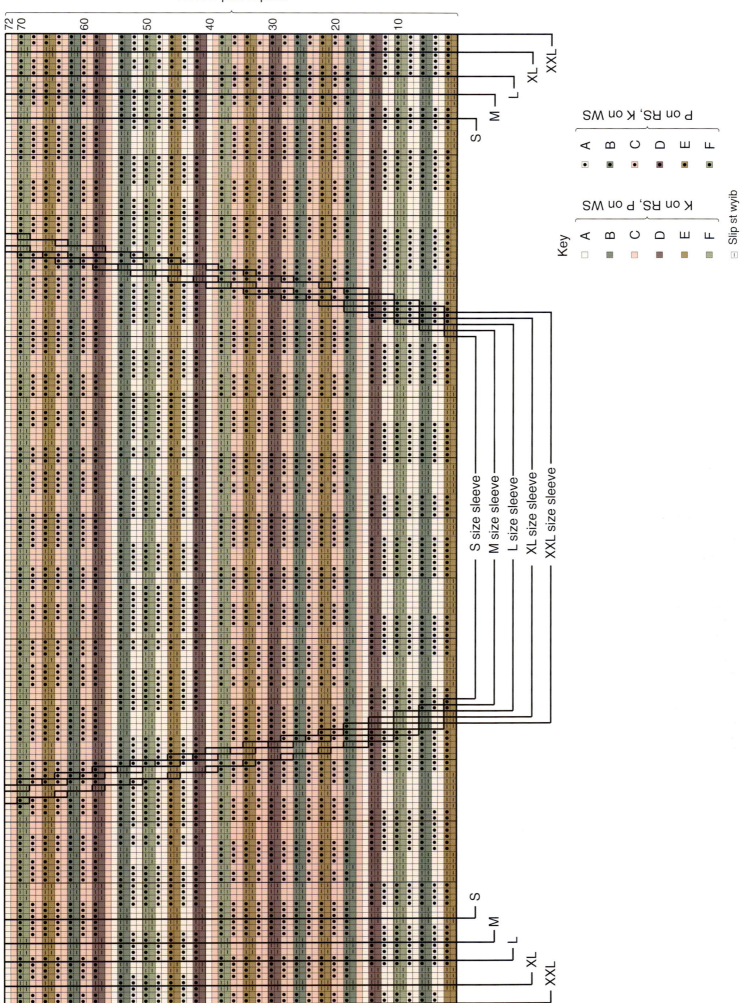

72 row patt repeat

Key

P on RS, K on WS

A •
B •
C •
D •
E •
F •

K on RS, P on WS

A
B
C
D
E
F

⊟ Slip st wyib

S size sleeve
M size sleeve
L size sleeve
XL size sleeve
XXL size sleeve

S
M
L
XL
XXL

Main image page 36

SIZE

8	10	12	14	16	18	20	22	
To fit bust								
82	87	92	97	102	107	112	117	cm
32	34	36	38	40	42	44	46	in

YARN

Rowan 4 ply Soft
and Scottish Tweed 4 ply

A	Soft Beetroot 382								
	9	9	10	11	11	12	12	13	x 50gm
B	Scot Lobster 017								
	2	2	2	2	2	2	2	2	x 25gm
C	Scot Apple 015								
	1	1	1	1	1	1	1	1	x 25gm
D	Scot Rust 009								
	1	1	1	1	1	1	1	1	x 25gm
E	Scot Thatch 018								
	1	1	1	1	1	1	1	1	x 25gm

NEEDLES

1 pair 2¾mm (no 12) (US 2) needles
1 pair 3¼mm (no 10) (US 3) needles

BUTTONS – 7 x 00408

TENSION

32 sts and 36 rows to 10 cm measured over pattern using 3¼mm (US 3) needles.

Pattern note: When working pattern from chart, follow the written instructions for rows 1 to 4, 19 to 22 and 35 to 38.

BACK
Using 2¾mm (US 2) needles and yarn A cast on 135 [141: 147: 157: 167: 177: 185: 199] sts.
Row 1 (RS): K1, *P1, K1, rep from * to end.
Row 2: P1, *K1, P1, rep from * to end.
These 2 rows form rib.
Work in rib for a further 18 rows, ending with RS facing for next row.
Change to 3¼mm (US 3) needles.
Row 1 (RS): Purl.
Row 2: K1 [0: 1: 0: 1: 0: 0: 1], *(K1, yfwd, K1) into next st, P3tog, rep from * to last 2 [1: 2: 1: 2: 1: 1: 2] sts, K2 [1: 2: 1: 2: 1: 1: 2].
Row 3: Purl.
Row 4: K1 [0: 1: 0: 1: 0: 0: 1], *P3tog, (K1, yfwd, K1) into next st, rep from * to last 2 [1: 2: 1: 2: 1: 1: 2] sts, K2 [1: 2: 1: 2: 1: 1: 2].
Beg and ending rows as indicated and using the **fairisle** technique as described on the information page, work chart rows 5 to 18.
Rows 19 to 22: As rows 1 to 4.
Work chart rows 23 to 34.
Rows 35 to 38: As rows 1 to 4.
Work chart rows 39 to 50.
These 50 rows form patt.
Cont in patt until back meas 32 [32: 31: 34: 33: 35: 34: 36] cm, ending with RS facing for next row.
Shape armholes
Keeping patt correct, cast off 7 [8: 8: 9: 9: 10: 10: 11] sts at beg of next 2 rows.
121 [125: 131: 139: 149: 157: 165: 177] sts.

Dec 1 st at each end of next 5 [5: 7: 7: 9: 9: 11: 11] rows, then on foll 2 [2: 1: 3: 4: 5: 5: 8] alt rows, then on foll 4th row.
105 [109: 113: 117: 121: 127: 131: 137] sts.
Cont straight until armhole meas 21 [21: 22: 22: 23: 23: 24: 24] cm, ending with RS facing for next row.
Shape shoulders and back neck
Cast off 8 [9: 10: 10: 10: 11: 12: 13] sts at beg of next 2 rows.
89 [91: 93: 97: 101: 105: 107: 111] sts.
Next row (RS): Cast off 8 [9: 10: 10: 10: 11: 12: 13] sts, patt until there are 13 [13: 13: 15: 15: 16: 16: 17] sts on right needle and turn, leaving rem sts on a holder.
Work each side of neck separately.
Cast off 4 sts at beg of next row.
Cast off rem 9 [9: 9: 11: 11: 12: 12: 13] sts.
With RS facing, rejoin yarns to rem sts, cast off centre 47 [47: 47: 47: 51: 51: 51: 51] sts, patt to end.
Complete to match first side, reversing shapings.

LEFT FRONT
Using 2¾mm (US 2) needles and yarn A cast on 67 [71: 73: 79: 83: 89: 93: 99] sts.
Work in rib as given for back for 20 rows, inc 1 [0: 1: 0: 1: 0: 0: 1] st at end of last row and ending with RS facing for next row.
68 [71: 74: 79: 84: 89: 93: 100] sts.
Change to 3¼mm (US 3) needles.
Row 1 (RS): Purl.
Row 2: K2 [2: 0: 2: 2: 0: 0: 2], *(K1, yfwd, K1) into next st, P3tog, rep from * to last 2 [1: 2: 1: 2: 1: 1: 2] sts, K2 [1: 2: 1: 2: 1: 1: 2].
Row 3: Purl.
Row 4: K2 [2: 0: 2: 2: 0: 0: 2], *P3tog, (K1, yfwd, K1) into next st, rep from * to last 2 [1: 2: 1: 2: 1: 1: 2] sts, K2 [1: 2: 1: 2: 1: 1: 2].
Beg and ending rows as indicated, work chart rows 5 to 18.
Rows 19 to 22: As rows 1 to 4.
Work chart rows 23 to 34.
Rows 35 to 38: As rows 1 to 4.
Work chart rows 39 to 50.
These 50 rows form patt.
Cont in patt until left front matches back to beg of armhole shaping, ending with RS facing for next row.
Shape armhole
Keeping patt correct, cast off 7 [8: 8: 9: 9: 10: 10: 11] sts at beg of next row.
61 [63: 66: 70: 75: 79: 83: 89] sts.
Work 1 row.
Dec 1 st at armhole edge of next 5 [5: 7: 7: 9: 9: 11: 11] rows, then on foll 2 [2: 1: 3: 4: 5: 5: 8] alt rows, then on foll 4th row.
53 [55: 57: 59: 61: 64: 66: 69] sts.
Cont straight until 29 [29: 29: 31: 31: 31: 33: 33] rows less have been worked than on back to beg of shoulder shaping, ending with **WS** facing for next row.
Shape neck
Keeping patt correct, cast off 11 [11: 11: 10: 12:

12: 11: 11] sts at beg of next row, then 7 sts at beg of foll alt row.
35 [37: 39: 42: 42: 45: 48: 51] sts.
Dec 1 st at neck edge of next 5 rows, then on foll 3 [3: 3: 4: 4: 4: 5: 5] alt rows, then on 2 foll 4th rows. 25 [27: 29: 31: 31: 34: 36: 39] sts.
Work 7 rows, ending with RS facing for next row.
Shape shoulder
Cast off 8 [9: 10: 10: 10: 11: 12: 13] sts at beg of next and foll alt row.
Work 1 row.
Cast off rem 9 [9: 9: 11: 11: 12: 12: 13] sts.

RIGHT FRONT
Using 2¾mm (US 2) needles and yarn A cast on 67 [71: 73: 79: 83: 89: 93: 99] sts.
Work in rib as given for back for 20 rows, inc 1 [0: 1: 0: 1: 0: 0: 1] st at beg of last row and ending with RS facing for next row.
68 [71: 74: 79: 84: 89: 93: 100] sts.
Change to 3¼mm (US 3) needles.
Row 1 (RS): Purl.
Row 2: K1 [0: 1: 0: 1: 0: 0: 1], *(K1, yfwd, K1) into next st, P3tog, rep from * to last 3 [3: 1: 3: 3: 1: 1: 3] sts, K3 [3: 1: 3: 3: 1: 1: 3].
Row 3: Purl.
Row 4: K1 [0: 1: 0: 1: 0: 0: 1], *P3tog, (K1, yfwd, K1) into next st, rep from * to last 3 [3: 1: 3: 3: 1: 1: 3] sts, K3 [3: 1: 3: 3: 1: 1: 3].
Beg and ending rows as indicated, work chart rows 5 to 18.
Rows 19 to 22: As rows 1 to 4.
Work chart rows 23 to 34.
Rows 35 to 38: As rows 1 to 4.
Work chart rows 39 to 50.
These 50 rows form patt.
Complete to match left front, reversing shapings.

SLEEVES
Using 2¾mm (US 2) needles and yarn A cast on 71 [71: 75: 75: 79: 79: 83: 83] sts.
Work in rib as given for back for 20 rows, inc 1 st at end of last row and ending with RS facing for next row.
72 [72: 76: 76: 80: 80: 84: 84] sts.
Change to 3¼mm (US 3) needles.
Row 1 (RS): Purl.
Row 2: *(K1, yfwd, K1) into next st, P3tog, rep from * to end.
Row 3: Purl.
Row 4: *P3tog, (K1, yfwd, K1) into next st, rep from * to end.
These 4 rows form patt.
Cont in patt, shaping sides by inc 1 st at each end of 3rd [3rd: 3rd: 3rd: 3rd: 3rd: next: next] and every foll 6th [6th: 6th: 6th: 6th: 6th: 6th: 4th] row to 98 [106: 106: 114: 114: 122: 128: 92] sts, then on every foll 8th [8th: 8th: 8th: 8th: 8th: -: 6th] row until there are 110 [112: 116: 118: 122: 124: -: 130] sts, taking inc sts into patt.
Cont straight until sleeve meas 45 [45: 46: 46: 47: 47: 46: 46] cm, ending with RS facing for next row.

Shape top
Keeping patt correct, cast off 7 [8: 8: 9: 9: 10: 10: 11] sts at beg of next 2 rows.
96 [96: 100: 100: 104: 104: 108: 108] sts.
Dec 1 st at each end of next 5 rows, then on foll alt row, then on every foll 4th row until 70 [70: 74: 74: 78: 78: 82: 82] sts rem.
Work 1 row.
Dec 1 st at each end of next and every foll alt row to 64 sts, then on foll 3 rows, ending with RS facing for next row. 58 sts.
Cast off 11 sts at beg of next 2 rows.
Cast off rem 36 sts.

MAKING UP
Press as described on the information page.
Join shoulder seams using back stitch, or mattress stitch if preferred.
Button band
Using 2¾ mm (US 2) needles and yarn A cast on 7 sts.
Work in rib as given for back until button band, when slightly stretched, fits up left front opening edge from cast-on edge to neck shaping, ending with RS facing for next row.
Break yarn and leave sts on a holder.
Slip stitch band in place.
Mark positions for 7 buttons on this band – first to come 2 cm up from cast-on edge, last to come just above neck shaping, and rem 5 buttons evenly spaced between.
Buttonhole band
Using 2¾ mm (US 2) needles and yarn A cast on 7 sts.
Work in rib as given for back until buttonhole

band, when slightly stretched, fits up right front opening edge from cast-on edge to neck shaping, with the addition of 6 buttonholes worked to correspond with positions marked for buttons as folls:
Buttonhole row (RS): Rib 2, work 2 tog, yrn, rib 3.
When band is complete, ending with RS facing for next row, do NOT break yarn.
Slip stitch band in place.
Neckband
With RS facing, using 2¾ mm (US 2) needles and yarn A, rib 7 sts of buttonhole band, pick up and knit 44 [44: 44: 45: 47: 47: 48: 48] sts up

right side of neck, 55 [55: 55: 55: 59: 59: 59: 59] sts from back, and 44 [44: 44: 45: 47: 47: 48: 48] sts down left side of neck, then rib 7 sts of button band.
157 [157: 157: 159: 167: 167: 169: 169] sts.
Work in rib as set by bands for 1 row, ending with RS facing for next row.
Row 2 (RS): Rib 2, work 2 tog, yrn, rib to end.
Work in rib for a further 4 rows, ending with **WS** facing for next row.
Cast off in rib (on **WS**).
See information page for finishing instructions, setting in sleeves using the set-in method.

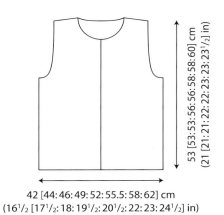

53 [53: 53: 56: 56: 56: 58: 60] cm
(21 [21: 21: 22: 22: 23: 23: 23½] in)

42 [44: 46: 49: 52: 55.5: 58: 62] cm
(16½ [17½: 18: 19½: 20½: 22: 23: 24½] in)

45 [45: 46: 46: 47: 47: 46: 46] cm
(17½ [17½: 18: 18½: 18½: 18: 18] in)

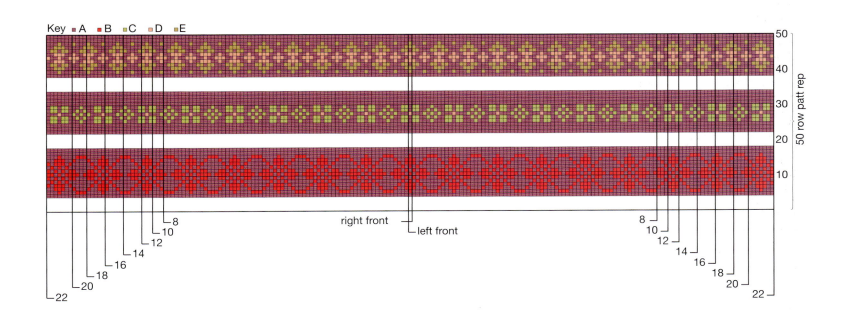

Key ▪A ▪B ▫C ▫D ▫E

50 row patt rep

right front   left front

8
10
12
14
16
18
20
22

131

Main image page 48

PAMPAS BY MARIE WALLIN

SIZE

	S	M	L	XL
	8/10	12/14	16/18	20/22

To fit bust

82-87	92-97	102-107	112-117	cm
32-34	36-38	40-42	44-46	in

YARN

Rowan Big Wool

	8	9	10	11	x 100gm

(photographed in Mulberry 042 and
Sugar Spun 016)

NEEDLES

1 pair 10mm (no 000) (US 15) needles
10.00mm (no 000) (US N15) crochet hook

BUTTONS – 3 x 00335 3 cm (1⅛ in)

diameter flat buttons

TENSION

10 sts and 14 rows to 10 cm measured over
pattern using 10mm (US 15) needles.

UK CROCHET ABBREVIATIONS

ch = chain; **ss** = slip stitch; **dc** = double
crochet; **tr** = treble.

US CROCHET ABBREVIATIONS

ch = chain; **ss** = slip stitch; **dc** = single
crochet; **tr** = double treble.

BACK

Using 10mm (US 15) needles cast on 45 [49:
57: 63] sts.
Rows 1 and 2: Knit.
Row 3 (RS): K0 [0: 0: 1], *P1, K1, rep from *
to last 1 [1: 1: 0] st, P1 [1: 1: 0].
Row 4: P0 [0: 0: 1], *K1, P1, rep from * to last
1 [1: 1: 0] st, K1 [1: 1: 0].
These 4 rows form patt.
Cont in patt, dec 1 st at each end of 3rd [3rd:
5th: 5th] and foll 8th row. 41 [45: 53: 59] sts.
Work 7 rows, end with RS facing for next row.
Inc 1 st at each end of next and foll 10th row,
taking inc sts into patt. 45 [49: 57: 63] sts.
Cont straight until back meas 32 [33: 34: 35] cm,
ending with RS facing for next row.
Shape armholes
Keeping patt correct, cast off 2 sts at beg of
next 2 rows. 41 [45: 53: 59] sts.
Dec 1 st at each end of next and foll alt row.
37 [41: 49: 55] sts.
Cont straight until armhole meas 20 [21: 22:
23] cm, ending with RS facing for next row.
Shape shoulders and collar extension
Cast off 10 [12: 15: 18] sts at beg of next
2 rows. 17 [17: 19: 19] sts.
Work a further 2 rows for collar extension,
ending with RS facing for next row.
Cast off.

LEFT FRONT

Using 10mm (US 15) needles cast on 23 [25:
29: 32] sts.
Rows 1 and 2: Knit.

Row 3 (RS): K0 [0: 0: 1], *P1, K1, rep from *
to last st, P1.
Row 4: *K1, P1, rep from * to last 1 [1: 1: 0] st,
K1 [1: 1: 0].
These 4 rows form patt.
Cont in patt, dec 1 st at beg of 3rd [3rd:
5th: 5th] and foll 8th row. 21 [23: 27: 30] sts.
Work 7 rows, ending with RS facing for next row.
Inc 1 st at beg of next and foll 10th row,
taking inc sts into patt. 23 [25: 29: 32] sts.
Cont straight until left front matches back to
beg of armhole shaping, ending with RS facing
for next row.
Shape armhole
Keeping patt correct, cast off 2 sts at beg of
next row. 21 [23: 27: 30] sts.
Work 1 row.
Dec 1 st at armhole edge of next and foll
alt row. 19 [21: 25: 28] sts.
Cont straight until left front matches back to
beg of shoulder shaping, ending with RS facing
for next row.
Shape shoulder and collar extension
Cast off 10 [12: 15: 18] sts at beg of next row.
9 [9: 10: 10] sts.
Work a further 3 rows for collar extension,
ending with RS facing for next row.
Cast off.

RIGHT FRONT

Using 10mm (US 15) needles cast on 23 [25:
29: 32] sts.
Rows 1 and 2: Knit.
Row 3 (RS): *P1, K1, rep from * to last 1 [1:
1: 0] st, P1 [1: 1: 0].
Row 4: P0 [0: 0: 1], *K1, P1, rep from * to
last st, K1.
These 4 rows form patt.
Cont in patt, dec 1 st at end of 3rd [3rd: 5th:
5th] and foll 8th row. 21 [23: 27: 30] sts.
Complete to match left front, reversing shapings.

SLEEVES

Using 10mm (US 15) needles cast on 25 [25:
27: 27] sts.
Rows 1 and 2: Knit.
Row 3 (RS): K1, *P1, K1, rep from * to end.
Row 4: P1, *K1, P1, rep from * to end.
These 4 rows form patt.
Cont in patt, shaping sides by inc 1 st at each
end of next and every foll 8th [6th: 6th: 6th]
row to 39 [35: 35: 43] sts, then on every foll -
[8th: 8th: 8th] row until there are - [41: 43: 45]
sts, taking inc sts into patt.
Cont straight until sleeve meas 43 [44: 45: 45] cm,
ending with RS facing for next row.
Shape top
Keeping patt correct, cast off 2 sts at beg of
next 2 rows. 35 [37: 39: 41] sts.
Dec 1 st at each end of next 2 rows, ending
with RS facing for next row. 31 [33: 35: 37] sts.
Cast off 8 [8: 9: 9] sts at beg of next 2 rows.
Cast off rem 15 [17: 17: 19] sts.
MAKING UP
Press as described on the information page.

Join shoulder and collar extension seams using
back stitch, or mattress stitch if preferred.
See information page for finishing instructions,
setting in sleeves using the set-in method.
Crochet edging
With RS facing and using 10.00mm (US N15)
crochet hook, attach yarn at base of one side
seam, 1 ch (does NOT count as st), work 1
round of dc evenly around entire hem, front
opening and collar edges, ensuring number of
dc worked is divisible by 6, ss to first dc, **turn.**
Next round (WS): 1 ch (does NOT count
as st), 1 dc into first dc, *miss 2 dc, 5 tr into next
dc, miss 2 dc, 1 dc into next dc, rep from * to end,
replacing dc at end of last rep with ss to first dc.
Fasten off.
Work crochet edging around lower edges of
sleeves in same way.
Button covers (make 3)
Using 10.00mm (US N15) crochet hook, make
3 ch and join with a ss to form a ring.
Round 1 (RS): 1 ch (does NOT count as st),
8 dc into ring, ss to first dc.
Round 2: 3 ch (counts as first tr), miss dc at
base of 3 ch, 1 tr into each dc to end, ss to top
of 3 ch at beg of round.
Fasten off.
Lay button onto WS of button cover. Run
gathering thread around top of last round and
pull up tightly, enclosing button.
Button loops (make 3)
Using 10.00mm (US N15) crochet hook, make
36 ch.
Row 1 (RS): 1 dc into 2nd ch from hook,
1 dc into each ch to end.
Fasten off.
Using photograph as a guide, form button loop
into shape as shown as sew onto fronts. Attach
buttons to correspond.

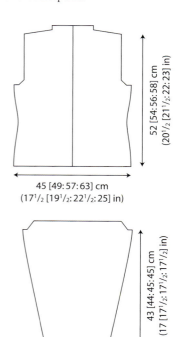

52 [54: 56: 58] cm
(20½ [21½: 22: 23] in)

45 [49: 57: 63] cm
(17½ [19½: 22½: 25] in)

43 [44: 45: 45] cm
(17 [17½: 17½: 17½] in)

Main image page 21, 50 & 51

MURMANSK BY GABRIELLE CARTER

YARN
Rowan Kid Classic and Wool Cotton

A	Kid Classic	1 x 50gm
B	Kid Classic	1 x 50gm
C	WoolCotton	1 x 50gm
D	Wool Cotton	1 x 50gm

1st colourway		**2nd colourway**
A	Smoke 831	Straw 851
B	Crystal 840	Battle 845
C	Misty 903	Chestnut 966
D	Antique 900	Antique 900

NEEDLES
1 pair 4mm (no 8) (US 6) needles
4.00mm (no 8) (US G6) crochet hook

EXTRAS – 3 x 00415 pins, 110 cm x 25 cm piece of lining fabric, same size piece of interfacing, and matching sewing thread

TENSION
23 sts and 28 rows to 10 cm measured over stocking stitch using 4mm (US 6) needles.

UK CROCHET ABBREVIATIONS
dc = double crochet.

US CROCHET ABBREVIATIONS
dc = single crochet.

BRACES (worked in one piece starting at lower edge of back)
Using 4mm (US 6) needles and yarn A cast on 8 sts.
Using the **intarsia** technique as described on the information page, work from chart, which is worked entirely in st st beg with a K row, as folls:
Inc 1 st at each end of 5th and foll 4th row, then on every foll 6th row until there are 42 sts.
Work 13 rows, ending after chart row 112 and with RS facing for next row.

Shape straps
Next row (RS): Patt 16 sts and turn, leaving rem sts on a holder.
Work each side of neck separately.
Dec 1 st at neck edge of 2nd and foll 3 alt rows, then on every foll 10th row until 8 sts rem.
Cont straight until chart row 300 has been completed, ending with RS facing for next row.
Cast off.
With RS facing, rejoin yarns to rem sts, cast off centre 10 sts, patt to end.
Complete to match first side, reversing shapings.

MAKING UP
Press as described on the information page.
With RS facing, using 4.00mm (US G6) crochet hook and yarn B, attach yarn at one end of cast-on edge and work 1 row of dc around entire row-end and neck edges, ending at other end of cast-on edge.
Fasten off.
Apply interfacing to WS of lining fabric. Cut out same size piece as knitted section from joined lining and interfacing, adding seam allowance along all edges. Fold seam allowance to WS, then slip stitch lining to WS of knitted section. Attach safety pins to back and strap edges.

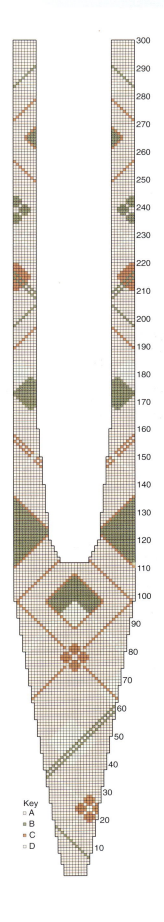

Key
- A
- B
- C
- D

Main image page 39

ORGANIC BAG BY BRONWEN HARLOWE

YARN
Rowan Tapestry and Kid Classic
A Tapestry Pot Pourri 172   4 x 50gm
B Kid Classic Bear 817   1 x 50gm
C Kid Classic Crushed Velvet 825   1 x 50gm

NEEDLES
1 pair 4mm (no 8) (US 6) needles
4.00mm (no 8) (US G6) crochet hook

EXTRAS – pair of bag handles x 00403

TENSION
22 sts and 30 rows to 10 cm measured over stocking stitch using 4mm (US 6) needles and yarn A (before felting)

UK CROCHET ABBREVIATIONS
ch = chain; **dc** = double crochet; **tr** = treble.

US CROCHET ABBREVIATIONS
ch = chain; **dc** = single crochet;
tr = double crochet.

FINISHED SIZE
Completed bag measures approx 29 cm (11½ in) wide and 26 cm (10¼ in) deep.

BAG
Using 4mm (US 6) needles and yarn A cast on 104 sts.
Beg with a K row, work in st st for 78 cm, ending with RS facing for next row.
Cast off.

BOBBLE STRANDS (make 12)
Using 4.00mm (US G6) hook and yarn B make 10 ch, ★(1 dc and 4 tr) into 2nd ch from hook (to form bobble), insert hook through centre of bobble and work 1 ch to anchor and close bobble, 10 ch, rep from ★ until strand is 30-40 cm long, varying the number of ch worked between each bobble.
Fasten off.
Make a further 5 bobble strands using yarn B, then a further 6 strands using yarn C.

MAKING UP
Do NOT press.
Fold bag in half, so that cast-on and cast-off edges match, and join side seams, beg 10 cm below cast-on and cast-off edges.

Using photograph as a guide, attach one end of each bobble strand to top opening edge of bag. Machine wash completed bag at 40° and leave to dry naturally, easing into shape.
Attach bag handles.

Main image page 36 & 37

DOTTY BY KAFFE FASSETT

SIZE
	S	M	L	XL	XXL	
To fit chest
	102	107	112	117	122	cm
	40	42	44	46	48	in

YARN
Rowan Felted Tweed and Tapestry
A Felted Tweed Phantom 153
   1   1   1   1   1 x 50gm
B Felted Tweed Dragon 147
   1   1   1   1   1 x 50gm
C Felted Tweed Camel 157
   4   4   4   4   5 x 50gm
D Tapestry Rustic 174
   4   4   5   5   5 x 50gm

NEEDLES
1 pair 3¼mm (no 10) (US 3) needles
1 pair 4mm (no 8) (US 6) needles

TENSION
24 sts and 32 rows to 10 cm measured over patterned stocking stitch using 4mm (US 6) needles.

BACK
Using 3¼mm (US 3) needles and yarn A cast on 127 [135: 143: 149: 157] sts.
Break off yarn A and join in yarn B.
Row 1 (RS): K1, ★P1, K1, rep from ★ to end.
Row 2: P1, ★K1, P1, rep from ★ to end.
These 2 rows form rib.
Break off yarn B and join in yarn C.
Cont in rib for a further 16 rows, ending with RS facing for next row.
Change to 4mm (US 8) needles.
Beg and ending rows as indicated, using the **fairisle** technique as described on the information page and repeating the 90 row patt repeat throughout, work in patt from chart, which is worked entirely in st st, as folls:
Work straight until back meas 32 [33: 32: 33: 32] cm, ending with RS facing for next row.

Shape armholes
Keeping patt correct, cast off 8 sts at beg of next 2 rows.
111 [119: 127: 133: 141] sts.★★
Dec 1 st at each end of next 7 [7: 5: 5: 5] rows, then on foll 3 [2: 3: 1: 1] alt rows, then on every foll 4th row until 87 [97: 107: 117: 125] sts rem.
Cont straight until armhole meas 24 [25: 26: 27: 28] cm, ending with RS facing for next row.

Shape shoulders and back neck
Cast off 7 [9: 10: 12: 13] sts at beg of next 2 rows.
73 [79: 87: 93: 99] sts.
Next row (RS): Cast off 7 [9: 10: 12: 13] sts, patt until there are 11 [12: 14: 15: 16] sts on right needle and turn, leaving rem sts on a holder.
Work each side of neck separately.
Cast off 4 sts at beg of next row.
Cast off rem 7 [8: 10: 11: 12] sts.

With RS facing, rejoin yarns to rem sts, cast off centre 37 [37: 39: 39: 41] sts, patt to end. Complete to match first side, reversing shapings.

FRONT
Work as given for back to ★★.
Dec 1 st at each end of next 7 [7: 5: 5: 5] rows, then on foll 3 [2: 3: 1: 1] alt rows, then on every foll 4th row until 89 [97: 107: 117: 125] sts rem.
Work 1 [1: 3: 9: 11] rows, ending with RS facing for next row.
Divide for neck
Next row (RS): Patt 44 [48: 53: 58: 62] sts and turn, leaving rem sts on a holder.
Work each side of neck separately.
Keeping patt correct, dec 1 st at neck edge of 2nd and foll 20 [19: 20: 20: 21] alt rows, then on 1 [2: 2: 2: 2] foll 4th rows **and at same time** dec 1 [0: 0: 0: 0] st at armhole edge of 2nd row.
21 [26: 30: 35: 38] sts.
Cont straight until front matches back to beg of shoulder shaping, ending with RS facing for next row.
Shape shoulder
Cast off 7 [9: 10: 12: 13] sts at beg of next and foll alt row.
Work 1 row.
Cast off rem 7 [8: 10: 11: 12] sts.
With RS facing, rejoin yarns to rem sts, K2tog, patt to end.

Complete to match first side, reversing shapings.

MAKING UP
Press as described on the information page. Join right shoulder seam using back stitch, or mattress stitch if preferred.
Neckband
With RS facing, using 3¼ mm (US 3) needles and yarn C, pick up and knit 56 [58: 60: 60: 62] sts down left side of neck, 1 st from base of V (mark this st with a coloured thread), 56 [58: 60: 60: 62] sts up right side of neck, then 46 [46: 48: 48: 50] sts from back.
159 [163: 169: 169: 175] sts.
Row 1 (WS): P1, ★K1, P1, rep from ★ to end.
This row sets position of rib.
Keeping rib correct, cont as folls:
Row 2: Rib to within 2 sts of marked st, K2tog tbl, K marked st, K2tog, rib to end.
Row 3: Rib to marked st, P marked st, rib to end.
Rows 4 and 5: As rows 2 and 3.
Break off yarn C and join in yarn B.
Rows 6 and 7: As rows 2 and 3.
Break off yarn B and join in yarn A.
Row 8: As row 2.
Cast off rem 151 [155: 161: 161: 167] sts in rib (on **WS**).
Join left shoulder and neckband seam.
Armhole borders (both alike)
With RS facing, using 3¼ mm (US 3) needles and yarn C, pick up and knit 135 [139: 143:

149: 153] sts evenly all round armhole edge.
Beg with row 2, work in rib as given for back for 5 rows, ending with RS facing for next row.
Break off yarn C and join in yarn B.
Work in rib for a further 2 rows.
Break off yarn B and join in yarn A.
Work in rib for 1 row more, ending with WS facing for next row.
Cast off in rib (on **WS**).
See information page for finishing instructions.

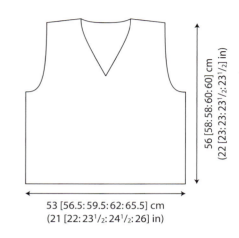

56 [58: 58: 60: 60] cm
(22 [23: 23: 23½: 23½] in)

53 [56.5: 59.5: 62: 65.5] cm
(21 [22: 23½: 24½: 26] in)

Key ☐ C ▨ D

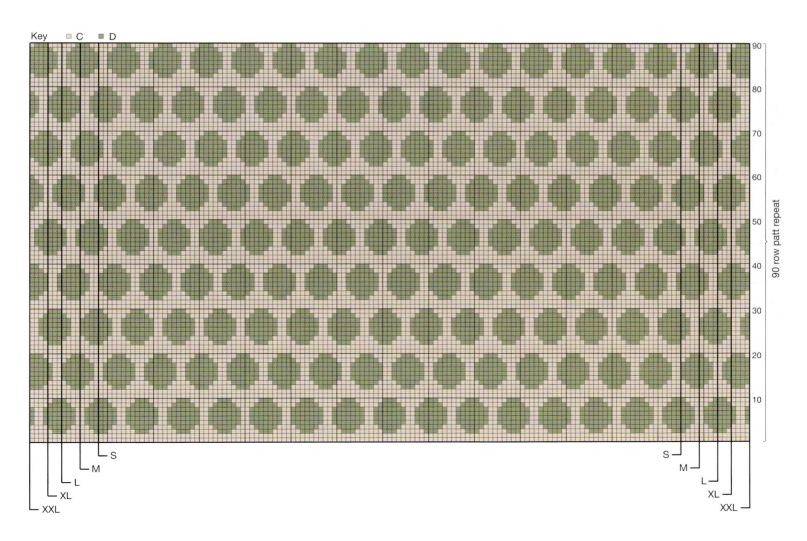

90 row patt repeat

Main image page 49

SHADED FLOWER BY KAFFE FASSETT

SIZE

8	10	12	14	16	18	20	22	
To fit bust

| 82 | 87 | 92 | 97 | 102 | 107 | 112 | 117 | cm |
| 32 | 34 | 36 | 38 | 40 | 42 | 44 | 46 | in |

YARN

Rowan Felted Tweed

A Phantom 153

| 5 | 5 | 5 | 6 | 6 | 6 | 7 | 7 | x 50gm |

B Rage 150

| 1 | 1 | 1 | 1 | 1 | 2 | 2 | 2 | x 50gm |

C Sigh 148

| 1 | 1 | 1 | 1 | 1 | 1 | 2 | 2 | x 50gm |

D Melody 142

| 2 | 2 | 2 | 2 | 2 | 2 | 2 | 2 | x 50gm |

E Pine 158

| 1 | 1 | 1 | 1 | 1 | 1 | 1 | 1 | x 50gm |

F Whisper 141

| 1 | 1 | 1 | 1 | 1 | 1 | 1 | 1 | x 50gm |

G Watery 152

| 1 | 1 | 1 | 1 | 1 | 1 | 1 | 1 | x 50gm |

H Ginger 154

| 2 | 2 | 2 | 2 | 2 | 2 | 2 | 2 | x 50gm |

J Dragon 147

| 1 | 1 | 1 | 1 | 1 | 1 | 1 | 1 | x 50gm |

NEEDLES

1 pair 3mm (no 11) (US 2/3) needles
1 pair 3¾mm (no 9) (US 5) needles
3mm (no 11) (US 2/3) circular needle

BUTTONS – 9 x 00408

TENSION

27 sts and 30 rows to 10 cm measured over patterned stocking stitch using 3¾mm (US 5) needles.

BACK

Using 3¾mm (US 5) needles and yarn A cast on 113 [119: 125: 133: 141: 149: 157: 165] sts.
Beg and ending rows as indicated, using the **fairisle** technique as described on the information page and repeating the 34 row patt repeat throughout, work in patt from chart, which is worked entirely in st st, as folls:
Work straight until back meas 31 [31: 30: 33: 32: 34: 33: 35] cm, ending with RS facing for next row.

Shape armholes

Keeping patt correct, cast off 4 [5: 5: 6: 6: 7: 7: 8] sts at beg of next 2 rows.
105 [109: 115: 121: 129: 135: 143: 149] sts.
Dec 1 st at each end of next 5 [5: 7: 7: 9: 9: 11: 11] rows, then on foll 1 [2: 2: 3: 3: 4: 4: 5] alt rows, then on foll 4th row.
91 [93: 95: 99: 103: 107: 111: 115] sts.
Cont straight until armhole meas 21 [21: 22: 22: 23: 23: 24: 24] cm, ending with RS facing for next row.

Shape shoulders and back neck

Cast off 8 [8: 8: 9: 9: 10: 11: 11] sts at beg of next 2 rows.
75 [77: 79: 81: 85: 87: 89: 93] sts.
Next row (RS): Cast off 8 [8: 8: 9: 9: 10:

11: 11] sts, patt until there are 11 [12: 13: 13: 14: 14: 14: 16] sts on right needle and turn, leaving rem sts on a holder.
Work each side of neck separately.
Cast off 4 sts at beg of next row.
Cast off rem 7 [8: 9: 9: 10: 10: 10: 12] sts.
With RS facing, rejoin yarns to rem sts, cast off centre 37 [37: 37: 37: 39: 39: 39: 39] sts, patt to end.
Complete to match first side, reversing shapings.

LEFT FRONT

Using 3¾mm (US 5) needles and yarn A cast on 57 [60: 63: 67: 71: 75: 79: 83] sts.
Beg and ending rows as indicated, work in patt from chart until left front matches back to beg of armhole shaping, ending with RS facing for next row.

Shape armhole

Keeping patt correct, cast off 4 [5: 5: 6: 6: 7: 7: 8] sts at beg of next row.
53 [55: 58: 61: 65: 68: 72: 75] sts.
Work 1 row.
Dec 1 st at armhole edge of next 5 [5: 7: 7: 9: 9: 11: 11] rows, then on foll 1 [2: 2: 3: 3: 4: 4: 5] alt rows, then on foll 4th row.
46 [47: 48: 50: 52: 54: 56: 58] sts.
Cont straight until 21 [21: 21: 23: 23: 23: 25: 25] rows less have been worked than on back to beg of shoulder shaping, ending with **WS** facing for next row.

Shape neck

Keeping patt correct, cast off 9 [9: 9: 8: 9: 9: 8: 8] sts at beg of next row, then 6 sts at beg of foll alt row.
31 [32: 33: 36: 37: 39: 42: 44] sts.
Dec 1 st at neck edge of next 4 rows, then on foll 3 [3: 3: 4: 4: 4: 5: 5] alt rows, then on foll 4th row.
23 [24: 25: 27: 28: 30: 32: 34] sts.
Work 4 rows, ending with RS facing for next row.

Shape shoulder

Cast off 8 [8: 8: 9: 9: 10: 11: 11] sts at beg of next and foll alt row.
Work 1 row.
Cast off rem 7 [8: 9: 9: 10: 10: 10: 12] sts.

RIGHT FRONT

Work to match left front, reversing shapings.

SLEEVES

Using 3mm (US 2/3) needles and yarn A cast on 63 [63: 65: 65: 67: 67: 69: 69] sts.
Joining in colours as required, work in striped g st as folls:
Rows 1 and 2: Using yarn A, knit.
Rows 3 and 4: Using yarn B, knit.
Rows 5 and 6: Using yarn C, knit.
Rows 7 and 8: Using yarn D, knit.
Change to 3¾mm (US 5) needles.
Beg and ending rows as indicated, work in patt from chart, shaping sides by inc 1 st at each end of 7th [7th: 7th: 5th: 5th: 7th: 5th: 5th] and

every foll 8th [8th: 8th: 8th: 8th: 6th: 6th: 6th] row to 79 [89: 87: 95: 97: 75: 79: 87] sts, then on every foll 10th [10th: 10th: –: –: 8th: 8th: 8th] row until there are 89 [91: 93: –: –: 99: 101: 103] sts, taking inc sts into patt.
Cont straight until sleeve meas 45 [45: 46: 46: 47: 47: 46: 46] cm, ending with RS facing for next row.

Shape top

Keeping patt correct, cast off 4 [5: 5: 6: 6: 7: 7: 8] sts at beg of next 2 rows.
81 [81: 83: 83: 85: 85: 87: 87] sts.
Dec 1 st at each end of next 5 rows, then on foll 2 alt rows, then on every foll 4th row until 57 [57: 59: 59: 61: 61: 63: 63] sts rem.
Work 1 row.
Dec 1 st at each end of next and every foll alt row to 53 sts, then on foll 5 rows, ending with RS facing for next row.
43 sts.
Cast off 8 sts at beg of next 2 rows.
Cast off rem 27 sts.

MAKING UP

Press as described on the information page.
Join shoulder seams using back stitch, or mattress stitch if preferred.

Neckband

With RS facing, using 3mm (US 2/3) needles and yarn D, beg and ending at front opening edges, pick up and knit 35 [35: 35: 36: 37: 37: 38: 38] sts up right side of neck, 45 [45: 45: 45: 47: 47: 47: 47] sts from back, then 35 [35: 35: 36: 37: 37: 38: 38] sts down left side of neck.
115 [115: 115: 117: 121: 121: 123: 123] sts.
★★Joining in and breaking off colours as required, work in striped g st as folls:
Row 1 (WS): Using yarn D, knit.
Rows 2 and 3: Using yarn C, knit.
Rows 4 and 5: Using yarn B, knit.
Rows 6 and 7: Using yarn A, knit.
Using yarn A, cast off.

Button band

With RS facing, using 3mm (US 2/3) needles and yarn D, pick up and knit 120 [120: 120: 127: 127: 134: 134: 134] sts down left front opening edge, from neckband pick-up row to cast-on edge.
Work as given for neckband from ★★.

Buttonhole band

With RS facing, using 3mm (US 2/3) needles and yarn D, pick up and knit 120 [120: 120: 127: 127: 134: 134: 134] sts up right front opening edge, from cast-on edge to neckband pick-up row.
Work as given for neckband from ★★, with the addition of 8 buttonholes worked in row 4 as folls:
Row 4 (buttonhole row) (RS): K2, *K2tog, yfwd, K14 [14: 14: 15: 15: 16: 16: 16], rep from * to last 6 sts, K2tog, yfwd, K4.
Join side seams.

Hem border

With RS facing, using 3mm (US 2/3) circular needle and yarn D, beg and ending at cast-off edges of bands, pick up and knit 62 [65: 68: 73: 76: 80: 84: 88] sts from left front cast-on edge, 112 [118: 124: 132: 140: 148: 156: 164] sts from cast-on edge of back, then 62 [65: 68: 73: 76: 80: 84: 88] sts from right front cast-on edge. 236 [248: 260: 278: 292: 308: 324: 340] sts. Joining in and breaking off colours as required, work in striped g st as folls:

Row 1 (WS): Using yarn D, cast on and K 10 sts, K to end.
246 [258: 270: 288: 302: 318: 334: 350] sts.
Rows 2 and 3: Using yarn C, knit.
Row 4 (RS): Using yarn B, K to last 4 sts, yfwd, K2tog (to make 9th buttonhole), K2.
Row 5: Using yarn B, knit.
Rows 6 and 7: Using yarn A, knit.
Using yarn A, cast off.
See information page for finishing instructions, setting in sleeves using the set-in method.

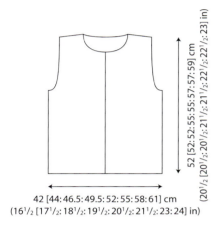

52 [52: 52: 55: 55: 57: 57: 59] cm
(20½ [20½: 20½: 21½: 21½: 22½: 22½: 23] in)

42 [44: 46.5: 49.5: 52: 55: 58: 61] cm
(16½ [17½: 18½: 19½: 20½: 21½: 23: 24] in)

45 [45: 46: 46: 47: 47: 46: 46] cm
(17½ [17½: 18: 18: 18½: 18½: 18: 18] in)

34 row patt repeat

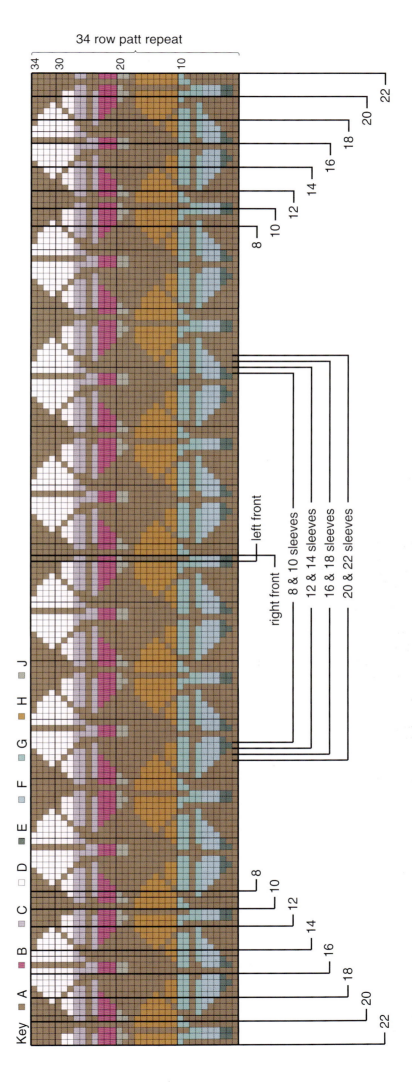

Main image page 56

SIZE

8	10	12	14	16	18	

To fit bust

82	87	92	97	102	107	cm
32	34	36	38	40	42	in

YARN

Rowan Wool Cotton and Felted Tweed

A Wool Cotton Dp Olive 907

5	5	5	6	6	6	x 50gm

B Wool Cotton Chestnut 966

3	3	3	3	3	4	x 50gm

C Wool Cotton Still 964

2	2	2	2	3	3	x 50gm

D Felted Tweed Herb 146

2	2	2	2	3	3	x 50gm

E Felted Tweed Pine 158

2	2	2	2	2	2	x 50gm

NEEDLES

1 pair 3¼ mm (no 10) (US 3) needles
1 pair 3¾ mm (no 9) (US 5) needles
Cable needle

BEADS AND SEQUINS – approx 320 [330: 340: 380: 400: 420] x beads, *Ref Glass Beads SB7 col. 16 Emerald from Creative Beadcraft Ltd and 1040 [1090: 1140: 1250: 1330: 1410] x sequins *Ref Flat Sequin FS6 col. 17 Emerald from Creative Beadcraft Ltd

TENSION

24 sts and 28 rows to 10 cm measured over patterned stocking stitch using 3¾ mm (US 5) needles.

SPECIAL ABBREVIATIONS

C2B = slip next st onto cable needle and leave at back of work, K1, then K1 from cable needle; **bead 1** = place a bead by bringing yarn to front (RS) of work and slipping bead up next to st just worked, slip next st purlwise from left needle to right needle and take yarn back to back (WS) of work, leaving bead sitting in front of slipped st on RS.

Beading note: Before starting to knit, thread beads onto yarn. To do this, thread a fine sewing needle (one that will easily pass through the beads) with sewing thread. Knot ends of thread and then pass end of yarn through this loop. Thread a bead onto sewing thread and then gently slide it along and onto knitting yarn. Continue in this way until required number of beads are on yarn. Do not place beads on edge sts of rows as this will interfere with sewing-up.

BACK

Using 3¼ mm (US 3) needles and yarn A cast on 103 [107: 111: 119: 127: 133] sts.
Row 1 (RS): P1 [3: 1: 1: 1: 4], *K5, P3, rep from * to last 6 [8: 6: 6: 6: 9] sts, K5, P1 [3: 1: 1: 1: 4].
Row 2: K1 [3: 1: 1: 1: 4], *P5, K3, rep from * to last 6 [8: 6: 6: 6: 9] sts, P5, K1 [3: 1: 1: 1: 4].

Rows 3 and 4: As rows 1 and 2.
Row 5: P1 [3: 1: 1: 1: 4], *K1, (C2B) twice, P3, rep from * to last 6 [8: 6: 6: 6: 9] sts, K1, (C2B) twice, P1 [3: 1: 1: 1: 4].
Row 6: As row 2.
Row 7: P1 [3: 1: 1: 1: 4], *(C2B) twice, K1, P3, rep from * to last 6 [8: 6: 6: 6: 9] sts, (C2B) twice, K1, P1 [3: 1: 1: 1: 4].
Row 8: As row 2.
Rows 9 to 20: As rows 5 to 8, 3 times.
Change to 3¾ mm (US 5) needles.
Beg and ending rows as indicated, using the **fairisle** technique as described on the information page and repeating the 44 row patt repeat throughout, work from chart for body as folls:
Dec 1 st at each end of 9th and every foll 6th row until 97 [101: 105: 113: 121: 127] sts rem.
Work 19 rows, ending with RS facing for next row.
Inc 1 st at each end of next and every foll 14th row until there are 103 [107: 111: 119: 127: 133] sts, taking inc sts into patt.
Cont straight until work meas 36 [36: 35: 38: 37: 39] cm, ending with RS facing for next row.

Shape armholes

Keeping patt correct, cast off 4 [5: 5: 6: 6: 7] sts at beg of next 2 rows.
95 [97: 101: 107: 115: 119] sts.
Dec 1 st at each end of next 5 [5: 5: 7: 7: 7] rows, then on foll 2 [2: 2: 2: 4: 4] alt rows, then on foll 4th row.
79 [81: 85: 87: 91: 95] sts.
Cont straight until armhole meas 21 [21: 22: 22: 23: 23] cm, ending with RS facing for next row.

Shape shoulders and back neck

Cast off 6 [6: 7: 7: 8: 8] sts at beg of next 2 rows.
67 [69: 71: 73: 75: 79] sts.
Next row (RS): Cast off 6 [6: 7: 7: 8: 8] sts, patt until there are 10 [11: 11: 12: 11: 13] sts on right needle and turn, leaving rem sts on a holder.
Work each side of neck separately.
Cast off 4 sts at beg of next row.
Cast off rem 6 [7: 7: 8: 7: 9] sts.
With RS facing, rejoin yarns to rem sts, cast off centre 35 [35: 35: 35: 37: 37] sts, patt to end.
Complete to match first side, reversing shapings.

FRONT

Work as given for back until 20 [20: 20: 20: 22: 22] rows less have been worked than on back to beg of shoulder shaping, ending with RS facing for next row.

Shape neck

Next row (RS): Patt 32 [33: 35: 36: 38: 40] sts and turn, leaving rem sts on a holder.
Work each side of neck separately.
Keeping patt correct, cast off 5 sts at beg of next row.
27 [28: 30: 31: 33: 35] sts.

Dec 1 st at neck edge of next 5 rows, then on foll 3 [3: 3: 3: 4: 4] alt rows, then on foll 4th row.
18 [19: 21: 22: 23: 25] sts.
Work 3 rows, ending with RS facing for next row.

Shape shoulder

Cast off 6 [6: 7: 7: 8: 8] sts at beg of next and foll alt row.
Work 1 row.
Cast off rem 6 [7: 7: 8: 7: 9] sts.
With RS facing, rejoin yarns to rem sts, cast off centre 15 sts, patt to end.
Complete to match first side, reversing shapings.

SLEEVES

Using 3¼ mm (US 3) needles and yarn A cast on 57 [57: 59: 59: 61: 61] sts.
Row 1 (RS): P2 [2: 3: 3: 4: 4], *K5, P3, rep from * to last 7 [7: 8: 8: 9: 9] sts, K5, P2 [2: 3: 3: 4: 4].
Row 2: K2 [2: 3: 3: 4: 4], *P5, K3, rep from * to last 7 [7: 8: 8: 9: 9] sts, P5, K2 [2: 3: 3: 4: 4].
Rows 3 and 4: As rows 1 and 2.

43 [44.5: 46.5: 49.5: 53: 55.5] cm
(17 [17½: 18½: 19½: 21: 22] in)

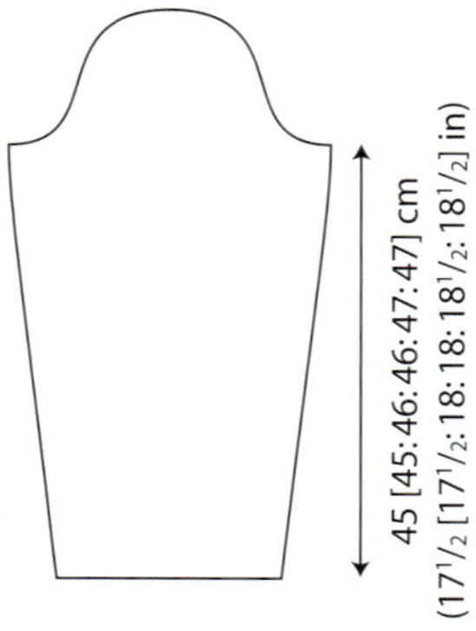

57 [57: 57: 60: 60: 62] cm
(22½ [22½: 22½: 23½: 23½: 24½] in)

45 [45: 46: 46: 47: 47] cm
(17½ [17½: 18: 18: 18½: 18½] in)

Row 5: P2 [2: 3: 3: 4: 4], ★K1, (C2B) twice, P3, rep from ★ to last 7 [7: 8: 8: 9: 9] sts, K1, (C2B) twice, P2 [2: 3: 3: 4: 4].
Row 6: As row 2.
Row 7: P2 [2: 3: 3: 4: 4], ★(C2B) twice, K1, P3, rep from ★ to last 7 [7: 8: 8: 9: 9] sts, (C2B) twice, K1, P2 [2: 3: 3: 4: 4].
Row 8: As row 2.
Rows 9 to 20: As rows 5 to 8, 3 times.
Change to 3¾ mm (US 5) needles.
Beg and ending rows as indicated, work from chart for sleeve, shaping sides by inc 1 st at each end of 7th [5th: 5th: 5th: 5th: 5th] and every foll 8th [6th: 6th: 6th: 6th: 6th] row to 81 [65: 65: 73: 73: 81] sts, then on every foll – [8th: 8th: 8th: 8th: 8th] row until there are – [83: 85: 87: 89: 91] sts, taking inc sts into patt. Cont straight until sleeve meas 45 [45: 46: 46: 47: 47] cm, ending with RS facing for

next row.
Shape top
Keeping patt correct, cast off 4 [5: 5: 6: 6: 7] sts at beg of next 2 rows. 73 [73: 75: 75: 77: 77] sts. Dec 1 st at each end of next 3 rows, then on foll alt row, then on every foll 4th row until 55 [55: 57: 57: 59: 59] sts rem.
Work 1 row.
Dec 1 st at each end of next and every foll alt row to 49 sts, then on foll 5 rows, ending with RS facing for next row.
39 sts.
Cast off 8 sts at beg of next 2 rows.
Cast off rem 23 sts.

MAKING UP
Press as described on the information page. Join right shoulder seam using back stitch, or mattress stitch if preferred.

Neck border
With RS facing, using 3¼ mm (US 3) needles and yarn A, pick up and knit 27 [27: 27: 27: 30: 30] sts down left side of neck, 15 sts from front, 27 [27: 27: 27: 30: 30] sts up right side of neck, then 46 [46: 46: 46: 48: 48] sts from back. 115 [115: 115: 115: 123: 123] sts.
Row 1 (WS): K3, ★P5, K3, rep from ★ to end.
Row 2: P3, ★K1, (C2B) twice, P3, rep from ★ to end.
Row 3: As row 1.
Row 4: P3, ★(C2B) twice, K1, P3, rep from ★ to end.
Rows 5 to 20: As rows 1 to 4, 4 times.
Cast off in patt (on **WS**).
See information page for finishing instructions, setting in sleeves using the set-in method.
Using photograph as a guide, sew sequins onto each rep of chart rows 23 and 32.

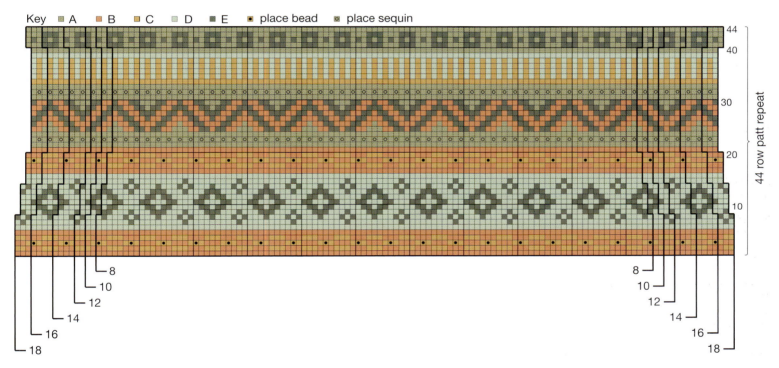

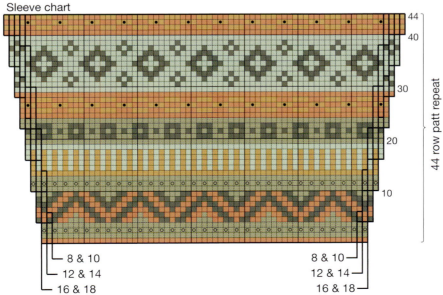

Sleeve chart

Main image page 72 & 73

AELF BY LEAH SUTTON

SIZE

8	10	12	14	16	18	
To fit bust						
82	87	92	97	102	107	cm
32	34	36	38	40	42	in

YARN

Rowan Kid Classic

6	6	6	7	7	8	x 50gm

(photographed in Lavender Ice 841)

NEEDLES

1 pair 4mm (no 8) (US 6) needles
1 pair 5mm (no 6) (US 8) needles

BUTTONS – 3 x 00319

TENSION

19 sts and 25 rows to 10 cm measured over stocking stitch using 5mm (US 8) needles.

BACK

Using 4mm (US 6) needles cast on 83 [87: 91: 97: 103: 107] sts.
Work in g st for 8 rows, ending with RS facing for next row.
Change to 5mm (US 8) needles.
Beg with a K row, work in st st, shaping side seams by dec 1 st at each end of 5th and every foll 4th row until 73 [77: 81: 87: 93: 97] sts rem.
Work 5 rows, ending with RS facing for next row.
Inc 1 st at each end of next and every foll 8th row until there are 79 [83: 87: 93: 99: 103] sts.
Cont straight until back meas 25 [25: 24: 27: 26: 28] cm, ending with RS facing for next row.

Shape armholes

Cast off 4 [5: 5: 6: 6: 7] sts at beg of next 2 rows.
71 [73: 77: 81: 87: 89] sts.
Dec 1 st at each end of next 3 [3: 3: 5: 5: 5] rows, then on foll 2 [2: 3: 2: 3: 3] alt rows.
61 [63: 65: 67: 71: 73] sts.
Cont straight until armhole meas 18 [18: 19: 19: 20: 20] cm, ending with RS facing for next row.

Shape back neck

Next row (RS): K18 [19: 20: 21: 22: 23] and turn, leaving rem sts on a holder.
Work each side of neck separately.
Dec 1 st at neck edge of next 3 rows, ending with RS facing for next row.
15 [16: 17: 18: 19: 20] sts.

Shape shoulder

Cast off.
With RS facing, rejoin yarn to rem sts, cast off centre 25 [25: 25: 25: 27: 27] sts, K to end.
Complete to match first side, reversing shapings.

LEFT FRONT

Using 4mm (US 6) needles cast on 39 [41: 43: 46: 49: 51] sts.
Work in g st for 8 rows, ending with RS facing

for next row.
Change to 5mm (US 8) needles.
Beg with a K row, work in st st, shaping side seams by dec 1 st at beg of 5th and every foll 4th row until 34 [36: 38: 41: 44: 46] sts rem.
Work 5 rows, ending with RS facing for next row.
Inc 1 st at beg of next and every foll 8th row until there are 37 [39: 41: 44: 47: 49] sts.
Cont straight until left front matches back to beg of armhole shaping, ending with RS facing for next row.

Shape armhole

Cast off 4 [5: 5: 6: 6: 7] sts at beg of next row.
33 [34: 36: 38: 41: 42] sts.
Work 1 row.

Shape front slope

Dec 1 st at armhole edge of next 3 [3: 3: 5: 5: 5] rows, then on foll 2 [2: 3: 2: 3: 3] alt rows **and at same time** dec 1 st at front slope edge of next and every foll alt row.
24 [25: 25: 26: 27: 28] sts.
Dec 1 st at front slope edge **only** of 2nd and foll 2 [2: 0: 0: 0: 0] alt rows, then on every foll 4th row until 15 [16: 17: 18: 19: 20] sts rem.
Cont straight until left front matches back to shoulder cast-off, ending with RS facing for next row.

Shape shoulder

Cast off.

RIGHT FRONT

Using 4mm (US 6) needles cast on 39 [41: 43: 46: 49: 51] sts.
Work in g st for 8 rows, ending with RS facing for next row.
Change to 5mm (US 8) needles.
Beg with a K row, work in st st, shaping side seams by dec 1 st at end of 5th and every foll 4th row until 34 [36: 38: 41: 44: 46] sts rem.
Complete to match left front, reversing shapings.

SLEEVES

Using 4mm (US 6) needles cast on 39 [39: 41: 41: 43: 43] sts.
Work in g st for 8 rows, ending with RS facing for next row.
Change to 5mm (US 8) needles.
Beg with a K row, work in st st, shaping sides by inc 1 st at each end of 5th [3rd: 3rd: 3rd: 3rd: 3rd] and every foll 6th [4th: 6th: 4th: 4th: 4th] row to 65 [43: 71: 49: 49: 55], then on every foll 8th [6th: –: 6th: 6th: 6th] row until there are 67 [69: –: 73: 75: 77] sts.
Cont straight until sleeve meas 45 [45: 46: 46: 47: 47] cm, ending with RS facing for next row.

Shape top

Cast off 4 [5: 5: 6: 6: 7] sts at beg of next 2 rows.
59 [59: 61: 61: 63: 63] sts.
Dec 1 st at each end of next 7 rows, then on every foll alt row to 29 sts, then on foll 5 rows, ending with RS facing for next row.

19 sts.
Cast off 4 sts at beg of next 2 rows.
Cast off rem 11 sts.

MAKING UP

Press as described on the information page.
Join both shoulder seams using back stitch, or mattress stitch if preferred.
See information page for finishing instructions, setting in sleeves using the set-in method.

Hem border

Using 5mm (US 8) needles cast on 11 sts.
Row 1 (RS): K2, *K2tog, (yfwd) twice, rep from * to last 3 sts, K2tog, K1.
13 sts.
Row 2: K3, *yfwd, K2tog, K1, rep from * to last st, K1.
Rows 3 and 4: Knit.
Rows 5 and 6: As rows 1 and 2.
16 sts.
Row 7: Knit.
Row 8: Cast off 5 sts, K to end.
11 sts.
These 8 rows form patt.
Cont in patt until straight edge of hem border fits around entire cast-on edge of back and fronts, ending after patt row 8 and with RS facing for next row.
Cast off.

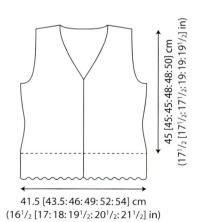

41.5 [43.5: 46: 49: 52: 54] cm
(16¹/₂ [17: 18: 19¹/₂: 20¹/₂: 21¹/₂] in)

Slip stitch hem border in place.

Right lapel

Using 4mm (US 6) needles cast on 2 sts.
Beg with a K row, work in st st, inc 1 st at beg of first row and at same edge of every row until there are 29 sts.
Work 1 row, ending with RS facing for next row.
Break yarn and leave sts on a holder.

Left lapel

Work as given for right lapel, reversing shaping.

Long lace strips (make 2)

Using 4mm (US 6) needles cast on 6 sts.
Row 1 (RS): K1, K2tog, yfwd, K2, (yfwd) twice, K1.
8 sts.
Row 2: K2, K1 tbl, K2tog, yfwd, K3.
Row 3: K1, K2tog, yfwd, K5.
Row 4: Cast off 2 sts (one st on right needle), K2tog, yfwd, K3.
6 sts.
These 4 rows form patt.★★
Work in patt for a further 8 rows, ending with RS facing for next row.
Break yarn and leave sts on a holder.

Medium lace strips (make 4)

Work as given for long lace strips to ★★.

Work in patt for a further 4 rows, ending with RS facing for next row.
Break yarn and leave sts on a holder.

Short lace strips (make 2)

Work as given for long lace strips to ★★.
Break yarn and leave sts on a holder.

Right collar

Using 4mm (US 6) needles and with RS facing, K across 6 sts of one long lace strip, (K across 6 sts of one medium lace strip) twice, K across 6 sts of one short lace strip.
24 sts.
Beg with a P row, work in st st for 7 rows, ending with RS facing for next row.
Break yarn and leave sts on a holder.

Left collar

Using 4mm (US 6) needles and with RS facing, K across 6 sts of one short lace strip, (K across 6 sts of one medium lace strip) twice, K across 6 sts of one long lace strip. 24 sts.
Beg with a P row, work in st st for 7 rows, ending with RS facing for next row.
Break yarn and leave sts on a holder.

Right front border

Using 4mm (US 6) needles cast on and K 50 [50: 48: 54: 52: 56] sts, with RS facing K across 29 sts of right lapel, then K across 24 sts of

right collar, turn and cast on 13 [13: 15: 15: 18: 18] sts.
116 [116: 116: 122: 123: 127] sts.
Work in g st for 2 rows, ending with **WS** facing for next row.
Row 3 (WS): K to last 48 [48: 46: 52: 50: 54] sts, cast off 2 sts, (K until there are 20 [20: 19: 22: 21: 23] sts on right needle after cast-off, cast off 2 sts) twice, K to end.
Row 4: K to end, casting on 2 sts over those cast off on previous row.
Work in g st for a further 3 rows, ending with RS facing for next row.
Cast off.

Left front border

Using 4mm (US 6) needles cast on and K 13 [13: 15: 15: 18: 18] sts, with RS facing K across 24 sts of left collar, then K across 29 sts of left lapel, turn and cast on 50 [50: 48: 54: 52: 56] sts.
116 [116: 116: 122: 123: 127] sts.
Work in g st for 7 rows, ending with RS facing for next row.
Cast off.
Join centre back neck row-end edges of borders, then slip stitch borders in place. Sew on buttons.

Main image page 80

TITANIA BY MARIE WALLIN

SIZE

	S	M	L	XL
	8/10	12/14	16/18	20/22
To fit bust				
	82-87	92-97	102-107	112-117 cm
	32-34	36-38	40-42	44-46 in

YARN

Rowan Romance, Kid Classic, Kidsilk Haze and Lurex Shimmer

A Romance Sparkle 095
| | 11 | 12 | 14 | 16 | x 50gm |
B Kid Classic Sherbet Dip 850
| | 1 | 1 | 1 | 1 | x 50gm |
C Kid Classic Lavender Ice 841
| | 1 | 1 | 1 | 1 | x 50gm |

D Kidsilk Haze Dewberry 600
| | 1 | 1 | 1 | 1 | x 25gm |
E Lurex Shimmer Gleam 336
| | 1 | 1 | 1 | 1 | x 25gm |

NEEDLES

1 pair 7mm (no 2) (US 10½) needles
Cable needle
2.50mm (no 12) (US C2) crochet hook
4.00mm (no 8) (US G6) crochet hook
6.00mm (no 4) (US J10) crochet hook

EXTRAS – 11 small *Ref Bali Silver Beads BS24 and 3 large silver beads *Ref Bali Silver Beads BS25, 6 large glass beads *Ref Glass

Bead GB68 col. 3 Purple from Creative Beadcraft Ltd and kilt pin.

TENSION

12 sts and 16 rows to 10 cm measured over stocking stitch using 7mm (US 10½) needles.

SPECIAL ABBREVIATIONS

C4B = slip next 2 sts onto cable needle and leave at back of work, K2, then K2 from cable needle; **Cr4R** = slip next 2 sts onto cable needle and leave at back of work, K2, then P2 from cable needle; **Cr4L** = slip next 2 sts onto cable needle and leave at front of work, P2, then K2 from cable needle; **Tw2** = K2tog

141

leaving sts on left needle, K first st again then slip both sts off left needle together; **wrap 3** = slip next 3 sts onto cable needle, wrap yarn twice round these 3 sts then K1, P1, K1 across 3 sts on cable needle.

UK CROCHET ABBREVIATIONS
ch = chain; **dc** = double crochet; **sp(s)** = space(es); **ss** = slip stitch; **tr(s)** = treble(s).

US CROCHET ABBREVIATIONS
ch = chain; **dc** = single crochet; **sp(s)** = space(es); **ss** = slip stitch; **tr(s)** = double crochet.

BACK
Using 7mm (US 10½) needles and yarn A cast on 62 [68: 76: 84] sts.
Row 1 (RS): P1 [4: 2: 2], (Tw2, P4) 0 [0: 1: 0] times, ★P4, Tw2, P4, rep from ★ to last 1 [4: 8: 2] sts, (P4, Tw2) 0 [0: 1: 0] times, P1 [4: 2: 2].
Row 2: K1 [4: 2: 2], (P2, K4) 0 [0: 1: 0] times, ★K4, P2, K4, rep from ★ to last 1 [4: 8: 2] sts, (K4, P2) 0 [0: 1: 0] times, K1 [4: 2: 2].
Rows 3 to 6: As rows 1 and 2, twice.
Row 7: As row 1.
Row 8: K1 [4: 2: 2], (inc once purlwise in each of next 2 sts, K4) 0 [0: 1: 0] times, ★K4, inc once purlwise in each of next 2 sts, K4, rep from ★ to last 1 [4: 8: 2] sts, (K4, inc once purlwise in each of next 2 sts) 0 [0: 1: 0] times, K1 [4: 2: 2].
74 [80: 92: 100] sts.
Row 9: P1 [4: 2: 2], (C4B, P4) 0 [0: 1: 0] times, ★P4, C4B, P4, rep from ★ to last 1 [4: 10: 2] sts, (P4, C4B) 0 [0: 1: 0] times, P1 [4: 2: 2].
Row 10: K1 [4: 2: 2], (P4, K4) 0 [0: 1: 0] times, ★K4, P4, K4, rep from ★ to last 1 [4: 10: 2] sts, (K4, P4) 0 [0: 1: 0] times, K1 [4: 2: 2].
Row 11: P1 [4: 2: 2], (K2, Cr4L, P2) 0 [0: 1: 0] times, ★P2, Cr4R, Cr4L, P2, rep from ★ to last 1 [4: 10: 2] sts, (P2, Cr4R, K2) 0 [0: 1: 0] times, P1 [4: 2: 2].
Row 12: K1 [4: 2: 2], (K2, P2) 0 [0: 2: 0] times, ★K2, P2, K4, P2, K2, rep from ★ to last 1 [4: 10: 2] sts, (K2, P2) 0 [0: 2: 0] times, K1 [4: 2: 2].
Row 13: P1 [4: 2: 2], (K2, P2, Cr4L) 0 [0: 1: 0] times, ★Cr4R, P4, Cr4L, rep from ★ to last 1 [4: 10: 2] sts, (Cr4R, P2, K2) 0 [0: 1: 0] times, P1 [4: 2: 2].
Row 14: K1 [4: 2: 2], (P2, K4, P2) 0 [0: 1: 0] times, ★P2, K8, P2, rep from ★ to last 1 [4: 10: 2] sts, (P2, K4, P2) 0 [0: 1: 0] times, K1 [4: 2: 2].
Row 15: P1 [4: 2: 2], K2, P8 [8: 4: 8], ★C4B, P8, rep from ★ to last 3 [6: 12: 4] sts, (C4B, P4) 0 [0: 1: 0] times, K2, P1 [4: 2: 2].
Row 16: As row 14.
Row 17: P1 [4: 2: 2], (K2, P2, Cr4R) 0 [0: 1: 0] times, ★Cr4L, P4, Cr4R, rep from ★ to last 1 [4: 10: 2] sts, (Cr4L, P2, K2) 0 [0: 1: 0] times, P1 [4: 2: 2].
Row 18: As row 12.
Row 19: P1 [4: 2: 2], (K2, Cr4R, P2) 0 [0: 1: 0] times, ★P2, Cr4L, Cr4R, P2, rep from ★ to last 1 [4: 10: 2] sts, (P2, Cr4L, K2) 0 [0: 1: 0] times, P1 [4: 2: 2].
Row 20: K1 [4: 2: 2], (P2tog, P2tog, K4) 0 [0: 1: 0] times, ★K4, (P2tog) twice, K4, rep from ★ to last 1 [4: 8: 2] sts, (K4, P2tog, P2tog) 0 [0: 1: 0] times, K1 [4: 2: 2].
62 [68: 76: 84] sts.
These 20 rows form patt.
Cont in patt for a further 7 rows, ending with **WS** facing for next row.
Row 28 (WS): Knit.
Row 29: P6 [11: 4: 2], P2tog, (P0 [0: 1: 1],

P2tog) 24 [22: 22: 26] times, P to end.
37 [45: 53: 57] sts.
Row 30: K1, ★P1, K1, rep from ★ to end.
Row 31: P1, ★K1, P1, rep from ★ to end.
Row 32: As row 30.
Row 33: P1, ★wrap 3, P1, rep from ★ to end.
Row 34: As row 30.
Row 35: P1, K1, P1, ★wrap 3, P1, rep from ★ to last 2 sts, K1, P1.
Row 36: As row 30.
Row 37: As row 33.
Rows 38 and 39: As rows 30 and 31.
Row 40: Knit.
Row 41: P6 [11: 4: 2], inc purlwise in next st, (P0 [0: 1: 1], inc purlwise in next st) 24 [22: 22: 26] times, P to end.
62 [68: 76: 84] sts.
Beg with row 2, work in patt for 39 rows, ending after patt row 20 and with RS facing for next row.
Next row (RS): P1 [4: 2: 2], (Tw2, P4) 0 [0: 1: 0] times, ★P4, Tw2, P4, rep from ★ to last 1 [4: 8: 2] sts, (P4, Tw2) 0 [0: 1: 0] times, P1 [4: 2: 2].
Next row: K1 [4: 2: 2], (P2, K4) 0 [0: 1: 0] times, ★K4, P2, K4, rep from ★ to last 1 [4: 8: 2] sts, (K4, P2) 0 [0: 1: 0] times, K1 [4: 2: 2].
Rep these 2 rows until back meas 62 [64: 66: 68] cm, ending with RS facing for next row.
Shape shoulder
Cast off all sts in patt.

LEFT FRONT
Using 7mm (US 10½) needles and yarn A cast on 32 [35: 39: 43] sts.
Row 1 (RS): P1 [4: 2: 2], (Tw2, P4) 0 [0: 1: 0] times, ★P4, Tw2, P4, rep from ★ to last st, P1.
Row 2: K1, ★K4, P2, K4, rep from ★ to last 1 [4: 8: 2] sts, (K4, P2) 0 [0: 1: 0] times, K1 [4: 2: 2].
Rows 3 to 6: As rows 1 and 2, twice.
Row 7: As row 1.
Row 8: K1, ★K4, inc once purlwise in each of next 2 sts, K4, rep from ★ to last 1 [4: 8: 2] sts, (K4, inc once purlwise in each of next 2 sts) 0 [0: 1: 0] times, K1 [4: 2: 2].
38 [41: 47: 51] sts.
Row 9: P1 [4: 2: 2], (C4B, P4) 0 [0: 1: 0] times, ★P4, C4B, P4, rep from ★ to last st, P1.
Row 10: K1, ★K4, P4, K4, rep from ★ to last 1 [4: 10: 2] sts, (K4, P4) 0 [0: 1: 0] times, K1 [4: 2: 2].
Row 11: P1 [4: 2: 2], (K2, Cr4L, P2) 0 [0: 1: 0] times, ★P2, Cr4R, Cr4L, P2, rep from ★ to last st, P1.
Row 12: K1, ★K2, P2, K4, P2, K2, rep from ★ to last 1 [4: 10: 2] sts, (K2, P2) 0 [0: 2: 0] times, K1 [4: 2: 2].
Row 13: P1 [4: 2: 2], (K2, P2, Cr4L) 0 [0: 1: 0] times, ★Cr4R, P4, Cr4L, rep from ★ to last st, P1.
Row 14: K1, ★P2, K8, P2, rep from ★ to last 1 [4: 10: 2] sts, (P2, K4, P2) 0 [0: 1: 0] times, K1 [4: 2: 2].
Row 15: P1 [4: 2: 2], K2, P8 [8: 4: 8], ★C4B, P8, rep from ★ to last 3 sts, K2, P1.
Row 16: As row 14.
Row 17: P1 [4: 2: 2], (K2, P2, Cr4R) 0 [0: 1: 0] times, ★Cr4L, P4, Cr4R, rep from ★ to last st, P1.
Row 18: As row 12.
Row 19: P1 [4: 2: 2], (K2, Cr4R, P2) 0 [0: 1: 0] times, ★P2, Cr4L, Cr4R, P2, rep from ★ to last st, P1.
Row 20: K1, ★K4, (P2tog) twice, K4, rep from ★ to last 1 [4: 10: 2] sts, (K4, P2tog, P2tog) 0 [0: 1: 0] times, K1 [4: 2: 2].

32 [35: 39: 43] sts.
These 20 rows form patt.
Cont in patt for a further 7 rows, ending with **WS** facing for next row.
Row 28 (WS): Knit.
Row 29: P1 [3: 5: 5], (P2tog) 15 [14: 14: 16] times, P to end.
17 [21: 25: 27] sts.
Row 30: K1, ★P1, K1, rep from ★ to end.
Row 31: P1, ★K1, P1, rep from ★ to end.
Row 32: As row 30.
Row 33: P1, ★wrap 3, P1, rep from ★ to last 0 [0: 0: 2] sts, (K1, P1) 0 [0: 0: 1] times.
Row 34: As row 30.
Row 35: P1, K1, P1, ★wrap 3, P1, rep from ★ to last 2 [2: 2: 0] sts, (K1, P1) 1 [1: 1: 0] times.
Row 36: As row 30.
Row 37: As row 33.
Rows 38 and 39: As rows 30 and 31.
Row 40: Knit.
Row 41: P1 [3: 5: 5], inc purlwise in each of next 15 [14: 14: 16] sts, P to end.
32 [35: 39: 43] sts.
Beg with row 2, work in patt for 39 rows, ending after patt row 20 and with RS facing for next row.
Next row (RS): P1 [4: 2: 2], (Tw2, P4) 0 [0: 1: 0] times, ★P4, Tw2, P4, rep from ★ to last st, P1.
Next row: K1, ★K4, P2, K4, rep from ★ to last 1 [4: 8: 2] sts, (K4, P2) 0 [0: 1: 0] times, K1 [4: 2: 2].
Rep these 2 rows until left front matches back to shoulder cast-off, ending with RS facing for next row.
Shape shoulder
Cast off all sts in patt.

RIGHT FRONT
Using 7mm (US 10½) needles and yarn A cast on 32 [35: 39: 43] sts.
Row 1 (RS): P1, ★P4, Tw2, P4, rep from ★ to last 1 [4: 8: 2] sts, (P4, Tw2) 0 [0: 1: 0] times, P1 [4: 2: 2].
Row 2: K1 [4: 2: 2], (P2, K4) 0 [0: 1: 0] times, ★K4, P2, K4, rep from ★ to last st, K1.
Rows 3 to 6: As rows 1 and 2, twice.
Row 7: As row 1.
Row 8: K1 [4: 2: 2], (inc once purlwise in each of next 2 sts, K4) 0 [0: 1: 0] times, ★K4, inc once purlwise in each of next 2 sts, K4, rep from ★ to last st, K1.
38 [41: 47: 51] sts.
Row 9: P1, ★P4, C4B, P4, rep from ★ to last 1 [4: 10: 2] sts, (P4, C4B) 0 [0: 1: 0] times, P1 [4: 2: 2].
Row 10: K1 [4: 2: 2], (P4, K4) 0 [0: 1: 0] times, ★K4, P4, K4, rep from ★ to last st, K1.
Row 11: P1, ★P2, Cr4R, Cr4L, P2, rep from ★ to last 1 [4: 10: 2] sts, (P2, Cr4R, K2) 0 [0: 1: 0] times, P1 [4: 2: 2].
Row 12: K1 [4: 2: 2], (K2, P2) 0 [0: 2: 0] times, ★K2, P2, K4, P2, K2, rep from ★ to last st, K1.
Row 13: P1, ★Cr4R, P4, Cr4L, rep from ★ to last 1 [4: 10: 2] sts, (Cr4R, P2, K2) 0 [0: 1: 0] times, P1 [4: 2: 2].
Row 14: K1 [4: 2: 2], (P2, K4, P2) 0 [0: 1: 0] times, ★P2, K8, P2, rep from ★ to last st, K1.
Row 15: P1, K2, P8, ★C4B, P8, rep from ★ to last 3 [6: 12: 4] sts, (C4B, P4) 0 [0: 1: 0] times, K2, P1 [4: 2: 2].
Row 16: As row 14.
Row 17: P1, ★Cr4L, P4, Cr4R, rep from ★ to last 1 [4: 10: 2] sts, (Cr4L, P2, K2) 0 [0: 1: 0] times, P1 [4: 2: 2].
Row 18: As row 12.
Row 19: P1, ★P2, Cr4L, Cr4R, P2, rep from ★

to last 1 [4: 10: 2] sts, (P2, Cr4L, K2) 0 [0: 1: 0] times, P1 [4: 2: 2].
Row 20: K1 [4: 2: 2], (P2tog, P2tog, K4) 0 [0: 1: 0] times, *K4, (P2tog) twice, K4, rep from * to last st, K1.
32 [35: 39: 43] sts.
These 20 rows form patt.
Cont in patt for a further 7 rows, ending with **WS** facing for next row.
Row 28 (WS): Knit.
Row 29: P1 [3: 5: 5], (P2tog) 15 [14: 14: 16] times, P to end. 17 [21: 25: 27] sts.
Row 30: K1, *P1, K1, rep from * to end.
Row 31: P1, *K1, P1, rep from * to end.
Row 32: As row 30.
Row 33: P1, (K1, P1) 0 [0: 0: 1] times, *wrap 3, P1, rep from * to end.
Row 34: As row 30.
Row 35: P1, (K1, P1) 1 [1: 1: 0] times, *wrap 3, P1, rep from * to last 2 sts, K1, P1.
Row 36: As row 30.
Row 37: As row 33.
Rows 38 and 39: As rows 30 and 31.
Row 40: Knit.
Row 41: P1 [3: 5: 5], inc purlwise in each of next 15 [14: 14: 16] sts, P to end.
32 [35: 39: 43] sts.
Beg with row 2, work in patt for 39 rows, ending after patt row 20 and with RS facing for next row.
Next row (RS): P1, *P4, Tw2, P4, rep from * to last 1 [4: 8: 2] sts, (P4, Tw2) 0 [0: 1: 0] times, P1 [4: 2: 2].
Next row: K1 [4: 2: 2], (P2, K4) 0 [0: 1: 0] times, *K4, P2, K4, rep from * to last st, K1.
Rep these 2 rows until right front matches back to shoulder cast-off, ending with RS facing for next row.
Shape shoulder
Cast off all sts in patt.

MAKING UP
Press as described on the information page.
Join shoulder seams using back stitch, or mattress stitch if preferred – fronts will meet at centre of back. Join side seams beg at cast-on edge and stopping approx 8 cm above smocked waist ribbing.
Front edging
With RS facing, using 6.00mm (US J10) crochet hook and yarn A, attach yarn at base of right front opening edge, 1 ch (does NOT count as st), work 1 row of dc up entire right front opening edge, then down entire left front opening edge to cast-on edge, ensuring there is an even number of sts, turn.
Row 1 (WS): 1 ch (does NOT count as st), 1

dc into each dc to end, turn.
Row 2: 3 ch (counts as first tr), miss dc at base of 3 ch, *1 tr between dc just missed and next dc, miss 1 dc, rep from * to end, turn.
Row 3: 3 ch (counts as first tr), miss tr at base of 3 ch, *1 tr between tr just missed and next tr, miss 1 tr, rep from * to end, working last tr between last tr and 3 ch at beg of previous row, turn.
Row 4: *3 ch, miss 2 tr, 1 dc between last tr just missed and next tr, rep from * to end, replacing dc at end of last rep with ss to top of 3 ch at beg of previous row.
Do NOT fasten off or turn.
Hem edging
With RS facing, now work across entire lower edge of fronts and back as folls: 1 ch (does NOT count as st), work 1 row of dc evenly along entire lower edge to beg of row 4 of front edging, turn.
Row 1 (WS): 1 ch (does NOT count as st), 1 dc into each dc to end, turn.
Rep this row once more.
Fasten off.
Armhole edgings (both alike)
With RS facing, using 6.00mm (US J10) crochet hook and yarn A, attach yarn at top of side seam, 1 ch (does NOT count as st), work 1 round of dc evenly around entire armhole edge, ending with ss to first dc, turn.
Round 1 (WS): 1 ch (does NOT count as st), 1 dc into each dc to end, ss to first dc, turn.
Rep this round once more.
Fasten off.
Large flower
With 4.00mm (US G6) crochet hook and yarn B, make 6 ch and join with a ss to form a ring.
Round 1 (RS): 3 ch (counts as first tr), 15 tr into ring, ss to top of 3 ch at beg of round. 16 sts.
Round 2: 5 ch (counts as 1 tr and 2 ch), 1 tr into st at base of 5 ch, *2 ch, miss 1 tr**, (1 tr, 2 ch and 1 tr) into next tr, rep from * to end, ending last rep at **, ss to 3rd of 5 ch at beg of round.
Round 3: Ss across and into first ch sp, 3 ch (counts as first tr), (1 tr, 2 ch and 2 tr) into same ch sp, *1 ch, miss 1 ch sp**, (2 tr, 2 ch and 2 tr) into next ch sp, rep from * to end, ending last rep at **, ss to top of 3 ch at beg of round.
Round 4: Ss across and into first ch sp, 3 ch (counts as first tr), 6 tr into same ch sp, *1 dc into next ch sp**, 7 tr into next ch sp, rep from * to end, ending last rep at **, ss to top of 3 ch at beg of round.
Fasten off.

Medium flower
With 4.00mm (US G6) crochet hook and yarn C, work as given for large flower to end of round 3.
Fasten off.
Small flower
With 2.50mm (US C2) crochet hook and yarn D, work as given for large flower to end of round 2.
Fasten off.
Leaf loops
With 4.00mm (US G6) crochet hook and one strand of each of yarn D and E held together, make 16 ch.
Round 1 (RS): 1 ss into 16th ch from hook, (15 ch, 1 ss into same place as last ss) twice. 3 loops.
Round 2: 1 ch (does NOT count as st), (28 dc into next loop, 1 ss into next ss) 3 times.
Round 3: Ss across and into 3rd dc of previous round, 1 ch (does NOT count as st), 1 dc into dc at base of 1 ch, 1 dc into each of next 23 dc, *miss (2 dc, 1 ss and 2 dc), 1 dc into each of next 24 dc, rep from * once more, 17 ch, 1 dc into 2nd ch from hook, 1 dc into each of next 15 ch, ss to first dc.
Fasten off.
Using photograph as a guide, sew flowers and leaf loops together. Attach beads as folls: attach 3 small silver beads to outer edge of each leaf loop, and one large silver bead to centre. Attach rem silver beads and glass beads to centre of medium flower. Attach joined flower and leaf loops to kilt pin to form corsage.

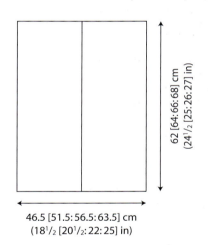

62 [64:66:68] cm
(24½ [25:26:27] in)

46.5 [51.5:56.5:63.5] cm
(18½ [20½: 22: 25] in)

Main image page 83

SIZE

8	10	12	14	16	18	
To fit bust						
82	87	92	97	102	107	cm
32	34	36	38	40	42	in

YARN

Rowan Romance, Kidsilk Haze and Soft Baby

A Romance Twinkle 091

7	8	8	9	9	10	x 50gm

B Kidsilk Haze Grace 580

2	2	2	2	2	2	x 25gm

C Soft Baby Princ. 003

2	2	2	2	2	2	x 50gm

NEEDLES

1 pair 6mm (no 4) (US 10) needles
1 pair 7mm (no 2) (US 10½) needles

TENSION

11½ sts and 15 rows to 10 cm measured over stocking stitch using 7mm (US 10½) needles and yarn A.

BACK

Using 7mm (US 10½) needles and yarn A cast on 45 [47: 49: 53: 57: 59] sts.
Beg with a K row, work in st st, shaping side seams by inc 1 st at each end of 9th and foll 8th row.
49 [51: 53: 57: 61: 63] sts.
Work 7 rows, ending with RS facing for next row.
Shape armholes
Cast off 3 sts at beg of next 2 rows.
43 [45: 47: 51: 55: 57] sts.
Dec 1 st at each end of next 3 rows.
37 [39: 41: 45: 49: 51] sts.
Cont straight until armhole meas 20 [20: 21: 21: 22: 22] cm, ending with RS facing for next row.
Shape shoulders and neck
Next row (RS): Cast off 4 [4: 5: 5: 6: 7] sts, K until there are 7 [8: 8: 9: 10: 10] sts on right needle and turn, leaving rem sts on a holder.
Work each side of neck separately.
Cast off 3 sts at beg of next row.
Cast off rem 4 [5: 5: 6: 7: 7] sts.
With RS facing, rejoin yarn to rem sts, cast off centre 15 [15: 15: 17: 17: 17] sts, K to end.
Complete to match first side, reversing shapings.

LEFT FRONT

Using 7mm (US 10½) needles and yarn A cast on 22 [23: 24: 26: 28: 29] sts.
Row 1 (RS): Knit.
Row 2: P4, wrap next st (by slipping next st onto right needle, taking yarn to opposite side of work between needles and then slipping same st back onto left needle – when working over wrapped sts work the st and the wrapped loop tog as 1 st) and turn.
Row 3: Knit.
Row 4: P10, wrap next st and turn.

Row 5: Knit.
Row 6: P16, wrap next st and turn.
Row 7: Knit.
Row 8: P to end.
Beg with a K row, work in st st for 6 rows, ending with RS facing for next row.
Shape front slope
Dec 1 st at end of next and 3 foll 4th rows **and at same time** inc 1 st at beg of next and foll 8th row.
20 [21: 22: 24: 26: 27] sts.
Work 3 rows, ending with RS facing for next row.
Shape armhole
Cast off 3 sts at beg and dec 1 st at end of next row.
16 [17: 18: 20: 22: 23] sts.
Work 1 row.
Dec 1 st at armhole edge of next 3 rows **and at same time** dec 1 st at front slope edge of 3rd row.
12 [13: 14: 16: 18: 19] sts.
Dec 1 st at front slope edge **only** of 4th and 1 [1: 0: 3: 2: 2] foll 4th rows, then on every foll 6th row until 8 [9: 10: 11: 13: 14] sts rem.
Cont straight until left front matches back to beg of shoulder shaping, ending with RS facing for next row.
Shape shoulder
Cast off 4 [4: 5: 5: 6: 7] sts at beg of next row.
Work 1 row.
Cast off rem 4 [5: 5: 6: 7: 7] sts.

RIGHT FRONT

Using 7mm (US 10½) needles and yarn A cast on 22 [23: 24: 26: 28: 29] sts.
Row 1 (RS): K4, wrap next st and turn.
Row 2: Purl.
Row 3: K10, wrap next st and turn.
Row 4: Purl.
Row 5: K16, wrap next st and turn.
Row 6: Purl.
Row 7: K to end.
Row 8: Purl.
Beg with a K row, work in st st for 6 rows, ending with RS facing for next row.
Shape front slope
Dec 1 st at beg of next and 3 foll 4th rows **and at same time** inc 1 st at end of next and foll 8th row.
20 [21: 22: 24: 26: 27] sts.
Complete to match left front, reversing shapings.

SLEEVES

Using 6mm (US 10) needles and yarn A cast on 25 [25: 27: 27: 29: 29] sts.
Row 1 (RS): K1, *P1, K1, rep from * to end.
Row 2: P1, *K1, P1, rep from * to end.
Row 3: As row 1.
Change to 7mm (US 10½) needles.
Beg with a P row, work in st st, shaping sides by inc 1 st at each end of 6th and every foll 6th row to 35 [35: 37: 37: 37: 37] sts, then on every foll 8th row until there are 41 [41: 43:

43: 45: 45] sts.
Cont straight until sleeve meas 43 [43: 44: 44: 45: 45] cm, ending with RS facing for next row.
Shape top
Cast off 3 sts at beg of next 2 rows.
35 [35: 37: 37: 39: 39] sts.
Dec 1 st at each end of next 4 rows, ending with RS facing for next row.
27 [27: 29: 29: 31: 31] sts.
Cast off 6 [6: 7: 7: 7: 7] sts at beg of next 2 rows.
Cast off rem 15 [15: 15: 15: 17: 17] sts.

MAKING UP

Press as described on the information page.
Join shoulder seams using back stitch, or mattress stitch if preferred.
Front band
With RS facing, using 6mm (US 10) needles and yarn A, beg and ending at cast-on edges, pick up and knit 48 [48: 49: 49: 50: 50] sts up right front opening edge, 20 [20: 20: 22: 22: 22] sts from back, then 48 [48: 49: 49: 50: 50] sts down left front opening edge.
116 [116: 118: 120: 122: 122] sts.
Cast off knitwise (on **WS**).
Tie
Using 6mm (US 10) needles and one strand each of yarn B and yarn C held together cast on 13 sts.
Work in g st for 2 rows, ending with RS facing for next row.
Now work in patt as folls:
Row 1 (RS): K7, yfwd, sl 1, K1, psso, yfwd, K4.
14 sts.
Row 2 and every foll alt row: K2, P to last 2 sts, K2.
Row 3: K6, (yfwd, sl 1, K1, psso) twice, yfwd, K4.
15 sts.
Row 5: K5, (yfwd, sl 1, K1, psso) 3 times, yfwd, K4.
16 sts.
Row 7: K4, (yfwd, sl 1, K1, psso) 4 times, yfwd, K4.
17 sts.
Row 9: K3, (yfwd, sl 1, K1, psso) 5 times, yfwd, K4.
18 sts.
Row 11: K4, (yfwd, sl 1, K1, psso) 5 times, K2tog, K2.
17 sts.
Row 13: K5, (yfwd, sl 1, K1, psso) 4 times, K2tog, K2.
16 sts.
Row 15: K6, (yfwd, sl 1, K1, psso) 3 times, K2tog, K2.
15 sts.
Row 17: K7, (yfwd, sl 1, K1, psso) twice, K2tog, K2.
14 sts.
Row 19: K8, yfwd, sl 1, K1, psso, K2tog, K2.
13 sts.

Row 20: As row 2.
These 20 rows form patt.
Cont in patt until tie meas approx 215 [220: 225: 230: 235: 240] cm, ending after patt row 19 and with **WS** facing for next row.
Work in g st for 2 rows, ending with **WS** facing for next row.
Cast off knitwise (on **WS**).
See information page for finishing instructions, setting in sleeves using the shallow set-in method. Slip stitch straight edge of tie to lower edge of back and fronts, positioning centre of tie at centre back.

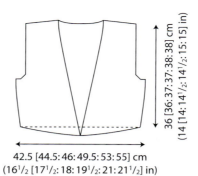

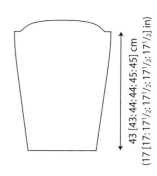

42.5 [44.5: 46: 49.5: 53: 55] cm
(16½ [17½: 18: 19½: 21: 21½] in)

36 [36: 37: 37: 38: 38] cm
(14 [14: 14½: 14½: 15: 15] in)

43 [43: 44: 44: 45: 45] cm
(17 [17: 17½: 17½: 17½: 17½] in)

Main image page 38

JUNO BY AMANDA CRAWFORD

SIZE

8	10	12	14	16	18	
To fit bust						
82	87	92	97	102	107	cm
32	34	36	38	40	42	in

YARN

Rowan Wool Cotton

17	18	19	20	21	23	x 50gm

Use yarn DOUBLE throughout.
(photographed in Mocha 965)

NEEDLES

1 pair 5½ mm (no 5) (US 9) needles
Cable needle

BUTTONS – 7 x 00408 or 7 x 00405

TENSION

16 sts and 23 rows to 10 cm measured over rib using 5½ mm (US 9) needles and yarn DOUBLE.

SPECIAL ABBREVIATIONS

C2B = slip next st onto cable needle and leave at back of work, K1, then K1 from cable needle; **C2F** = slip next st onto cable needle and leave at front of work, K1, then K1 from cable needle; **CR3R** = slip next st onto cable needle and leave at back of work, K2, then P1 from cable needle; **Cr3L** = slip next 2 sts onto cable needle and leave at front of work, P1, then K2 from cable needle; **C4B** = slip next 2 sts onto cable needle and leave at back of work, K2, then K2 from cable needle; **C4F** = slip next 2 sts onto cable needle and leave at front of work, K2, then K2 from cable needle; **CR4R** = slip next 2 sts onto cable needle and leave at back of work, K2, then P2 from cable needle; **Cr4L** = slip next 2 sts onto cable needle and leave at front of work, P2, then K2 from cable needle.

BACK

Using 5½ mm (US 9) needles and yarn DOUBLE cast on 60 [64: 68: 72: 76: 82] sts.
Row 1 (RS): K0 [1: 0: 1: 0: 0], P1 [2: 1: 2: 1: 0], *K2, P2, rep from * to last 3 [1: 3: 1: 3: 2] sts, K2 [1: 2: 1: 2: 2], P1 [0: 1: 0: 1: 0].
Row 2: P0 [1: 0: 1: 0: 0], K1 [2: 1: 2: 1: 0], *P2, K2, rep from * to last 3 [1: 3: 1: 3: 2] sts, P2 [1: 2: 1: 2: 2], K1 [0: 1: 0: 1: 0].
These 2 rows form rib.
Cont in rib, shaping side seams by inc 1 st at each end of 15th and every foll 16th row until there are 66 [70: 74: 78: 82: 88] sts, taking inc sts into rib.
Cont straight until back meas 28 [28: 27: 30: 29: 31] cm, ending with RS facing for next row.

Shape armholes

Keeping rib correct, cast off 3 [4: 4: 5: 5: 6] sts at beg of next 2 rows.
60 [62: 66: 68: 72: 76] sts.
Dec 1 st at each end of next 3 rows, then on foll 1 [1: 2: 2: 3: 4] alt rows.
52 [54: 56: 58: 60: 62] sts.
Cont straight until armhole meas 18 [18: 19: 19: 20: 20] cm, ending with RS facing for next row.

Shape back neck

Next row (RS): Rib 13 [14: 15: 16: 16: 17] and turn, leaving rem sts on a holder.
Work each side of neck separately.
Cast off 6 sts at beg of next row.
7 [8: 9: 10: 10: 11] sts.
Dec 1 st at neck edge of next 2 rows, ending with RS facing for next row.

Shape shoulder

Cast off rem 5 [6: 7: 8: 8: 9] sts.
With RS facing, rejoin yarn to rem sts, cast off centre 26 [26: 26: 26: 28: 28] sts, rib to end.

Complete to match first side, reversing shapings.

LEFT FRONT
Using 5½ mm (US 9) needles and yarn DOUBLE cast on 33 [35: 37: 39: 41: 44] sts.
Row 1 (RS): K0 [1: 0: 1: 0: 0], P1 [2: 1: 2: 1: 0], *K2, P2, rep from * to last 2 sts, K2.
Row 2: *P2, K2, rep from * to last 3 [1: 3: 1: 3: 2] sts, P2 [1: 2: 1: 2: 2], K1 [0: 1: 0: 1: 0].
These 2 rows form rib.
Cont in rib, shaping side seam by inc 1 st at beg of 15th and every foll 16th row until there are 36 [38: 40: 42: 44: 47] sts, taking inc sts into rib.
Cont straight until left front matches back to beg of armhole shaping, ending with RS facing for next row.
Shape armhole
Keeping rib correct, cast off 3 [4: 4: 5: 5: 6] sts at beg of next row.
33 [34: 36: 37: 39: 41] sts.
Work 1 row.
Shape front slope
Dec 1 st at armhole edge of next 3 rows, then on foll 1 [1: 2: 2: 3: 4] alt rows **and at same time** dec 1 st at front slope edge of next 5 [5: 7: 7: 9: 9] rows, then on foll 0 [0: 0: 0: 0: 1] alt row.
24 [25: 24: 25: 24: 24] sts.
Dec 1 st at front slope edge **only** of next [next: next: 2nd: 2nd] and foll 5 [5: 1: 1: 0: 0] rows, then on foll 12 [12: 14: 14: 14: 13] alt rows, then on foll 4th row. 5 [6: 7: 8: 8: 9] sts.
Cont straight until left front matches back to shoulder cast-off, ending with RS facing for next row.
Shape shoulder
Cast off rem 5 [6: 7: 8: 8: 9] sts.

RIGHT FRONT
Using 5½ mm (US 9) needles and yarn DOUBLE cast on 33 [35: 37: 39: 41: 44] sts.
Row 1 (RS): *K2, P2, rep from * to last 3 [1: 3: 1: 3: 2] sts, K2 [1: 2: 1: 2: 2], P1 [0: 1: 0: 1: 0].
Row 2: P0 [1: 0: 1: 0: 0], K1 [2: 1: 2: 1: 0], *P2, K2, rep from * to last 2 sts, P2.
These 2 rows form rib.
Cont in rib, shaping side seam by inc 1 st at end of 15th and every foll 16th row until there are 36 [38: 40: 42: 44: 47] sts, taking inc sts into rib.
Complete to match left front, reversing shapings.

SLEEVES
Using 5½ mm (US 9) needles and yarn DOUBLE cast on 38 [38: 40: 40: 42: 42] sts.
Row 1 (RS): P0 [0: 1: 1: 2: 2], *K2, P2, rep from * to last 2 [2: 3: 3: 0: 0] sts, K2 [2: 2: 2: 0: 0], P0 [0: 1: 1: 0: 0].
Row 2: K0 [0: 1: 1: 2: 2], *P2, K2, rep from * to last 2 [2: 3: 3: 0: 0] sts, P2 [2: 2: 2: 0: 0], K0 [0: 1: 1: 0: 0].
These 2 rows form rib.
Cont in rib, shaping sides by inc 1 st at each end of 9th [7th: 7th: 7th: 7th: 5th] and every foll 12th [10th: 12th: 10th: 10th: 8th] row to 44 [42: 56: 54: 54: 46] sts, then on every foll 14th [12th: -: 12th: 12th: 10th] row until there are 52 [54: -: 58: 60: 62] sts, taking inc sts into rib.
Cont straight until sleeve meas 45 [45: 46: 46: 47: 47] cm, ending with RS facing for next row.
Shape top
Keeping rib correct, cast off 3 [4: 4: 5: 5: 6] sts at beg of next 2 rows.

46 [46: 48: 48: 50: 50] sts.
Dec 1 st at each end of next 3 rows, then on foll alt row, then on every foll 4th row until 30 [30: 32: 32: 34: 34] sts rem.
Work 1 row.
Dec 1 st at each end of next and every foll alt row to 26 sts, then on foll 5 rows, ending with RS facing for next row.
Cast off rem 16 sts.

MAKING UP
Press as described on the information page.
Join both shoulder seams using back stitch, or mattress stitch if preferred.
Button border
With RS facing, using 5½ mm (US 9) needles and yarn DOUBLE, pick up and knit 50 [50: 50: 54: 54: 54] sts down left front opening edge, from beg of front slope shaping to cast-on edge.
Row 1 (WS): P2, *K2, P2, rep from * to end.
Row 2: K2, *P2, K2, rep from * to end.
These 2 rows form rib.
Work in rib for a further 3 rows, ending with RS facing for next row.
Cast off in rib.
Buttonhole border
With RS facing, using 5½ mm (US 9) needles and yarn DOUBLE, pick up and knit 50 [50: 50: 54: 54: 54] sts up right front opening edge, from cast-on edge to beg of front slope shaping.
Work in rib as given for button border for 1 row, ending with RS facing for next row.
Row 2 (RS): rib 2 [2: 2: 1: 1: 1], *yrn (to make a buttonhole), work 2 tog, rib 7 [7: 7: 8: 8: 8], rep from * 4 times more, yrn (to make 6th buttonhole), work 2 tog, rib 1.
Work in rib for a further 3 rows, ending with RS facing for next row.
Cast off in rib.
Collar
Using 5½ mm (US 9) needles and yarn DOUBLE cast on 38 sts.
Work in g st for 2 rows, ending with RS facing for next row.
Row 3 (RS): K12, (inc once in each of next 2 sts, K4) twice, inc once in each of next 2 sts, K12. 44 sts.
Row 4: P2, K2, P2, K6, (P4, K4) 3 times, (K2, P2) twice.
Row 5: C2B, P2, C2B, P1, P2tog tbl, yrn (to make a buttonhole), P3, C4B, (P4, C4B) twice, P6, C2F, P2, C2F.
Row 6: As row 4.
Cont in cable patt as folls:
Row 1 (RS): C2B, P2, C2B, P5, Cr3R, (Cr4L, Cr4R) twice, Cr3L, P5, C2F, P2, C2F.
Row 2: P2, K2, P2, K5, P2, K3, P4, K4, P4, K3, P2, K5, P2, K2, P2.
Row 3: C2B, P2, C2B, P4, Cr3R, P3, C4F, P4, C4B, P3, Cr3L, P4, C2F, P2, C2F.
Row 4: P2, K2, P2, K4, P2, (K4, P4) twice, K4, P2, K4, P2, K2, P2.
Row 5: C2B, P2, C2B, P4, K2, P2, (Cr4R, Cr4L) twice, P2, K2, P4, C2F, P2, C2F.
Row 6: (P2, K2, P2, K4) twice, P4, (K4, P2, K2, P2) twice.
Row 7: C2B, P2, C2B, P4, K2, P2, K2, P4, C4B, P4, K2, P2, K2, P4, C2F, P2, C2F.
Row 8: As row 6.
Row 9: C2B, P2, C2B, P4, K2, P2, (Cr4L, Cr4R) twice, P2, K2, P4, C2F, P2, C2F.
Row 10: As row 4.
Row 11: C2B, P2, C2B, P4, Cr3L, P3, C4F, P4, C4B, P3, Cr3R, P4, C2F, P2, C2F.
Row 12: As row 2.
Row 13: C2B, P2, C2B, P5, Cr3L, (Cr4R,

Cr4L) twice, Cr3R, P5, C2F, P2, C2F.
Row 14: P2, K2, P2, K6, (P4, K4) twice, P4, K6, P2, K2, P2.
Row 15: C2B, P2, C2B, P6, (C4B, P4) twice, C4B, P6, C2F, P2, C2F.
Row 16: As row 14.
These 16 rows form cable patt.
Cont in patt until collar meas 10 cm, ending with RS facing for next row.
Place marker at end of last row.
Cont in patt until marked edge of collar, when slightly stretched, fits up right front slope, across back neck and down left front slope, ending with RS facing for next row.
Place marker at end of last row.
Cont in patt until collar meas approx 10 cm from second marker, ending after patt row 15 and with WS facing for next row.
Next row (WS): P2, K2, P2, K6, *(P2tog) twice, K4, rep from * once more, (P2tog) twice, K6, P2, K2, P2. 38 sts.
Work in g st for 3 rows, ending with **WS** facing for next row.
Cast off knitwise (on **WS**).
See information page for finishing instructions, setting in sleeves using the set-in method.
Using photograph as a guide, sew collar to neck edge, matching collar markers to ends of pick-up rows of front borders at beg of front slope shaping. Sew on buttons, attaching one to left front end of collar as in photograph to correspond with buttonhole in collar.

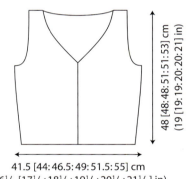

48 [48: 48: 51: 51: 53] cm
(19 [19: 19: 20: 20: 21] in)

41.5 [44: 46.5: 49: 51.5: 55] cm
(16½ [17½: 18½: 19½: 20½: 21½] in)

45 [45: 46: 46: 47: 47] cm
(17½ [17½: 18: 18: 18½: 18½] in)

Main image page 87 & 88

COSY MUFFLER BY NIKKI RYAN

YARN
Rowan Big Wool and Kid Classic
A Big Wool W. Berry 025   2 x 100gm
B Kid Classic Victoria 852   2 x 50gm
C Kid Classic Frilly 844   1 x 50gm

CROCHET HOOKS
3.50mm (no 9) (US E4) crochet hook
9.00mm (no 00) (US M13) crochet hook

TENSION
21 sts to 10 cm and 4 rows to 9.5 cm measured
over mesh pattern using 3.50mm (US E4)
hook and Kid Classic.

UK CROCHET ABBREVIATIONS
ch = chain; **tr** = treble; **dtr** = double treble;
sp(s) = space(s); **ss** = slip stitch.

US CROCHET ABBREVIATIONS
ch = chain; **tr** = double crochet; **dtr** = treble;
sp(s) = space(s); **ss** = slip stitch.

FINISHED SIZE
Completed muff measures approx 33 cm
(13 in) long, excluding ruffles.

MUFF
First section
Using 9.00mm (US M13) hook and yarn A
make 48 ch and join with a ss to form a ring.
Round 1 (RS): 7 ch (counts as 1 dtr and
3 ch), miss ch at base of 7 ch and next 3 ch,
★1 dtr into next ch, 3 ch, miss 3 ch, rep from
★ to end, ss to 4th of 7 ch at beg of round.
48 sts, 12 ch sps.
Round 2: 7 ch (counts as 1 dtr and 3 ch),
miss st at base of 7 ch and next 3 ch, ★1 dtr
into next dtr, 3 ch, miss 3 ch, rep from ★ to
end, ss to 4th of 7 ch at beg of round.
★★Break off yarn A and join in yarn B.
Change to 3.50mm (US E4) hook.
Round 3: 7 ch (counts as 1 dtr and 3 ch), miss
st at base of 7 ch, 1 dtr into first ch sp, ★3 ch,

1 dtr into next dtr, 3 ch, 1 dtr into next ch sp,
rep from ★ to end, 3 ch, ss to 4th of 7 ch at beg
of round.
96 sts, 24 ch sps.
Join in yarn C.
Round 4: Using yarn C, 6 ch (counts as 1 dtr
and 2 ch), miss st at base of 6 ch and next 3 ch,
★1 dtr into next dtr, 2 ch, miss 3 ch, rep from ★
to end, ss to 4th of 6 ch at beg of round.
Round 5: Using yarn B, 5 ch (counts as 1 dtr
and 1 ch), miss st at base of 5 ch and next 2 ch,
★1 dtr into next dtr, 1 ch, miss 2 ch, rep from ★
to end, ss to 4th of 5 ch at beg of round.
Break off yarn B and cont using yarn C only.
Round 6: 7 ch (counts as 1 dtr and 3 ch), miss
(st at base of 7 ch, 1 ch, 1 dtr and 1 ch), ★1 dtr
into next dtr, 3 ch, miss (1 ch, 1 dtr and 1 ch),
rep from ★ to end, ss to 4th of 7 ch at beg
of round.
48 sts, 12 ch sps.
Round 7: 3 ch (counts as first tr), miss st at
base of 3 ch, 3 tr into first ch sp, ★1 tr into next
dtr, 3 tr into next ch sp, rep from ★ to end, ss to
top of 3 ch at beg of round.
Fasten off.
Second section
With RS facing, using 9.00mm (US M13) hook
and yarn A, rejoin yarn to foundation ch of first
section at base of 7 ch at beg of round 1.
Next round (RS): 7 ch (counts as 1 dtr and
3 ch), miss ch at base of 7 ch and next 3
foundation ch, ★1 dtr into next ch (this is ch at
base of a dtr), 3 ch, miss 3 ch, rep from ★ to
end, ss to 4th of 7 ch at beg of round.
48 sts, 12 ch sps.
Complete as for first section from ★★.
First ruffle
With RS facing, using 3.50mm (US E4)
hook and yarn C, rejoin yarn to base of
7 ch at beg of round 6 of first section, 4 ch
(counts as first dtr), 6 dtr around stem of
first st of round 6 (this is first 4 ch of 7 ch at
beg of round), 1 dtr into base of centre tr of
round 7 worked into first ch sp of round 6, 7

dtr around stem of next dtr of round 6, miss
first 2 ch sps of round 5, 1 dtr into dtr between
next 2 ch sps of round 5, ★7 dtr around stem of
next dtr of round 6, miss 1 ch sp of round 6, 1
dtr into base of centre tr of round 7 worked
into next ch sp of round 6, 7 dtr around stem
of next dtr of round 6, miss 3 ch sps of round
5, 1 dtr into dtr between next 2 ch sps of
round 5, rep from ★ to end, ss to top of 4 ch at
beg of round.
Fasten off.
Second ruffle
With RS facing, using 3.50mm (US E4) hook
and yarn B, rejoin yarn to base of 5 ch at beg
of round 5 of first section, 4 ch (counts as first
dtr), 6 dtr around stem of first st of round 5
(this is first 4 ch of 5 ch at beg of round), 1 dtr
into first ch sp of round 5, 7 dtr around stem of
next dtr of round 5, miss first ch sp of round 4,
1 dtr into next ch sp of round 4, ★7 dtr around
stem of next dtr of round 5, miss 1 ch sp of
round 5, 1 dtr into next ch sp of round 5, 7 dtr
around stem of next dtr of round 5, miss next
ch sp of round 4, 1 dtr into next ch sp of
round 4, rep from ★ to end, ss to top of 4 ch at
beg of round.
Fasten off.
Third ruffle
Using yarn C, work ruffle around ch sps of
round 4 in same way as given for second ruffle.
Fourth ruffle
Using yarn B, work ruffle around ch sps of
round 3 in same way as given for second ruffle.
Fifth, sixth and seventh ruffles
Using 9.00mm (US M13) hook and yarn A,
work ruffles around ch sps of rounds 2 and 1 of
first section, and round 1 of second section in
similar way as given for second ruffle.
Eighth, ninth, tenth and eleventh ruffles
Work to match first, second, third and fourth
ruffles but working into second section.

MAKING UP
Do NOT press.

Main image page 75

EVELEEN BY LOIS DAYKIN

SIZE

8	10	12	14	16	18	
To fit bust						
82	87	92	97	102	107	cm
32	34	36	38	40	42	in

YARN

Rowan 4 ply Soft, Kidsilk Haze and Lurex Shimmer

A	4 Ply Soft Victoria 390						
	6	6	7	7	8	8	x 50gm
B	★Kidsilk Haze Dewberry 600						
	1	1	1	1	1	1	x 25gm
C	4 Ply Soft Daydream 378						
	1	1	1	1	1	1	x 50gm
D	★Kidsilk Haze Fondant 630						
	1	1	1	1	1	1	x 25gm
E	4 Ply Soft Fairy 395						
	1	1	1	1	1	1	x 50gm
F	★Kidsilk Haze Jelly 597						
	1	1	1	1	1	1	x 25gm
G	4 Ply Soft Leafy 367						
	1	1	1	1	1	1	x 50gm
H	Lurex Shimmer Bronze 335						
	2	2	2	2	2	2	x 25gm

★Use Kidsilk Haze DOUBLE throughout.

NEEDLES

1 pair 2¾ mm (no 12) (US 2) needles
1 pair 3¼ mm (no 10) (US 3) needles

RIBBON – 150 cm of narrow satin ribbon

TENSION

28 sts and 36 rows to 10 cm measured over stocking stitch using 3¼ mm (US 3) needles and 4 ply Soft.

SPECIAL ABBREVIATIONS

sl 2 = slip 2 sts as though to K2tog; **p2sso** = pass 2 slipped sts over; **cluster 2** = with yarn at WS (front) of work slip next 2 sts onto right needle, take yarn to back (RS) of work between needles, slip same 2 sts back onto left needle, bring yarn to front (WS) of work between needles and slip same 2 sts back onto right needle; **cluster 3** = with yarn at WS (front) of work slip next 3 sts onto right needle, take yarn to back (RS) of work between needles, slip same 3 sts back onto left needle, bring yarn to front (WS) of work between needles and slip same 3 sts back onto right needle; **cluster 5** = with yarn at WS (front) of work slip next 5 sts onto right needle, take yarn to back (RS) of work between needles, slip same 5 sts back onto left needle, bring yarn to front (WS) of work between needles and slip same 5 sts back onto right needle.

BACK

Using 3¼ mm (US 3) needles and yarn H cast on 133 [133: 155: 155: 155: 177] sts.
Row 1 (RS): K1, ★yfwd, (K1 tbl, P3) 5 times, K1 tbl, yfwd, K1, rep from ★ to end.
145 [145: 169: 169: 169: 193] sts.

Row 2: P1, ★P2, (K3, P1) 4 times, K3, P3, rep from ★ to end.
Break off yarn H and join in yarn A.
Row 3: K1, ★yfwd, K1 tbl, yfwd, (K1 tbl, P3) 5 times, (K1 tbl, yfwd) twice, K1, rep from ★ to end.
169 [169: 197: 197: 197: 225] sts.
Row 4: P1, ★P4, (K3, P1) 4 times, K3, P5, rep from ★ to end.
Row 5: K1, ★yfwd, K1 tbl, yfwd, sl 1, K1, psso, yfwd, (K1 tbl, P2tog, P1) 5 times, K1 tbl, yfwd, K2tog, yfwd, K1 tbl, yfwd, K1, rep from ★ to end.
163 [163: 190: 190: 190: 217] sts.
Row 6: P1, ★P6, (K2, P1) 4 times, K2, P7, rep from ★ to end.
Row 7: K1, ★K1 tbl, (yfwd, sl 1, K1, psso) twice, yfwd, (K1 tbl, P2) 5 times, K1 tbl, yfwd, (K2tog, yfwd) twice, K1 tbl, K1, rep from ★ to end.
175 [175: 204: 204: 204: 233] sts.
Row 8: P1, ★P7, (K2, P1) 4 times, K2, P8, rep from ★ to end.
Row 9: K1, ★K1, (yfwd, K2tog) twice, yfwd, K1 tbl, yfwd, (K1 tbl, P2tog) 5 times, (K1 tbl, yfwd) twice, (sl 1, K1, psso, yfwd) twice, K2, rep from ★ to end.
169 [169: 197: 197: 197: 225] sts.
Row 10: P1, ★P9, (K1, P1) 4 times, K1, P10, rep from ★ to end.
Row 11: Sl 1, K1, psso, ★(yfwd, K2tog) 3 times, K1 tbl, yfwd, (K1 tbl, P1) 5 times, K1 tbl, yfwd, K1 tbl, (sl 1, K1, psso, yfwd) 3 times, sl 2, K1, p2sso, rep from ★ to last 27 sts, (yfwd, K2tog) 3 times, K1 tbl, yfwd, (K1 tbl, P1) 5 times, K1 tbl, yfwd, K1 tbl, (sl 1, K1, psso, yfwd) 3 times, P2tog.
Row 12: As row 10.
Row 13: K1, ★(K2tog, yfwd) twice, K2tog, K1, K1 tbl, yfwd, (sl 1, K1, psso) twice, sl 1, K2tog, psso, (K2tog) twice, yfwd, K1 tbl, K1, sl 1, K1, psso, (yfwd, sl 1, K1, psso) twice, K1, rep from ★ to end.
133 [133: 155: 155: 155: 177] sts.
Row 14: Cluster 2, ★P7, cluster 5, P7, cluster 3, rep from ★ to last 21 sts, P7, cluster 5, P7, cluster 2.
These 14 rows form patt.
Using yarn A throughout, rep last 14 rows 8 [8: 8: 9: 9: 9] times more, ending with RS facing for next row.
Next row (RS): K2 [5: 4: 4: 8: 10], K2tog, ★K7 [13: 4: 7: 15: 5], K2tog, rep from ★ to last 3 [6: 5: 5: 9: 11] sts, K to end.
118 [124: 130: 138: 146: 154] sts.
Beg with a P row, work in st st for 3 rows.
Join in yarn H.
Using yarn H, work in g st for 3 rows.
Using yarn A, purl 1 row.
Next row (eyelet row) (RS): Using yarn A, K1 [4: 2: 1: 5: 4], ★K2tog, yfwd, K2, K2tog, yfwd, K4, rep from ★ to last 7 [10: 8: 7: 11: 10] sts, K2tog, yfwd, K2, K2tog, yfwd, K1 [4: 2: 1: 5: 4].
Using yarn A and beg with a P row, work

in st st for 3 rows, ending with RS facing for next row.
Using yarn H, work in g st for 3 rows.
Break off yarn H and cont using yarn A **only**.
Beg with a P row, work in st st as folls:
Work 5 rows, ending with RS facing for next row.
Shape armholes
Cast off 6 [7: 7: 8: 8: 9] sts at beg of next 2 rows.
106 [110: 116: 122: 130: 136] sts.
Dec 1 st at each end of next 5 [5: 7: 7: 9: 9] rows, then on foll 1 [2: 2: 2: 2: 3] alt rows, then on foll 4th row. 92 [94: 96: 102: 106: 110] sts.
Cont straight until armhole meas 18 [18: 19: 19: 20: 20] cm, ending with RS facing for next row.
Shape back neck
Next row (RS): K36 [37: 38: 41: 42: 44] and turn, leaving rem sts on a holder.
Work each side of neck separately.
Cast off 8 sts at beg of next row, then 7 sts at beg of foll alt row, ending with RS facing for next row.
21 [22: 23: 26: 27: 29] sts.
Shape shoulder
Cast off 6 [6: 7: 8: 8: 9] sts at beg of next and foll alt row **and at same time** dec 1 st at neck edge of foll 3 rows.
Work 1 row.
Cast off rem 6 [7: 6: 7: 8: 8] sts.
With RS facing, rejoin yarn to rem sts, cast off centre 20 [20: 20: 20: 22: 22] sts, K to end.
Complete to match first side, reversing shapings.

FRONT

Work as given for back to beg of armhole shaping, ending with RS facing for next row.
Shape armholes and place chart
Next row (RS): Cast off 6 [7: 7: 8: 8: 9] sts, K until there are 17 [19: 22: 25: 29: 32] sts on right needle, work next 72 sts as row 1 of chart, K to end.
Next row: Cast off 6 [7: 7: 8: 8: 9] sts, P until there are 17 [19: 22: 25: 29: 32] sts on right needle, work next 72 sts as row 2 of chart, P to end. 106 [110: 116: 122: 130: 136] sts.
These 2 rows set position of chart.
Working rem 40 rows of chart and then completing front in st st using yarn A only, cont as folls:
Dec 1 st at each end of next 5 [5: 7: 7: 9: 9] rows, then on foll 1 [2: 2: 2: 2: 3] alt rows, then on foll 4th row. 92 [94: 96: 102: 106: 110] sts.
Cont straight until 24 [24: 24: 24: 26: 26] rows less have been worked than on back to beg of shoulder shaping, ending with RS facing for next row.
Shape neck
Next row (RS): K38 [39: 40: 43: 45: 47] and turn, leaving rem sts on a holder.
Work each side of neck separately.
Cast off 6 sts at beg of next row, then 5 sts at beg of foll alt row.

27 [28: 29: 32: 34: 36] sts.
Dec 1 st at neck edge of next 5 rows, then on foll 2 [2: 2: 2: 3: 3] alt rows, then on 2 foll 4th rows. 18 [19: 20: 23: 24: 26] sts.
Work 3 rows, ending with RS facing for next row.

Shape shoulder
Cast off 6 [6: 7: 8: 8: 9] sts at beg of next and foll alt row.
Work 1 row.
Cast off rem 6 [7: 6: 7: 8: 8] sts.
With RS facing, rejoin yarn to rem sts, cast off centre 16 sts, K to end.
Complete to match first side, reversing shapings.

SLEEVES

Using 2¾ mm (US 2) needles and yarn H work picot cast-on as folls: cast on 3 [4: 3: 4: 3: 4] sts, cast off 2 sts, slip st on right needle back onto left needle (1 [2: 1: 2: 1: 2] sts on left needle), ★cast on 5 sts, cast off 2 sts, slip st on right needle back onto left needle (3 more sts on left needle), rep from ★ until there are 79 [80: 85: 86: 91: 92] sts on left needle, cast on a further 1 [2: 1: 2: 1: 2] sts.
80 [82: 86: 88: 92: 94] sts.
Work in g st for 2 rows, ending with RS facing for next row.
Break off yarn H and join in yarn A.
Change to 3¼ mm (US 3) needles.
Beg with a K row, work in st st for 2 rows, ending with RS facing for next row.

Shape top
Cast off 6 [7: 7: 8: 8: 9] sts at beg of next

2 rows.
68 [68: 72: 72: 76: 76] sts.
Dec 1 st at each end of next 3 rows, then on foll 2 alt rows, then on every foll 4th row until 46 [46: 50: 50: 54: 54] sts rem.
Work 1 row.
Dec 1 st at each end of next and every foll alt row to 38 sts, then on foll 5 rows, ending with RS facing for next row. 28 sts.
Cast off 5 sts at beg of next 2 rows.
Cast off rem 18 sts.

MAKING UP

Press as described on the information page.
Join right shoulder seam using back stitch, or mattress stitch if preferred.

Neck border
With RS facing, using 2¾ mm (US 2) needles and yarn H, pick up and knit 32 [32: 32: 32: 34: 34] sts down left side of front neck, 16 sts from front, 32 [32: 32: 32: 34: 34] sts up right side of front neck, 20 sts down right side of back neck, 19 [19: 19: 19: 21: 21] sts from back, then 20 sts up left side of back neck.
139 [139: 139: 139: 145: 145] sts.

Row 1 (WS): Knit.
Work picot cast-off as folls: cast off 2 sts, ★slip st on right needle back onto left needle, cast on 2 sts, cast off 5 sts, rep from ★ to end, casting off 4 sts at end of last rep.
See information page for finishing instructions, setting in sleeves using the set-in method.
Using photograph as a guide, thread ribbon through eyelet row and tie ends in a bow at centre front.

53 [53:54:58:59:59] cm
(21 [21:21½:23:23:23] in)

42 [44.5:46.5:49.5:52:55] cm
(16½ [17½:18½:19½:20½:21½] in)

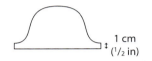

1 cm
(½ in)

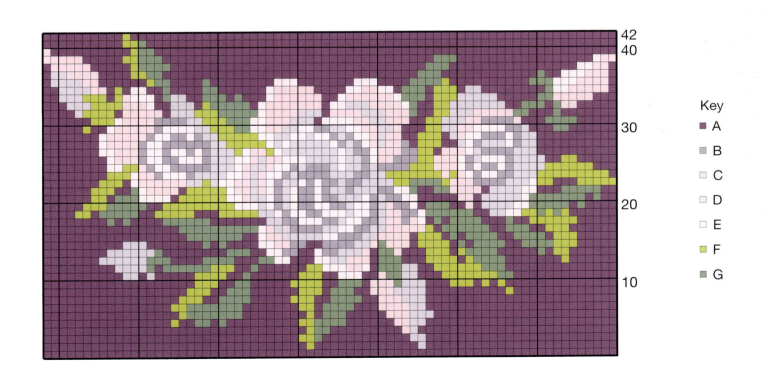

Key

- A
- B
- C
- D
- E
- F
- G

Main image page 25

SIZE

	S	M	L	XL	XXL	
To fit chest
	102	107	112	117	122	cm
	40	42	44	46	48	in

YARN

Rowan Big Wool and Big Wool Fusion

A	Big Wool Smoky 007

	8	9	9	10	10	x 100gm

B	Big Wool Fusion Soot 006

	1	1	1	1	1	x 100gm

C	Big Wool Smudge 019

	1	1	1	1	1	x 100gm

NEEDLES

1 pair 9mm (no 00) (US 13) needles
1 pair 10mm (no 000) (US 15) needles

TENSION

9 sts and 12½ rows to 10 cm measured over stocking stitch using 10mm (US 15) needles.

BACK

Using 9mm (US 13) needles and yarn A cast on 52 [54: 56: 60: 62] sts.
Row 1 (RS): P0 [0: 1: 0: 0], K1 [2: 2: 1: 2], *P2, K2, rep from * to last 3 [0: 1: 3: 0] sts, P2 [0: 1: 2: 0], K1 [0: 0: 1: 0].
Row 2: K0 [0: 1: 0: 0], P1 [2: 2: 1: 2], *K2, P2, rep from * to last 3 [0: 1: 3: 0] sts, K2 [0: 1: 2: 0], P1 [0: 0: 1: 0].
These 2 rows form rib.
Work in rib for a further 8 rows, ending with RS facing for next row.
Change to 10mm (US 15) needles.
Row 1 (RS): Rib 11 [12: 13: 15: 16], K30, rib to end.
Row 2: Rib 11 [12: 13: 15: 16], P30, rib to end.
These 2 rows set the sts.
Cont as set until back meas 39 [40: 38: 39: 37] cm, ending with RS facing for next row.
Shape raglan armholes
Keeping patt correct, cast off 3 sts at beg of next 2 rows.
46 [48: 50: 54: 56] sts.
Dec 1 st at each end of next and 4 [4: 4: 3: 3] foll 4th rows, then on foll 0 [1: 2: 5: 6] alt rows. 36 sts.
Work 1 row, ending with RS facing for next row.
Next row (RS): K1, P2, sl 1, K1, psso, K to last 5 sts, K2tog, P2, K1.
Next row: P1, K2, P to last 3 sts, K2, P1.
Next row: K1, P2, sl 1, K1, psso, K to last 5 sts, K2tog, P2, K1.
Next row: P1, K2, P2tog, P to last 5 sts, P2tog tbl, K2, P1.
Rep last 2 rows 4 times, ending with RS facing for next row.
Cast off rem 14 sts.

FRONT

Work as given for back until 4 rows less have been worked than on back to beg of raglan

armhole shaping, ending with RS facing for next row.
Place chart
Next row (RS): Patt 16 [17: 18: 20: 21] sts, work next 20 sts as row 1 of chart, patt to end.
Next row: Patt 16 [17: 18: 20: 21] sts, work next 20 sts as row 2 of chart, patt to end.
These 2 rows set the sts.
Keeping chart correct as now set until all 21 rows have been worked and then working sts above chart in st st using yarn A, cont as folls:
Work 2 rows, ending with RS facing for next row.
Shape raglan armholes
Keeping patt correct, cast off 3 sts at beg of next 2 rows.
46 [48: 50: 54: 56] sts.
Dec 1 st at each end of next and 4 [4: 4: 3: 3] foll 4th rows, then on foll 0 [1: 2: 5: 6] alt rows. 36 sts.
Work 1 row, ending with RS facing for next row.
Next row (RS): K1, P2, sl 1, K1, psso, K to last 5 sts, K2tog, P2, K1.
Next row: P1, K2, P to last 3 sts, K2, P1.
Next row: K1, P2, sl 1, K1, psso, K to last 5 sts, K2tog, P2, K1.
Next row: P1, K2, P2tog, P to last 5 sts, P2tog tbl, K2, P1.
Rep last 2 rows once more, ending with RS facing for next row. 26 sts.
Shape neck
Next row (RS): K1, P2, sl 1, K1, psso, K3 and turn, leaving rem sts on a holder.
Work each side of neck separately.
Next row: Cast off 4 sts (one st on right needle), K1, P1.
Next row: P3tog and fasten off.
With RS facing, rejoin yarn to rem sts, cast off centre 10 sts, K to last 5 sts, K2tog, P2, K1.
Complete to match first side, reversing shapings.

SLEEVES

Using 9mm (US 13) needles and yarn A cast on 24 [26: 26: 28: 28] sts.
Row 1 (RS): P0 [0: 0: 1: 1], K1 [2: 2: 2: 2], *P2, K2, rep from * to last 3 [0: 0: 1: 1] sts, P2 [0: 0: 1: 1], K1 [0: 0: 0: 0].
Row 2: K0 [0: 0: 1: 1], P1 [2: 2: 2: 2], *K2, P2, rep from * to last 3 [0: 0: 1: 1] sts, K2 [0: 0: 1: 1], P1 [0: 0: 0: 0].
These 2 rows form rib.
Work in rib for a further 8 rows, ending with RS facing for next row.
Change to 10mm (US 15) needles.
Row 1 (RS): Inc in first st, rib 2 [3: 3: 4: 4], K18, rib to last st, inc in last st.
Row 2: Rib 4 [5: 5: 6: 6], P18, rib to end.
These 2 rows set the sts.
Cont as set, shaping sides by inc 1 st at each end of 3rd [5th: 3rd: 3rd: 3rd] and every foll 4th [6th: 4th: 6th: 4th] row to 30 [42: 32: 46: 36] sts, then on every foll 6th [–: 6th: –: 6th] row until there are 40 [–: 44: –: 48] sts, taking

65 [67: 67: 69: 69] cm (25½ [26½: 26½: 26½: 27: 27] in)

58 [60: 62: 66.5: 69] cm
(23 [23½: 24½: 26: 27] in)

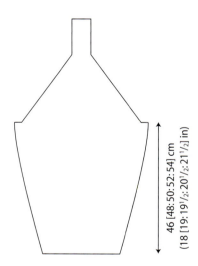

46 [48: 50: 52: 54] cm
(18 [19: 19½: 20½: 21½] in)

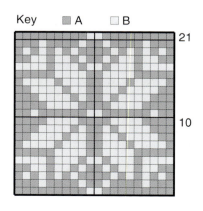

Key ■ A □ B

21

10

inc sts into rib.
Cont straight until sleeve meas 46 [48: 50: 52: 54] cm, ending with RS facing for next row.
Shape raglan
Cast off 3 sts at beg of next 2 rows.
34 [36: 38: 40: 42] sts.
Dec 1 st at each end of next 7 rows, then on every foll alt row until 10 sts rem.
Work 9 rows, ending with RS facing for next row.
Left sleeve only
Work 1 row.
Cast off 4 sts at beg of next row, then 3 sts at beg of foll alt row.
Right sleeve only
Cast off 4 sts at beg of next row, then 3 sts at beg of foll alt row.
Work 1 row.
Both sleeves
Cast off rem 3 sts.

MAKING UP
Press as described on the information page.
Join both front and right back raglan seams using back stitch, or mattress stitch if preferred.
Neckband
With RS facing, using 9mm (US 13) needles and yarn A, pick up and knit 10 sts from top of left sleeve, 6 sts down left side of neck, 12 sts from front, 6 sts up right side of neck, 10 sts from top of right sleeve, then 18 sts from back. 62 sts.
Row 1 (WS): P2, ★K2, P2, rep from ★ to end.
Row 2: K2, ★P2, K2, rep from ★ to end.
These 2 rows form rib.
Work in rib for a further 15 rows, ending with RS facing for next row.
Cast off in rib.
See information page for finishing instructions.
Using photograph as a guide and yarn C, oversew along the 2 P sts either side of centre st st panels on back, front and sleeves.

Main image page 17

RUFFLE SCARF BY NIKKI RYAN

YARN
Rowan Kid Classic
3 x 50gm
(photographed in Crystal 840)

CROCHET HOOK
3.50mm (no 9) (US E4) crochet hook

TENSION
21 sts to 10 cm and 4 rows to 9.5 cm measured over mesh pattern using 3.50mm (US E4) hook.

UK CROCHET ABBREVIATIONS
ch = chain; **dtr** = double treble;
sp(s) = space(s); **ss** = slip stitch.

UK CROCHET ABBREVIATIONS
ch = chain; **dtr** = treble;
sp(s) = space(s); **ss** = slip stitch.

FINISHED SIZE
Completed scarf measures 9.5 cm (3¾ in) wide and 124 cm (49 in) long, excluding ruffles.

SCARF
Mesh section
Using 3.50mm (US E4) hook make 267 ch.
Row 1 (RS): 1 dtr into 11th ch from hook, (3 ch, miss 3 ch, 1 dtr into next ch) 11 times, mark dtr just worked with a coloured thread, ★3 ch, miss 3 ch, 1 dtr into next ch, rep from ★ to end.
65 ch sps.
Fasten off.
Row 2 (RS): Rejoin yarn to marked dtr, 54 ch, 1 dtr into 11th ch from hook, (3 ch, miss 3 ch, 1 dtr into next ch) 10 times, 3 ch, miss 3 ch, 1 dtr into marked dtr, mark dtr just worked with a coloured thread, (3 ch, miss 3 ch, 1 dtr into next dtr) 11 times, turn, miss dtr just worked, 1 ss into each of next 24 sts, turn, 24 ch, 1 ss into last dtr worked in this row before turning, ★3 ch, miss 3 ch, 1 dtr into next dtr, rep from ★ to end.
Fasten off.
Row 3 (RS): Rejoin yarn to marked dtr, 54 ch, 1 dtr into 11th ch from hook, (3 ch, miss 3 ch, 1 dtr into next ch) 10 times, 3 ch, miss 3 ch, 1 dtr into marked dtr, mark dtr just worked with a coloured thread, (3 ch, miss 3 ch, 1 dtr into next dtr) 11 times, (3 ch, miss 3 ch, 1 dtr into next ch) 5 times, ★3 ch, miss 3 ch, 1 dtr into next dtr, rep from ★ to end.
Fasten off.
Row 4 (RS): Rejoin yarn to marked dtr, 54 ch, 1 dtr into 11th ch from hook, (3 ch, miss 3 ch, 1 dtr into next ch) 10 times, 3 ch, miss 3 ch, 1 dtr into marked dtr, ★3 ch, miss 3 ch, 1 dtr into next dtr, rep from ★ to end.
Do NOT fasten off.
Ruffle
Now work first band of ruffles into mesh of row 4 as folls:
Row 5 (RS): 4 ch (counts as first dtr), 6 dtr around stem of last dtr of row 4, 1 dtr into last ch sp of row 4, ★working down dtr from top towards bottom of st: 7 dtr around stem of next dtr of row 4, 1 dtr into previous ch sp of row 3★★, working down dtr from top towards bottom of st: 7 dtr around stem of next dtr of row 4, 1 dtr into next ch sp of row 3, rep from ★ to end, ending last rep at ★★ and noting that for last 12 sps of mesh you will be working into ch sp formed by foundation ch at beg of row 4 instead of ch sps formed by row 3.
Fasten off.
Rejoin yarn to top of dtr at end of row 3 and work next band of ruffles into mesh of row 3 in same way.
In same way, work ruffles along rows 2 and 1.

MAKING UP
Do NOT press.

Main image page 15

CELTIC BY MARTIN STOREY

SIZE

8	10	12	14	16	18	20	22	

To fit bust

| 82 | 87 | 92 | 97 | 102 | 107 | 112 | 117 | cm |
| 32 | 34 | 36 | 38 | 40 | 42 | 44 | 46 | in |

YARN

Rowan Felted Tweed and Kid Classic
A Felted Tweed Carbon 159

| 7 | 7 | 7 | 8 | 8 | 8 | 9 | 9 | x 50gm |

B Kid Classic Smoke 831

| 2 | 2 | 2 | 2 | 2 | 2 | 2 | 2 | x 50gm |

NEEDLES

1 pair 3¼ mm (no 10) (US 3) needles
1 pair 3¾ mm (no 9) (US 5) needles
Cable needle

ZIP – Open-ended zip to fit

TENSION

23 sts and 32 rows to 10 cm measured over stocking stitch using 3¾ mm (US 5) needles and yarn A.

Pattern note: The number of sts varies whilst working the chart. All sts counts given assume there are 44 sts in chart **at all times**. When working shaping through chart sts, ensure extra sts are decreased (or cast off) to balance the extra sts that have been increased.

SPECIAL ABBREVIATIONS

C4B = slip next 2 sts onto cable needle and leave at back of work, K2, then K2 from cable needle; **C4F** = slip next 2 sts onto cable needle and leave at front of work, K2, then K2 from cable needle; **C6B** = slip next 3 sts onto cable needle and leave at back of work, K3, then K3 from cable needle; **C6F** = slip next 3 sts onto cable needle and leave at front of work, K3, then K3 from cable needle; **Cr5R** = slip next 2 sts onto cable needle and leave at back of work, K3, then P2 from cable needle; **Cr5L** = slip next 3 sts onto cable needle and leave at front of work, P2, then K3 from cable needle; **dec7** = with yarn at front of work slip next 4 sts onto right needle, *lift 2nd st on right needle over first st and off right needle, slip first st on right needle back onto left needle, lift 2nd st on left needle over first st and off left needle, slip first st on left needle back onto right needle, rep from * twice more, slip first st on right needle back onto left needle and K this st; **inc2** = (K1 tbl, K1) into next st, insert left needle point behind vertical strand that runs downwards from between 2 sts just made and K1 tbl into this loop.

BACK

Using 3¼ mm (US 3) needles and yarn B cast on 84 [88: 92: 100: 106: 114: 120: 126] sts.
Work in g st for 7 rows, ending with **WS** facing for next row.
Row 8 (WS): K6 [8: 10: 14: 17: 21: 24: 27], M1, K2, M1, K1, M1, K13, M1, K2, M1, K1, M1, K13, M1, K2, M1, K1, M1, K2, M1, K2, M1, K1, M1, K13, M1, K2, M1, K1, M1, K13, M1, K2, M1, K1, M1, K to end. 102 [106: 110: 118: 124: 132: 138: 144] sts.
Break off yarn B and join in yarn A.
Change to 3¾ mm (US 5) needles.

Place charts

Row 1 (RS): P6 [8: 10: 14: 17: 21: 24: 27], work next 44 sts as row 1 of chart, P2, work next 44 sts as row 1 of chart, P to end.
Row 2: K6 [8: 10: 14: 17: 21: 24: 27], work next 44 sts as row 2 of chart, K2, work next 44 sts as row 2 of chart, K to end.
These 2 rows set the sts – 2 charts with rev st st between and at sides.
Cont as set, shaping side seams by inc 1 st at each end of 9th and every foll 10th row until there are 116 [120: 124: 132: 138: 146: 152: 158] sts, taking inc sts into rev st st.
Cont straight until back meas 28 [28: 27: 30: 29: 31: 30: 32] cm, ending with RS facing for next row.

Shape armholes

Keeping patt correct, cast off 5 [6: 6: 7: 7: 8: 8: 9] sts at beg of next 2 rows.
106 [108: 112: 118: 124: 130: 136: 140] sts.
Dec 1 st at each end of next 3 [3: 5: 5: 7: 7: 9: 9] rows, then on foll 3 [3: 2: 3: 2: 4: 3: 3] alt rows, then on foll 4th row.
92 [94: 96: 100: 104: 106: 110: 114] sts.
Cont straight until armhole meas 19 [19: 20: 20: 21: 21: 22: 22] cm, ending with RS facing for next row.

Shape shoulders and back neck

Cast off 9 [9: 9: 10: 10: 11: 11: 12] sts at beg of next 2 rows.
74 [76: 78: 80: 84: 84: 88: 90] sts.
Next row (RS): Cast off 9 [9: 9: 10: 10: 11: 11: 12] sts, patt until there are 12 [13: 14: 14: 15: 14: 16: 16] sts on right needle and turn, leaving rem sts on a holder.
Work each side of neck separately.
Cast off 4 sts at beg of next row.
Cast off rem 8 [9: 10: 10: 11: 10: 12: 12] sts.
With RS facing, rejoin yarn to rem sts, cast off centre 32 [32: 32: 32: 34: 34: 34: 34] sts dec 6 sts evenly, patt to end.
Complete to match first side, reversing shapings.

LEFT FRONT

Using 3¼ mm (US 3) needles and yarn B cast on 43 [45: 47: 51: 54: 58: 61: 64] sts.
Work in g st for 7 rows, ending with **WS** facing for next row.
Row 8 (WS): K2, M1, K2, M1, K1, M1, K13, M1, K2, M1, K1, M1, K13, M1, K2, M1, K1, M1, K to end.
52 [54: 56: 60: 63: 67: 70: 73] sts.
Break off yarn B and join in yarn A.
Change to 3¾ mm (US 5) needles.

Place chart

Row 1 (RS): P6 [8: 10: 14: 17: 21: 24: 27], work next 44 sts as row 1 of chart, P2.
Row 2: K2, work next 44 sts as row 2 of chart, K to end.

These 2 rows set the sts – chart with rev st st at both sides.
Cont as set, shaping side seam by inc 1 st at beg of 9th and every foll 10th row until there are 59 [61: 63: 67: 70: 74: 77: 80] sts, taking inc sts into rev st st.
Cont straight until left front matches back to beg of armhole shaping, ending with RS facing for next row.

Shape armhole

Keeping patt correct, cast off 5 [6: 6: 7: 7: 8: 8: 9] sts at beg of next row.
54 [55: 57: 60: 63: 66: 69: 71] sts.
Work 1 row.
Dec 1 st at armhole edge of next 3 [3: 5: 5: 7: 7: 9: 9] rows, then on foll 3 [3: 2: 3: 2: 4: 3: 3] alt rows, then on foll 4th row.
47 [48: 49: 51: 53: 54: 56: 58] sts.
Cont straight until 17 [17: 17: 19: 19: 19: 21: 21] rows less have been worked than on back to beg of shoulder shaping, ending with **WS** facing for next row.

Shape neck

Keeping patt correct, cast off 10 [10: 10: 9: 10: 10: 9: 9] sts at beg of next row.
37 [38: 39: 42: 43: 44: 47: 49] sts.
Dec 1 st at neck edge of next 7 rows, then on foll 4 [4: 4: 5: 5: 5: 6: 6] alt rows.
26 [27: 28: 30: 31: 32: 34: 36] sts.
Work 1 row, ending with RS facing for next row.

Shape shoulder

Cast off 9 [9: 9: 10: 10: 11: 11: 12] sts at beg of next and foll alt row.
Work 1 row.
Cast off rem 8 [9: 10: 10: 11: 10: 12: 12] sts.

RIGHT FRONT

Using 3¼ mm (US 3) needles and yarn B cast on 43 [45: 47: 51: 54: 58: 61: 64] sts.
Work in g st for 7 rows, ending with **WS** facing for next row.
Row 8 (WS): K6 [8: 10: 14: 17: 21: 24: 27], M1, K2, M1, K1, M1, K13, M1, K2, M1, K1, M1, K13, M1, K2, M1, K1, M1, K2.
52 [54: 56: 60: 63: 67: 70: 73] sts.
Break off yarn B and join in yarn A.
Change to 3¾ mm (US 5) needles.

Place chart

Row 1 (RS): P2, work next 44 sts as row 1 of chart, P to end.
Row 2: K6 [8: 10: 14: 17: 21: 24: 27], work next 44 sts as row 2 of chart, K2.
These 2 rows set the sts – chart with rev st st at both sides.
Cont as set, shaping side seam by inc 1 st at end of 9th and every foll 10th row until there are 59 [61: 63: 67: 70: 74: 77: 80] sts, taking inc sts into rev st st.
Complete to match left front, reversing shapings.

SLEEVES

Using 3¼ mm (US 3) needles and yarn B cast on 57 [57: 59: 59: 61: 61: 63: 63] sts.
Work in g st for 7 rows, ending with **WS**

facing for next row.
Row 8 (WS): K11 [11: 12: 12: 13: 13: 14: 14],
M1, K2, M1, K1, M1, K13, M1, K2, M1, K1,
M1, K13, M1, K2, M1, K1, M1, K to end.
66 [66: 68: 68: 70: 70: 72: 72] sts.
Break off yarn B and join in yarn A.
Change to 3¾ mm (US 5) needles.
Place chart
Row 1 (RS): P11 [11: 12: 12: 13: 13: 14: 14],
work next 44 sts as row 1 of chart, P to end.
Row 2: K11 [11: 12: 12: 13: 13: 14: 14], work
next 44 sts as row 2 of chart, K to end.
These 2 rows set the sts – chart with rev st st at
both sides.
Cont as set, shaping sides by inc 1 st at each
end of 11th [9th: 9th: 9th: 9th: 7th: 7th: 7th]
and every foll 14th [12th: 14th: 12th: 12th:
10th: 10th: 10th] row to 74 [72: 86: 84: 84:
76: 80: 92] sts, then on every foll 16th [14th: –:
14th: 14th: 12th: 12th: 12th] row until there are
82 [84: –: 88: 90: 92: 94: 96] sts, taking inc sts
into rev st st.
Cont straight until sleeve meas 45 [45: 46: 46:
47: 47: 46: 46] cm, ending with RS facing for
next row.
Shape top
Keeping patt correct, cast off 5 [6: 6: 7: 7:
8: 8: 9] sts at beg of next 2 rows.
72 [72: 74: 74: 76: 76: 78: 78] sts.
Dec 1 st at each end of next 3 rows, then on
foll 3 alt rows, then on every foll 4th row until
50 [50: 52: 52: 54: 54: 56: 56] sts rem.
Work 1 row.

Dec 1 st at each end of next and every foll alt
row to 42 sts, then on foll 9 rows, ending with
RS facing for next row.
Cast off rem 24 sts dec 3 sts evenly.

MAKING UP
Press as described on the information page.
Join shoulder seams using back stitch, or
mattress stitch if preferred.
Front bands (both alike)
With RS facing, using 3¼ mm (US 3) needles
and yarn B, pick up and knit 100 [100: 100:
105: 105: 110: 108: 113] sts evenly along front
opening edge, between cast-on edge and neck
shaping.
Work in g st for 2 rows, ending with **WS**
facing for next row.
Cast off knitwise (on **WS**).
Collar
With RS facing, using 3¼ mm (US 3) needles
and yarn B, beg and ending at cast-off edges of
front bands, pick up and knit 34 [34: 34: 35: 36:
36: 37: 37] sts up right side of neck, 37 [37: 37:
37: 39: 39: 39: 39] sts from back, then 34 [34:
34: 35: 36: 36: 37: 37] sts down left side of
neck.
105 [105: 105: 107: 111: 111: 113: 113] sts.
Work in g st for 10 cm, ending with **WS** of
collar (RS of body) facing for next row.
Cast off knitwise (on **WS**).
See information page for finishing instructions,
setting in sleeves using the set-in method and
inserting zip into front opening.

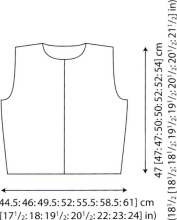

42.5 [44.5: 46: 49.5: 52: 55.5: 58.5: 61] cm
(16½ [17½: 18: 19½: 20½: 22: 23: 24] in)

47 [47: 47: 50: 50: 52: 52: 54] cm
(18½ [18½: 18½: 19½: 19½: 20½: 20½: 21½] in)

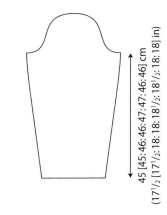

45 [45: 46: 46: 47: 47: 46: 46] cm
(17½ [17½: 18: 18: 18½: 18½: 18: 18] in)

Key

☐ K on RS,
  P on WS

▪ P on RS,
  K on WS

▱ C4B

▱ C4F

▱ Cr5R

▱ Cr5L

▱ C6B

▱ C6F

☑ M1

☒ inc 2

▾ inc purlwise

⊞ K1 tbl

▨ dec 7

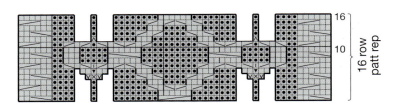

16

10

16 row patt rep

Main image page 86

PAISLEY BY MARTIN STOREY

SIZE

	S	M	L	XL	
	8/10	12/14	16/18	20/22	
To fit bust					
	82-87	92-97	102-107	112-117	cm
	32-34	36-38	40-42	44-46	in

YARN
Rowan Kid Classic

A Victoria 852					
	15	16	18	19	x 50gm
B Smoke 831					
	4	4	4	5	x 50gm
C Crystal 840					
	3	4	4	4	x 50gm
D Spruce 853					
	2	2	3	3	x 50gm
E Straw 851					
	1	2	2	2	x 50gm

NEEDLES
1 pair 4mm (no 8) (US 6) needles
1 pair 5mm (no 6) (US 8) needles

BEADS – approx 166 pearl beads *Ref Pearl Bead P6. col. white from Creative Bead Craft Ltd. 1 x large kilt pin 00414 or 00412

TENSION
19 sts and 25 rows to 10 cm measured over patterned stocking stitch using 5mm (US 8) needles.

SPECIAL ABBREVIATIONS
MB = (K1, P1, K1) all into next st, turn and P3, turn and K3, turn and P3, turn and sl 1, K2tog, psso.

BACK
Using 4mm (US 6) needles and yarn B cast on 115 [125: 135: 147] sts.
Work in g st for 2 rows, ending with RS facing for next row.
Change to 5mm (US 8) needles.
Beg and ending rows as indicated and using the **fairisle** technique as described on the information page for rows 1 to 61, working chart rows 1 to 64 once only and then repeating chart rows 65 to 88 throughout, work from chart for back as folls:
Work 48 rows, ending with RS facing for next row.
Dec 1 st at each end of next and every foll 10th row to 101 [111: 121: 133] sts, then on every foll 8th row to 95 [105: 115: 127] sts, then on every foll 6th row until 89 [99: 109: 121] sts rem.
Work 9 rows, ending with RS facing for next row.
Inc 1 st at each end of next and every foll 12th row until there are 95 [105: 115: 127] sts, taking inc sts into patt.
Cont straight until back meas 79 [80: 81: 82] cm, ending with RS facing for next row.
Shape armholes
Keeping patt correct, cast off 6 sts at beg of

next 2 rows.
83 [93: 103: 115] sts.
Dec 1 st at each end of next 5 [7: 9: 11] rows, then on foll 3 [4: 4: 5] alt rows, then on foll 4th row. 65 [69: 75: 81] sts.
Cont straight until armhole meas 22 [23: 24: 25] cm, ending with RS facing for next row.
Shape shoulders and back neck
Cast off 5 [6: 7: 8] sts at beg of next 2 rows. 55 [57: 61: 65] sts.
Next row (RS): Cast off 5 [6: 7: 8] sts, patt until there are 10 [10: 10: 11] sts on right needle and turn, leaving rem sts on a holder.
Work each side of neck separately.
Cast off 4 sts at beg of next row.
Cast off rem 6 [6: 6: 7] sts.
With RS facing, rejoin yarn to rem sts, cast off centre 25 [25: 27: 27] sts, patt to end.
Complete to match first side, reversing shapings.

LEFT FRONT
Using 4mm (US 6) needles and yarn B cast on 60 [65: 70: 76] sts.
Work in g st for 2 rows, ending with RS facing for next row.
Change to 5mm (US 8) needles.
Beg and ending rows as indicated but **omitting** part paisley motifs and bobbles that fall along front opening edge, work from chart for back as folls:
Work 48 rows, ending with RS facing for next row.
Dec 1 st at beg of next and every foll 10th row to 53 [58: 63: 69] sts, then on every foll 8th row to 50 [55: 60: 66] sts, then on every foll 6th row until 47 [52: 57: 63] sts rem.
Work 9 rows, ending with RS facing for next row.
Inc 1 st at beg of next and every foll 12th row until there are 50 [55: 60: 66] sts, taking inc sts into patt.
Cont straight until left front matches back to beg of armhole shaping, ending with RS facing for next row.
Shape armhole
Keeping patt correct, cast off 6 sts at beg of next row. 44 [49: 54: 60] sts.
Work 1 row.
Dec 1 st at armhole edge of next 5 [7: 9: 11] rows, then on foll 3 [4: 4: 5] alt rows, then on foll 4th row.
35 [37: 40: 43] sts.
Cont straight until 31 [31: 33: 33] rows less have been worked than on back to beg of shoulder shaping, ending with **WS** facing for next row.
Shape neck
Keeping patt correct, cast off 4 sts at beg of next row. 31 [33: 36: 39] sts.
Dec 1 st at neck edge of next and every foll alt row until 16 [18: 20: 23] sts rem.
Work 1 row, ending with RS facing for next row.

Shape shoulder
Cast off 5 [6: 7: 8] sts at beg of next and foll alt row.
Work 1 row.
Cast off rem 6 [6: 6: 7] sts.

RIGHT FRONT
Using 4mm (US 6) needles and yarn B cast on 60 [65: 70: 76] sts.
Work in g st for 2 rows, ending with RS facing for next row.
Change to 5mm (US 8) needles.
Beg and ending rows as indicated but **omitting** part paisley motifs and bobbles that fall along front opening edge, work from chart for back as folls:
Work 48 rows, ending with RS facing for next row.
Dec 1 st at end of next and every foll 10th row to 53 [58: 63: 69] sts, then on every foll 8th row to 50 [55: 60: 66] sts, then on every foll 6th row until 47 [52: 57: 63] sts rem.
Work 9 rows, ending with RS facing for next row.
Complete to match left front, reversing shapings.

SLEEVES
Using 4mm (US 6) needles and yarn D cast on 65 [67: 69: 71] sts.
Work in g st for 2 rows, ending with RS facing for next row.
Change to 5mm (US 8) needles.
Beg and ending rows as indicated and using the **fairisle** technique as described on the information page for rows 1 to 47, working chart rows 1 to 50 once only and then repeating chart rows 51 to 74 throughout, work from chart for sleeve as folls:
Work 26 rows, ending with RS facing for next row.
Inc 1 st at each end of next and every foll 28th row until there are 71 [73: 75: 77] sts, taking inc sts into patt.
Cont straight until sleeve meas 44 [45: 46: 46] cm, ending with RS facing for next row.
Shape top
Keeping patt correct, cast off 6 sts at beg of next 2 rows.
59 [61: 63: 65] sts.
Dec 1 st at each end of next 5 rows, then on foll 3 alt rows, then on every foll 4th row until 35 [37: 39: 41] sts rem.
Work 1 row.
Dec 1 st at each end of next and every foll alt row to 29 sts, then on foll 5 rows, ending with RS facing for next row.
Cast off rem 19 sts.

MAKING UP
Press as described on the information page.
Join shoulder seams using back stitch, or mattress stitch if preferred.
Left front band
With RS facing, using 5mm (US 8) needles

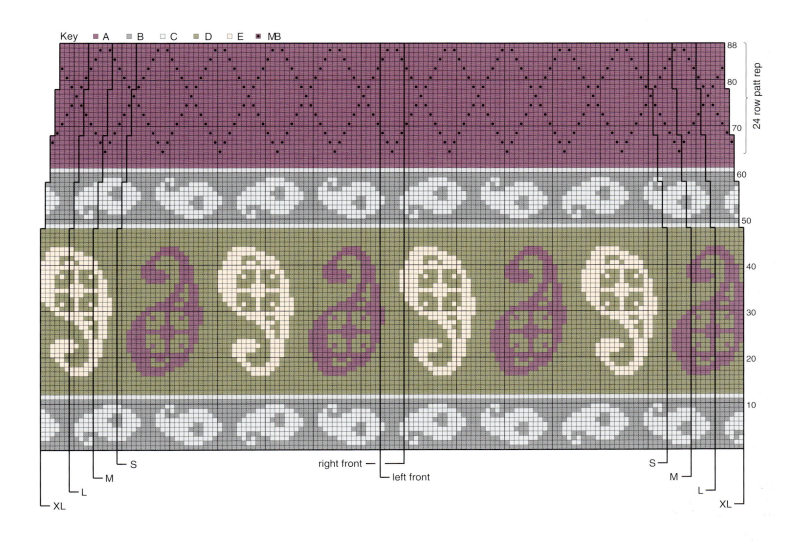

Key ■ A ■ B □ C ■ D □ E ■ MB

88
80
70
60
50
40
30
20
10

24 row patt rep

S
M
L
XL

right front
left front

S
M
L
XL

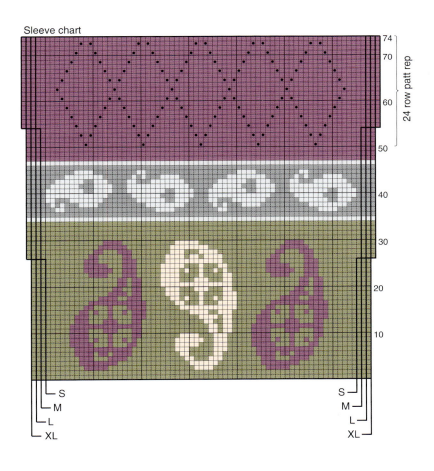

Sleeve chart

74
70
60
50
40
30
20
10

24 row patt rep

S
M
L
XL

S
M
L
XL

and yarn B, pick up and knit 171 [175: 177: 181] sts evenly down left front opening edge, from neck shaping to cast-on edge.

Place chart

Row 1 (WS): K2, P0 [3: 4: 8], work next 167 sts as row 1 of chart for front band, P0 [1: 2: 2], K2.

Row 2: K2 [3: 4: 4], work next 167 sts as row 2 of chart for front band, K2 [5: 6: 10].

These 2 rows set the sts.

Cont as now set until chart row 12 has been completed, ending with **WS** facing for next row.

Break off contrasts and cont using yarn B only. Change to 4mm (US 6) needles.

Work in g st for 2 rows, ending with **WS** facing for next row.

Cast off knitwise (on **WS**).

Right front band

With RS facing, using 5mm (US 8) needles and yarn B, pick up and knit 171 [175: 177: 181] sts evenly up right front opening edge, from cast-on edge to neck shaping.

Place chart

Row 1 (WS): K2, P0 [1: 2: 2], work next 167 sts as row 1 of chart for front band, P0 [3: 4: 8], K2.

Row 2: K2 [5: 6: 10], work next 167 sts as row 2 of chart for front band, K2 [3: 4: 4].

These 2 rows set the sts.

Complete to match left front band.

Collar

Using 4mm (US 6) needles and yarn B cast on 117 [117: 123: 123] sts.

Work in g st for 2 rows, ending with RS facing for next row.

Change to 5mm (US 8) needles.

Place chart

Row 1 (RS): K2 [2: 5: 5], work next 113 sts as row 1 of chart for collar, K2 [2: 5: 5].

Row 2: K2, P0 [0: 3: 3], work next 113 sts as

row 2 of chart for collar, P0 [0: 3: 3], K2.

These 2 rows set the sts.

Cont as now set until chart row 44 has been completed, ending with RS facing for next row.

Break off contrasts and cont using yarn D only.

Next row (RS): Knit.

Next row: K2, P to last 2 sts, K2.

Rep last 2 rows once more.

Cast off 11 [11: 12: 12] sts at beg of next 8 rows.

Cast off rem 29 [29: 27: 27] sts.

Matching row-end edges of collar to cast-off edges of front bands, sew shaped cast-off edge of collar to neck edge.

See information page for finishing instructions, setting in sleeves using the set-in method. Using photograph as a guide, outline large paisley motifs of charts in chain stitch, using yarn B to outline motifs in yarn E, and yarn C for motifs in yarn A. Attach pearl beads to centres of all motifs as in photograph.

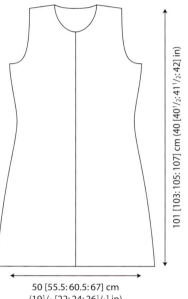

101 [103:105:107] cm (40 [40½: 41½: 42] in)

50 [55.5:60.5:67] cm (19½ [22: 24: 26½] in)

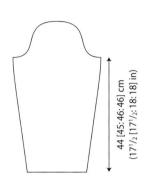

44 [45: 46: 46] cm (17½ [17½: 18: 18] in)

Collar chart

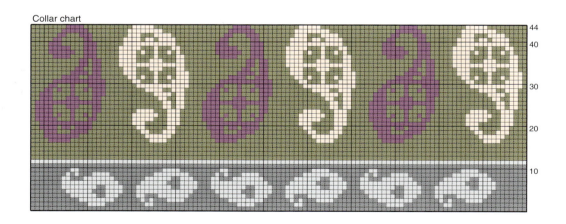

Front band chart

Main image page 24

KAY BY LEAH SUTTON

SIZE

S	M	L	XL	
8/10	12/14	16/18	20/22	

To fit bust

82-87	92-97	102-107	112-117	cm
32-34	36-38	40-42	44-46	in

YARN

Rowan Big Wool and Kidsilk Spray
A BigWool Black 008

7	8	9	10	x 100gm

B Kidsilk Spray Graphite 570

1	1	1	1	x 25gm

NEEDLES

1 pair 4mm (no 8) (US 6) needles
1 pair 9mm (no 00) (US 13) needles
1 pair 10mm (no 000) (US 15) needles

BUTTONS - 3 x 00407

TENSION

8 sts and 12 rows to 10 cm measured over stocking stitch using yarn A and 10mm (US 15) needles.

BACK

Using 10mm (US 15) needles and yarn A cast on 41 [45: 49: 53] sts.
Beg with a K row, work in st st until back meas 28 [29: 29: 29] cm, ending with RS facing for next row.
Shape raglan armholes
Cast off 2 sts at beg of next 2 rows.
37 [41: 45: 49] sts.
Dec 1 st at each end of next and every foll 4th row to 25 [31: 35: 41] sts, then on foll 0 [3: 4: 7] alt rows. 25 [25: 27: 27] sts.
Work 1 row, ending with RS facing for next row.
Shape back neck
Next row (RS): K2tog, K1 and turn, leaving rem sts on a holder.
Work each side of neck separately.
Next row: P2tog and fasten off.
With RS facing, rejoin yarn to rem sts, cast off centre 19 [19: 21: 21] sts (one st on right needle), K2tog.
Next row: P2tog and fasten off.

LEFT FRONT

Using 10mm (US 15) needles and yarn A cast on 18 [20: 22: 24] sts.
Beg with a K row, work in st st until left front matches back to beg of raglan armhole shaping, ending with RS facing for next row.
Shape raglan armhole
Cast off 2 sts at beg of next row.
16 [18: 20: 22] sts.
Work 1 row.
Dec 1 st at armhole edge of next and every foll 4th row to 10 [13: 15: 18] sts, then on foll 0 [3: 4: 7] alt rows, ending with **WS** facing for next row. 10 [10: 11: 11] sts.
Shape neck
Cast off 6 [6: 7: 7] sts at beg of next row.

4 sts.
Next row (RS): (K2tog) twice.
Next row: P2tog and fasten off.

RIGHT FRONT

Work to match left front, reversing shapings.

SLEEVES

Using 9mm (US 13) needles and yarn A cast on 19 [19: 21: 21] sts.
Beg with a P row, work in rev st st for 8 rows, ending with RS facing for next row.
Change to 10mm (US 15) needles.
Beg with a K row, work in st st, shaping sides by inc 1 st at each end of 3rd and every foll 4th row to 27 [33: 33: 39] sts, then on every foll 6th row until there are 35 [37: 39: 41] sts.
Cont straight until sleeve meas 43 [44: 45: 45] cm, ending with RS facing for next row.
Shape raglan
Cast off 2 sts at beg of next 2 rows.
31 [33: 35: 37] sts.
Dec 1 st at each end of next and every foll alt row until 7 sts rem.
Work 1 row, ending with RS facing for next row.
Cast off.

MAKING UP

Press as described on the information page.
Join raglan seams using back stitch, or mattress stitch if preferred.
Button band
Using 9mm (US 13) needles and yarn A cast on 9 sts.
Beg with a P row, work in rev st st until band, when slightly stretched, fits up left front opening edge to neck shaping, ending with RS facing for next row.
Break yarn and leave sts on a holder.
Slip stitch band in place.
Buttonhole band
Using 9mm (US 13) needles and yarn A cast on 9 sts.
Beg with a P row, work in rev st st until band, when slightly stretched, fits up right front opening edge to a point 2 rows below neck shaping, ending with RS facing for next row.
Next row (buttonhole row) (RS): P3, P2tog, yrn, P4.
Work a further 1 row, ending with RS facing for next row.
Do NOT break yarn.
Slip stitch band in place.
Collar
With RS facing, using 9mm (US 13) needles and yarn A, P 9 sts of buttonhole band, pick up and knit 7 [7: 8: 8] sts up right side of neck, 7 sts from right sleeve, 20 [20: 22: 22] sts from back, 7 sts from left sleeve, and 7 [7: 8: 8] sts down left side of neck, then P 9 sts of button band.
66 [66: 70: 70] sts.
Row 1 (WS): K9, P to last 9 sts, K9.
Row 2: P9, K to last 9 sts, P9.

These 2 rows form patt.
Work in patt for a further 3 rows, ending with RS facing for next row.
Row 6 (buttonhole row) (RS): P3, P2tog, yrn, patt to end.
Patt 7 rows.
Row 14: As row 6.
Patt a further 2 rows, ending with **WS** facing for next row.
Cast off in patt (on **WS**).
See information page for finishing instructions.
Leaves (make 10)
Using 4mm (US 6) needles and yarn B cast on 6 sts.
Row 1 (RS): K1, K2tog, (yfwd) twice, K2tog, K1.
Row 2: P2, (P1, K1) into double yfwd of previous row, P2.
Rep rows 1 and 2, 14 times more.
Cast off.
Folding leaf to form a V shape, sew leaves to fronts as in photograph.

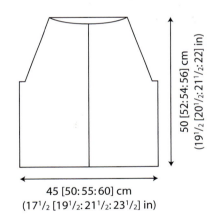

50 [52: 54: 56] cm
(19½ [20½: 21½: 22] in)

45 [50: 55: 60] cm
(17½ [19½: 21½: 23½] in)

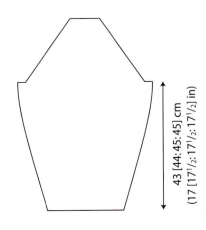

43 [44: 45: 45] cm
(17 [17½: 17½: 17½] in)

Main image page 71

SIZE

8   10   12   14   16   18   20   22
To fit bust
82 87 92 97 102 107 112 117 cm
32 34 36 38 40 42 44 46   in

YARN

Rowan Kidsilk Night and Lurex Shimmer
A Kidsilk Night Fountain 612
   4   4   4   5   5   5   6   6   x 25gm
B Lurex Shimmer Gleam 336
   1   1   1   1   1   1   1   1   x 25gm

NEEDLES

1 pair 3¾ mm (no 9) (US 5) needles
2.00mm (no 14) (US B1) crochet hook
4.00mm (no 8) (US G6) crochet hook

BEADS – 13 large fancy beads *Ref Bali

Silver Bead B524, and approx 380 [390: 400:
420: 440: 460: 480: 500] each of small clear
beads *Ref Glass Bead GB7 col. 10 grey and
dark faceted beads *Ref Glass Bead GB7 col. 3
Gunmetal all from Creative Bead Craft Ltd.

TENSION

22 sts and 30 rows to 10 cm measured over
stocking stitch using 3¾ mm (US 5) needles
and yarn A.

SPECIAL ABBREVIATIONS

bead 1 = place a bead by bringing yarn to
front (RS) of work and slipping bead up next
to st just worked, slip next st purlwise from left
needle to right needle and take yarn back to
back (WS) of work, leaving bead sitting in
front of slipped st on RS.

UK CROCHET ABBREVIATIONS

ch = chain; **dc** = double crochet;
ss = slip stitch; **tr** = treble.

US CROCHET ABBREVIATIONS

ch = chain; **dc** = single crochet;
ss = slip stitch; **tr** = double crochet.

Beading note: Before starting to knit, thread
small faceted beads onto yarn. To do this, thread
a fine sewing needle (one that will easily pass
through the beads) with sewing thread. Knot
ends of thread and then pass end of yarn
through this loop. Thread a bead onto sewing
thread and then gently slide it along and onto
knitting yarn. Continue in this way until
required number of beads are on yarn – thread
beads onto yarn in alternate colours. Chart
shows which colour bead to use. If next bead
on yarn is incorrect colour, break yarn, remove
incorrect colour bead and rejoin yarn. Do not
place beads on edge sts of rows as this will
interfere with sewing-up.

BACK

Using 3¾ mm (US 5) needles and yarn A cast
on 93 [97: 101: 107: 115: 121: 127: 135] sts.
Beg and ending rows as indicated, working

chart rows 1 to 36 **once only** and then
repeating chart rows 37 to 48 **throughout**,
cont in patt from chart as folls:
Work 42 [42: 40: 48: 46: 52: 48: 54] rows,
ending with RS facing for next row. (Back
should meas 14 [14: 13: 16: 15: 17: 16: 18] cm.)

Shape armholes

Keeping patt correct, cast off 4 [5: 5: 6: 6: 7:
7: 8] sts at beg of next 2 rows.
85 [87: 91: 95: 103: 107: 113: 119] sts.
Dec 1 st at each end of next 3 [3: 5: 5: 7:
7: 9: 9] rows, then on foll 3 [3: 2: 2: 3: 3: 2: 4]
alt rows.
73 [75: 77: 81: 83: 87: 91: 93] sts.
Cont straight until armhole meas 18 [18: 19:
19: 20: 20: 21: 21] cm, ending with RS facing
for next row.

Shape back neck

Next row (RS): Patt 21 [22: 23: 25: 25:
27: 29: 30] sts and turn, leaving rem sts on
a holder.
Work each side of neck separately.
Cast off 4 sts at beg of next row, ending with
RS facing for next row.
17 [18: 19: 21: 21: 23: 25: 26] sts.

Shape shoulder

Cast off 6 [7: 7: 8: 8: 9: 10: 11] sts at beg of next
row, then 4 sts at beg of foll row.
Cast off rem 7 [7: 8: 9: 9: 10: 11: 11] sts.
With RS facing, rejoin yarn to rem sts, cast off
centre 31 [31: 31: 31: 33: 33: 33: 33] sts, patt
to end.
Complete to match first side, reversing
shapings.

LEFT FRONT

Using 3¾ mm (US 5) needles and yarn A cast
on 51 [53: 55: 58: 62: 65: 68: 72] sts.
Beg and ending rows as indicated, cont in patt
from chart as folls:
Work 4 rows, ending with RS facing for
next row.

Shape front slope

Keeping patt correct, dec 1 st at end of next
and foll 11 [11: 11: 7: 8: 5: 6: 3] alt rows, then
on every foll 4th row until 36 [38: 40: 43: 47:
50: 54: 58] sts rem.
Work 3 [3: 1: 1: 1: 1: 3: 3] rows, ending with
RS facing for next row. (Left front should now
match back to beg of armhole shaping.)

Shape armhole

Keeping patt correct, cast off 4 [5: 5: 6: 6:
7: 7: 8] sts at beg and dec 1 [1: 0: 0: 0: 0: 1: 1] st
at end of next row.
31 [32: 35: 37: 41: 43: 46: 49] sts.
Work 1 row.
Dec 1 st at armhole edge of next 3 [3: 5: 5: 7:
7: 9: 9] rows, then on foll 3 [3: 2: 2: 3: 3: 2: 4]
alt rows **and at same time** dec 1 st at front
slope edge of 3rd [3rd: next: next: next: next:
3rd: 3rd] and every foll 4th row.
23 [24: 25: 27: 27: 29: 32: 32] sts.
Dec 1 st at front slope edge **only** of 2nd [2nd:
4th: 4th: 4th: 4th: 2nd: 2nd] and every foll 4th
row until 13 [14: 15: 17: 17: 19: 21: 22] sts rem.

Cont straight until left front matches back to
beg of shoulder shaping, ending with RS facing
for next row.

Shape shoulder

Cast off 6 [7: 7: 8: 8: 9: 10: 11] sts at beg of
next row.
Work 1 row.
Cast off rem 7 [7: 8: 9: 9: 10: 11: 11] sts.

RIGHT FRONT

Using 3¾ mm (US 5) needles and yarn A cast
on 51 [53: 55: 58: 62: 65: 68: 72] sts.
Beg and ending rows as indicated, cont in patt
from chart as folls:
Work 4 rows, ending with RS facing for
next row.

Shape front slope

Keeping patt correct, dec 1 st at beg of next
and foll 11 [11: 11: 7: 8: 5: 6: 3] alt rows, then
on every foll 4th row until 36 [38: 40: 43: 47:
50: 54: 58] sts rem.
Complete to match left front, reversing
shapings.

SLEEVES

Using 3¾ mm (US 5) needles and yarn A cast
on 71 [71: 73: 73: 75: 75: 77: 77] sts.
Beg and ending rows as indicated, working
chart rows 1 to 36 **once only** and then
repeating chart rows 37 to 48 **throughout**,
cont in patt from chart, shaping sides by dec
1 st at each end of 13th and every foll 10th
row until 61 [61: 63: 63: 65: 65: 67: 67] sts rem.
Work 15 rows, ending with RS facing for
next row.
Inc 1 st at each end of next and every foll
6th [6th: 6th: 6th: 6th: 4th: 4th: 4th] row to
67 [75: 73: 81: 81: 69: 73: 79] sts, then on every
foll 8th [8th: 8th: 8th: 8th: 6th: 6th: 6th] row
until there are 77 [79: 81: 83: 85: 87: 89: 91] sts,
taking inc sts into patt.
Cont straight until sleeve meas 44 [44: 45: 45:
46: 46: 45: 45] cm, ending with RS facing for
next row.

Shape top

Cast off 4 [5: 5: 6: 6: 7: 7: 8] sts at beg of next
2 rows.
69 [69: 71: 71: 73: 73: 75: 75] sts.
Dec 1 st at each end of next 7 rows, then on
every foll alt row to 31 sts, then on foll 7 rows,
ending with RS facing for next row.
17 sts.
Cast off 3 sts at beg of next 2 rows.
Cast off rem 11 sts.

MAKING UP

Press as described on the information page.
Join both shoulder seams using back stitch, or
mattress stitch if preferred.
See information page for finishing instructions,
setting in sleeves using the set-in method.

Hem edging

With RS facing, using 2.00mm (US B1)
crochet hook and yarn A, attach yarn to cast-
on edge at left front opening edge, 1 ch (does

NOT count as st), work 1 row of dc evenly along entire cast-on edge, working a multiple of 4 sts plus 1, turn.

Row 1 (WS): 1 ch (does NOT count as st), 1 dc into each dc to end, turn.

Row 2: 1 ch (does NOT count as st), 1 dc into first dc, ★miss 1 dc, 5 tr into next dc, miss 1 dc, 1 dc into next dc, rep from ★ to end.
Do NOT fasten off.

Front edging

With RS facing, using 2.00mm (US B1) crochet hook and yarn A, 1 ch (does NOT count as st), work 1 row of dc evenly up right front opening edge, across back neck and down left front opening edge to beg of last row of hem edging, turn.

Row 1 (RS): 1 ch (does NOT count as st), 1 dc into each dc to end, turn.

Row 2: 1 ch (does NOT count as st), 1 dc into first dc, 7 ch (to form button loop), 1 dc into each dc to end.
Fasten off.

Beg and ending at shoulder seams, thread lengths of yarn A through front edging and pull up to gather edge slightly. Fasten off securely. Attach one large bead to left front opening edge to correspond with button loop.

Crochet flowers (make 12)

Using 4.00mm (US G6) crochet hook and one strand each of yarn A and B held together make 5 ch and join with a ss to form a ring.

Round 1 (RS): 3 ch (counts as first tr), 13 tr into ring, ss to top of 3 ch at beg of round.
Fasten off.

Using photograph as a guide, sew flowers in place along front opening edges, attaching one large and 4 small (2 of each colour) beads to each flower.

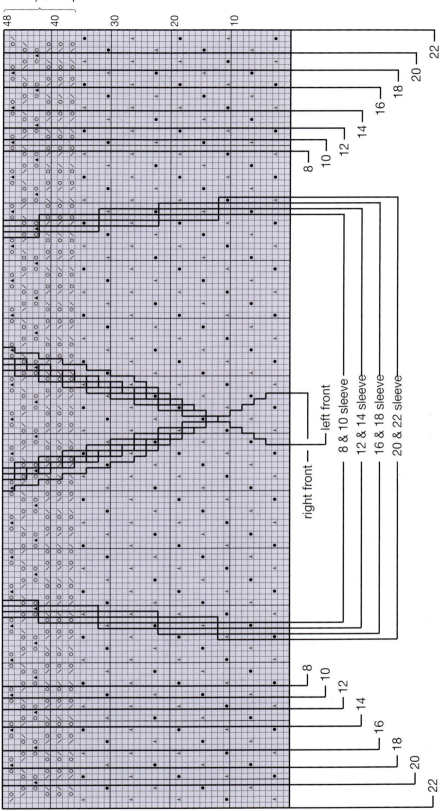

12 row patt rep

right front — left front

8 & 10 sleeve
12 & 14 sleeve
16 & 18 sleeve
20 & 22 sleeve

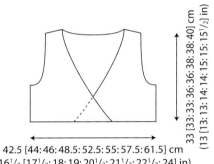

42.5 [44: 46: 48.5: 52.5: 55: 57.5: 61.5] cm
(16½ [17½: 18: 19: 20½: 21½: 22½: 24] in)

33 [33: 33: 36: 36: 38: 38: 40] cm
(13 [13: 13: 14: 14: 15: 15: 15½] in)

44 [44: 45: 45: 46: 46: 45: 45] cm
(17½ [17½: 17½: 17½: 18: 18: 17½: 17½] in)

Key

	K on RS, P on WS
⊙	yfwd
⊠	K2tog
⊘	K2tog tbl
◀	sl1, K2tog, psso
●	bead 1 using dark bead
⊡	bead 1 using clear bead

Main image page 9 & 19

ANYA BY MARIE WALLIN

SIZE

8	10	12	14	16	18	20	22	
To fit bust								
82	87	92	97	102	107	112	117	cm
32	34	36	38	40	42	44	46	in

YARN

Rowan Kid Classic, Kidsilk Haze and Kidsilk Night

A Kid Classic Smoke 831

4	5	5	5	5	5	6	6	x 50gm

B ★Kidsilk Haze Smoke 605

2	2	2	2	3	3	3	3	x 25gm

C ★Kidsilk Haze Wicked 599

2	2	3	3	3	3	3	3	x 25gm

D ★Kidsilk Haze Pearl 590

1	1	1	1	1	1	1	1	x 25gm

E ★Kidsilk Night Moonlight 608

1	1	1	1	1	1	1	1	x 25gm

★Use Kidsilk Haze and Kidsilk Night DOUBLE throughout.

NEEDLES

1 pair 3¾mm (no 9) (US 5) needles
1 pair 4mm (no 8) (US 6) needles
Cable needle

BEADS – GB7 Glass Beads, approx 220 [220: 230: 240: 260: 260: 280: 280] x col. 10 Grey, 510 [530: 550: 570: 600: 620: 650: 670] x col. 3 Gunmetal and 110 [120: 120: 130: 130: 140: 140: 150] x col. 6 Black faceted beads. All from Creative Bead Craft Ltd.

TENSION

24 sts and 27 rows to 10 cm measured over patterned stocking stitch using 4mm (US 6) needles.

SPECIAL ABBREVIATIONS

C2B = slip next st onto cable needle and leave at back of work, K1, then K1 from cable needle;
C2F = slip next st onto cable needle and leave at front of work, K1, then K1 from cable needle;
Cr2R = slip next st onto cable needle and leave at back of work, K1, then P1 from cable needle;
Cr2L = slip next st onto cable needle and leave at front of work, P1, then K1 from cable needle;
bead 1 = place a bead by bringing yarn to front (RS) of work and slipping bead up next to st just worked, slip next st purlwise from left needle to right needle and take yarn back to back (WS) of work, leaving bead sitting in front of slipped st on RS.

Beading note: Before starting to knit, thread beads onto yarn. To do this, thread a fine sewing needle (one that will easily pass through the beads) with sewing thread. Knot ends of thread and then pass end of yarn through this loop. Thread a bead onto sewing thread and then gently slide it along and onto knitting yarn. Continue in this way until required number of beads are on yarn. Do not place beads on edge sts of rows as this will interfere with sewing-up.

BACK and FRONT (both alike)

Using 3¾mm (US 5) needles and yarn A cast on 102 [106: 110: 118: 126: 132: 140: 146] sts.
Row 1 (RS): K1 [3: 0: 0: 0: 0: 2: 0], P2 [2: 0: 2: 0: 0: 2: 0], K2 [2: 0: 2: 0: 2: 2: 0], P1 [1: 1: 1: 0: 1: 1: 1], ★P1, K2, P3, C2B, P2, C2B, P3, K2, P1, rep from ★ to last 6 [8: 1: 5: 0: 3: 7: 1] sts, P1 [1: 1: 1: 0: 1: 1: 1], K2 [2: 0: 2: 0: 2: 2: 0], P2 [2: 0: 2: 0: 0: 2: 0], K1 [3: 0: 0: 0: 0: 2: 0].
Row 2: P1 [3: 0: 0: 0: 0: 2: 0], K2 [2: 0: 2: 0: 0: 2: 0], P2 [2: 0: 2: 0: 2: 2: 0], K1 [1: 1: 1: 0: 1: 1: 1], ★K1, P2, K3, P2, K2, P2, K3, P2, K1, rep from ★ to last 6 [8: 1: 5: 0: 3: 7: 1] sts, K1 [1: 1: 1: 0: 1: 1: 1], P2 [2: 0: 2: 0: 2: 2: 0], K2 [2: 0: 2: 0: 0: 2: 0], P1 [3: 0: 0: 0: 0: 2: 0].
Row 3: K1 [3: 0: 0: 0: 0: 2: 0], P2 [2: 0: 2: 0: 0: 2: 0], K2 [2: 0: 2: 0: 2: 2: 0], P1 [1: 1: 1: 0: 1: 1: 1], ★P1, K2, P2, (Cr2R, Cr2L) twice, P2, K2, P1, rep from ★ to last 6 [8: 1: 5: 0: 3: 7: 1] sts, P1 [1: 1: 1: 0: 1: 1: 1], K2 [2: 0: 2: 0: 2: 2: 0], P2 [2: 0: 2: 0: 0: 2: 0], K1 [3: 0: 0: 0: 0: 2: 0].
Row 4: P1 [3: 0: 0: 0: 0: 2: 0], K2 [2: 0: 2: 0: 0: 2: 0], P2 [2: 0: 2: 0: 2: 2: 0], K1 [1: 1: 1: 0: 1: 1: 1], ★K1, P2, K2, P1, K2, P2, K2, P1, K2, P2, K1, rep from ★ to last 6 [8: 1: 5: 0: 3: 7: 1] sts, K1 [1: 1: 1: 0: 1: 1: 1], P2 [2: 0: 2: 0: 2: 2: 0], K2 [2: 0: 2: 0: 0: 2: 0], P1 [3: 0: 0: 0: 0: 2: 0].
Row 5: K1 [3: 0: 0: 0: 0: 2: 0], P2 [2: 0: 2: 0: 0: 2: 0], K2 [2: 0: 2: 0: 2: 2: 0], P1 [1: 1: 1: 0: 1: 1: 1], ★P1, K2, P2, K1, P2, C2F, P2, K1, P2, K2, P1, rep from ★ to last 6 [8: 1: 5: 0: 3: 7: 1] sts, P1 [1: 1: 1: 0: 1: 1: 1], K2 [2: 0: 2: 0: 2: 2: 0], P2 [2: 0: 2: 0: 0: 2: 0], K1 [3: 0: 0: 0: 0: 2: 0].
Row 6: As row 4.
Row 7: K1 [3: 0: 0: 0: 0: 2: 0], P2 [2: 0: 2: 0: 0: 2: 0], K2 [2: 0: 2: 0: 2: 2: 0], P1 [1: 1: 1: 0: 1: 1: 1], ★P1, K2, P2, (Cr2L, Cr2R) twice, P2, K2, P1, rep from ★ to last 6 [8: 1: 5: 0: 3: 7: 1] sts, P1 [1: 1: 1: 0: 1: 1: 1], K2 [2: 0: 2: 0: 2: 2: 0], P2 [2: 0: 2: 0: 0: 2: 0], K1 [3: 0: 0: 0: 0: 2: 0].
Row 8: As row 2.
Rows 9 to 16: As rows 1 to 8.
Change to 4mm (US 6) needles.
Beg with a K row, work in st st for 2 rows, inc 1 st at beg of first of these rows and ending with RS facing for next row.
103 [107: 111: 119: 127: 133: 141: 147] sts.
Beg and ending rows as indicated, using the **fairisle** technique as described on the information page, and working chart rows 1 to 106 once only and then repeating chart rows 107 and 108 throughout, work from chart as folls:
Cont in patt until work meas 39 [39: 38: 41: 40: 42: 41: 43] cm, ending with RS facing for next row.

Shape armholes

(**Note**: armhole shaping is **NOT** shown on chart.)
Keeping patt correct, cast off 4 [5: 5: 6: 6: 7: 7: 8] sts at beg of next 2 rows.
95 [97: 101: 107: 115: 119: 127: 131] sts.
Dec 1 st at each end of next 5 [5: 7: 7: 9: 9: 11: 11] rows, then on foll 2 [2: 1: 2: 2: 2: 2: 3] alt

rows, then on foll 4th row.
79 [81: 83: 87: 91: 95: 99: 101] sts.
Cont straight until armhole meas 21 [21: 22: 22: 23: 23: 24: 24] cm, ending with RS facing for next row.

Shape shoulders

Cast off 6 [6: 6: 7: 7: 8: 9: 9] sts at beg of next 4 rows, then 5 [6: 7: 7: 8: 8: 8: 9] sts at beg of foll 2 rows. 45 [45: 45: 45: 47: 47: 47: 47] sts.

Shape funnel neck

Change to 3¾mm (US 5) needles.
Work a further 27 rows on these 45 [45: 45: 45: 47: 47: 47: 47] sts only, ending with **WS** facing for next row.
Using a 4mm (US 6) needle, cast off in patt (on **WS**).

SLEEVES

Using 3¾mm (US 5) needles and yarn A cast on 58 [58: 60: 60: 62: 62: 64: 64] sts.
Row 1 (RS): P0 [0: 0: 0: 1: 1: 2: 2], K1 [1: 2: 2: 2: 2: 2: 2], P1, ★P1, K2, P3, C2B, P2, C2B, P3, K2, P1, rep from ★ to last 2 [2: 3: 3: 4: 4: 5: 5] sts, P1, K1 [1: 2: 2: 2: 2: 2: 2], P0 [0: 0: 0: 1: 1: 2: 2].
Row 2: K0 [0: 0: 0: 1: 1: 2: 2], P1 [1: 2: 2: 2:

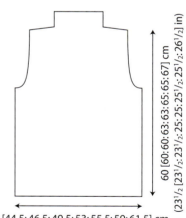

60 [60: 60: 63: 63: 65: 65: 67] cm
(23½ [23½: 23½: 25: 25: 25½: 25½: 26½] in)

43 [44.5: 46.5: 49.5: 53: 55.5: 59: 61.5] cm
(17 [17½: 18½: 19½: 21: 22: 23: 24] in)

44 [44: 45: 45: 46: 46: 45: 45] cm
(17½ [17½: 17½: 17½: 18: 18: 17½: 17½] in)

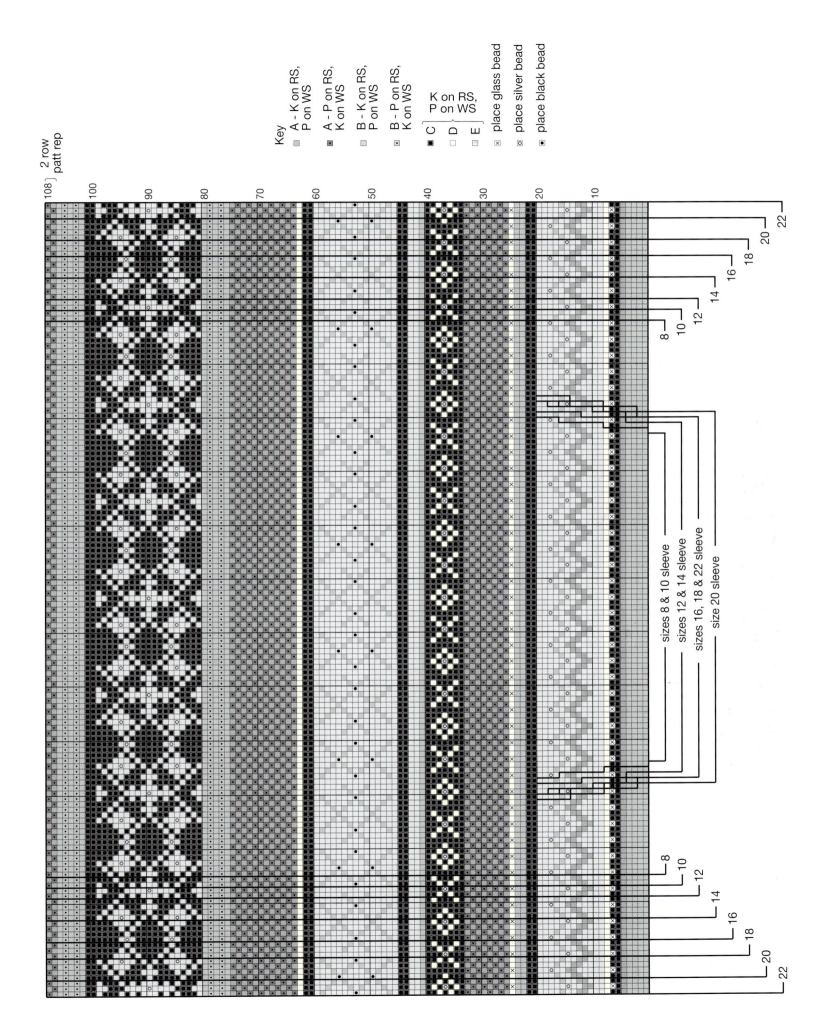

Key

A - K on RS,
P on WS

A - P on RS,
K on WS

B - K on RS,
P on WS

B - P on RS,
K on WS

K on RS,
P on WS

C
D
E

place glass bead

place silver bead

place black bead

2 row
patt rep

108

100

90

80

70

60

50

40

30

20

10

sizes 8 & 10 sleeve

sizes 12 & 14 sleeve

sizes 16, 18 & 22 sleeve

size 20 sleeve

2: 2: 2], K1, *K1, P2, K3, P2, K2, P2, K3, P2, K1, rep from * to last 2 [2: 3: 3: 4: 4: 5: 5] sts, K1, P1 [1: 2: 2: 2: 2: 2: 2], K0 [0: 0: 0: 1: 1: 2: 2].
Row 3: P0 [0: 0: 0: 0: 1: 1: 2: 2], K1 [1: 2: 2: 2: 2: 2: 2], P1, *P1, K2, P2, (Cr2R, Cr2L) twice, P2, K2, P1, rep from * to last 2 [2: 3: 3: 4: 4: 5: 5] sts, P1, K1 [1: 2: 2: 2: 2: 2: 2], P0 [0: 0: 0: 1: 1: 2: 2].
Row 4: K0 [0: 0: 0: 1: 1: 2: 2], P1 [1: 2: 2: 2: 2: 2: 2], K1, *K1, P2, K2, P2, K2, P2, K1, rep from * to last 2 [2: 3: 3: 4: 4: 5: 5] sts, K1, P1 [1: 2: 2: 2: 2: 2: 2], K0 [0: 0: 0: 1: 1: 2: 2].
Row 5: P0 [0: 0: 0: 1: 1: 2: 2], K1 [1: 2: 2: 2: 2: 2: 2], P1, *P1, K2, P2, K1, P2, C2F, P2, K1, P2, K2, P1, rep from * to last 2 [2: 3: 3: 4: 4: 5: 5] sts, P1, K1 [1: 2: 2: 2: 2: 2: 2], P0 [0: 0: 0: 1: 1: 2: 2].
Row 6: As row 4.
Row 7: P0 [0: 0: 0: 0: 1: 1: 2: 2], K1 [1: 2: 2: 2: 2: 2: 2], P1, *P1, K2, P2, (Cr2L, Cr2R) twice, P2, K2, P1, rep from * to last 2 [2: 3: 3: 4: 4: 5: 5] sts, P1, K1 [1: 2: 2: 2: 2: 2: 2], P0 [0: 0: 0: 1: 1: 2: 2].
Row 8: As row 2.
Rows 9 to 16: As rows 1 to 8.
Change to 4mm (US 6) needles.
Beg with a K row, work in st st for 2 rows, inc

1 st at beg of first of these rows and ending with RS facing for next row.
59 [59: 61: 61: 63: 63: 65: 65] sts.
Row 19 (RS): K1, *P1, K1, rep from * to end.
Row 20: As row 19.
These 2 rows form moss st.
Cont in moss st, inc 1 st at each end of 3rd [3rd: 3rd: next: next: next: next] and foll 0 [0: 8th: 6th: 6th: 6th: 6th: 0] row.
61 [61: 65: 65: 67: 67: 69: 67] sts.
Work 7 [7: 3: 1: 5: 1: 1: 3] rows, ending with RS facing for next row. (12 [12: 16: 10: 14: 10: 10: 6] rows of moss st completed.)
Beg and ending rows as indicated, work from chart as folls:
Inc 1 st at each end of next [next: 5th: 5th: 5th: 5th: 3rd] and every foll 8th [8th: 8th: 8th: 6th: 6th: 6th] row to 71 [81: 81: 85: 87: 75: 79: 87] sts, then on every foll 10th [-: 10th: -: -: 8th: 8th: 8th] row until there are 79 [-: 83: -: -: 89: 91: 93] sts, taking inc sts into patt.
Cont straight until sleeve meas approx 44 [44: 45: 45: 46: 46: 45: 45] cm, ending after same

chart row as on back and front to armhole shaping and with RS facing for next row.
Shape top
(**Note:** sleeve top shaping is **NOT** shown on chart.)
Keeping patt correct, cast off 4 [5: 5: 6: 6: 7: 7: 8] sts at beg of next 2 rows.
71 [71: 73: 73: 75: 75: 77: 77] sts.
Dec 1 st at each end of next 3 rows, then on foll alt row, then on every foll 4th row until 53 [53: 55: 55: 57: 57: 59: 59] sts rem.
Work 1 row.
Dec 1 st at each end of next and every foll alt row to 47 sts, then on foll 3 rows, ending with RS facing for next row. 41 sts.
Cast off 8 sts at beg of next 2 rows.
Cast off rem 25 sts.

MAKING UP
Press as described on the information page.
Join shoulder and funnel neck seams using back stitch, or mattress stitch if preferred.
See information page for finishing instructions, setting in sleeves using the set-in method.

Main image page 20

SIZE

8	10	12	14	16	18	20	22	
To fit bust

| 82 | 87 | 92 | 97 | 102 | 107 | 112 | 117 | cm |
| 32 | 34 | 36 | 38 | 40 | 42 | 44 | 46 | in |

YARN
Rowan Wool Cotton, Kidsilk Haze and Kidsilk Night
A Wool Cotton Misty 903

9	10	10	11	11	12	12	13	x 50gm

B Kidsilk Haze Smoke 605

1	1	1	1	1	1	1	1	x 25gm

C Kidsilk Night Moonlight 608

1	1	1	1	1	1	1	1	x 25gm

D Kidsilk Night Starlight 607

1	1	1	1	1	1	1	1	x 25gm

NEEDLES
1 pair 3¼mm (no 10) (US 3) needles
1 pair 4mm (no 8) (US 6) needles
1 pair 5mm (no 6) (US 8) needles
1 pair 8mm (no 0) (US 11) needles

TENSION
22 sts and 30 rows to 10 cm measured over stocking stitch using 4mm (US 6) needles and yarn A.

BACK
Using 3¼mm (US 3) needles and yarn A cast on 97 [101: 105: 111: 119: 125: 131: 139] sts.
Row 1 (RS): K1, *P1, K1, rep from * to end.

Row 2: P1, *K1, P1, rep from * to end.
These 2 rows form rib.
Cont in rib for a further 7 rows, ending with **WS** facing for next row.
Row 10 (WS): Purl.
Change to 4mm (US 6) needles.
Beg with a K row, work in st st for 8 rows.
Dec 1 st at each end of next and every foll 8th row to 91 [95: 99: 105: 113: 119: 125: 133] sts, then on every foll 6th row until 83 [87: 91: 97: 105: 111: 117: 125] sts rem.
Work 9 rows, ending with RS facing for next row.
Inc 1 st at each end of next and every foll 6th row until there are 93 [97: 101: 107: 115: 121: 127: 135] sts.
Cont straight until back meas 40 [40: 39: 42: 41: 43: 42: 44] cm, ending with RS facing for next row.
Shape armholes
Cast off 5 [6: 6: 7: 7: 8: 8: 9] sts at beg of next 2 rows.
83 [85: 89: 93: 101: 105: 111: 117] sts.
Dec 1 st at each end of next 3 [3: 5: 5: 7: 7: 9: 9] rows, then on foll 2 [2: 1: 1: 2: 2: 1: 3] alt rows. 73 [75: 77: 81: 83: 87: 91: 93] sts.
Cont straight until armhole meas 20 [20: 21: 21: 22: 22: 23: 23] cm, ending with RS facing for next row.
Shape shoulders and back neck
Next row (RS): Cast off 8 [9: 9: 10: 10: 11: 12: 13] sts, K until there are 13 [13: 14: 15: 15:

16: 17: 17] sts on right needle and turn, leaving rem sts on a holder.
Work each side of neck separately.
Cast off 4 sts at beg of next row.
Cast off rem 9 [9: 10: 11: 11: 12: 13: 13] sts.
With RS facing, rejoin yarn to rem sts, cast off centre 31 [31: 31: 31: 33: 33: 33: 33] sts, K to end.
Complete to match first side, reversing shapings.

FRONT
Work as given for back until 14 [14: 14: 16: 16: 16: 18: 18] rows less have been worked than on back to beg of shoulder shaping, ending with RS facing for next row.
Shape neck
Next row (RS): K24 [25: 26: 29: 29: 31: 34: 35] and turn, leaving rem sts on a holder.
Work each side of neck separately.
Dec 1 st at neck edge of next 6 rows, then on foll 1 [1: 1: 2: 2: 2: 3: 3] alt rows.
17 [18: 19: 21: 21: 23: 25: 26] sts.
Work 5 rows, ending with RS facing for next row.
Shape shoulder
Cast off 8 [9: 9: 10: 10: 11: 12: 13] sts at beg of next row.
Work 1 row.
Cast off rem 9 [9: 10: 11: 11: 12: 13: 13] sts.
With RS facing, rejoin yarn to rem sts, cast off centre 25 [25: 25: 23: 25: 25: 23: 23] sts,

K to end.
Complete to match first side, reversing shapings.

SLEEVES

Using 8mm (US 11) needles and one strand each of yarn B, C and D held together cast on 47 [47: 49: 49: 51: 51: 53: 53] sts.
Beg with a K row, work in st st for 13 rows, ending with WS facing for next row.
Row 14 (WS): (P8 [8: 8: 8: 9: 9: 9: 9], P2tog) twice, P7 [7: 9: 9: 7: 7: 9: 9], (P2tog, P8 [8: 8: 9: 9: 9: 9]) twice.
43 [43: 45: 45: 47: 47: 49: 49] sts.
Change to 4mm (US 6) needles.
Join in yarn A.
Row 15: Using yarn A K1, *using yarns B, C and D held together K1, using yarn A K1, rep from * to end.
Row 16: Using yarns B, C and D held together P1, *using yarn A P1, using yarns B, C and D held together P1, rep from * to end.
Rows 17 to 20: As rows 15 and 16, twice.
Break off yarns B, C and D and cont using yarn A only.
Beg with a K row, work in st st, shaping sides by inc 1 st at each end of 5th and every foll 4th row to 57 [63: 61: 67: 67: 73: 73: 79] sts, then on every foll 6th row until there are 77 [79: 81: 83: 85: 87: 89: 91] sts.
Cont straight until sleeve meas 45 [45: 46: 46: 47: 47: 46: 46] cm, ending with RS facing for next row.

Shape top

Cast off 5 [6: 6: 7: 7: 8: 8: 9] sts at beg of next 2 rows.
67 [67: 69: 69: 71: 71: 73: 73] sts.
Dec 1 st at each end of next 7 rows, then on every foll alt row to 29 sts, then on foll 5 rows, ending with RS facing for next row. 19 sts.
Cast off 3 sts at beg of next 2 rows.
Cast off rem 13 sts.

MAKING UP

Press as described on the information page.
Join right shoulder seam using back stitch, or mattress stitch if preferred.
Collar
With RS facing, using 3¼ mm (US 3) needles and yarn A, pick up and knit 15 [15: 15: 17: 17: 17: 19: 19] sts down left side of neck, 25 [25: 25: 23: 25: 25: 23: 23] sts from front, 15 [15: 15: 17: 17: 17: 19: 19] sts up right side of neck, then 38 [38: 38: 38: 40: 40: 40: 40] sts from back.
93 [93: 93: 95: 99: 99: 101: 101] sts.
Beg with row 2, work in rib as given for back for 19 rows, ending with RS facing for next row.
Break off yarn A and join in one strand of yarns B, C and D held together.
Change to 5mm (US 8) needles.
Beg with a K row, work in st st for 6 rows.
Cast off.
See information page for finishing instructions, setting in sleeves using the set-in method.

42.5 [44: 46: 48.5: 52.5: 55: 57.5: 61.5] cm
(16½ [17½: 18: 19: 20½: 21½: 22½: 24] in)

60 [60: 60: 63: 63: 65: 65: 67] cm
(23½ [23½: 23½: 25: 25: 25½: 25½: 26½] in)

45 [45: 46: 46: 47: 47: 46: 46] cm
(17½ [17½: 18: 18: 18½: 18½: 18: 18] in)

Main image page 54

SIZE

	S	M	L	XL	
	8/10	12/14	16/18	20/22	
To fit bust					
	82-87	92-97	102-107	112-117	cm
	32-34	36-38	40-42	44-46	in

YARN

Rowan Felted Tweed, Kid Classic, 4 ply Soft and Lurex Shimmer

A	Felted Tweed Phantom		153		
	7	8	9	10	x 50gm
B	Kid Clas Bear 817				
	2	2	2	2	x 50gm
C	4ply Soft Black 383				
	1	1	1	1	x 50gm
D	Felted Tweed Ginger 154				
	1	1	1	1	x 50gm
E	*Lurex Shimmer Bronze 335				
	1	1	1	1	x 25gm
F	Lurex Shimmer Pewter 333				
	1	1	1	1	x 25gm

*Use Lurex Shimmer DOUBLE.

NEEDLES

1 pair 3¼ mm (no 10) (US 3) needles
1 pair 3¾ mm (no 9) (US 5) needles
1 pair 5mm (no 6) (US 8) needles
2 double-pointed 3¼ mm (no 10) (US 3) needles
2 double-pointed 3¾ mm (no 9) (US 5) needles
Cable needle

BEADS – approx 85 x 01016 beads

TENSION

23 sts and 32 rows to 10 cm measured over pattern using yarn A and 3¾ mm (US 5) needles.

SPECIAL ABBREVIATIONS

C6B = slip next 3 sts onto cable needle and leave at back of work, K3, then K3 from cable needle; **C6F** = slip next 3 sts onto cable needle and leave at front of work, K3, then K3 from cable needle; **Cr4R** = slip next st onto cable needle and leave at back of work, K3, then P1 from cable needle; **Cr4L** = slip next 3 sts onto cable needle and leave at front of work, P1, then K3 from cable needle.

BACK

Using 3¾ mm (US 5) needles and yarn A cast on 101 [113: 127: 141] sts.
Row 1 (RS): K6 [3: 1: 8], (yfwd, sl 1, K1, psso, K2tog, K4, yfwd, K1) 1 [0: 1: 1] times, *yfwd, K4, sl 1, K1, psso, K2tog, yfwd, K1, yfwd, sl 1, K1, psso, K2tog, K4, yfwd, K1, rep from * to last 14 [2: 9: 16] sts, (yfwd, K4, sl 1, K1, psso, K2tog, yfwd) 1 [0: 1: 1] times, K6 [2: 1: 8].
Row 2 and every foll alt row: Purl.
Row 3: K6 [3: 1: 8], (yfwd, K1, sl 1, K2tog, psso, K4, yfwd, K1) 1 [0: 1: 1] times, *yfwd, K4, K3tog, (K1, yfwd) twice, K1, sl 1, K2tog, psso,

AUTUMN LEAVES BY MARTIN STOREY

163

K4, yfwd, K1, rep from * to last 14 [2: 9: 16] sts, (yfwd, K4, K3tog, K1, yfwd) 1 [0: 1: 1] times, K6 [2: 1: 8].

Row 5: K6 [3: 1: 8], (yfwd, K2, sl 1, K1, psso, K5) 1 [0: 1: 1] times, *K4, K2tog, K2, yfwd, K1, yfwd, K2, sl 1, K1, psso, K5, rep from * to last 14 [2: 9: 16] sts, (K4, K2tog, K2, yfwd) 1 [0: 1: 1] times, K6 [2: 1: 8].

Row 7: K6 [3: 1: 8], (yfwd, K3, sl 1, K1, psso, K4) 1 [0: 1: 1] times, *K3, K2tog, K3, yfwd, K1, yfwd, K3, sl 1, K1, psso, K4, rep from * to last 14 [2: 9: 16] sts, (K3, K2tog, K3, yfwd) 1 [0: 1: 1] times, K6 [2: 1: 8].

Row 9: K6 [3: 1: 8], (yfwd, K4, sl 1, K1, psso, K2tog, yfwd, K1) 1 [0: 1: 1] times, *yfwd, sl 1, K1, psso, K2tog, K4, yfwd, K1, yfwd, K4, sl 1, K1, psso, K2tog, yfwd, K1, rep from * to last 14 [2: 9: 16] sts, (yfwd, sl 1, K1, psso, K2tog, K4, yfwd) 1 [0: 1: 1] times, K6 [2: 1: 8].

Row 11: K6 [3: 1: 8], (yfwd, K4, K3tog, K1, yfwd, K1) 1 [0: 1: 1] times, *yfwd, K1, sl 1, K2tog, psso, K4, yfwd, K1, yfwd, K4, K3tog, K1, yfwd, K1, rep from * to last 14 [2: 9: 16] sts, (yfwd, K1, sl 1, K2tog, psso, K4, yfwd) 1 [0: 1: 1] times, K6 [2: 1: 8].

Row 13: K10 [3: 5: 12], (K2tog, K2, yfwd, K1) 1 [0: 1: 1] times, *yfwd, K2, sl 1, K1, psso, K9, K2tog, K2, yfwd, K1, rep from * to last 14 [2: 9: 16] sts, (yfwd, K2, sl 1, K1, psso) 1 [0: 1: 1] times, K10 [2: 5: 12].

Row 15: K9 [3: 4: 11], (K2tog, K3, yfwd, K1) 1 [0: 1: 1] times, *yfwd, K3, sl 1, K1, psso, K7, K2tog, K3, yfwd, K1, rep from * to last 14 [2: 9: 16] sts, (yfwd, K3, sl 1, K1, psso) 1 [0: 1: 1] times, K9 [2: 4: 11].

Row 16: As row 2.
These 16 rows form patt.
Cont in patt, shaping side seams by dec 1 st at each end of 5th and every foll 10th row to 95 [107: 121: 135] sts, then on every foll 8th row until 91 [103: 117: 131] sts rem.
Cont straight until back meas 21 [22: 23: 24] cm, ending with RS facing for next row.
Inc 1 st at each end of next and every foll 10th row until there are 101 [113: 127: 141] sts, taking inc sts into patt.
Work 9 rows, ending with RS facing for next row.

Shape armholes
Keeping patt correct, cast off 6 [7: 8: 9] sts at beg of next 2 rows. 89 [99: 111: 123] sts.
Dec 1 st at each end of next 3 [5: 7: 9] rows, then on foll 3 [4: 5: 6] alt rows, then on foll 4th row. 75 [79: 85: 91] sts.
Cont straight until armhole meas 20 [21: 22: 23] cm, ending with RS facing for next row.

Shape shoulders and back neck
Next row (RS): Cast off 5 [6: 7: 8] sts, patt until there are 9 [10: 11: 13] sts on right needle and turn, leaving rem sts on a holder.
Work each side of neck separately.
Cast off 4 sts at beg of next row.
Cast off rem 5 [6: 7: 9] sts.
With RS facing, rejoin yarn to rem sts, cast off centre 47 [47: 49: 49] sts, patt to end.
Complete to match first side, reversing shapings.

LEFT FRONT
Using 3¾ mm (US 5) needles and yarn A cast on 51 [57: 64: 71] sts.
Row 1 (RS): K6 [3: 1: 8], (yfwd, sl 1, K1, psso, K2tog, K4, yfwd, K1) 1 [0: 1: 1] times, *yfwd, K4, sl 1, K1, psso, K2tog, yfwd, K1, yfwd, sl 1, K1, psso, K2tog, K4, yfwd, K1, rep from * to end.
Row 2 and every foll alt row: Purl.
Row 3: K6 [3: 1: 8], (yfwd, K1, sl 1, K2tog, psso, K4, yfwd, K1) 1 [0: 1: 1] times, *yfwd, K4,

K3tog, (K1, yfwd) twice, K1, sl 1, K2tog, psso, K4, yfwd, K1, rep from * to end.
Row 5: K6 [3: 1: 8], (yfwd, K2, sl 1, K1, psso, K5) 1 [0: 1: 1] times, *K4, K2tog, K2, yfwd, K1, yfwd, K2, sl 1, K1, psso, K5, rep from * to end.
Row 7: K6 [3: 1: 8], (yfwd, K3, sl 1, K1, psso, K4) 1 [0: 1: 1] times, *K3, K2tog, K3, yfwd, K1, yfwd, K3, sl 1, K1, psso, K4, rep from * to end.
Row 9: K6 [3: 1: 8], (yfwd, K4, sl 1, K1, psso, K2tog, yfwd, K1) 1 [0: 1: 1] times, *yfwd, sl 1, K1, psso, K2tog, K4, yfwd, K1, yfwd, K4, sl 1, K1, psso, K2tog, yfwd, K1, rep from * to end.
Row 11: K6 [3: 1: 8], (yfwd, K4, K3tog, K1, yfwd, K1) 1 [0: 1: 1] times, *yfwd, K1, sl 1, K2tog, psso, K4, yfwd, K1, yfwd, K4, K3tog, K1, yfwd, K1, rep from * to end.
Row 13: K10 [3: 5: 12], (K2tog, K2, yfwd, K1) 1 [0: 1: 1] times, *yfwd, K2, sl 1, K1, psso, K9, K2tog, K2, yfwd, K1, rep from * to end.
Row 15: K9 [3: 4: 11], (K2tog, K3, yfwd, K1) 1 [0: 1: 1] times, *yfwd, K3, sl 1, K1, psso, K7, K2tog, K3, yfwd, K1, rep from * to end.
Row 16: As row 2.
These 16 rows form patt.
Cont in patt, shaping side seams by dec 1 st at beg of 5th and every foll 10th row to 48 [54: 61: 68] sts, then on every foll 8th row until 46 [52: 59: 66] sts rem.
Cont straight until left front meas 21 [22: 23: 24] cm, ending with RS facing for next row.
Inc 1 st at beg of next and every foll 10th row until there are 49 [55: 62: 69] sts, taking inc sts into patt.
Work 7 rows, ending with RS facing for next row.

Shape front slope
Keeping patt correct, dec 1 st at end of next and foll 10 alt rows **and at same time** inc 1 st at beg of 3rd and foll 10th row.
40 [46: 53: 60] sts.
Work 1 row, ending with RS facing for next row.

Shape armhole
Keeping patt correct, cast off 6 [7: 8: 9] sts at beg and dec 1 st at end of next row.
33 [38: 44: 50] sts.
Work 1 row.
Dec 1 st at armhole edge of next 3 [5: 7: 9] rows, then on foll 3 [4: 5: 6] alt rows, then on foll 4th row **and at same time** dec 1 st at front slope edge of next and foll 4 [2: 3: 1] alt rows, then on every foll 4th row.
20 [22: 24: 27] sts.
Dec 1 st at front slope edge **only** of 4th [4th: 2nd: 2nd] and every foll 4th row until 10 [12: 14: 17] sts rem.
Cont straight until left front matches back to beg of shoulder shaping, ending with RS facing for next row.

Shape shoulder
Cast off 5 [6: 7: 8] sts at beg of next row.
Work 1 row.
Cast off rem 5 [6: 7: 9] sts.

RIGHT FRONT
Using 3¾ mm (US 5) needles and yarn A cast on 51 [57: 64: 71] sts.
Row 1 (RS): K1, *yfwd, K4, sl 1, K1, psso, K2tog, yfwd, K1, yfwd, sl 1, K1, psso, K2tog, K4, yfwd, K1, rep from * to last 14 [2: 9: 16] sts, (yfwd, K4, sl 1, K1, psso, K2tog, yfwd) 1 [0: 1: 1] times, K6 [2: 1: 8].
Row 2 and every foll alt row: Purl.
Row 3: K1, *yfwd, K4, K3tog, (K1, yfwd) twice, K1, sl 1, K2tog, psso, K4, yfwd, K1, rep

from * to last 14 [2: 9: 16] sts, (yfwd, K4, K3tog, K1, yfwd) 1 [0: 1: 1] times, K6 [2: 1: 8].
Row 5: K1, *K4, K2tog, K2, yfwd, K1, yfwd, K2, sl 1, K1, psso, K5, rep from * to last 14 [2: 9: 16] sts, (K4, K2tog, K2, yfwd) 1 [0: 1: 1] times, K6 [2: 1: 8].
Row 7: K1, *K3, K2tog, K3, yfwd, K1, yfwd, K3, sl 1, K1, psso, K4, rep from * to last 14 [2: 9: 16] sts, (K3, K2tog, K3, yfwd) 1 [0: 1: 1] times, K6 [2: 1: 8].
Row 9: K1, *yfwd, sl 1, K1, psso, K2tog, K4, yfwd, K1, yfwd, K4, sl 1, K1, psso, K2tog, yfwd, K1, rep from * to last 14 [2: 9: 16] sts, (yfwd, sl 1, K1, psso, K2tog, K4, yfwd) 1 [0: 1: 1] times, K6 [2: 1: 8].
Row 11: K1, *yfwd, K1, sl 1, K2tog, psso, K4, yfwd, K1, yfwd, K4, K3tog, K1, yfwd, K1, rep from * to last 14 [2: 9: 16] sts, (yfwd, K1, sl 1, K2tog, psso, K4, yfwd) 1 [0: 1: 1] times, K6 [2: 1: 8].
Row 13: K1, *yfwd, K2, sl 1, K1, psso, K9, K2tog, K2, yfwd, K1, rep from * to last 14 [2: 9: 16] sts, (yfwd, K2, sl 1, K1, psso) 1 [0: 1: 1] times, K10 [2: 5: 12].
Row 15: K1, *yfwd, K3, sl 1, K1, psso, K7, K2tog, K3, yfwd, K1, rep from * to last 14 [2: 9: 16] sts, (yfwd, K3, sl 1, K1, psso) 1 [0: 1: 1] times, K9 [2: 4: 11].
Row 16: As row 2.
These 16 rows form patt.
Cont in patt, shaping side seams by dec 1 st at end of 5th and every foll 10th row to 48 [54: 61: 68] sts, then on every foll 8th row until 46 [52: 59: 66] sts rem.
Complete to match left front, reversing shapings.

SLEEVES
Using 3¾ mm (US 5) needles and yarn A cast on 57 [59: 61: 63] sts.
Row 1 (RS): K2 [3: 4: 5], *yfwd, sl 1, K1, psso, K2tog, K4, yfwd, K1, yfwd, K4, sl 1, K1, psso, K2tog, yfwd, K1, rep from * to last 1 [2: 3: 4] sts, K1 [2: 3: 4].
Row 2 and every foll alt row: Purl.
Row 3: K2 [3: 4: 5], *yfwd, K1, sl 1, K2tog, psso, K4, yfwd, K1, yfwd, K4, K3tog, K1, yfwd, K1, rep from * to last 1 [2: 3: 4] sts, K1 [2: 3: 4].
Row 5: K2 [3: 4: 5], *yfwd, K2, sl 1, K1, psso, K9, K2tog, K2, yfwd, K1, rep from * to last 1 [2: 3: 4] sts, K1 [2: 3: 4].
Row 7: K2 [3: 4: 5], *yfwd, K3, sl 1, K1, psso, K7, K2tog, K3, yfwd, K1, rep from * to last 1 [2: 3: 4] sts, K1 [2: 3: 4].
Row 9: (Inc in first st) 0 [0: 0: 1] times, K2 [3: 4: 4], *yfwd, K4, sl 1, K1, psso, K2tog, yfwd, K1, yfwd, sl 1, K1, psso, K2tog, K4, yfwd, K1, rep from * to last 1 [2: 3: 4] sts, K1 [2: 3: 3], (inc in last st) 0 [0: 0: 1] times.
57 [59: 61: 65] sts.
Row 11: (Inc in first st) 0 [1: 1: 0] times, K2 [2: 3: 6], *yfwd, K4, K3tog, (K1, yfwd) twice, K1, sl 1, K2tog, psso, K4, yfwd, K1, rep from * to last 1 [2: 3: 5] sts, K1 [1: 2: 5], (inc in last st) 0 [1: 1: 0] times.
57 [61: 63: 65] sts.
Row 13: (Inc in first st) 1 [0: 0: 0] times, K1 [4: 5: 6], *K4, K2tog, K2, yfwd, K1, yfwd, K2, sl 1, K1, psso, K5, rep from * to last 1 [3: 4: 5] sts, K0 [3: 4: 5], (inc in last st) 1 [0: 0: 0] times. 59 [61: 63: 65] sts.
Row 15: K3 [4: 5: 6], *K3, K2tog, K3, yfwd, K1, yfwd, K3, sl 1, K1, psso, K4, rep from * to last 2 [3: 4: 5] sts, K2 [3: 4: 5].
Row 16: As row 2.
These 16 rows form patt and beg sleeve shaping.
Cont in patt, shaping sides by inc 1 st at each end of 11th [9th: 7th: 3rd] and every foll

14th [12th: 12th: 10th] row to 75 [71: 83: 75] sts, then on every foll - [14th: -: 12th] row until there are - [79: -: 87] sts, taking inc sts into patt. Cont straight until sleeve meas 44 [45: 46: 46] cm, ending with RS facing for next row.

Shape top
Keeping patt correct, cast off 6 [7: 8: 9] sts at beg of next 2 rows. 63 [65: 67: 69] sts.
Dec 1 st at each end of next 3 rows, then on foll 3 alt rows, then on every foll 4th row until 37 [39: 41: 43] sts rem.
Work 1 row.
Dec 1 st at each end of next and foll 1 [2: 3: 4] alt rows, then on foll 5 rows, ending with RS facing for next row.
Cast off rem 23 sts.

MAKING UP
Press as described on the information page.
Join shoulder seams using back stitch, or mattress stitch if preferred.
Front bands (both alike)
Using 5mm (US 8) needles and yarn B cast on 28 sts.
Working rows 1 and 2 **once only** and then repeating rows 3 to 40 throughout, work in patt from chart until band, when slightly stretched, fits up front opening edge, up front slope and across to centre back neck, ending with RS facing for next row.
Cast off.
Join cast-off ends of bands, then slip stitch bands in place.
See information page for finishing instructions, setting in sleeves using the set-in method.
Leaf A (make 4)
Using double-pointed 3¼ mm (US 3) needles and yarn C cast on 5 sts.
Row 1 (RS): K5, ★without turning work push these 5 sts to opposite end of needle and bring yarn to opposite end of work, pulling it quite tightly across back of these 5 sts. Using other needle K these 5 sts again; rep from ★ until stalk is 3 cm long.
Change to 3¼ mm (US 3) needles and cont as folls:
Row 1 (RS): K1, (inc in next st, K1) twice. 7 sts.
Row 2 and every foll alt row to row 14: Purl.
Row 3: K3, M1, K1, M1, K3. 9 sts.
Row 5: K4, M1, K1, M1, K4. 11 sts.
Row 7: K5, M1, K1, M1, K5. 13 sts.
Row 9: K6, M1, K1, M1, K6. 15 sts.
Row 11: K7, M1, K1, M1, K7. 17 sts.
Row 13: K8, M1, K1, M1, K8. 19 sts.
Row 15: Cast off 3 sts (one st on right needle), K5, M1, K1, M1, K9. 18 sts.
Row 16 (WS): Cast off 3 sts, P to end. 15 sts.
Row 17: As row 11.
Row 18: Purl.
Row 19: As row 13. 19 sts.
Row 20: Purl.
Beg with a K row, work in st st as folls:
Cast off 3 sts at beg of next 2 rows. 13 sts.
Work 4 rows.
Cast off 3 sts at beg of next 2 rows. 7 sts.
Row 29 (RS): sl 1, K1, psso, K3, K2tog.
Row 30: P5.
Row 31: sl 1, K1, psso, K1, K2tog.
Row 32: P3.
Row 33: sl 1, K2tog, psso and fasten off.
Leaf B (make 2)
Using double-pointed 3¾ mm (US 5) needles and yarn D cast on 3 sts.
Row 1 (RS): K3, ★without turning work push these 3 sts to opposite end of needle and bring yarn to opposite end of work, pulling it

quite tightly across back of these 3 sts. Using other needle K these 3 sts again; rep from ★ until stalk is 3 cm long.
Change to 3¾ mm (US 5) needles and cont as folls:
Row 1 (RS): K1, P1, K1.
Row 2: Inc knitwise in first st, P1, inc knitwise in last st. 5 sts.
Row 3: (P1, K1) twice, P1.
Row 4: Inc knitwise in first st, K1, P1, K1, inc knitwise in last st. 7 sts.
Row 5: (K1, P1) 3 times, K1.
Row 6: Inc knitwise in first st, (P1, K1) twice, P1, inc knitwise in last st. 9 sts.
These 6 rows form moss st and beg shaping.
Keeping moss st correct, inc 1 st at each end of 2nd and foll alt row. 13 sts.
★★Cast off 2 sts at beg of next 2 rows. 9 sts.
Inc 1 st at each end of 2nd and foll alt row. 13 sts.
Rep from ★★ once more.
Cast off 2 sts at beg of next 2 rows. 9 sts.
Work 1 row.
Dec 1 st at each end of next 3 rows, ending with RS facing for next row. 3 sts.
Row 29: sl 1, P2tog, psso and fasten off.
Leaf C (make 4)
Using double-pointed 3¾ mm (US 5) needles and yarn E DOUBLE cast on 5 sts.
Row 1 (RS): K5, ★without turning work push these 5 sts to opposite end of needle and bring yarn to opposite end of work, pulling it quite tightly across back of these 5 sts. Using other needle K these 5 sts again; rep from ★ until stalk is 3 cm long.
Change to 3¾ mm (US 5) needles and cont as folls:
Row 1 (RS): K2, yfwd, K1, yfwd, K2. 7 sts.
Row 2 and every foll alt row: Purl.
Row 3: K3, yfwd, K1, yfwd, K3. 9 sts.
Row 5: K4, yfwd, K1, yfwd, K4. 11 sts.
Row 7: K5, yfwd, K1, yfwd, K5. 13 sts.
Row 9: K6, yfwd, K1, yfwd, K6. 15 sts.
Row 11: sl 1, K1, psso, K to last 2 sts, K2tog.
Row 12: Purl.

Rows 13 to 22: As rows 11 and 12, 5 times. 3 sts.
Row 23: sl 1, K2tog, psso and fasten off.
Using photograph as a guide, sew leaves onto fronts, leaving stalk sections free. Using yarn F, embroider back stitch veins onto leaf A. Using yarn C, embroider back stitch veins onto leaf B. Attach beads around edge of leaf C as in photograph.

57 [59: 61: 63] cm (22½ [23: 24: 25] in)

44 [49: 55: 61.5] cm (17½ [19½: 21½: 24] in)

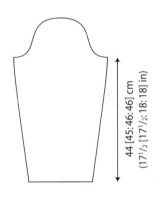

44 [45: 46: 46] cm (17½ [17½: 18: 18] in)

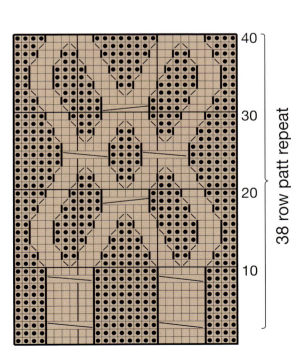

38 row patt repeat

Key
- ☐ K on RS, P on WS
- ▣ P on RS, K on WS
- C6B
- C6F
- Cr4R
- Cr4L

Main image page 11

VIKTOR BY MARIE WALLIN

SIZE

	S	M	L	XL	XXL	
To fit chest						
	102	107	112	117	122	cm
	40	42	44	46	48	in

YARN

Rowan Tapestry and Kid Classic
A Tapestry Leadmine 177

	11	12	12	13	14	x 50gm

B Kid Classic Smoke 831

	2	2	2	2	3	x 50gm

NEEDLES

1 pair 3¾ mm (no 9) (US 5) needles
1 pair 4mm (no 8) (US 6) needles

TENSION

23 sts and 28 rows to 10 cm measured over patterned stocking stitch using 4mm (US 6) needles.

Pattern note: The charts are an odd number of rows. On the first and every foll alt rep of chart, odd numbered rows are RS K rows, and even numbered rows are WS P rows. On the second and every foll alt rep of chart, odd numbered rows are **WS** P rows, and even numbered rows are **RS** K rows.

BACK and FRONT (both alike)
Using 3¾ mm (US 5) needles and yarn A cast on 126 [134: 142: 146: 154] sts.
Row 1 (RS): K2, *P2, K2, rep from * to end.
Row 2: P2, *K2, P2, rep from * to end.
These 2 rows form rib.
Work in rib for a further 18 rows, inc [dec: dec: inc: inc] 1 st at end of last row and ending with RS facing for next row.
127 [133: 141: 147: 155] sts.
Change to 4mm (US 6) needles.
Beg and ending rows as indicated, using the **fairisle** technique as described on the information page for the centre section and repeating the 45 row patt repeat throughout, work from chart for body, which is worked entirely in st st beg with a K row, as folls:
Cont straight until work meas 39 [40: 39: 40: 39] cm, ending with RS facing for next row.
Shape raglan armholes
Keeping patt correct, cast off 8 sts at beg of next 2 rows.
111 [117: 125: 131: 139] sts.
Dec 1 st at each end of next 1 [1: 5: 9: 11] rows, then on 1 [0: 0: 0: 0] foll 4th row, then on every foll alt row until 45 [45: 47: 47: 49] sts rem.
Work 1 row, ending with RS facing for next row.
Cast off.

SLEEVES

Using 3¾ mm (US 5) needles and yarn A cast on 62 [66: 66: 70: 70] sts.
Work in rib as given for back and front for

20 rows, inc [dec: inc: dec: inc] 1 st at end of last row and ending with RS facing for next row.
63 [65: 67: 69: 71] sts.
Change to 4mm (US 6) needles.
Beg and ending rows as indicated, using the **fairisle** technique as described on the information page for the centre section and repeating the 45 row patt repeat throughout, work from chart for sleeve, which is worked entirely in st st beg with a K row, as folls:

Inc 1 st at each end of 3rd and every foll 4th row to 95 [97: 93: 91: 93] sts, then on every foll 6th row until there are 109 [113: 115: 117: 121] sts.
Cont straight until sleeve meas 50 [52: 54: 56: 58] cm, ending with RS facing for next row.
Shape raglan
Cast off 8 sts at beg of next 2 rows.
93 [97: 99: 101: 105] sts.
Dec 1 st at each end of next and every foll alt

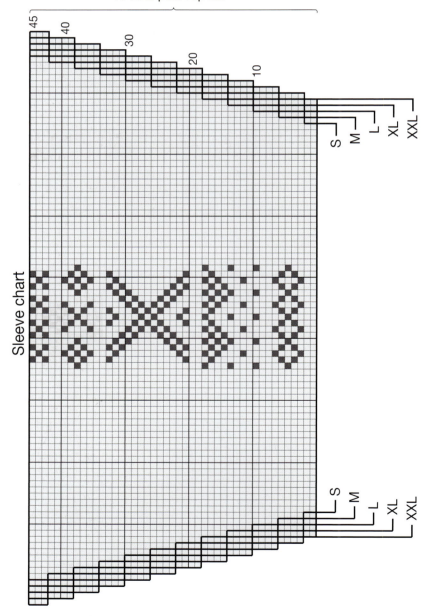

45 row patt repeat

Sleeve chart

166

row until 25 sts rem.
Work 1 row, ending with RS facing for
next row.
Break yarns and leave sts on a holder.

MAKING UP
Press as described on the information page.
Join both front and right back raglan seams
using back stitch, or mattress stitch if preferred.
Neckband
With RS facing, using 3¾ mm (US 5) needles
and yarn A, work across 25 sts on left sleeve
holder as folls: P2, patt 21 sts, P2, pick up and
knit 46 [46: 46: 46: 50] sts from front, work
across 25 sts on right sleeve holder as folls:
P2, patt 21 sts, P2, then pick up and knit
46 [46: 46: 46: 50] sts from back.
142 [142: 142: 142: 150] sts.
Row 1 (WS): (P2, K2) 12 [12: 12: 12: 13]
times, patt 21 sts, (K2, P2) 12 [12: 12: 12: 13]
times, K2, patt 21 sts, K2.
Row 2: P2, patt 21 sts, P2, (K2, P2) 12 [12: 12:
12: 13] times, patt 21 sts, (P2, K2) 12 [12: 12:
12: 13] times.
These 2 rows set the sts.
Cont as set for a further 14 rows, ending with
WS facing for next row.
Cast off in patt.
See information page for finishing instructions.

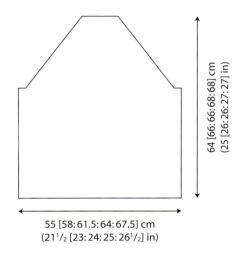

55 [58: 61.5: 64: 67.5] cm
(21½ [23: 24: 25: 26½] in)

64 [66: 66: 68: 68] cm
(25 [26: 26: 27: 27] in)

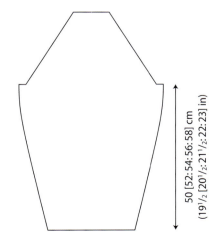

50 [52: 54: 56: 58] cm
(19½ [20½: 21½: 22: 23] in)

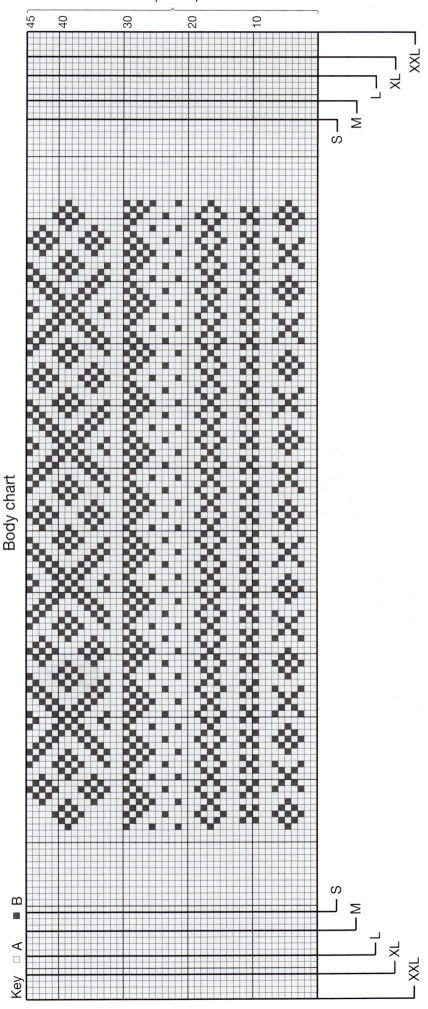

Body chart

45 row patt repeat

Key □ A ■ B

Main image page 74

SIZE

8	10	12	14	16	18	20	22	
To fit bust

82	87	92	97	102	107	112	117	cm
32	34	36	38	40	42	44	46	in

YARN

Rowan Wool Cotton

10	11	11	12	12	13	14	14	x 50gm
(photographed in Grand 954)

NEEDLES

1 pair 3¼ mm (no 10) (US 3) needles
1 pair 4mm (no 8) (US 6) needles
3¼ mm (no 10) (US 3) circular needle
Cable needle

BEADS – 664 [664: 671: 671: 691: 691: 698: 698] x 01007 beads

TENSION

28½ sts and 30 rows to 10 cm measured over pattern using 4mm (US 6) needles.

SPECIAL ABBREVIATIONS

C4B = slip next 2 sts onto cable needle and leave at back of work, K2, then K2 from cable needle; **C4F** = slip next 2 sts onto cable needle and leave at front of work, K2, then K2 from cable needle.

Beading note: Before starting to knit neckband, thread beads onto yarn. To do this, thread a fine sewing needle (one that will easily pass through the beads) with sewing thread. Knot ends of thread and then pass end of yarn through this loop. Thread a bead onto sewing thread and then gently slide it along and onto knitting yarn. Continue in this way until required number of beads are on yarn.

Pattern note: When working patt from chart, do not work the yfwd inc unless there are sufficient sts to work the corresponding K2tog or sl 1, K1, psso dec.

BACK

Using 3¼ mm (US 3) needles cast on 111 [117: 123: 129: 137: 147: 153: 161] sts.
Row 1 (RS): K1, *P1, K1, rep from * to end.
Row 2: P1, *K1, P1, rep from * to end.
These 2 rows form rib.
Work in rib for 1 row more.
Row 4 (WS): Rib 6 [9: 12: 4: 8: 13: 5: 9], M1, *rib 11, M1, rep from * to last 6 [9: 12: 4: 8: 13: 5: 9] sts, rib to end.
121 [127: 133: 141: 149: 159: 167: 175] sts.
Change to 4mm (US 6) needles.
Beg and ending rows as indicated and repeating the 8 row patt rep throughout, work in patt from chart for back as folls:
Work 10 rows, ending with RS facing for next row.
Keeping patt correct, dec 1 st at each end of next and every foll 6th row until 111 [117: 123: 131: 139: 149: 157: 165] sts rem.

Work 9 rows, ending with RS facing for next row.
Inc 1 st at each end of next and every foll 8th row until there are 121 [127: 133: 141: 149: 159: 167: 175] sts, taking inc sts into patt.
Cont straight until back meas 31 [31: 30: 33: 32: 34: 33: 35] cm, ending with RS facing for next row.

Shape armholes

Keeping patt correct, cast off 6 [7: 7: 8: 8: 9: 9: 10] sts at beg of next 2 rows.
109 [113: 119: 125: 133: 141: 149: 155] sts.★★
Dec 1 st at each end of next 7 [7: 9: 9: 11: 11: 13: 13] rows, then on foll 1 [2: 2: 2: 2: 4: 4: 5] alt rows.
93 [95: 97: 103: 107: 111: 115: 119] sts.
Cont straight until armhole meas 19 [19: 20: 20: 21: 21: 22: 22] cm, ending with RS facing for next row.

Shape back neck

Next row (RS): Patt 21 [22: 23: 26: 27: 29: 31: 33] sts and turn, leaving rem sts on a holder.
Work each side of neck separately.
Work 5 rows, ending with RS facing for next row.

Shape shoulder

Cast off rem 21 [22: 23: 26: 27: 29: 31: 33] sts.
With RS facing, rejoin yarn to rem sts, cast off centre 51 [51: 51: 51: 53: 53: 53: 53] sts, patt to end.
Complete to match first side.

FRONT

Work as given for back to ★★.
Dec 1 st at each end of next 6 [6: 8: 8: 10: 10: 12: 12] rows, ending with RS facing for next row.
97 [101: 103: 109: 113: 121: 125: 131] sts.

Shape front neck

Next row (RS): K2tog, patt 21 [23: 24: 27: 28: 32: 34: 37] sts and turn, leaving rem sts on a holder.
22 [24: 25: 28: 29: 33: 35: 38] sts.
Work each side of neck separately.
Dec 1 st at armhole edge of 2nd and foll 0 [1: 1: 1: 1: 3: 3: 4] alt rows.
21 [22: 23: 26: 27: 29: 31: 33] sts.
Cont straight until front matches back to shoulder cast-off, ending with RS facing for next row.

Shape shoulder

Cast off rem 21 [22: 23: 26: 27: 29: 31: 33] sts.
With RS facing, rejoin yarn to rem sts, cast off centre 51 [51: 51: 51: 53: 53: 53: 53] sts, patt to last 2 sts, K2tog.
Complete to match first side, reversing shapings.

SLEEVES

Using 3¼ mm (US 3) needles cast on 57 [57: 59: 59: 63: 63: 65: 65] sts.
Work in rib as given for back for 3 rows, ending with **WS** facing for next row.
Row 4 (WS): Rib 6 [6: 7: 7: 9: 9: 10: 10], M1,

(rib 11, M1) 4 times, rib to end.
62 [62: 64: 64: 68: 68: 70: 70] sts.
Change to 4mm (US 6) needles.
Beg and ending rows as indicated and repeating the 8 row patt rep throughout, work in patt from chart for sleeve, shaping sides by inc 1 st at each end of 3rd and every foll 4th row to 66 [72: 70: 76: 72: 78: 82: 88] sts, then on every foll 6th row until there are 100 [102: 104: 106: 108: 110: 112: 114] sts, taking inc sts into patt.
Cont straight until sleeve meas 43 [43: 44: 44: 45: 45: 44: 44] cm, ending with RS facing for next row.

Shape top

Keeping patt correct, cast off 6 [7: 7: 8: 8: 9: 9: 10] sts at beg of next 2 rows.
88 [88: 90: 90: 92: 92: 94: 94] sts.
Dec 1 st at each end of next 13 rows, then on every foll alt row to 50 sts, then on foll 13 rows, ending with RS facing for next row.
24 sts.
Cast off 5 sts at beg of next 2 rows.
Cast off rem 14 sts.

MAKING UP

Press as described on the information page.
Join right shoulder seam using back stitch, or

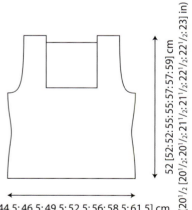

52 [52: 52: 55: 55: 57: 57: 59] cm
(20½ [20½: 20½: 21½: 21½: 22½: 22½: 23] in)

42.5 [44.5: 46.5: 49.5: 52.5: 56: 58.5: 61.5] cm
(16½ [17½: 18½: 19½: 20½: 22: 23: 24] in)

43 [43: 44: 44: 45: 45: 44: 44] cm
(17 [17: 17½: 17½: 17½: 17½: 17½: 17½] in)

mattress stitch if preferred.

Neckband

With RS facing and using 3¼ mm (US 3)
circular needle, pick up and knit 48 [48: 49: 49:
50: 50: 51: 51] sts down left side of front neck,
47 [47: 47: 47: 49: 49: 49: 49] sts from front,
48 [48: 49: 49: 50: 50: 51: 51] sts up right side
of front neck, 4 sts down right side of back
neck, 47 [47: 47: 47: 49: 49: 49: 49] sts from
back, then 4 sts up left side of back neck.
198 [198: 200: 200: 206: 206: 208: 208] sts.
Row 1 (WS): P1, ★inc purlwise in next st, P1,
rep from ★ to last st, P1. 296 [296: 299: 299:
308: 308: 311: 311] sts.
Row 2: K1, ★inc in next st, K1, rep from
★ to last 1 [1: 0: 0: 1: 1: 0: 0] st, K1 [1: 0: 0: 1:
1: 0: 0].
443 [443: 448: 448: 461: 461: 466: 466] sts.
Row 3: P1, ★inc purlwise in next st, P1, rep
from ★ to last 0 [0: 1: 1: 0: 0: 1: 1] st, P0 [0: 1: 1:
0: 0: 1: 1].
664 [664: 671: 671: 691: 691: 698: 698] sts.
Cast off knitwise, placing a bead (by inserting
right needle into next st, sliding bead up next
to right needle and then completing st in usual
way) on every cast-off st.
See information page for finishing instructions,
setting in sleeves using the set-in method.

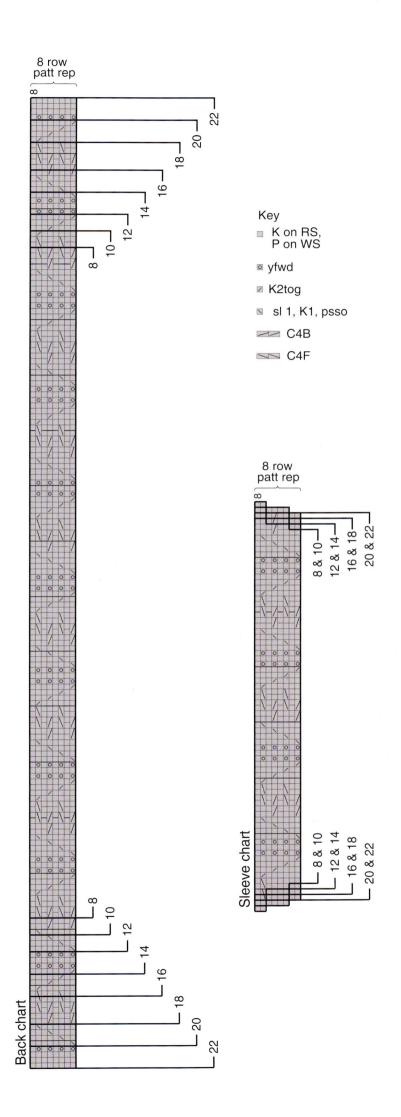

Key

◻ K on RS,
P on WS

⊙ yfwd

☑ K2tog

◩ sl 1, K1, psso

▱ C4B

▱ C4F

Main image page 16

SADIE BY SARAH HATTON

SIZE

8	10	12	14	16	18	
To fit bust						
82	87	92	97	102	107	cm
32	34	36	38	40	42	in

YARN
Rowan Wool Cotton

9	10	10	11	12	12	x 50gm

(photographed in Smart 963)

NEEDLES
1 pair 3¼ mm (no 10) (US 3) needles
1 pair 4mm (no 8) (US 6) needles

TENSION
21 sts and 34 rows to 10 cm measured over pattern using 4mm (US 6) needles.

BACK
Using 3¼ mm (US 3) needles cast on 93 [97: 101: 107: 113: 119] sts.
Row 1 (RS): K1, *P1, K1, rep from * to end.
Row 2: P1, *K1, P1, rep from * to end.
These 2 rows form rib.
Cont in rib for a further 4 rows, dec 1 st at end of last row and ending with RS facing for next row.
92 [96: 100: 106: 112: 118] sts.
Change to 4mm (US 6) needles.
Beg with a K row, work in st st for 6 rows.
Row 7 (RS): Purl.
Row 8: K1, *yfwd, K2tog, rep from * to last st, K1.
Row 9: As row 8.
Row 10: Knit.
These 10 rows form patt.
Cont in patt, shaping side seams by dec 1 st at each end of 5th and foll 20th row.
88 [92: 96: 102: 108: 114] sts.
Cont straight until back meas 40 [40: 39: 42: 41: 43] cm, ending with RS facing for next row.
Shape armholes
Keeping patt correct, cast off 4 [5: 5: 6: 6: 7] sts at beg of next 2 rows.
80 [82: 86: 90: 96: 100] sts.
Dec 1 st at each end of next 3 rows, then on foll 1 [1: 2: 2: 3: 3] alt rows.
72 [74: 76: 80: 84: 88] sts.
Cont straight until armhole meas 19 [19: 20: 20: 21: 21] cm, ending with RS facing for next row.
Shape back neck
Next row (RS): Patt 19 [20: 21: 23: 24: 26] sts and turn, leaving rem sts on a holder.
Work each side of neck separately.
Cast off 3 sts at beg of next and foll alt row.
13 [14: 15: 17: 18: 20] sts.
Shape shoulder
Cast off 6 [7: 7: 8: 9: 10] sts at beg of next row.
Work 1 row.
Cast off rem 7 [7: 8: 9: 9: 10] sts.
With RS facing, rejoin yarn to rem sts, cast off centre 34 [34: 34: 34: 36: 36] sts, patt to end.
Complete to match first side, reversing

shapings.
LEFT FRONT
Using 3¼ mm (US 3) needles cast on 46 [48: 50: 54: 56: 60] sts.
Row 1 (RS): *K1, P1, rep from * to end.
Row 2: As row 1.
These 2 rows form rib.
Cont in rib for a further 4 rows, dec 0 [0: 0: 1: 0: 1] st at end of last row and ending with RS facing for next row.
46 [48: 50: 53: 56: 59] sts.
Change to 4mm (US 6) needles.
Beg with a K row, work in st st for 6 rows.
Row 7 (RS): Purl.
Row 8: K1, *yfwd, K2tog, rep from * to last 1 [1: 1: 0: 1: 0] st, K1 [1: 1: 0: 1: 0].
Row 9: K1 [1: 1: 2: 1: 2], *yfwd, K2tog, rep from * to last st, K1.
Row 10: Knit.
These 10 rows form patt.
Cont in patt, shaping side seam by dec 1 st at beg of 5th and foll 20th row.
44 [46: 48: 51: 54: 57] sts.
Cont straight until left front matches back to beg of armhole shaping, ending with RS facing for next row.
Shape armhole
Keeping patt correct, cast off 4 [5: 5: 6: 6: 7] sts at beg of next row.
40 [41: 43: 45: 48: 50] sts.
Work 1 row.
Dec 1 st at armhole edge of next 3 rows, then on foll 1 [1: 2: 2: 3: 3] alt rows.
36 [37: 38: 40: 42: 44] sts.
Cont straight until 43 [43: 43: 45: 45: 45] rows less have been worked than on back to beg of shoulder shaping, ending with **WS** facing for next row.
Shape neck
Keeping patt correct, cast off 6 [6: 6: 5: 6: 6] sts at beg of next row.
30 [31: 32: 35: 36: 38] sts.
Dec 1 st at neck edge of next 7 rows, then on foll 10 [10: 10: 11: 11: 11] alt rows.
13 [14: 15: 17: 18: 20] sts.
Work 15 rows, ending with RS facing for next row.
Shape shoulder
Cast off 6 [7: 7: 8: 9: 10] sts at beg of next row.
Work 1 row.
Cast off rem 7 [7: 8: 9: 9: 10] sts.

RIGHT FRONT
Using 3¼ mm (US 3) needles cast on 46 [48: 50: 54: 56: 60] sts.
Row 1 (RS): *P1, K1, rep from * to end.
Row 2: As row 1.
These 2 rows form rib.
Cont in rib for a further 4 rows, dec 0 [0: 0: 1: 0: 1] st at beg of last row and ending with RS facing for next row.
46 [48: 50: 53: 56: 59] sts.
Change to 4mm (US 6) needles.
Beg with a K row, work in st st for 6 rows.
Row 7 (RS): Purl.

Row 8: K1 [1: 1: 2: 1: 2], *yfwd, K2tog, rep from * to last st, K1.
Row 9: K1, *yfwd, K2tog, rep from * to last 1 [1: 1: 0: 1: 0] st, K1 [1: 1: 0: 1: 0].
Row 10: Knit.
These 10 rows form patt.
Cont in patt, shaping side seam by dec 1 st at end of 5th and foll 20th row.
44 [46: 48: 51: 54: 57] sts.
Complete to match left front, reversing shapings.

SLEEVES
Using 3¼ mm (US 3) needles cast on 47 [47: 49: 49: 51: 51] sts.
Work in rib as given for back for 6 rows, dec 1 st at end of last row and ending with RS facing for next row.
46 [46: 48: 48: 50: 50] sts.
Change to 4mm (US 6) needles.
Beg with a K row, work in st st for 6 rows, inc 0 [1: 1: 1: 1: 1] st at each end of 5th of these rows.
46 [48: 50: 50: 52: 52] sts.
Row 7 (RS): (Inc in first st) 1 [0: 0: 0: 0: 0] times, P to last 1 [0: 0: 0: 0: 0] st, (inc in last st) 1 [0: 0: 0: 0: 0] times.
48 [48: 50: 50: 52: 52] sts.
Row 8: K1, *yfwd, K2tog, rep from * to last st, K1.
Row 9: As row 8.
Row 10: Knit.
These 10 rows form patt and beg sleeve shaping.
Cont in patt, shaping sides by inc 1 st at each end of 5th [next: next: next: next: next] and every foll 8th [6th: 8th: 6th: 6th: 6th] row to 76 [52: 82: 60: 58: 66] sts, then on every foll 10th [8th: –: 8th: 8th: 8th] row until there are 78 [80: –: 84: 86: 88] sts, taking inc sts into patt.
Cont straight until sleeve meas 43 [43: 44: 44: 45: 45] cm, ending with RS facing for next row.
Shape top
Keeping patt correct, cast off 4 [5: 5: 6: 6: 7] sts at beg of next 2 rows.
70 [70: 72: 72: 74: 74] sts.
Dec 1 st at each end of next 7 rows, then on every foll alt row to 26 sts, then on foll 3 rows, ending with RS facing for next row.
Cast off 4 sts at beg of next 2 rows.
Cast off rem 12 sts.

MAKING UP
Press as described on the information page.
Join both shoulder seams using back stitch, or mattress stitch if preferred.
Left front band
With RS facing and using 3¼ mm (US 3) needles, pick up and knit 114 [114: 114: 120: 120: 124] sts down left front opening edge, from neck shaping to cast-on edge.
Work in rib as given for right front for 5 rows, ending with RS facing for next row.
Cast off in rib.

Right front band

With RS facing and using 3¼ mm (US 3) needles, pick up and knit 114 [114: 114: 120: 120: 124] sts up right front opening edge, from cast-on edge to neck shaping.

Work in rib as given for left front for 5 rows, ending with RS facing for next row.

Cast off in rib.

Neckband

With RS facing and using 3¼ mm (US 3) needles, cast on 38 sts, beg and ending at cast-off edge of front bands, pick up and knit 39 [39: 39: 40: 41: 41] sts up right side of neck, 49 [49: 49: 49: 51: 51] sts from back, then 39 [39: 39: 40: 41: 41] sts down left side of neck, turn and cast on 38 sts.

203 [203: 203: 205: 209: 209] sts.

Beg with row 2, work in rib as given for back for 6 rows, ending with **WS** facing for next row.

Cast off in rib (on **WS**).

See information page for finishing instructions, setting in sleeves using the set-in method.

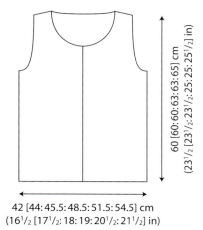

42 [44: 45.5: 48.5: 51.5: 54.5] cm
(16¹/₂ [17¹/₂: 18: 19: 20¹/₂: 21¹/₂] in)

60 [60: 60: 63: 63: 65] cm
(23¹/₂ [23¹/₂: 23¹/₂: 25: 25: 25¹/₂] in)

43 [43: 44: 44: 45: 45] cm
(17 [17: 17¹/₂: 17¹/₂: 17¹/₂: 17¹/₂] in)

Main image page 84, 85, 87 & 88

ARWEN BY MARIE WALLIN

SIZE

S	M	L	
8/10	12/14	16/18	
To fit bust			
82–87	92–97	102–107	cm
32–34	36–38	40–42	in

YARN

Rowan Kidsilk Night and Kidsilk Haze

A	Kidsilk Night Macbeth 614			
	24	25	26	x 25gm
B	Kidsilk Haze Violetta	633		
	1	1	1	x 25gm
C	Kidsilk Haze Liqueur 595			
	1	2	2	x 25gm
D	Kidsilk Haze Nightly 585			
	1	1	1	x 25gm

NEEDLES

1 pair 3¼mm (no 10) (US 3) needles
2.50mm (no 12) (US C2) crochet hook

BEADS – 10 x 01005 large beads, approx 700 x 01009 small beads and 10 x GB79 8mm round silver lined glass bead col. 3 Purple from Creative Bead Craft Ltd.

EXTRAS – piece of lining fabric (for bodice) approx 110 cm x 43 cm, 4 m of 128 cm wide tulle netting (for underskirt), 5 hook and eye fasteners, matching sewing thread and 3m of 5cm mole velvet or satin ribbon in a tonally matching colour.

TENSION

27 sts and 34 rows to 10 cm measured over stocking stitch using 3¼mm (US 3) needles and yarn A.

UK CROCHET ABBREVIATIONS

ch = chain; **dc** = double crochet;
ss = slip stitch; **sp** = space; **tr** = treble;
dtr = double treble.

US CROCHET ABBREVIATIONS

ch = chain; **dc** = single crochet; **ss** = slip stitch; **sp** = space; **tr** = double crochet; **dtr** = treble.

BODICE FRONT

Using 3¼mm (US 3) needles and yarn A cast on 100 [114: 130] sts.
Beg with a K row, work in st st, shaping side seams by inc 1 st at each end of 11th and every foll 10th row until there are 110 [124: 140] sts.
Cont straight until bodice front meas 18 cm, ending with RS facing for next row.

Shape armholes
Cast off 3 [4: 5] sts at beg of next 2 rows.
104 [116: 130] sts.
Dec 1 st at each end of next 1 [3: 5] rows, then on foll 1 [2: 3] alt rows, then on every foll 4th row until 96 [102: 110] sts rem.
Cont straight until armhole meas 6 [7: 8] cm, ending with RS facing for next row.

Shape neck
Next row (RS): K40 [43: 46] and turn, leaving rem sts on a holder.
Work each side of neck separately.
Cast off 5 sts at beg of next row, 4 sts at beg of foll alt row, 3 sts at beg of foll 2 alt rows, and 2 sts at beg of foll alt row.
23 [26: 29] sts.
Dec 1 st at neck edge of next 5 rows, then on every foll alt row until 5 [8: 11] sts rem.
Work 5 rows, ending with RS facing for next row.

Shape shoulder
Cast off 2 [4: 5] sts at beg of next row.
Work 1 row.
Cast off rem 3 [4: 6] sts.
With RS facing, rejoin yarn to rem sts, cast off centre 16 [16: 18] sts, K to end.
Complete to match first side, reversing shapings.

BODICE RIGHT BACK

Using 3¼mm (US 3) needles and yarn A cast on 50 [57: 65] sts.
Beg with a K row, work in st st, shaping side seam by inc 1 st at beg of 11th and every foll 10th row until there are 55 [62: 70] sts.
Cont straight until bodice right back matches bodice front to beg of armhole shaping, ending with RS facing for next row.

Shape armhole
Cast off 3 [4: 5] sts at beg of next row.
52 [58: 65] sts.
Work 1 row.
Dec 1 st at armhole edge of next 1 [3: 5] rows, then on foll 1 [2: 3] alt rows, then on every foll 4th row until 48 [51: 55] sts rem.
Cont straight until 7 rows less have been worked than on bodice front to beg of shoulder shaping, ending with **WS** facing for next row.

Shape neck
Cast off 26 [26: 27] sts at beg of next row, 7 sts at beg of foll alt row, and 5 sts at beg of foll 2 alt rows, ending with RS facing for next row.
5 [8: 11] sts.

Shape shoulder
Cast off 2 [4: 5] sts at beg of next row.
Work 1 row.
Cast off rem 3 [4: 6] sts.

BODICE LEFT BACK

Using 3¼mm (US 3) needles and yarn A cast on 50 [57: 65] sts.
Beg with a K row, work in st st, shaping side seam by inc 1 st at end of 11th and every foll 10th row until there are 55 [62: 70] sts.
Complete to match bodice right back, reversing shapings.

FRONT AND SIDE SKIRT PANELS
(make 5)
Using 3¼mm (US 3) needles and yarn A cast on 122 [138: 154] sts.
Beg with a K row, work in st st until skirt panel meas 115 [116: 117] cm, ending with RS facing for next row.
Cast off.

CENTRE BACK SKIRT PANEL

Using 3¼mm (US 3) needles and yarn A cast on 122 [138: 154] sts.
Beg with a K row, work in st st until skirt panel meas 105 [106: 107] cm, ending with RS facing for next row.

Divide for back opening
Next row (RS): K61 [69: 77] and turn, leaving rem sts on a holder.
Work each side separately.
Cont straight until skirt panel meas 10 cm from beg of back opening, ending with RS facing for next row.
Cast off.
With RS facing, rejoin yarn to rem sts, K to end.
Complete to match first side.

MAKING UP

Press as described on the information page.
From lining fabric, cut out same size pieces as knitted bodice front and backs, adding seam allowance along all edges.
Join both shoulder seams using back stitch, or mattress stitch if preferred.

Neck edging
Using 2.50mm (US C2) crochet hook and yarn A, attach yarn to top of right back opening edge and, with **WS** facing, work 1 row of dc evenly around entire neck edge, working a multiple of 7 sts and ending at top of left back opening edge, turn.
Row 1 (RS): 1 ch (does NOT count as st), 1 dc into each of first 6 dc, ★turn, 7 ch, miss 5 dc, 1 dc into next dc, turn, (6 dc, 5 ch and 6 dc) into ch sp just formed★★, 1 dc into each of next 7 dc of previous row, rep from ★ to end, ending last rep at ★★, 1 dc into last dc, turn.
Row 2: 4 ch (counts as first dtr), miss first 7 dc, ★(1 tr, 3 ch, ss to 3rd ch from hook) 4 times into next 5-ch loop, 1 tr into same 5-ch loop, miss 6 dc★★, 1 dtr into next dc, miss 6 dc, rep from ★ to end, ending last rep at ★★, 1 dtr into dc at beg of previous row.
Fasten off.

Armhole edgings (both alike)
Using 2.50mm (US C2) crochet hook and yarn A, attach yarn to top of one side seam edge and, with RS facing, work 1 row of dc evenly around entire armhole edge, turn.
Row 1 (RS): 1 ch (does NOT count as st), 1 dc into each dc to end.
Fasten off.

Flower centres (make 10)
Using 2.50mm (US C2) crochet hook and yarn B, make 6 ch and join with a ss to form a ring.
Round 1 (RS): 3 ch (counts as first tr), 15 tr into ring, ss to top of 3 ch at beg of round.
16 sts.
Round 2: 3 ch (counts as first tr), 1 tr into st at base of 3 ch, 2 tr into each tr to end, ss to top

of 3 ch at beg of round.
32 sts.
Fasten off.

Flowers (make 10)
Using 3¼ mm (US 3) needles and yarn C cast on 37 sts.
Row 1 (RS): K1, *P1, K1, rep from * to end.
Row 2: P1, *K1, P1, rep from * to end.
Row 3: K1, *P1, M1P, K1, rep from * to end. 55 sts.
Row 4: P1, *K2, P1, rep from * to end.
Row 5: K1, *P2, M1P, K1, rep from * to end. 73 sts.
Row 6: P1, *K3, P1, rep from * to end.
Row 7: K1, *P3, M1P, K1, rep from * to end. 91 sts.
Row 8: P1, *K4, P1, rep from * to end.
Row 9: K1, *P4, M1P, K1, rep from * to end. 109 sts.
Row 10: P1, *K5, P1, rep from * to end.
Row 11: K1, *P5, M1P, K1, rep from * to end. 127 sts.
Row 12: P1, *K6, P1, rep from * to end.
Cast off in patt.
Using photograph as a guide, roll up cast-on edge and sew together. Lay flower centre over centre of flower and sew in place. Attach one large bead at centre, then 8 small beads around this bead, attaching beads through all layers. Attach beads to outer layer of flower as folls: bring a length of yarn C through from WS just near cast-off edge at centre of one K st. Thread 5 small beads onto yarn and take yarn back to WS just under outer edge of flower centre, leaving a line of 5 beads sitting over K st ridge. Make a further 6 lines of small beads on flower in same way.

Leaves (make 20)
Using 3¼ mm (US 3) needles and yarn D cast on 5 sts.
Row 1 (RS): K2, yfwd, K1, yfwd, K2. 7 sts.
Row 2 and every foll alt row: Purl.
Row 3: K3, yfwd, K1, yfwd, K3. 9 sts.
Row 5: K4, yfwd, K1, yfwd, K4. 11 sts.
Row 7: K5, yfwd, K1, yfwd, K5. 13 sts.
Row 9: sl 1, K1, psso, K9, K2tog. 11 sts.
Row 11: sl 1, K1, psso, K7, K2tog. 9 sts.
Row 13: sl 1, K1, psso, K5, K2tog. 7 sts.
Row 15: sl 1, K1, psso, K3, K2tog. 5 sts.
Row 17: sl 1, K1, psso, K1, K2tog. 3 sts.
Row 19: sl 1, K2tog, psso and fasten off.
Using photograph as a guide, attach 11-13 small beads around outer edge of leaf. Attach cast-on edges of 2 leaves under outer edge of each flower as in photograph.
Join bodice side seams. Join all skirt panels together along row-end edges to form one large tube. Run gathering threads around upper (cast-off) edges and pull up to fit cast-on edge of bodice. Matching bodice and centre back skirt panel opening edges and with **WS** together (so seam shows on RS), sew skirt panels to bodice.
Make up bodice lining and tulle skirt sections in same way. Fold seam allowance to WS around armhole, neck and back opening edges and slip lining and tulle inside knitted sections. Slip stitch lining in place around armhole, neck and back opening edges, and slip stitch lower edge of lining to waist seam of knitted sections. Attach hook and eye fasteners evenly spaced along back opening edges to fasten back of dress.
Using photograph as a guide, attach 2 flowers and leaves to each shoulder seam. Attach rem 6 flowers and leaves to skirt sections, attaching flowers through both knitted skirt and tulle and

lifting up knitted sections so that skirt forms swag effect above each flower.
To finish, the dress must be worn with ribbon, wrapped twice around the waist and tied in a bow at the back. This is to ensure a snug fit.

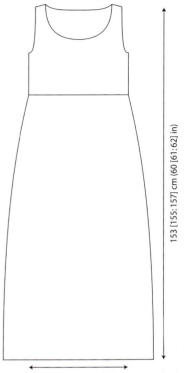

153 [155: 157] cm (60 [61: 62] in)

40.5 [46: 52] cm (16 [18: 20½] in)

Main image page 45

SIZE

	S	M	L	XL	
	8/10	12/14	16/18	20/22	
To fit bust					
	82-87	92-97	102-107	112-117	cm
	32-34	36-38	40-42	44-46	in

YARN

Rowan Felted Tweed

		S	M	L	XL	
A	Treacle 145					
		3	3	4	4	x 50gm
B	Rage 150					
		2	2	2	3	x 50gm
C	Pine 158					
		2	2	2	2	x 50gm
D	Ginger 154					
		3	3	3	3	x 50gm
E	Pickle 155					
		2	2	2	2	x 50gm
F	Whisper 141					
		2	2	2	2	x 50gm
G	Midnight 133					
		2	2	2	2	x 50gm
H	Bilberry 151					
		2	2	2	2	x 50gm
I	Herb 146					
		2	2	2	2	x 50gm
J	Sigh 148					
		2	2	2	2	x 50gm

CROCHET HOOK

4.00mm (no 8) (US G6) crochet hook

TENSION

18 sts and 12½ rows to 10 cm measured over pattern using 4.00mm (US G6) hook.

UK CROCHET ABBREVIATIONS

ch = chain; **dc** = double crochet;
sp(s) = space(s); **ss** = slip stitch;
tr(s) = treble(s); **tr2tog** = *yoh and insert hook as indicated, yoh and draw loop through, yoh and draw through 2 loops, rep from * once more, yoh and draw through all 3 loops on hook; **tr3tog** = *yoh and insert hook as indicated, yoh and draw loop through, yoh and draw through 2 loops, rep from * twice more, yoh and draw through all 4 loops on hook; **yoh** = yarn over hook.

US CROCHET ABBREVIATIONS

ch = chain; **dc** = single crochet;
sp(s) = space(s); **ss** = slip stitch;
tr(s) = double crochet; **tr2tog** = *yoh and insert hook as indicated, yoh and draw loop through, yoh and draw through 2 loops, rep from * once more, yoh and draw through all 3 loops on hook; **tr3tog** = *yoh and insert hook as indicated, yoh and draw loop through, yoh and draw through 2 loops, rep from * twice more, yoh and draw through all 4 loops on hook; **yoh** = yarn over hook.

BACK

Using 4.00mm (US G6) hook and yarn A make 98 [110: 122: 134] ch.

HICKORY BY MARIE WALLIN

Foundation row (RS): 1 dc into 2nd ch from hook, 1 dc into each ch to end, turn. 97 [109: 121: 133] sts.

Next row: 1 ch (does NOT count as st), 1 dc into each dc to end, turn.
Joining in and breaking off colours as required, cont in patt as folls:

Row 1 (RS): Using yarn B, 1 ch (does NOT count as st), 1 dc into first dc, *miss 2 dc, 5 tr into next dc, miss 2 dc, 1 dc into next dc, rep from * to end, turn.

Row 2: Using yarn C, 3 ch (counts as first tr), 2 tr into dc at base of 3 ch, *miss 2 tr, 1 dc into next tr, miss 2 tr**, 5 tr into next dc, rep from * to end, ending last rep at **, 3 tr into last dc, turn.

Row 3: Using yarn D, 1 ch (does NOT count as st), 1 dc into tr at end of previous row, *miss 2 tr, 5 tr into next dc, miss 2 tr, 1 dc into next tr, rep from * to end, working dc at end of last rep into top of 3 ch at beg of previous row, turn.

Row 4: Using yarn E, as row 2.
Row 5: Using yarn F, as row 3.
Row 6: Using yarn A, as row 2.
Row 7: Using yarn B, as row 3.
Row 8: Using yarn G, 3 ch (counts as first tr), miss dc at base of 3 ch, 1 tr into each tr and dc to end, turn.
Row 9: Using yarn D, 3 ch (counts as first tr), miss tr at end of previous row, *1 tr between tr just missed and next tr, miss 1 tr, rep from * to end, working last tr between tr and 3 ch at beg of previous row, turn.
Row 10: Using yarn H, as row 9.
Row 11: Using yarn E, as row 9.
Row 12: Using yarn A, as row 9.
Row 13: Using yarn B, 1 ch (does NOT count as st), 1 dc into first tr, *miss 2 tr, 5 tr into next tr, miss 2 tr, 1 dc into next tr, rep from * to end, working last dc into top of 3 ch at beg of previous row, turn.
Row 14: Using yarn G, as row 2.
Row 15: Using yarn D, as row 3.
Row 16: Using yarn I, as row 2.
Row 17: Using yarn J, as row 3.
Row 18: Using yarn H, as row 2.
Row 19: Using yarn C, as row 8.
Row 20: Using yarn D, as row 9.
Row 21: Using yarn F, as row 9.
Row 22: Using yarn J, as row 9.
Row 23: Using yarn I, as row 9.
Row 24: Using yarn A, as row 9.
Row 25: Using yarn B, as row 13.
Rows 2 to 25 **only** form patt.
Work in patt for a further 27 rows, ending after patt row 4 and with RS facing for next row. (Back should meas 43 cm.)

Shape armholes
Place markers at both ends of last row to denote base of armholes.
Keeping colours correct as set, work 1 row.
Row 2: ss across first dc, next 2 tr and into 3rd tr of first group of trs, 1 ch (does NOT count as st), 1 dc into same place as last ss

– 3 sts decreased, *miss 2 tr, 5 tr into next dc, miss 2 tr, 1 dc into next tr, rep from * until dc has been worked into 3rd tr of last tr group and turn, leaving rem 3 sts unworked – 3 sts decreased.
Row 3: As row 2. 85 [97: 109: 121] sts.
Row 4: 3 ch (does NOT count as st), miss dc at base of 3 ch, tr2tog over next 2 tr – 2 sts decreased, 1 tr into each st to last 3 sts, tr3tog over last 3 sts – 2 sts decreased, turn. 81 [93: 105: 117] sts.
Row 5: 3 ch (does NOT count as st), miss tr3tog at base of 3 ch, tr2tog placing first "leg" between tr3tog and next tr at end of previous row and 2nd "leg" between last 2 tr of previous row – 2 sts decreased, *miss 1 tr, 1 tr between tr just missed and next tr, rep from * until (2 tr and tr2tog) rem at end of row, tr3tog placing "legs" between next 3 sts – 2 sts decreased, turn. 77 [89: 101: 113] sts.
Rows 6 and 7: As row 5. 69 [81: 93: 105] sts.
Row 8: 3 ch (does NOT count as st), miss tr3tog at base of 3 ch, 1 tr between tr3tog and next tr at end of previous row – 1 st decreased, *miss 1 tr, 1 tr between tr just missed and next tr, rep from * until (1 tr and tr2tog) rem at end of row, tr2tog placing "legs" between next 2 sts – 1 st decreased, turn. 67 [79: 91: 103] sts.
Working next row in same way as patt row 3 but keeping colour and patt stripe sequence correct, work 1 row.
M, L and XL sizes
Rep armhole dec row 2, - [1: 3: 4] times more. - [73: 73: 79] sts.
All sizes
Cont in patt for a further 19 [19: 18: 19] rows, ending after patt row 8 [9: 10: 12].
Shape back neck
Keeping colours correct as set, cont as folls:
Next row: 3 ch (counts as first tr), patt next 16 [19: 19: 21] sts, tr3tog over next 3 sts and turn, leaving rem sts unworked.
18 [21: 21: 23] sts.
Working decrease in same way as for armhole shaping, dec 2 sts at neck edge (beg) of next row.
16 [19: 19: 21] sts.
Fasten off.
Return to last complete row worked, miss centre 27 [27: 27: 29] sts, rejoin appropriate yarn between st just missed and next st, 3 ch (does NOT count as st), tr2tog over next 2 sts, patt to end, turn.
18 [21: 21: 23] sts.
Working decrease in same way as for armhole shaping, dec 2 sts at neck edge (end) of next row. 16 [19: 19: 21] sts.
Fasten off.

LEFT FRONT
Using 4.00mm (US G6) hook and yarn A make 50 [56: 62: 68] ch.

Foundation row (RS): 1 dc into 2nd ch from hook, 1 dc into each ch to end, turn. 49 [55: 61: 67] sts.

Next row: 1 ch (does NOT count as st), 1 dc into each dc to end, turn.

Joining in and breaking off colours as required and beg with patt row 1, cont in patt as given for back as folls:

Work 43 rows, ending after patt row 19 and with **WS** facing for next row.

Shape front slope

Working all decreases as set by back, dec 1 st at beg of next and 2 foll alt rows. 46 [52: 58: 64] sts.

Work 2 rows.

Dec 3 sts at front slope edge of next row. 43 [49: 55: 61] sts.

Work 1 row, ending after patt row 4 and with RS facing for next row. (Left front should match back to beg of armhole shaping.)

Shape armhole

Place marker at end of last row to denote base of armhole.

Work 1 row.

Dec 3 sts at each end of next row, then 3 sts at armhole edge of foll row. 34 [40: 46: 52] sts.

Dec 2 sts at armhole edge of next 4 rows **and at same time** dec 1 st at front slope edge of next and foll alt row. 24 [30: 36: 42] sts.

Dec 1 st at each end of next row. 22 [28: 34: 40] sts.

Work 3 [1: 1: 1] rows.

Dec 0 [3: 3: 3] sts at armhole edge of next 0 [1: 2: 2] rows. 22 [25: 28: 34] sts.

Work 0 [1: 0: 0] row.

Dec 3 sts at front slope edge of next row **and at same time** dec 0 [0: 3: 3] sts at armhole edge. 19 [22: 22: 28] sts.

Work 2 rows, dec 0 [0: 0: 3] sts at armhole edge of first of these rows. 19 [22: 22: 25] sts.

Dec 1 st at front slope edge of next and foll 2 alt rows. 16 [19: 19: 22] sts.

Work a further 11 [12: 13: 8] rows, ending after patt row 10 [11: 12: 7].

XL size only

Dec 1 st at front slope edge of next row. 21 sts.

Work 4 rows, ending after patt row 12.

Keeping colours correct as set by patt, rep last row twice more.

All sizes

Fasten off.

RIGHT FRONT

Work to match left front, reversing all shapings.

SLEEVES

Using 4.00mm (US G6) hook and yarn A make 50 [50: 56: 56] ch.

Foundation row (RS): 1 dc into 2nd ch from hook, 1 dc into each ch to end, turn. 49 [49: 55: 55] sts.

Next row: 1 ch (does NOT count as st), 1 dc into each dc to end, turn.

Joining in and breaking off colours as required, cont in patt as given for back as folls:

Work 7 rows.

Row 8: Using yarn G, 3 ch (counts as first tr), 1 tr into dc at base of 3 ch − 1 st increased, 1 tr into each tr and dc to last dc, 2 tr into last dc − 1 st increased, turn. 51 [51: 57: 57] sts.

Work 1 row.

Row 10: Using yarn H, 3 ch (counts as first tr), miss tr at end of previous row, 2 tr between tr just missed and next tr − 1 st increased, miss 1 tr, ★1 tr between tr just missed and next tr, miss 1 tr, rep from ★ to end, working last tr between tr and 3 ch at beg of previous row, 1 tr into same place as last tr worked − 1 st increased, turn. 53 [53: 59: 59] sts.

Working all increases as set by last 3 rows, inc 1 st at each end of 2nd row. 55 [55: 61: 61] sts.

Work 7 rows.

Inc 1 st at each end of next and foll 2 alt rows. 61 [61: 67: 67] sts.

Rep last 12 rows twice more. 73 [73: 79: 79] sts.

Cont straight until sleeve meas 43 [43: 45: 45] cm, ending after patt row 4 and with RS facing for next row.

Shape top

Place markers at both ends of last row to denote top of sleeve seam.

Work 1 row.

Working all shaping as given for back, dec 3 sts at each end of next 2 rows. 61 [61: 67: 67] sts.

Dec 2 sts at each end of next 5 rows. 41 [41: 47: 47] sts.

Work 1 row.

Dec 3 sts at each end of next 2 rows. 29 [29: 35: 35] sts.

Fasten off.

MAKING UP

Press as described on the information page.

Join shoulder seams.

Front border

With RS facing, using 4.00mm (US G6) hook and yarn A, attach yarn at base of right front opening edge, 1 ch (does NOT count as st), work in dc evenly up entire right front opening and neck edge, across back neck and down left front slope and opening edge to base of left front opening edge, turn.

Joining in and breaking off colours as required, cont as folls:

Row 1 (WS): Using yarn B, 1 ch (does NOT count as st), 1 dc into each dc to end, turn.

This row forms dc fabric.

Cont in dc fabric in stripe sequence as folls:

Row 2: Using yarn F.

Row 3: Using yarn D.

Row 4: Using yarn G.

Row 5: Using yarn E.

Row 6: Using yarn C.

Row 7: Using yarn D.

Row 8: Using yarn J.

Row 9: Using yarn I.

Row 10: Using yarn H.

Row 11: Using yarn F.

Row 12: Using yarn B.

Rows 13 and 14: Using yarn A.

Fasten off.

Belt

Using 4.00mm (US G6) hook and yarn A make a ch approx 135 cm long.

Row 1 (RS): 1 dc into 2nd ch from hook, 1 dc into each ch to end, turn.

Row 2: 1 ch (does NOT count as st), 1 dc into each dc to end, turn.

This row forms dc fabric.

Joining in and breaking off colours as required, cont in dc fabric in stripe sequence as folls:

Row 3: Using yarn B.

Row 4: Using yarn F.

Row 5: Using yarn D.

Row 6: Using yarn G.

Row 7: Using yarn E.

Row 8: Using yarn C.

Row 9: Using yarn D.

Row 10: Using yarn J.

Row 11: Using yarn I.

Row 12: Using yarn H.

Row 13: Using yarn F.

Row 14: Using yarn B.

Rows 15 and 16: Using yarn A.

Fasten off.

See information page for finishing instructions, setting in sleeves using the set-in method.

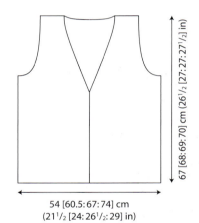

67 [68: 69: 70] cm (26½ [27: 27: 27½] in)

54 [60.5: 67: 74] cm
(21½ [24: 26½: 29] in)

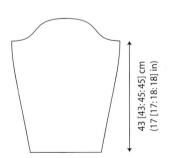

43 [43: 45: 45] cm
(17 [17: 18: 18] in)

Main image page 81

SIZE

8	10	12	14	16	18	20	22	

To fit bust

82	87	92	97	102	107	112	117	cm
32	34	36	38	40	42	44	46	in

YARN

Rowan Romance

12	12	13	14	15	16	16	17	x 50gm

(photographed in Shimmer 092 and
Starlight 094)

NEEDLES

1 pair 7mm (no 2) (US 10½) needles

TENSION

12½ sts and 15 rows to 10 cm measured over
rib using 7mm (US 10½) needles.

BACK and FRONT (both alike)

Using 7mm (US 10½) needles cast on 53 [55:
59: 63: 67: 71: 73: 77] sts.
Row 1 (RS): K0 [0: 1: 0: 0: 1: 2: 0], P1 [2: 3:
0: 2: 3: 3: 1], *K3, P3, rep from * to last 4 [5: 1:
3: 5: 1: 2: 4] sts, K3 [3: 1: 3: 3: 3: 1: 2: 3], P1 [2: 0:
0: 2: 0: 0: 1].
Row 2: P0 [0: 1: 0: 0: 1: 2: 0], K1 [2: 3: 0: 2:
3: 3: 1], *P3, K3, rep from * to last 4 [5: 1: 3:
5: 1: 2: 4] sts, P3 [3: 1: 3: 3: 3: 1: 2: 3], K1 [2: 0: 0:
2: 0: 0: 1].
These 2 rows form rib.
Cont in rib for a further 10 rows, ending with
RS facing for next row.
Dec 1 st at each end of next and foll 6th row.
49 [51: 55: 59: 63: 67: 69: 73] sts.
Work 11 rows, ending with RS facing for
next row.
Inc 1 st at each end of next and foll 10th row.
53 [55: 59: 63: 67: 71: 73: 77] sts.
Cont straight until work meas 33 [33: 34:
37: 36: 38: 37: 39] cm, ending with RS facing
for next row.

Shape armholes

Keeping rib correct, dec 1 st at each end of
next 2 [2: 3: 3: 3: 4: 4: 4] rows.
49 [51: 53: 57: 61: 63: 65: 69] sts.
Cont straight until armhole meas 18 [18: 19:
19: 20: 20: 21: 21] cm, ending with RS facing
for next row.

Shape shoulders and neck

Next row (RS): Rib 6 [7: 8: 10: 11: 12: 13:

15] and turn, leaving rem sts on a holder.
Work each side of neck separately.
Cast off 4 sts at beg of next row.
Cast off rem 2 [3: 4: 6: 7: 8: 9: 11] sts.
With RS facing, rejoin yarn to rem sts,
cast off centre 37 [37: 37: 37: 39: 39: 39: 39] sts,
rib to end.
Complete to match first side, reversing shapings.

SLEEVES

Using 7mm (US 10½) needles cast on 33 [33:
33: 33: 35: 35: 35: 35] sts.
Row 1 (RS): K0 [0: 0: 0: 1: 1: 1: 1], P3, *K3,
P3, rep from * to last 0 [0: 0: 0: 1: 1: 1: 1] sts,
K0 [0: 0: 0: 1: 1: 1: 1].
Row 2: P0 [0: 0: 0: 1: 1: 1: 1], K3, *P3, K3,
rep from * to last 0 [0: 0: 0: 1: 1: 1: 1] sts,
P0 [0: 0: 0: 1: 1: 1: 1].
These 2 rows form rib.
Cont in rib, shaping sides by inc 1 st at each
end of 7th [7th: 3rd: 3rd: 3rd: 3rd: 3rd: 3rd] and
every foll 10th [10th: 8th: 8th: 6th: 6th: 6th:
6th] row to 45 [45: 49: 49: 43: 43: 53: 53] sts,
then on every foll - [-: -: -: 8th: 8th: 8th: 8th]
row until there are - [-: -: -: 53: 53: 55: 55] sts,
taking inc sts into rib.
Cont straight until sleeve meas 45 [45: 46: 46:
47: 47: 46: 46] cm, ending with RS facing for
next row.

Shape top

Keeping rib correct, dec 1 st at each end of
next 2 [2: 4: 4: 4: 4: 4: 4] rows.
41 [41: 41: 41: 45: 45: 47: 47] sts.
Cast off 10 [10: 10: 10: 11: 11: 12: 12] sts at beg
of next 2 rows.
Cast off rem 21 [21: 21: 21: 23: 23: 23: 23] sts.

MAKING UP

Press as described on the information page.
Join right shoulder seam using back stitch, or
mattress stitch if preferred.

Collar

With RS facing and using 7mm (US 10½)
needles, pick up and knit 3 sts down left side of
front neck, 37 [37: 37: 37: 39: 39: 39: 39] sts
from front, 3 sts up right side of front neck,
3 sts down right side of back neck, 36 [36: 36:
36: 40: 40: 40: 40] sts from back, then 3 sts up
left side of back neck.
85 [85: 85: 85: 91: 91: 91: 91] sts.

Row 1 (RS of collar, WS of body): K2,
*P3, K3, rep from * to last 5 sts, P3, K2.
Row 2: P2, *K3, P3, rep from * to last 5 sts,
K3, P2.
These 2 rows form rib.
Cont in rib until collar meas 28 cm.
Cast off in rib.
See information page for finishing instructions,
setting in sleeves using the shallow set-in
method.

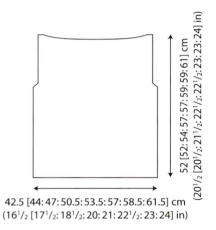

42.5 [44: 47: 50.5: 53.5: 57: 58.5: 61.5] cm
(16½ [17½: 18½: 20: 21: 22½: 23: 24] in)

52 [52: 54: 57: 57: 59: 59: 61] cm
(20½ [20½: 21½: 21½: 22½: 23: 23: 24] in)

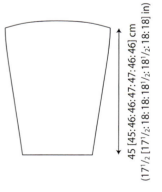

45 [45: 46: 46: 47: 47: 46: 46] cm
(17½ [17½: 18: 18: 18½: 18½: 18: 18] in)

INFORMATION

TENSION

Obtaining the correct tension is perhaps the single factor which can make the difference between a successful garment and a disastrous one. It controls both the shape and size of an article, so any variation, however slight, can distort the finished garment. Different designers feature in our books and it is **their** tension, given at the **start** of each pattern, which you must match. We recommend that you knit a square in pattern and/or stocking stitch (depending on the pattern instructions) of perhaps 5 – 10 more stitches and 5 – 10 more rows than those given in the tension note. Mark out the central 10cm square with pins. If you have too many stitches to 10cm try again using thicker needles, if you have too few stitches to 10cm try again using finer needles. Once you have achieved the correct tension your garment will be knitted to the measurements indicated in the size diagram shown at the end of the pattern.

SIZING & SIZE DIAGRAM NOTE

The instructions are given for the smallest size. Where they vary, work the figures in brackets for the larger sizes. **One set of figures refers to all sizes.** Included with most patterns in this magazine is a **'size diagram'**, or sketch of the finished garment and its dimensions. To help you choose the size of garment to knit please refer to the NEW sizing guide on page 102.

CHART NOTE

Many of the patterns in the book are worked from charts. Each square on a chart represents a stitch and each line of squares a row of knitting. Each colour used is given a different letter and these are shown in the **materials** section, or in the **key** alongside the chart of each pattern. When working from the charts, read odd rows (K) from right to left and even rows (P) from left to right, unless otherwise stated.

KNITTING WITH COLOUR

There are two main methods of working colour into a knitted fabric: **Intarsia** and **Fairisle** techniques. The first method produces a single thickness of fabric and is usually used where a colour is only required in a particular area of a row and does not form a repeating pattern across the row, as in the fairisle technique.
Intarsia: The simplest way to do this is to cut short lengths of yarn for each motif or block of colour used in a row. Then joining in the various colours at the appropriate point on the row, link one colour to the next by twisting them around each other where they meet on the wrong side to avoid gaps. All ends can then either be darned along the colour join lines, as each motif is completed or then can be " knitted-in" to the fabric of the knitting as each colour is worked into the pattern. This is done in much the same way as"weaving-in" yarns when working the Fairisle technique and does save time darning-in ends. It is essential that the tension is noted for **Intarsia** as this may vary from the stocking stitch if both are used in the same pattern.
Fair isle type knitting: When two or three colours are worked repeatedly across a row, strand the yarn **not** in use loosely behind the stitches being worked. If you are working with more than two colours, treat the "floating" yarns as if they were one yarn and always spread the stitches to their correct width to keep them elastic. It is advisable not to carry the stranded or "floating" yarns over more than three stitches at a time, but to weave them under and over the colour you are working. The "floating" yarns are therefore caught at the back of the work.

FINISHING INSTRUCTIONS

After working for hours knitting a garment, it seems a great pity that many garments are spoiled because such little care is taken in the pressing and finishing process. Follow the following tips for a truly professional-looking garment.

PRESSING

Block out each piece of knitting and following the instructions on the ball band press the garment pieces, omitting the ribs. Tip: Take special care to press the edges, as this will make sewing up both easier and neater. If the ball band indicates that the fabric is not to be pressed, then covering the blocked out fabric with a damp white cotton cloth and leaving it to stand will have the desired effect. Darn in all ends neatly along the selvage edge or a colour join, as appropriate.

STITCHING

When stitching the pieces together, remember to match areas of colour and texture very carefully where they meet. Use a seam stitch such as back stitch or mattress stitch for all main knitting seams and join all ribs and neckband with mattress stitch, unless otherwise stated.

CONSTRUCTION

Having completed the pattern instructions, join left shoulder and neckband seams as detailed above. Sew the top of the sleeve to the body of the garment using the method detailed in the pattern, referring to the appropriate guide:
Straight cast-off sleeves: Place centre of cast-off edge of sleeve to shoulder seam. Sew top of sleeve to body, using markers as guidelines where applicable.
Square set-in sleeves: Place centre of cast-off edge of sleeve to shoulder seam. Set sleeve head into armhole, the straight sides at top of sleeve to form a neat right-angle to cast-off sts at armhole on back and front.
Shallow set-in sleeves: Place centre of cast off edge of sleeve to shoulder seam. Match decreases at beg of armhole shaping to decreases at top of sleeve. Sew sleeve head into armhole, easing in shapings.
Set- in sleeves: Place centre of cast-off edge of sleeve to shoulder seam. Set in sleeve, easing sleeve head into armhole.

Join side and sleeve seams.
Slip stitch pocket edgings and linings into place.
Sew on buttons to correspond with buttonholes.
Ribbed welts and neckbands and any areas of garter stitch should not be pressed.

WORKING A LACE PATTERN

When working a lace pattern it is important to remember that if you are unable to work both the increase and corresponding decrease and vica versa, the stitches should be worked in stocking stitch.

 = Easy, straight forward knitting

 = Suitable for the average knitter

 = For the more experienced knitter

ABBREVIATIONS

K	knit
P	purl
st(s)	stitch(es)
inc	increas(e)(ing)
dec	decreas(e)(ing)
st st	stocking stitch (1 row K , 1 row P)
g st	garter stitch (K every row)
beg	begin(ning)
foll	following
rem	remain(ing)
rev st st	reverse stocking stitch (1 row K , 1 row P)
rep	repeat
alt	alternate
cont	continue
patt	pattern
tog	together
mm	millimetres
cm	centimetres
in(s)	inch(es)
RS	right side
WS	wrong side
sl 1	slip one stitch
psso	pass slipped stitch over
p2sso	pass 2 slipped stitches over
tbl	through back of loop
M1	make one stitch by picking up horizontal loop before next stitch and knitting into back of it
M1P	make one stitch by picking up horizontal loop before next stitch and purling into back of it
yfwd	yarn forward
yrn	yarn round needle
meas	measures
0	no stitches, times or rows
-	no stitches, times or rows for that size
yon	yarn over needle
yfrn	yarn forward round needle
wyib	with yarn at back

CROCHET TERMS

UK crochet terms and abbreviations have been used throughout. The list below gives the US equivalent where they vary.

ABBREV.	UK	US
dc	double crochet	single crochet
htr	half treble	half double crochet
tr	treble	double crochet
dtr	double treble	treble

Bead Stockist
Creative Bead Craft Ltd.
Unit 2, Asheridge Business Centre, Asheridge Rd, Chesham, Buckinghamshire HB5 2PT. England.
Tel: +44 (0)1494 778818
Email: beads@creativebeadcraft.co.uk
Website: www.creativebeadcraft.co.uk

BUTTONS, BUCKLES AND BEADS

Grey
00332

Grey
00315

Grey
00316

Grey
00317

Natural
00333

Natural
00318

Grey
00319

Abalone
00322

Shell
00320

Shell
00321

Metal
00337

Metal
00338

Grey
00347

Grey
00348

Natural
00349

Natural
00350

Brass
00410

Brass
00409

Brass
00408

Silver
00405

Silver
00406

Silver
00407

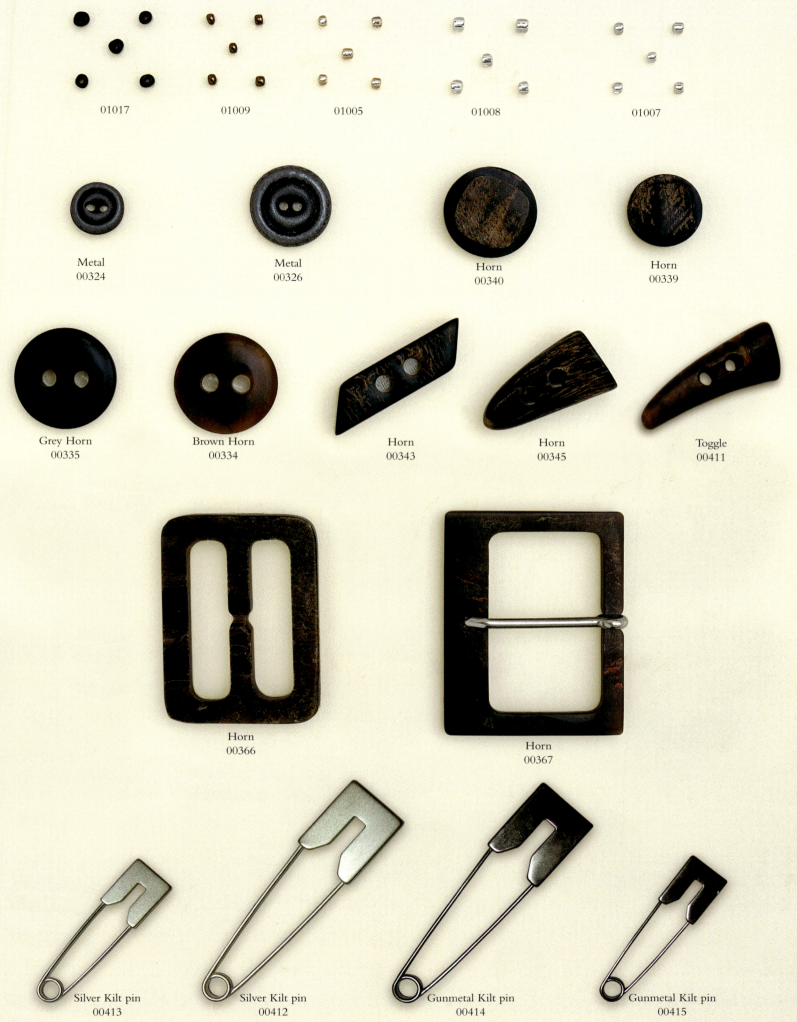

01017

01009

01005

01008

01007

Metal
00324

Metal
00326

Horn
00340

Horn
00339

Grey Horn
00335

Brown Horn
00334

Horn
00343

Horn
00345

Toggle
00411

Horn
00366

Horn
00367

Silver Kilt pin
00413

Silver Kilt pin
00412

Gunmetal Kilt pin
00414

Gunmetal Kilt pin
00415

00377

01022

00351

00369

00353

00368

00378

01013

01021

00379

00372

01019

00352

00370

00380

00355

00381

01023

01020

00371

00383

00358

01014

00354

00374

00375

00384

01016

00357

01015

01006

00356

00373

00359

00382

01018

00385

00376

00398

00401

00389

00391

00364

00394

00360

00386

00393

00388

00363

00400

00390

00397

00396

00395

00399

00362

00392

00387

00361

Bag
Handles

Bag Handles pictured are approx
50% of actual size.

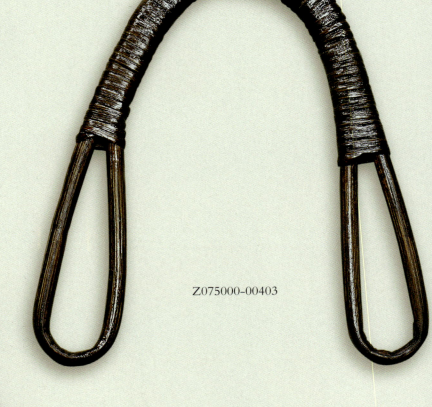

Z075000-00403

Z075000-00404

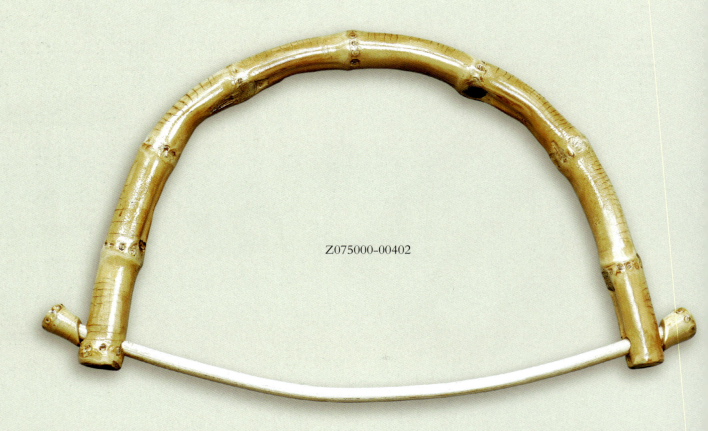

Z075000-00402

Rowan Overseas Stockists

For more information on overseas stockists and Mail Order details please contact the Rowan distributor / agent listed under each country. 'ROWAN AT ....' stockists carry a large range of Rowan Yarns.

AUSTRALIA

DISTRIBUTOR : Australian Country Spinners, 314 Albert Street, Brunswick, Victoria 3056. Tel : (03) 9380 3888.

Albert Park – Wool Baa, 124 Bridport Street, VIC 3206 Tel (03) 9690 6633 Email: sales@woolbaa.com, www.woolbaa.com
Byron Bay – Byron Bay Craft, Shop 6 Rear 14 Middleton Street, NSW 2481 Tel (02) 6680 9951
Canberra – The Shearing Shed, 7B Manuka Court, Bougainville Street, Manuka, ACT 2603. Tel (02) 6295 0061.
Hawthorn – Calico & Chintz, 99 Auburn Rd, VIC 3123. Tel (03) 9813 5634
Innaloo – The Wool Shack, PO Box 228, WA 6918 Tel (08) 9446 6344 Email: info@thewoolshack.com, www.thewoolshack.com
LINFIELD – ROWAN AT Greta's Handcrafts Centre, 321 Pacific Highway, Lindfield, NSW 2070. Tel (02) 9416 2489
Malvern East – Marta's Yarns, 33 Waverley Road, VIC 3145 Tel (03) 9572 0319
MELBOURNE – ROWAN AT Sunspun, 185 Canterbury Road, VIC 3126. Tel (03) 9830 1609 Email: shop@sunspun.com.au, www.sunspun.com.au
Mittagong – Victoria House Needlecraft P/L, Hume H'way, NSW 2575. Tel (02) 4871 1682
Moorabbin – Wool Shop Direct, 461 South Road, VIC 3189 Tel (03) 9533 1233
Mosman Park – Calico and Ivy, 1 Glyde Street, 6012 Tel (08) 9383 3794 Email: calicohs@ozemail.com.au, www.calicohouse.com.au
Nundle – Nundle Woollen Mill, 1 Oakenville St, NSW. Tel (02) 6769 3330
Pennant Hills – Cherryhills, Shop 6, 354 Pennant Hills Road, NSW 2121 Tel (02) 9484 0212
Prahran – AK Tradions of the Silk Road, 524 Malvern Road, Hawksburn Village, VIC 3181 Tel (03) 9510 0588
Queens Park – Atelier Kumi, 2a Ashton Street, NSW 2022. Tel (02) 9369 3705
Sydney – Tapestry Craft, 50 York Street, NSW 2000 Tel (02) 929 8588
Williamstown – Stitchery Blue, 95a Ferguson Street, VIC 3016. Tel (03) 9397 2005

AUSTRIA

DISTRIBUTOR: Coats Harlander GmbH, Autokaderstrasse 31, A-1210 Wien. Tel (01) 27716 – 0 Fax (01) 27716 - 228

WIEN – ROWAN AT Zwei Glatt Zwei Verkehrt – Josefstaedter Str. 14, A-1080. Tel/Fax 0043/1/4035735 Email: wolle@zweiglattzweiverkehrt.at www.zweiglattzweiverkehrt.at
FELDKIRCH – ROWAN AT Zum Schwarzen Schaf, Schlossergasse 1, A-6800 Tel 0043/552281072 Email: wolle@amazingthings.at www.amazingthings.at

BELGIUM

DISTRIBUTOR: Pavan, Meerlaanstraat 73, 9860 Balegem Tel (09) 221 8594 Fax (09) 221 5662

ANTWERPEN – ROWAN AT Lana, Anselmostraat 92, 2018 Tel (03) 238 70 17 Email: info@lana-antwerpen.be
Brugge – Stikkestek, Walweinstraat 3, 8000 Tel (050) 34 03 45
Brussel – Art et Fil, 25, Rue du Baillie, 1000. Tel (02) 647 64 51
Brussel – L'Atelier de la Passion, 7, Av. St. Pancratius, 1950 Kraainem Tel 02 725 53 23
Brussel – La Filandihre, 121 Rue Vander Elst, 1170. Tel (02) 742 08 42
Gavere-Asper – Pas 42, Stationstraat 143, 9890. Tel 0495 82 53 47
Gent – Stoffenidee, Hoogpoort 8, 9000. Tel (09) 233 3748
Hasselt – Handmade, Diesterstraat 3, 3500. Tel (011) 22 20 28 Email: info@hand-made.be
Hemiksem – De Schaepestalle, Provinciale Steenweg 153, 2620 Tel/fax (03) 877 70 23
Kortrijk – Alle steken op een rij, Grote Kring 14, 8500
LEUVEN – ROWAN AT 't Wolwinkeltje, Parijsstraat 25, 3000 Tel/fax (016) 22 75 48
Leuven – D-Yarns, Van Langendoncklaan 17, 3012 Wilsele Tel 016 20 13 81
ST-NIKLAAS – ROWAN AT 't Wolleken, Ankerstraat 28, 9100 Tel (03) 777 64 15
Wavre – L'Arbrelaine, 7 rue des Brasseries, 1300 Tel 010 22 76 10
WILSELE – ROWAN AT D. Yarns, P Van Langendoncklaan 17 Tel (016) 20 13 81

CANADA

DISTRIBUTOR: Diamond Yarn, 9697 St Laurent, Montreal, Quebec H3L 2N1 Tel (514) 388-6188 / Diamond Yarn (Toronto), 155 Martin Ross, Unit 3, Toronto, Ontario M3J 2L9. Tel (416) 736-6111 Email: diamond@diamondyarn.com www.diamondyarn.com

ALBERTA

Calgary – Gina Brown's, 107 – 5718, 1A Street S.W., T2H 0E8. Tel (403) 255-2200 E-mail: ginabrown's@hotmail.com
Calgary – Knit One, Chat Too, 509-1851 Sirocco Dr. SW, T3H 4R5 Tel (403) 685 5556 E-mail: allison@knitonechattoo.com
Calgary – Pudding Yarn, 1516-6th St., SW, T2R 0Z8 Tel (403) 244 2996 Toll Free 1-888-355-0555
Calgary – Make One Yarn Studio, 841 1st Ave NE, T2E 0C2 Tel (403) 802 4770
Edmonton – Wool Revival, 6513-112 Avenue, T5W 0P1. Tel (780) 471-2749

BRITISH COLUMBIA

Courtenay – Uptown Yarns, 206-307 Fifth St., V9N 1J9 Tel/Fax (250) 338 1940 E-mail: uptownyarns@yahoo.ca
Duncan – The Loom, Whippletree Junction, Box H, 4705 Trans Canada Hwy, V9L 6E1. Tel (250) 746-5250
Kelowna – Art of Yarn, 102-3010 Pandosy St., V1Y 1W2. Tel (250) 717 3247
Richmond – Wool & Wicker, 120-12051 2nd Ave Tel (604) 275 1239 Toll Free 1-877-966-5945 www.woolandwicker.com
Vancouver – ROWAN AT Urban Yarns, 1-4421 West 10th Ave., V6R 2H8 Tel (604) 228 1122 E-mail: urbanyarns@telus.net www.urbanyarns.ca
Victoria – Beehive Wool Shop, 1700 Douglas Street, V8W 2G7. Tel : (250) 385 2727. Toll Free 1-888-334-9005 E-mail: beehivewool@telus.net
West Vancouver – The Knit & Stitch Shoppe, 2460a Marine Drive, V7V 1L3. Tel (604) 922-1023 Toll Free 1-800-565-KNIT (5648) Email ingy@knit-n-stitch.com www.knit-n-stitch.com

MANITOBA

WINNIPEG – ROWAN AT Ram Wools, 1266 Fife Street, R2X 2N6. Tel (204) 949-6868 Toll Free 1-800-263-8002 Fax (204) 947-0024 Email yarn@ramwools.com www.ramwools.com MAIL ORDER AVAILABLE

NEW BRUNSWICK

Cricket Cove – Cricket Cove, 836 Main St., E5H 1A2 Tel (506) 456 3897 Fax (506 529 3333 E-mail: cricketcove@hotmail.com

NOVA SCOTIA

Baadeck – Baadeck Yarns, 16 Chebucto St, B0E 1B0. Tel (902) 295-3303 Toll Free 1-877-707-5512 Email: baadeckyarns@ns.sympatico.ca
Dartmouth – Tangled Skeins, 158A Portland St, Dartmouth, B2Y 1J1. Tel (902) 464 0387

ONTARIO

ANCASTER – ROWAN AT The Needle Emporium, 420 Wilson St. East, L9G 4S4. Tel 01 800 667-9167 www.needleemporium.com Mail Order Service
AURORA – ROWAN AT Knit or Knot, 14800 Yonge St. (Aurora Shopping Centre) L4G 1N3 Tel 905 713 1818 Toll Free 1/877- 272-9665 (mail order service available)
Kingston – Gwin Gryffon, 157 Wellington St. K7L 3E1 Tel (613) 549 5546 www.gwingryffon.com
LONDON – ROWAN AT Needles & Pins Inc., 205 Oxford St. #103, N6A 5G6 Tel 519 642 3445 Email: ellen@needlesandpins.ca www.needlesandpins.ca
Milton – Main St. Yarns, 15 Martin St. Unit AM8, L9T 2R1 Tel 905 693-4299 email: info@mainstyarns.com www.mainstyarns.com
Ottawa – Wool 'n' Things, 1439 Youville Drive, Unit 20, K1C 4M8 Tel 613 841 8689 Email: gisele@woolnthings.com www.woolnthings.com
STE. CATHARINES – ROWAN AT Serendipity, 23 Duke St. L2R 5W1 Tel (905) 685 1183 www.wowbeads.ca
TORONTO – ROWAN AT Passionknit, 3232 Yonge St. M4N 2L4 Tel: 416 322 0688 Tel: 1-800-701-7610 (Mail order service available)
TORONTO – ROWAN AT Romni Wools Ltd, 658 Queen St. West M6J 1E6 Tel (416) 703 0202 Mail Order Service available
TORONTO – ROWAN AT Village Yarns, 4895 Dundas Street West, M9A 1B2 Tel (416) 232-2361 www.villageyarns.com
TORONTO – ROWAN AT The Naked Sheep, 2144A Queen St. E., M4E 1E3 Tel (416) 691-6320 Fax (416) 691-6321
UNIONVILLE – ROWAN AT Mary's Yarn Shop, 136 Main St, L3R 2G5 Tel (905) 479-6576 Mail Order Service available
WATERLOO – ROWAN AT Cloth and Clay, #45-75 King St.. S., Waterloo Town Square, N2J 1P2 Tel (519) 886 7400
WINDSOR – ROWAN AT Knit One, Purl One, 1674 Ottawa St. N8Y 1R1 Tel (519) 973 4606

QUEBEC

Montreal – A la Tricoteuse, 779 Rachel Est, H2J 2H4 Tel (514) 527-2451
Montreal – Moulinee Yarns, 2679 Notre-Dame Ouest, H3G 1N9 Tel (514) 935-4401 Email: svetlana@moulineyarns.com, www.moulineyarns.com
Pte Claire – Les Lainages Du Petit Mouton, 2958 Boul. St-Jean, H9R 3J1 Tel 514 694 6268

SASKATCHEWAN

Regina – Hip 2 Knit, 2227 – 14th Ave., S4P 0X8. Tel 306 585 7557

DENMARK

AALBORG – ROWAN AT Design Vaerkstedet, Boulevarden 9, 9000. Tel 98 12 07 13 Fax 98 13 02 13
AARHUS C – ROWAN AT Inger's, Volden 19, 8000 Tel 86 19 40 44
Copenhagen – Wilfert's, Gammel Kongevej 102, 1850 Frederiksberg. Tel/Fax 33 22 54 90. Email: wilfert@webspeed.dk www.wilferts.dk
Kobenhaven K – Uldstedet, Fiolstraede 13, 1171. Tel/Fax 33 91 1771 Email: uldstedet@get2net.dk, www.uldstedet.dk
KOBENHAVN K – ROWAN AT Sommerfuglen, Vandkunsten 3, 1467 Tel/Fax 33 32 82 90. Email: mail@sommerfuglen.dk www.sommerfuglen.dk
Lyngby – Uldstedet, Gl. Jernbanevej 7, 2800. Tel 45 88 1088 Fax 45 93 41 77 Email: uldstedet@get2net.dk www.uldstedet.dk
ROSKILDE – ROWAN AT Garnhokeren, Karen Olsdatterstraede 9, 4000 Tel/Fax 46 37 20 63

EIRE

Dublin – Springwools Ltd, The Olde Sawmills, Walkinstown, Dublin 12. Tel:+353 1 450 9134 Fax: +353 1 450 9233 Email: sales@springwools.com www.springwools.com
Co. Wicklow – The Wool Shop, 71 Main Street, Bray. Tel/Fax: +3531 2760029

FINLAND

DISTRIBUTOR: Coats Opti Oy, Ketjutie 3, 04220 Kerava Tel: (358) 9 274871 Fax: (358) 9 2748 7330 Email: coatsopti.sales@coats.com

FRANCE

DISTRIBUTOR: Coats France/Steiner Freres, 100 Avenue du General de Gaulle, 18 500 Mehun-sur-Yevre Tel 02 48 23 12 30 Fax 02 48 23 12 40

Besançon – La Pastourelle, 4 rue Delavelle, 25000. Tel 03 81 80 96 51
Bordeaux – Boutique Can-Elle, 49 rue du Tondu, 33000. Tel 05 56 96 51 38
Brissac Quince – Picoti Picota la boutique, 15 Place Georges Clemenceau, 49320. Tel 02 41 44 16 00
Challans – Autrement, Passage Carnot, 85000. Tel 02 51 93 54 69
Dijon – Planete Laines, 20 rue du Chateau, 21000. Tel 03 80 30 37 96
GRENOBLE – ROWAN AT Perles & Moi, 2 rue Casimir Perier, 38000. Tel 04 76 56 18 37 Fax 04 76 53 99 16
Le Havre – Feelaine, 90 bis rue Victor Hugo, 76600. Tel 02 35 43 19 92
Lyon – Morceaux Choisis, 49 rue Franklin, 69002. Tel 04 78 37 39 63
Marly le Roi – Juste un Petit Point, 5 Grand'Rue. Tel 01 39 16 04 02
Molsheim – Laine et Lin, 19 rue de Strasbourg, 67120. Tel 03 88 38 87 60
Narbonne – Atelier Jade, 1 bis rue Louis Blanc, 11100. Tel 04 68 32 72 41
Orsay – Anatis, 3-5 rue du Dct Lauriot. Tel 01 69 07 15 15
PARIS (3) – ROWAN AT Entree des Fournisseurs, 8 rue des Francs Bourgeois. Tel 01 48 87 58 98 Fax 01 48 87 77 40. Email: edf@club-internet.fr www.entreedesfournisseurs.com
PARIS (7) – ROWAN AT Le Bon Marche, 115 rue du Bac, 75007. Tel 01 44 39 80 00 Fax 01 44 39 80 50
Paris (9) – Lecomptoir, 26 rue Cadet, 75009. Tel 01 42 46 20 72
Paris (16) – Les Tricots De Coco, 35 rue Davioud, 75016. Tel 01 45 20 11 80
Ramonville – Le Sabot des Laines, 15 avenue d'Occitanie, 31520. Tel 05 61 73 14 38
Rennes – L'écheveau, 11 rue de la Monnaie, 35000. Tel 02 99 79 14 86
Rennes – LTM, 11 rue Poullain Duparc, 35000. Tel 02 99 78 20 60
Rouen – Travaux d'Aiguilles, 25 rue Cauchoise, 76000. Tel 02 35 70 38 50
Sarzeau – Les Chemins Buissonniers, 1 Place Marie le Franc, 56370 Tel 02 97 48 08 30
STRASBOURG – ROWAN AT Elle Tricote, 8 rue du coq, 67000 Tel 03 88 23 03 13 Fax 03 88 23 01 69 Email elletricote@agat.net www.elletricote.com
Thonon Les Bains – Au Vieux Rouet, 7 rue Ferdinand Dubouloz, 74200. Tel 04 50 71 07 33

GERMANY

DISTRIBUTOR: Coats GmbH, Kaiserstrasse 1, 79341 Kenzingen Tel 7644 802 185 www.coatsgmbh.de

Aachen – Goerg + Goerg Wolle, Annastrasse 18, 52062 Tel 0241/4705913 Fax 0241/4705919 E-mail: magoerg@gmx.de, www.goerg-wolle.de
Adelsdorf-Aisch – Das Strickforum – Hoehenstrasse 3, 91325 Tel 09195/50515 E-mail: info@dasstrickforum.de, www.dasstrickforum.de
Ahaus – Die newue WollPalette, Bahnhofstrasse 96, 48683 Tel 02561/2241 Fax 02563/98209 E-mail: info@wollpalette.de, www.wollpalette.de
Ahrweiler – Dat Laedche, Niederhut Str. 17, 53474 Tel 02641/4464 E-mail: dat_laedche_adams@t-online.de
Bad Lauterberg – Naehzentrum, Hauptstr. 165, 37431 Tel 05524/5354
Bad Neuenahr-Ahrweiler – Dat Lädche, Niederhutstr. 17, 53474 Tel 02641/4464 E-mail: dat_laedche_adams@t-lonline.de
Backnang – Wollstube Wollin, Eduard-Breuninger-Str. 7A, 71522, Tel 07191/902828 Fax 07191/341726 E-mail: wollstabe-wollin@t-online.de
Bargteheide – Wollstudio Bargteheide, Bahnhofstrasse 7, 22941 Tel/Fax 04532-287818 E-mail: wollstudio@web, www.wollstudio-bargteheide.de
BAYREUTH – ROWAN AT Strick-Art, Sophienstrasse 20, 95444, Tel 0921/5304870 E-mail: strickwerk@gmx.de
Berlin – Frau Wolle – Bismarckstrasse. 76, 12157 Tel 030/8559181 Fax 030/85605172 E-mail: frauwolle@web.de, www.frau-wolle-berlin.de
Berlin – Holz + Wolle, Warnemuender Strasse 29, 14199 Tel 030/83222762
Berlin – Loops Maschenpower, Woerthestrasse 19, 10405 Tel 030/44054934
Bielefeld – Wollzauber, Vilsendorfer Strasse 45, 33739 Tel/Fax 05206/2992
Bonn – Wollkorbchen, Oststr. 6, 53173, Tel 0228/363379 Fax 0228/363377 E-mail: wollkoerbchen@gmx.de
Bonn – Patent, Koblenzer Strasse 18, 53179 Tel 0228/93399175 Fax 0228/93399173 E-mail: info@patent-wolle.de, www.patent-woll.de
Braunschweig – Stil-Blute, Pestalozzistr. 17, 38114 Tel 0531-1226736 E-mail: sanne_wenke@web.de, www.stil-bluete.net
Buchholz-Sproetze – Arladne Wolle und Mehr, Niedersachsenstrasse 8, 21244 Tel 04186-888931 E-mail: arladne-wolle@t-online.de, www.arladne-wolle-und-mehr.de
Dannenberg – Der rote Faden, Lange Strasse 32, 29451 Tel 05861-986050
Detmold – Handarbeiten Mueller, Krumme Strasse 19, 32756 Tel 05231/28216 E-mail: info@handarbeitenmueller.de, www.handarbeitenmueller.de
Dortmund – Wolle, Tee und mehr ....., Neuer Graben 89, 44137 Tel 0231-9509360 Fax 0231-9509365 E-mail: winfried.gutbier@t-online.de
Dresden – Strick und Faden, Rothenburger Strasse 14, 01099 Tel 0351/8104086 E-mail: Kristina.ring@tiscali.de
Dusseldorf – Woll Duo, Scharnhorstrasse 16, 40477 Tel 0211/467776 Fax 0211/44022040
Eberswalde – Eberswalder Blitz Handels GmbH, Eisenbahnstrasse 92-93, 16225 Tel 03338-752547 Fax 03334-202030 E-mail: hanisch@eberswalder-blitz.de
Elmshorn – Strickcafe, Kirchenstrasse 8, 25335 Tel 04121/2611751 Fax 04121/103055 E-mail: Katrin.Melcher@onlinehome.de
Erfurt – Wolle Werkstatt, Paulstrasse 29-30, 99084 Tel 0361/7892727 E-mail: knotakt@wolle-werkstatt.de, www.wolle-werkstatt.de
Essen – Wollstudio, Frankenstrasse 99, 45134 Tel 0201/442168
Esslingen – Phantasia, Apothekergasse 13, 73728, Tel 0711/523979 Fax 0711/523979
Flensburg – Strick Chic GmbH, Grosse Strasse 53-55, 24937 Tel 0461/23942 E-mail: daubrawa@t-online.de
Freiburg – Nadel & Faden, Carl-Kistner-Strasse 19, 79115 Tel 0761/441044 Fax 0761/441045 E-mail: nadel-faden@t-online.de, www.nadel-faden.de
Gifhorn – Heidis Masche, Steinweg 60, 38518 Tel/Fax 05371/53260
Hamburg – Pur-Pur-Wolle, Heussweg 41B, Karl-Schneider Passagen, 20255 Tel 040/4904579 Email: info@purpurwolle.de, www.purpurwolle.de
Hamburg – Woll Boutique, Wandsbeker Chaussee 315, 22089 Tel 040/2007620 E-mail: service@wollboutique.de, www.wollboutique.de
Hamburg – Lanaria, Hudtwalckerstrasse 24, 22299 Tel 040/47195680 E-mail: nadja@koch-muehler.de
Hannover – Tiedemann, Podbielskistrasse 5, 30163, Tel 0511/621290
Hattingen – Handarbeiten Schueth, Grosse Weilstr. 11, 45525 Tel 02324/22686 Fax 02324/570354
Hirschaid – Textiles Gestalten, Jungenhofenerweg 41, 96114 Tel 09543/419572 Fax 09543/419572
Homburg – Filatum, Saarbrucker Strasse 3, 66424 Tel 06841-171500 Fax 06841-171301 E-mail: Ibeyersdorf@t-online.de
Höxter – Betty's Wollboutique, Westerbachstrasse 5, 37671 Tel 05271/959550
Itzehoe – Allerhand von Hand, Oelmuehlengang 2, 25524. Tel 04821/2807
JUELICH – ROWAN AT Wolle & Design – Wolfshovener Str. 76, 52428 Tel 02461/54735 Fax 02461/4535 E-mail: info@wolleunddesign.de www.wolleunddesign.de
Karlsruhe – Wollstube, Elbinger Strasse 14 A, 76139 Tel/Fax 0721/689656
Kassel – Fil-Wolle, Friedrich-Ebert-Str. 1, 34117 Tel 0561/710029 Fax 0561/33815
Kelkheim – Kelkheimer Masche uvg, Hoechster Strasse 8, 65779 Tel: 06195-975678 Fax 06195-977167
Kiel – Damaschkeweg 50A, 24113 Tel 0431/651231 E-mail: doerte_dietrich@arcor.de
Köln – 'Casa Lana', Schwertnergasse 1, 50667 Tel 0221/256588 Fax 0221/254644 E-mail: casalana@aol.de
Köln – Woll-Laden Ziebeil, Honinger Weg 166, 50969 Tel 0221/3602701
Leimen – Kreativwerkstatt Tausendschon, Bahnhofstr. 45, 69181. Tel/Fax 06224/50560
Melle – Jutta s Laedchen, Haferstrasse 2, 49324 Tel 05422-49646 E-mail: jutta.mertelsmann@t-online.de
Moenchengladbach – Wolln wir mal, Hauptstrasse 95, 41236, Tel 02166/139980 Fax 02166/139981
Nassau an der Lahn – Friedhelm Gras, Obertal 18, 56377. Tel 0260/4476
Neunkirchen – Lind Wurm, Bahnhofstrasse 44, 66538 Tel 06821-179691 Fax 06821-179692
Neuss – Schweizer Stubli, Kraemerstrasse 7, 41460 Tel 02131-25057
Nuernberg – Tolle Wolle, Weinmarkt 10, 90403, Tel 0911/209497
Oberursel – Wolllaus, Rathausplatz 6, 61440 Tel 06171/586555
Oppenheim – Wolle in der Villa, Friedrich-Ebert-Str. 83, 55276, Tel/Fax 06133/2131 E-mail: wolle-seufert@t-online.de
Osnabrueck – Woll-Perle, Hakenstrasse 3, 49074, Tel 0541/258561
Potsdam – Daenische Handarbeiten, Friedrich-Ebert-Str. 27, 14467 Tel 0331/2800609 E-mail: sybilleadler@onlinehome.de
Reutlingen – Wolle & Mehr, Metzgerstr 64, 72764. Tel 07121/310488
Saarbruecken – Tausendschon, Mainzer Strasse 24 Tel 0681/9880181 Fax 0681/9880182 E-mail: mail@strickstduschon.de, www.strickstduschon.de
Salzhausen – Wollart, Eyendorferstrasse 3, 21376 Tel 04172/969123 Fax 04172/969122 E-mail: info@wollart.de www.wollart.de
SCHONAU – ROWAN AT Wollmond, Weinstrasse 12, 86956, Tel 08861/7137317 Fax 08861/7137318 E-mail: info@wollmond.de, www.wollmond.de
Schorndorf – Wollwerk Kreativ, Johannesstrasse 39, 73614 Tel 07181/41245 Fax 07181/258311Email: monika@zvw.de
Stuttgart – Fifco Strick-Art – Alexanderstr 51, 70182. Tel 0711/245218
Uelzen – Wolle und Handarbeiten, Veersser Strasse 15, 29525 Tel 0581/73137

Ulm – Wolle & Ideen, Pfauengasse 17, 89073 Tel 0731/619491
Undorf – Rosi s Wollstube, Dachred 21, 93152 Tel 09404-649299
Waldkirch – Nadel & Faden, Lange Strasse 21, 79183. Tel 07681-4749130
Weilhelm – Die Strickliesel, Obere Stadt 4, 82362 Tel 0881-9278206
Wenden – Handarbeiten, Severinusstrasse 2, 57482 Tel 02762/490291 Fax 02762/490292
Wetter – Pur Pur, Am Wilshause 28, 58300 Tel 02335/845174 Fax 02335/845174 E-mail: purpur-laedchen@gmx.de
Wolfenbuttel – Wollrausch, Harzstrasse 16, 38300 Tel 05337-94915 E-mail: maridadi@t-online.de
Wuppertal – Strick und Stick, Friedrichstr. 42, 42105, Tel 0202/7585966 Fax 0202/7585949

HOLLAND

DISTRIBUTOR: de Afstap, Oude Leliestraat 12, 1015 AW Amsterdam Tel 020-6231445, www.afstap.nl
AMERSFOORT – ROWAN AT H. W. Mur, Langestraat 13, 3811 AA. Tel 033 461 7837
AMSTERDAM - ROWAN AT de Afstap (Lonnie Bussink), Oude Leliestraat 12, 1015 AW. Tel 020-6231445 Fax 020-4278522
Amsterdam – 't Wolhuys, Raadhuisstraat 263, 2406 AD.
BERGEN – ROWAN AT Finlandia, Kleine Dorpsstraat 26, 1861 KN. Tel 0725 894642
DALEN – ROWAN AT Breiweb, Hoofdstraat 44, 7751 GD. Tel 052 4551597 Email: info@breiweb.nl www.breiweb.nl
Etten-Leur – De Wolboetiek, Bisschopsmolenstraat 169, 4076 AL. Tel 076-5022597
Haarlem – Wollana, Tempelierstraat 64-68, 2012 EH. Tel 023-5312470
HUISSEN – ROWAN AT t'Hobby hoekje, Langestraat 29, 6851 AL. Tel 026-3253507
LEIDEN – ROWAN AT Ribbels, Pieterskerk-Choorsteeg 18, 2311 TR. Tel 071 5133126
Maastricht – Buttons & Beads, Minckelersstraat 16, 6211 GX. Tel 043-325 2458
NIEUWPOORT – ROWAN AT De Schapekop, Hoogstraat 30, 2965 AL. Tel 0184-602678
OLDENZAAL – ROWAN AT Lohuis, Steenstraat 26, 7571 BK. Tel 05415-12626
s'Hertogenbosch – De Vuurvogel, Hinthamerstraat 214F, 5211 MX. Tel 073-613 2457
Sittard – Wollstreet, Rijksweg Noord 61, 6131 CJ. Tel 0464-586330
Someren – Het Weverke, Molenstraat 24, 5711EW. Tel 0493-492092
UTRECHT – ROWAN AT Modilaine, Lijnmarkt 22, 3511 KH. Tel 030-2328911
ZUIDLAREN – ROWAN AT Ryahuis (Lucy van Zanten), Telefoonstraat 26, 9471 EN. Tel 050-4092618

HONG KONG

DISTRIBUTOR: East Unity Company Limited, Unit B2, 7/F Block B, Kailey Industrial Centre, 12 Fung Yip Street, Chai Wan. Tel (852) 2869 7110 Fax (852) 2537 6952 Email: eastuni@netvigator.com

ICELAND

DISTRIBUTOR: ROWAN AT Storkurinn, Laugavegi 59, ICE -101. Tel 551 8258 Fax 562 8252 Email: malin@mmedia.is
REYKJAVIK - ROWAN AT Storkurinn, Laugavegi 59, 101 Reykjavik Tel 551 8258 Fax 562 8252. Email: malin@mmedia.is

ITALY

DISTRIBUTOR: Dl Srl, Via Piave 24-26, 20016 Pero, Milian. Tel 02 339 101 80

JAPAN

DISTRIBUTOR: Puppy Co Ltd, T151-0051, 3-16-5 Sendagaya, Shibuyaku, Tokyo Tel 03-5412-7001 Email: info@rowan-jaeger.com
Hiroshima – Puppy Hiroshima Top, 5-28 Hacchobori Nakaku Tel/Fax 082-222-0537
Hokkaido – Puppy Sapporo Komiyamaya, Nishi 2, Minami 3 Chuoku Sapporo Tel/Fax 011-221-0565
Kitakyushu – Izutsuya Department Store, 2-4 Higashiko Kokurakitaku Tel/Fax 093-522-2729
Kobe – Union Wool, 1-30-22 Kitanagasadori Chuoku, 650-0012 Tel 078-331-8854
Osaka – Masuzakiya, 4-5-4 Kawaramachi Chuoku, 541-0048 Tel 06-6222-1110
Tokyo – Rowan & Jaeger Shop, Ebisu Mitsukoshi 2F, 4-20-7 Ebisu Shibuyaku, 150-6090 Tel 03-5423-1602
Tokyo – Mitsubaya, 1-1-1 Minamiaoyama Minatoku, 107-0062 Tel 03-3404-1677
Tokyo – Hobby & Craft Salon, 8F Mitsukoshi new bldng, 1-4-1 Nihonbashi Muromachi Chuoku, 103-8001. Tel 03-3273-6500

KOREA

DISTRIBUTOR: Coats Korea Co. Ltd., 5F Kuckdong B/D, 935-40 Bangbae-Dong, Seocho-Gu, Seoul Tel: 82-2-521-6262, Fax: 82-2-521-5181 E-mail: rozenpark@coats.com
Seoul – My Knit Studio, (3F) 121 Kwan Hoon Dong, Chongro-ku Tel 822 722 0006 Email: myknit@myknit.com, www.myknit.com

NEW ZEALAND

Auckland – Alterknitives, PO Box 47961, Tel : (64 9) 376 0337
Christchurch – Knit World, 189 Peterborough St Tel: 03 379 2300
Dunedin – Knit World, 26 The Octagon Tel: 03 477 0400
Lower Hutt – Knit World (Mail Order Only), PO Box 30 645 Tel: 04 586 4530 E-mail: info@knitting.co.nz
Taupo – The Stitchery, Suncourt Shopping Centre, Tamamutu St. Tel: (64 7) 378 9195 E-mail: stitchery@xtra.co.nz
Wellington – Knit World, Shop 210b, Left Bank, Cuba Mall Tel: 04 385 1918

NORWAY

DISTRIBUTOR: Coats Knappehuset AS – Pb 100 Ulset, 5873 Bergen. Tel (47) 55 53 93 00 Fax (47) 55 53 93 93
Bergen – Pinnsvin Design, Jonsvollsgt. 9, 5011. Tel 99 37 09 12, www.pinnsvindesign.no
Dombas – Tusen og En Trad, 2660. Tel 61 24 16 50
Oslo – Bentes Boutique, Gjovikgt. 1, 0470. Tel 22 18 26 39
Oslo – Guanako Garn & Design, Seilduksgt. 7, 0553. Tel 23 22 98 11
Oslo – Tjorven Garn og Gaver, Valkyriegt. 17, 0366. Tel 22 69 33 60

SINGAPORE

DISTRIBUTOR: Golden Dragon Store, 101 Upper Cross St. #02-51, People's Park Centre, 058357. Tel (65) 65358454 Email: gdscraft@hotmail.com

SPAIN

DISTRIBUTOR: -Barcelona – Oyambre, Pau Claris 145, 08009 Tel/Fax: (34) 93 4872672
Barcelona – Oyambre, Pau Claris 145, 08009 Tel/Fax: (34) 93 4872672

SOUTH AFRICA

Johannesburg – Arthur Bales Ltd, 62 4th Avenue, Linden, Johannesburg 2195 Tel (27) 118 882 401 Fax (27) 117 826 137 E-mail: arthurb@new.co.za

SWEDEN

DISTRIBUTOR: Coats Expotex AB, Division Craft, Box 297, 401 24 Göteborg Tel (46) 33 720 79 00 Fax (46) 31 47 16 50
Ahus – PPCO, Gamla Skeppsbron 10, 296 31 Tel (044) 24 05 21
Borås – Stickat och Klart, Hallbergsgatan 2, 503 30 Tel (033) 10 32 38
Brastad – Gullmarens stickverkstad/Garn Torpet, Frojdendal 132, Samstad, 454 91 Tel (0523) 44005
Goteborg – Strikk, Vallgatan 22, 411 16 Tel (031) 711 37 99 www.strikkdesign.com
Malmo – Irmas Hus, Kalendegatan 13, 211 35 Tel (040) 611 08 00
STOCKHOLM – ROWAN AT Wincent, Norrtullsgatan 65, 113 45 Tel (08) 33 70 60. E-mail: wincent@chello.se www.wincentgarner.se & www.wincentyarn.com
Stockholm – Garnverket, Hantverkargatan 14, 112 21 Tel (08) 651 78 08 www.garnverket.com
Stockholm – NK Tyg & Sy, Hamngatan 18-20, 111 77 Tel (08) 762 88 50
Uppsala - Yll & Tyll, Bredgrand 7c, 753 20 Tel (018) 10 51 90 www.yllotyll.com

SWITZERLAND

DISTRIBUTOR: Coats Stroppel AG, CH-5300 Turgi (AG).
Aarau – Mode + Wolle, Graben 30, 5000 Tel 0041/628246611 Fax 0041/628246544 E-mail: bpeter@mode-wolle.ch
BERN – ROWAN AT WollWirrWare, Astrid Balli, Wylestrasse 53, 3014 Tel 0041/31332 06 33 E-mail: info@wollwirrware.ch
Buchs – Wool Art, Bahnhofstr. 57, Parkhof, 9470 Tel/Fax 0041/81/756 56 66
Burgdorf – Woll-Laden, Barbara Zueger, Muehlegasse 4, 3401 Burgdorf Tel (0041) 344313753 www.woll-laden.ch
Rapperswil – Pingouin-Wolle GmgH, Zentrum Sonnenhof, 8640 Tel (0041) 552104347 Fax (0041) 552104347 E-mail: pingouin.wolle@bluewin.ch
Wettingen – Lana Luna...mehr als Wolle, Landstrasse 28, 5430 Tel (0041) 564300026
Zurich – Handart, Neumarkt 10, 8001 Tel 0041/12515757
ZURICH – ROWAN AT Vilfil, Kreuzstrasse 39, Beim Kreuzplatz, 8032 Tel 0041/13839903

TAIWAN

DISTRIBUTOR: Laiter Wool Knitting Co Ltd, 10-1 313 Lane, Sec 3, Chung Ching North Road, Taipei Tel: (886) 2 2596 0269 Fax: (886) 2 2598 0619
DISTRIBUTOR: Mon Cher Coporation, 9F No 117 Chung Sun First Road, Kaoshiung Tel: (886) 7 9711988 Fax: (886) 9711666

UNITED STATES OF AMERICA

DISTRIBUTOR: WESTMINSTER FIBERS INC, 4 Townsend West, Suite 8, Nashua, New Hampshire 03063 Tel (603) 886 5041/5043 Email info@westminsterfibers.com

ALABAMA
Huntsville - Yarn Expressions, 8415 Whitesburg Dr., 35802 Tel (800) 833-6133 www.yarnexpressions.com

ALASKA
Anchorage – Far North Yarn Company, 2636 Spenard Rd, Ste 6, 99503 Tel (907) 258-5648

ARIZONA
Scottsdale – Jessica Knits, 8275 E. Bell Rd., #1186, 85260. Tel (480) 515-4454
Surprise – Needler's Nest, 12133 W Bell Rd, Ste 102, 85374 Tel (888) 550-4411

ARKANSAS
LITTLE ROCK – ROWAN AT The Handworks Gallery, 2911 Kavanaugh, 72205 Tel (501) 664 6300 www.handworksgallery.com
Fayetteville – Hand Held – A Knitting Gallery, 119 North East Avenue, 72701 Tel (479) 582-2910

CALIFORNIA
Alameda – Yarn!, 2311 Santa Clara, 94501 Tel (510) 522-9276
Alpine – Lori's Frames, Fibers and Frills, 2206 Alpine Blvd., 91901 Tel (619) 659-9784
ANAHEIM HILLS – ROWAN AT Velona Needlecraft, 5701 M Santa Ana Canyon Road, 92807 Tel (800) 972-1570
Bakersfield – Classy Knits & Yarns, 1833 F Street, 93306 Tel: (661) 325-7226
BERKELEY – ROWAN AT Stash, 1820 Solano Ave, Ste. B-2, 94707 Tel (510) 558-9276
Dana Point – Strands, 34212 Violet Lantern, 92629 Tel (949) 496-4021
El Cerrito – Skein Lane, 7512 Fairmount, 94530 Tel: (510) 525-1828 www.skeinlane.com
Encinitas – Common Threads, 466 South Coast Hwy., #101, 92024 Tel (760) 436-6119 www.fiberartshop.com
Half Moon Bay – Fengari, 400 Main St, 94019 Tel (650) 726-2550
Ladera Ranch – La Petite Knitterie, 25642 Crown Valley Parkway, E3, 92694 Tel (949) 347-7073
Laguna Beach – Strands & Stitches, 1516 South Coast Hwy., 92651 Tel: (949) 497-5648
LAGUNA HILLS – ROWAN AT Yarn Lady, 24371 Avenida de la Carlota, 92653 Tel (888) 770-7809 www.yarnlady.com
La Jolla - Knitting in La Jolla, 909 Prospect St., 92037 Tel (800) 956-5648
LONG BEACH – ROWAN AT Alamitos Bay Yarn Co, 174 Marina Dr, 90803 Tel (562) 799-8484 www.yarncompany.com
LOS ALTOS - ROWAN AT Uncommon Threads, 293 State Street, 94022 Tel (650) 941-1815 www.uncommonthreadsyarn.com
Los Angeles – The Knitter's Studio, 8118 West Third St, 90048 Tel (323) 655-6487
Los Angeles – Black Sheep Knittery, 6324 Yucca St, 90028 Tel (323) 464-2253
Los Angeles – Jennifer Knits, 108 Barrington Walk, 90049 Tel (310) 471-8733
Mendocino – Mendocino Yarn, 45066 Ukiah Str, 95460 Tel (888) 530 - 1400
Mill Valley – Studio Knit Inc., 320 Miller Ave, 94941 Tel (415) 389-9994
Napa – Yarns On First, 1305 First St., 94559 Tel (707) 967-0779
OAKLAND – ROWAN AT The Knitting Basket, 2054 Mountain Blvd, 94611 Tel (800) 654-4887
OAKLAND – ROWAN AT Article Pract, 5010 Telegraph Ave, 94609 Tel (510) 595-7875
Pacific Grove – Monarch Knitting & Quilting, 529 Central Avenue, 93950 Tel (831) 647-9276
Pasadena – Elegance Designer Yarns, 975 E. Green St, Ste 102, 91101 Tel (626) 792-2404
Pasedena – Skein, 1101 East Walnut St, 91106 Tel (626) 577/2035
Petaluma – Knitterly, 260 Petaluma Blvd. North, 94952 Tel (707) 762-9276
Pleasanton – Main Street Knits, 205A Main Street, 94566 Tel (925) 249-9276
Redondo Beach – L'Atelier, 1714 ? Catalina, 90277 Tel (800) 833 6133
ROCKLIN – ROWAN AT Filati Yarns, 4810 Granite Dr, Ste A-7, 95677 Tel (800) 398 - 9043
St. HELENA – ROWAN AT Muse, 1400 Oak Ave., 94574 Tel: (707) 967-9500
San Diego – The Grove at Juniper and 30th, 3010 Juniper St. 92104 Tel (619) 284-7684
SAN FRANCISCO - ROWAN AT Greenwich Yarns, 2073 Greenwich Street, 94123 Tel (415) 567-2535
SAN FRANCISCO – ROWAN AT Imaginknit, 3897 18th Street, 94114 Tel: (415) 621-6642 www.imagiknit.com
San Francisco – Urban Knitting Studio, 320 Fell St, 94102 Tel (415) 552-5333
San Francisco – Noe Knit, 3957 24th St., 94114 Tel (415) 970-9750
San Jose – CommuKNITy, 1345 The Alameda, 95126 Tel (408) 293-9333
Santa Barbara – BB's Knits, 3030 State St, 93105 Tel (805) 569-0531
Santa Monica – L'Atelier, 1202 Montana Ave 90403 Tel (800) 493-1244
SANTA MONICA – ROWAN AT Wild Fiber, 1453 E. 14th Street, 90404 Tel (310) 458-2748
SARATOGA – ROWAN AT Knitting Arts, 14567 Big Basin Way, 95070 Tel: (408) 867-5010 www.goknit.com
Studio City – La Knitterie Parisienne, 12642-44 Ventura Blvd, 91604 Tel (818) 766-1515
THOUSAND OAKS – ROWAN AT Eva's Needleworks, 1321 East Thousand Oaks Blvd, 91362 Tel (805) 379 – 0722
TRUCKEE – ROWAN AT Jimmy Beans Wool, 10065 Donner Pass Road, 96161 Tel (530) 582-9530 www.jimmybeanswool.com
Valley Village – Stitch Café, 12443 Magnolia Blvd, 91607 Tel (818) 980-1234
Ventura – Anacapa Fine Yarns, 4572 Telephone Rd #909, 93003 Tel (805) 654-9500
Walnut Creek – Fash-Ion Knit, 1538 Newell Avenue, 94596 Tel (925) 943-3994
West Hollywood - Knit Café, 8441 Melrose Ave, 90069 Tel (323) 658-5648

COLORADO
CENTENNIAL – ROWAN AT Knitty Cat, 7475 E. Arapahoe Road #15, 80112 Tel: (720) 493-5648
Fort Collins – Lambspun of Colorado, 1101 East Lincoln Ave., 80524 Tel (800) 558-5262
Grand Junction – Cozy, Knit & Purl, 2490 Patterson Rd., 81505 Tel (970) 464-1088
Highlands Ranch – String, LLC, 9325 Dorchester St, Ste #121, 80129 Tel (303) 470-6335
Littleton – A Knitted Peace, 5654-C South Prince St., 80120 Tel: (303) 730-0366
Steamboat Springs – Knitch – The Drawn Thread, 80488 Tel (970) 871-9640

CONNECTICUT
Avon – The Wool Connection, 34 East Main Street, Old Avon Village North, 06001 Tel (800) 933-9665 www.woolconnection.com
Greenwich - The Knitting Niche Inc., 115 Mason St, 06830 Tel (203) 869-6205
Mystic – Mystic River Yarns, 14 Holmes Street, 06355 Tel (860) 536-4305
New Milford – Village Sheep, 369 Litchfield Road, 06776 Tel (860) 354-5442
Westport – Knitting Central, 582 Post Rd East, 06880 Tel (203) 454-4300
Woodbridge - Yarn Barn, 1666 Litchfield Turnpike, 06525 Tel (203) 389-5117

DISTRICT OF COLUMBIA
GEORGETOWN - ROWAN AT Stitch DC Georgetown, 1071 Wisconsin Ave, NW 20007 Tel (202) 333 5648
WASHINGTON – ROWAN AT Stitch DC, 731A 8th Street, SE, 20003 Tel (202) 544-8900

FLORIDA
Hollywood – The Yarn Tree, 2000-3 Harrison St, 33067 Tel (954) 921-1160

IDAHO
Boise – Drop A Stitch, 413 South 8th St, Ste.A. 83702 Tel (208) 331-3767
Eagle – Handmade, 124 E State St, 83616 Tel (208) 938-8341

ILLINOIS
CHICAGO – ROWAN AT Knitting Workshop, 2218 N Lincoln Ave, 60614, Tel (773) 929-5776
Chicago – Arcadia Knitting, 1613 W. Lawrence Ave., 60640, Tel (773) 293-1211
Chicago – Nina, 1655 W. Division St., 60622 Tel (773) 486-8996
Geneva – Wool & Co Simple Gifts, 23 South 3rd St, 60134 Tel (630) 232-2305 www.woolandcompany.com
Northbrook - Three Bags Full, 1130 Shermer Rd, 60062 Tel (847) 291-9933
OAK PARK – ROWAN AT Tangled Web Fibers, 177 S Oak Park Road, 60302, Tel (708) 445-8335

INDIANA
Fort Wayne - Cass Street Depot, 1044 Cass Street, 46802 Tel (260) 420-2277
INDIANAPOLIS – ROWAN AT Mass Avenue Knit Shop, 862 Virginia Avenue, 46203 Tel (800) 675-8565
Newburgh – The Village Knitter, 8a West Jennings St. 47630 Tel (812) 842-2360
Valparaiso – Sheeps Clothing, 257 Indiana Ave., 46383 Tel: (219) 462-1700

IOWA
West Des Moines – Purls – The Yarn Studio, 4800 Mills Civic Pkwy., #104, 50265 Tel (515) 223-9000

KANSAS
LAWRENCE - ROWAN AT The Yarn Barn, 930 Mass Ave, 66044 Tel (800) 468-0035

LOUISIANA
New Orleans – Garden District Needleworks Shop, LLC, 2011 Magazine St., 70130 Tel (504) 558 0221, www.gardendistrictneedlework.com

MAINE
FREEPORT - ROWAN AT Grace Robinson & Co, 208 US Rte 1, Ste 1, 04032 Tel (207) 865-6110, www.yarnandneedlepoint.com
Portland – Knit Wit, 247A Congress St., 04101. Tel (207) 774-6444

MARYLAND
BALTIMORE - ROWAN AT Woolworks, 6117 Falls Rd, 21209 Tel (410) 337-9030
Bethesda - Knit and Stitch = Bliss, 4706 Bethesda Ave, 20814 Tel (866) 563-3353 www.knitandstitch.com
Bethesda - Yarns International, 5110 Ridgefield Road, 20816 Tel (301) 913-2980 www.yarnsinternational.com

Rockville – Woolwinders & Knitting, 404 King Farm Blvd, 20850.
Tel (240) 632-9276 www.woolwinders.com
MASSACHUSETTS
BROOKLINE VILLAGE – ROWAN AT A Good Yarn, 4 Station
Street, 02445. Tel (617) 731 4900
CAMBRIDGE – ROWAN AT Woolcott & Co., 61 JFK Street, 02138-
4931 Tel (617) 547-2837
Concord – Needle Arts of Concord, 100 Commonwealth Ave., 01742
Tel: (978) 371-0424
Harvard – The Fiber Loft/Bare Hill Studio, 9 Massachusetts Ave. (Rt. 111)
01451 Tel (978) 456-8669 www.thefiberloft.com
LEXINGTON – ROWAN AT Wild & Woolly Studio, 7A Meriam St,
02420 Tel (781) 861-7717
LENOX – ROWAN AT Colorful Stitches, 48 Main St. 01240
Tel (413) 637-8206 www.colorful-stitches.com
Milton - Snow Goose, 10 Bassett St, Milton Market Pl, 02186,
Tel (617) 698-1190
Needham – The Black Sheep Knitting Co, 1500 Highland Avenue, 02492
Tel(781) 444-0694
Northampton – Northampton Wools, 11 Pleasant St, 01060
Tel (413) 586-4331
UXBRIDGE – ROWAN AT Knitting Garden – 19 Depot St., 01569
Tel (888) 381-9276 www.theknittinggarden.com
MICHIGAN
Ada – Clever Ewe, 7205 Thornapple River Dr., 49301.
Tel: (616) 682-1545
Ann Arbor – Knit a Round Yarn Shop, 2663 Plymouth Rd, 48105
Tel (734) 998-3771
Ann Arbor – Flying Sheep Yarns, 1954 S. Industrial Hwy. Ste.B 48104
Tel (734) 623-1640
BIRMINGHAM - ROWAN AT Knitting Room, 251 Merrill, 48009
Tel (248) 540-3623 www.knittingroom.com
Commerce – Knitters Kove, 4088 Haggerty Road, 48390
Tel (248) 366-8136
HOLLAND – ROWAN AT Lizzie Ann's Wool Company, 54 East 8th
St., 49423 Tel(616) 392-2035
Lambertville – Vintage Yarns, 3478 W. Sterns Rd., 48144
Tel (734) 854 5648 www.vintageyarns.com
Mount Clemens – Sweet Celeste, 64 Cherry St., 48043
Tel (586) 783 6243
Rochester – Skeins on Main Yarn Co, 428 Main Street, 48307
Tel (248) 656-9300
TRAVERSE CITY – ROWAN AT Yarn Quest, 819 S. Garfield Ave.,
49684 Tel: (231) 929-4277
MINNESOTA
Maple Grove – The Yarn Café, 12688 Bass Lake Rd., 55369
Tel (763) 478-2899
MINNEAPOLIS - ROWAN AT Linden Hills Yarn, 2720 W. 43rd St,
55410 Tel (612) 929-1255
MINNEAPOLIS – ROWAN AT Needlework Unlimited, 4420 Drew
Ave., S, 55410 Tel (612) 925-2454 www.needleworkunlimited.com
ST PAUL - ROWAN AT The Yarnery KMK Crafts, 840 Grand Ave.
55105 Tel (651) 222-5793
ST PETER – ROWAN AT Tangled Skein Yarn Shop, 217 W. Park
Row, 56082 Tel: (507) 934-2433
WHITE BEAR LAKE – ROWAN AT A Sheepy Yarn Shoppe, 2185
Third St, 55110 Tel (800) 480-5462
MISSISSIPPI
Natchez – Natchez Needlearts, 508 Franklin Street, 39120
Tel (601) 446-8335
MISSOURI
Florissant – Myer's House/Weaving Dept., 180 Dunn Rd., 63031
Tel (866) 921-7800
Saint Louis – Threadquarters, 717 N. New Ballas Rd., 63141
Tel (314) 432-2555
Springfield – Simply Fibers, 2744 South Campbell Ave., 65807
Tel (417) 881-9276
NEBRASKA
OMAHA - ROWAN AT Personal Threads Boutique,
8025 W Dodge Rd, 68114 Tel (402) 391-7733 www.personalthreads.com
NEVADA
RENO – ROWAN AT Jimmy Beans Wool, 5000 Smithridge Rd.,
#A11, 89502 Tel: (775) 827-9276 www.jimmybeanswool.com
NEW HAMPSHIRE
Nashua – Ewe'll Love It, 100 Main Street, 03060. Tel (603) 578-2630
New London – Knit New London, 428 Main St., 03257
Tel (603) 526-6923
NEW JERSEY
Haddonfield – Woolplay, 22 N. Haddon Ave., 08033
Tel 856 428 0110
Princeton – Glenmarle Woolworks, 301 N. Harrison Street, 08540
Tel (609) 921-3022 www.glenmarlewoolworks.com
RED BANK – ROWAN AT Wooly Monmouth, 9 Monmouth St,
07701 Tel (732) 224-9276
Westfield – Knit A Bit, 66 Elm St., 07090 Tel (908) 301-005
NEW MEXICO
Santa Fe - Needle's Eye, 839 Paseo de Peralta, Ste.O, 87501
Tel (505) 982 0706
NEW YORK
BEDFORD HILLS – ROWAN AT Lee's Yarn Center, 733 N Bedford
Rd, 10507 Tel (914) 244-3400 www.leesyarn.com
New York – Seaport Yarns, 135 William St., 5Fl., 10038
Tel (212) 608-3100
New York City – The Yarn Company, 2274 Broadway, 10024
Tel (212) 787-7878
NEW YORK CITY - ROWAN AT Yarn Connection, 218 Madison
Ave, 10016 Tel (212) 684-5099
New York City - Purl, 137 Sullivan St, 10012 Tel (212) 420-8796
www.purlsoho.com
New York City – Downtown Yarns, 45 Avenue A, 10009
Tel (212) 995-5991
Skaneateles – Elegant Needles, 7 Jordan Street, 13152
Tel (315) 685-9276, www.elegantneedles.com
Staten Island – Yarn Girl, 851 Castleton Ave., 10310
Tel (718) 447 6117
Syosset – Simply Knitting, 39 Berry Hill Road, 11791. Tel (516) 921-0888
NORTH CAROLINA
GREENSBORO – ROWAN AT Yarns Etc., 231 South Elm St, 27401
Tel (336) 370-1233
RALEIGH – ROWAN AT GREAT YARNS, 1208 Ridge Road, 27607
Tel (919) 832-3599
Southern Pines – Bella Filati, 275-B NE Broad St, 28387
Tel: (910) 692-3528, www.bellafilati.com
NORTH DAKOTA
Fargo – Yarn Renaissance, 2615 S. University Drive, 58103
Tel (701) 280-1478

OHIO
CINCINNATI - ROWAN AT One More Stitch, 2030 Madison Road,
45208. Tel (513) 533 1170
CLEVELAND – ROWAN AT Fine Points, 12620 Larchmere Blvd,
44120 Tel (216) 229-6644 www.finepoints.com
Terrace Park - Fiberge, 702 Indian Hill Rd., 45174
Tel (513) 831 9276
Toledo – FiberWorks Knitting & Weaving, 2007 Glendale Ave, 43614.
Tel (419) 389-1821
OKLAHOMA
Guthrie – Sealed with a Kiss, 109 E. Oklahoma, 73044
Tel (405) 282-8649
Tulsa – Naturally Needlepoint, 5800 South Lewis, Ste. 147, 74105
Tel (918) 747-8838
Tulsa – Loops, 2042 Utica Sq., 74114 Tel (918) 742-9276
OREGON
ASHLAND - ROWAN AT Web-sters, 11 North Main St, 97520
Tel (800) 482-9801, www.yarnatwebsters.com
Bend – Juniper Fiberworks, 143 SW Century Dr., Ste. B., 97702
Tel (541) 318-0726, www.juniperfiberworks.com
Bethany – Knitting Bee, 18305 NW West Union Road, 97229
Tel (503) 439-3316
CARLTON – ROWAN AT Woodland Woolworks, 100 E Washington
St., 97111 Tel (800) 547-3725, www.woodlandwoolworks.com
Eugene – The Knit Shop Inc., 2821 Oak St., 97405
Tel: (541) 434-0430
Lake Oswego – Molehill Farm, 16722 SW Boones Ferry Rd., 97035
Tel: (503) 697-9554
PORTLAND– ROWAN AT Lint, 1700 NW Marshall, 97209
Tel (503) 226-8500, www.lintinc.com
Portland – Northwest Wools, 3524 SW Troy St, 97219
Tel (503) 244-5024
PORTLAND – ROWAN AT Yarn Garden, 1413 SE Hawthorne Blvd,
97214 Tel (503) 239-7950
PENNSYLVANIA
Kennett Square – Wool Gathering, 131 East State St., 19348
Tel (610) 444-8236
Lahaska – The Stitch Inn, 5788 Route 202, 18931
Tel (215) 794-4120
PHILADELPHIA - ROWAN AT Rosie's Yarn Cellar, 2017 Locust
Street, 19103 Tel (215) 977-9276
Philadelphia – Tangled Web, 7900 Germantown Ave, 19118
Tel (215) 242-1271
SEWICKLEY – ROWAN AT Yarns Unlimited, 435 Beaver St, 15143
Tel (412) 741-8894
RHODE ISLAND
TIVERTON - ROWAN AT Sakonnet Purls, 3988 Main Rd, 02878
Tel (888) 624-9902 www.letsknit.com
SOUTH CAROLINA
Aiken – Barbara Sue Brodie Needlepoint & Yarn, 345 Hayne Ave., SW,
29801 Tel (803) 644-0990
Charleston – Knit, 87 Wentworth St., 29401 Tel (843) 937-8500
TENNESSEE
Memphis – The Yarn Studio, 816 S. Cooper St., 38104 Tel: (901) 276-5442
NASHVILLE – ROWAN AT Angel Hair Yarn Co, 4117 Hillsboro
Pike, #102, 37215 Tel (615) 269-8833 www.angelhairyarn.com
TEXAS
AUSTIN – ROWAN AT Hill Country Weavers, 1701 South Congress,
78704 Tel (512) 707-7396
HOUSTON – ROWAN AT Yarns 2 Ewe Inc, 603 West 19th St, 77008
Tel (713) 880-5648
PLANO – ROWAN AT Woolie Ewe, 1301 Custer Rd. #328, 75075
Tel (972) 424-3163
San Antonio – The Yarn Barn of San Antonio, 4300 McCullough,
78212 Tel (210) 826-3679
UTAH
Sandy – Unraveled Sheep, 9312 South 700 East, 84070
Tel (801) 255-6833
VERMONT
Essex Junction – Kaleidoscope Yarns, 15 Pearl St., 05452
Tel (802) 288-9200
Norwich – Northern Nights Yarn Shop, 289 Main St., 05055
Tel (802) 649-2000
Woodstock – The Whippletree, 7 Central St, 05091
Tel (802) 457-1325
VIRGINIA
ALEXANDRIA – ROWAN AT Knit Happens Inc, 127A N.
Washington St, 22314 Tel (703) 836-0039
Charlottesville – It's A Stitch Inc, 188 Zan Road 22901.
Tel (434) 973-0331
RICHMOND – ROWAN AT The Knitting Basket, 5812 Grove Ave,
23226 Tel (804) 282-2909
Richmond – Lettuce Knit, 3030 Stony Point Rd., 23235
Tel (804) 323-5777
Vienna – Uniquities, 421-D Church St., NE 22180
Tel (703) 242-0520
Williamsburg – Knitting Sisters, 1915 Pocahontas Trail, 23185
Tel (757) 258-5005
WASHINGTON
BAINBRIDGE ISLAND – ROWAN AT Churchmouse Yarn and
Teas, 118 Madrone Lane, 98110 Tel (206) 780-2686
BELLEVUE – ROWAN AT Hilltop Yarns East, 10635 NE 8th St.,
Ste. 104, 98004 Tel (425) 452-1248
KENT – ROWAN AT Pastimes Yarns & Sitting Room, 321 West
Smith Street, 98032 Tel (877) 520-9276, www.pastimesyarn.com
Mill Creek – Main Street Yarn, 15217 Main St., Ste. 106, 98012
Tel (425) 337-9606
Olympia – Canvas Works, 525 Columbia St., 98501.
Tel (360) 352-4481, www.canvasworks.net
SEATTLE – ROWAN AT The Weaving Works, 4717 Brooklyn Ave,
N.E., 98105 Tel (888) 524-1221 www.weavingworks.com
SEATTLE – ROWAN AT Hilltop Yarn, 2224 Queen Ann Ave. N.,
98109 Tel (206) 282-1332 www.hilltopyarn.com
Seattle – Tricoter, 3121 East Madison St., 98112
Tel (206) 328-6505
Shoreline – Serial Yarn & Tea Shop, 19500 Ballinger Way NE, #110,
98155 Tel (206) 361 7256
Spokane – A Grand Yarn, 1314 S. Grand Blvd., #1, 99202
Tel (509) 455 8213
WISCONSIN
Appleton – ROWAN AT Jane's Knitting Hutch, 132 E. Wisconsin
Ave., 54911 Tel (920) 954-9001
Elm Grove - The Yarn House, 940 Elm Grove Rd, 53122
Tel (262) 786-5660
MILWAUKEE - ROWAN AT Ruhama's, 420 E Silver Spring Dr.,
53217 Tel (888) 669-4726 www.ruhamas.com

Portsmouth – Anne-Louise Wool Shop, 204 Copnor Rd., PO3 5DA. Tel: 023-9264-4242

Romsey – Foster A Hobby, 5 The Cornmarket, SO51 8GB. Tel: 01794 516429

SOUTHAMPTON – ROWAN AT John Lewis, West Quay Shopping Centre, SO15 1GY. Tel: 0238 021 6400 Mail Order

Winchester – C & H Fabrics, 8 High St, SO23 9JX. Tel: 01962 843355 Knitting up service available

HERTFORDSHIRE

Boreham Wood – The Wool Shop, 29 Shenley Road, WD6 1EB. Tel: 0208 9052499 Mail Order

Bushey – Mavis, 44 High Street, WD23 3HL. Tel: 0208 950 5445, www.mavis-crafts.com Mail Order

St Albans – Alison's Wool Shop, 63 Hatfield Road, AL1 4JE. Tel: 01727 833738

WATFORD – ROWAN AT John Lewis, The Harlequin, High St, WD2 8HL. Tel: 01923 244266 Mail Order

WELWYN GARDEN CITY – ROWAN AT John Lewis., AL7 1LT. Tel: 01707 323456 Mail Order

ISLE OF MAN

Peel – Fabric Centre, 2 Crown Street, IM5 1AJ. Tel: 01624 844991 Mail Order

KENT

CANTERBURY – ROWAN AT C & H Fabrics, 2 St George's Street, CT1 2SR. Tel: 01227 459760 Knitting up service available

Deal – Swantitch Ltd, 82-84 High Street, CT14 6EG. Tel: 01304 366915

GREENHITHE – ROWAN AT John Lewis, Bluewater, DA9 9SA. Tel: 01322 624123 Mail Order

Maidstone – C & H Fabrics, 68 Week Street, ME14 1RJ. Tel: 01622 762060 Knitting up service available

Pettswood – Curtain Scene, 115 Queensway, BR5 1DG. Tel: 01689 822654

Sevenoaks – The Curtain Scene, 5 London Road, TN13 1AH. Tel: 01732 459708 Email: enquiries@uknit.co.uk, www.uknit.co.uk

TUNBRIDGE WELLS – ROWAN AT C & H Fabrics, 113/115 Mount Pleasant, TN1 1QS. Tel: 01892 522618 Knitting up service available

LANCASHIRE

BARNOLDSWICK – ROWAN AT Whichcrafts?, 29 Church St, BB18 5UR. Tel: 01282 851003 Email: crafts@whichcrafts.co.uk, www.whichcrafts.co.uk Mail Order

Preston – Bow Peep, 136 Liverpool Road (next to the Red Lion), Longton, PR4 5AU. Tel: 01772 614508 Mail Order

RAMSBOTTOM – ROWAN AT Clark Craft Products, Empire Works, Railway Street, Bury, BL0 9AS. Tel: 01706 826479

LEICESTERSHIRE

Hinckley – Busy Fingers, 104 Castle Street, LE10 1DD. Tel: 01455 631033

Leicester – Ryte Lynes, 4 Shaftesbury Road, LE3 0QN. Tel: 0116 254 1063 Mail Order

Leicester – Button Boutique, 8-10 Malcolm Arcade, Cank Street, LE1 4FT. Tel: 0116 271 9707

MOUNTSORREL – ROWAN AT Blackberry Yarns, 89/91 Loughborough Road, LE12 7AP. Tel: 0116 237 6171 Mail Order www.blackberry-yarns.co.uk

LINCOLNSHIRE

Lincoln – Needle 'N' Craft, 15 Sincil Street, LN5 7ET. Tel: 01522 529339

LONDON – CENTRAL

ROWAN AT Liberty, Regent St, W1. Tel: 020 7734 1234 Mail Order

ROWAN AT John Lewis, Oxford Street, W1. Tel: 020 7629 7711 Mail Order

ROWAN AT Peter Jones, Sloane Square, SW1. Tel: 020 7730 3434 Mail Order

Chiswick – Creations, 29 Turnham Green Terrace, W4 1RS. Tel: 020 8747 9697 Mail Order, Knitting up service available

LONDON – NORTH

ROWAN AT John Lewis, Brent Cross Shopping Centre, NW4. Tel: 020 8202 6535 Mail Order

Finsbury Park - Lenarow, 169 Blackstock Road, N4 2JS. Tel: 020 7359 1274 Email: michael@lenarow.co.uk, www.lenarow.co.uk

LONDON – SOUTH

Barnes – Creations, 79 Church Road, SW13 9HH. Tel: 020 8563 2970 Mail Order, Knitting up service available

LONDON – WEST

West Ealing – Bunty's at Daniels, 132-138 Uxbridge Road, W13 8QS. Tel: 020 8567 8729 Email: enquiries@bunty-wool.co.uk, www.bunty-wool.co.uk

MERSEYSIDE

LIVERPOOL – ROWAN AT John Lewis, Basnett Street, L24 9HH. Tel: 0151 709 7070 Mail Order

Prescot – Prescot Knitting Co Limited, 32 Eccleston Street, L34 5QJ. Tel: 0151 426 5264

St Helens – The Knitting Centre, 9 Westfield Street, WA10 1QA. Tel: 01744 23993

MIDDLESEX

Shepperton – Arts & Yarns, Squires Garden Centre, Halliford Road, TW17 8RU. Tel: 01932 781141 Mail Order

MONMOUTHSHIRE (ALSO SEE WALES)

Monmouth – B's Hive, 20/22 Church Street, NP25 3BU. Tel: 01600 713548 Mail Order, Knitting up service available

NORFOLK

Diss – Diss Wool & Craft Shop, 2 Cobbs Yard, St Nicholas Street, IP22 4LB. Tel: 01379 650640

East Dereham – Central Norfolk Knitting Machines, 4 Aldiss Court, NR19 1TS. Tel: 01362 694744

NORWICH – ROWAN AT John Lewis, All Saints Green, NR1 3LX. Tel: 01603 660021 Mail Order

Norwich – Norwich Sewing Centre, 1 St Augustine Street, NR3 1LQ. Tel: 01603 621147

Sheringham – Creative Crafts, 47 Station Road, NR26 8RG. Tel: 01263 823153 Email: info@creative-crafts.co.uk, www.creative-crafts.co.uk

NORTHAMPTONSHIRE

Weedon – The Bramble Patch, West Street, NN12 8HP. Tel: 01327 342212 Email: patchwork@thebramblepatch.co.uk, www.thebramblepatch.co.uk

NOTTINGHAMSHIRE

Beeston – Yarn, 55 Chilwell Road, NG9 1EN. Tel: 0115 925 3606, www.yarn-in-notts.co.uk

NOTTINGHAM – ROWAN AT John Lewis, Victoria Centre, NG1 3QA. Tel: 0115 941 8282 Mail Order

OXFORDSHIRE

Abingdon – Masons, 39 Stert Street, OX14 3JF. Tel: 01235 520107

BURFORD – ROWAN AT Burford Needlecraft Shop, 117 High St, OX18 4RG. Tel: 01993 822136 Email: rbx20@dial.pipex.com, www.needlework.co.uk Mail Order

SHETLAND ISLES

Lerwick – Fibres, 133 Commercial Street, ZE1 0DL. Tel: 01595 695575

SHROPSHIRE

Shrewsbury – R.K.M., 4A Roushill, SY1 1PQ. Tel: 01743 245623, www.rkmwools.co.uk

SOMERSET

Minehead – Jana Henrie, High St, Porlock, TA24 8SP. Tel: 01643 862058

Taunton – Hayes Wools Ltd, 150 East Reach, TA1 3HT Tel: 01823 284768

Wincanton – Good Yarns, 38 High St, BA9 9JF. Tel: 01963 33834

STAFFORDSHIRE

Lichfield – The Knitting Corner, Unit 6, Curborough Hall Farm, Watery Lane, WS13 8ES

NEWCASTLE-UNDER-LYME – ROWAN AT K2 Tog, 97 High Street, Wolstanton, ST5 0EP. Tel: 01782 862332 Email: sales@cucumberpatch.com, www.cucumberpatch.com Mail Order

Stafford – Knits & Kneedles, 7 Northwalls, ST16 3AD. Tel: 01785 224221.

SUFFOLK

Wickham Market – Quilters Haven Ltd, 68 High St, IP13 0QU. Tel: 01728 746275, Email: quilters.haven@btinternet.com, www.quilters-haven.co.uk Mail Order

Woodbridge – Anjays Fabrics, 11 Gobbitts Yard, IP12 1DD. Tel: 01394 387593

SURREY

Camberley – Army & Navy, 45-51 Park Street, GU15 3PG. Tel: 08701 607230

Caterham on the Hill – The Yarn House, 27 High Street, CR3 5UE. Tel: 01883 345220, Email: sales@theyarnhouse.co.uk, www.theyarnhouse.co.uk

Cheam – Whichcraft, 7 Station Road, SM3 8SD. Tel: 0208 643 3211

GUILDFORD – ROWAN AT Pandora, 196 High Street, GU1 3HZ. Tel: 01483 572558 Email: sales@stitch1knit1.com, www.stitch1knit1.com

KINGSTON – ROWAN AT John Lewis, Wood Street, KT1 1TE. Tel: 020 8547 3000 Mail Order

EAST SUSSEX

BRIGHTON – ROWAN AT C & H Fabrics, 179 Western Road, BN1 2BA. Tel: 01273 321959 Knitting up service available

Eastbourne – C & H Fabrics, 82/86 Terminus Road, BN21 3LX. Tel: 01323 410428 Knitting up service available

FOREST ROW – ROWAN AT Village Crafts, The Square, RH18 5ES. Tel: 01342 823238. Email: village.crafts@virgin.net or shop@village-crafts.co.uk, www.village-crafts.co.uk

WEST SUSSEX

ARUNDEL – ROWAN AT David's Needle-Art, 37 Tarrant Street, BN18 9DG. Tel: 01903 882761 Fax: 01903 885822 Mail Order

Chichester – C & H Fabrics, 33/34 North Street, PO19 1LX. Tel: 01243 783300 Knitting up service available

Horsham – The Fabric Shop, 62 Swan Walk, RH12 1PT. Tel: 01403 217945

SHOREHAM BY SEA – ROWAN AT Shoreham Knitting, 19 East Street, BN43 5ZE. Tel: 01273 461029 Fax: 01273 465407 Email: sales@englishyarns.co.uk, www.englishyarns.co.uk Mail Order

Worthing – The Fabric Shop, 55 Chapel Road, BN11 1EF. Tel: 01903 207389 Mail Order

TEESIDE (FORMERLY CLEVELAND)

HARTLEPOOL – ROWAN AT Bobby Davison, 101 Park Road, TS26 9HP. Tel: 01429 861300 Email: sales@woolsworldwide.com, www.woolsworldwide.com Mail Order

TYNE AND WEAR

NEWCASTLE UPON TYNE – ROWAN AT John Lewis, Eldon Sq, NE99 1AB. Tel: 0191 232 5000 Mail Order

Whitley Bay – Ring a Rosie, 169 Park View, NE26 3RE. Tel: 0191 252 8874

WARWICKSHIRE

Leamington Spa – Web of Wool, 53 Regent Grove, Holly Walk, CV32 4PA. Tel: 01926 311614, www.webofwool.co.uk

SHIPSTON-ON-STOUR – ROWAN AT Shipston-on-Stour Needlecraft, 24/26 Sheep Street, CV36 4AF. Tel: 01608 661616

Warwick – Warwick Wools, 17 Market Place, CV34 4SA. Tel: 01926 492853 Mail Order

WEST MIDLANDS

BIRMINGHAM – ROWAN AT House of Fraser, Corporation Street, B2 5JS. Tel: 0121 236 3333

Coventry – Busy Fingers, 29 City Arcade, CV1 3HX. Tel: 02476 559644 Mail Order, Knitting up service available

Coventry – Mrs T's, 55 Winsford Avenue, Allesley Park, CV5 9JG. Tel: 02467 713105 Mail Order, Knitting up service available

SOLIHULL – ROWAN AT John Lewis, Touchwood, B90 4SH. Tel: 0121 704 1121 Mail Order

WOLVERHAMPTON – ROWAN AT Beatties, 71-78 Victoria Street, WV1 3PQ. Tel: 01902 422311 Mail Order

WILTSHIRE

Calne – Handi Wools, 3 Oxford Road, SN11 8AA. Tel: 01249 812081

Pewsey – The Wool Shop, 45-47 North Street, SN9 5ES. Tel: 01672 564585

Trowbridge – Fabric Magic, Station Approach, Off Stallard Street, BA14 8HW. Tel: 01225 768833

WORCESTERSHIRE

Kidderminster – Woolwise, 10 Lower Mill Street, DY11 6UO. Tel: 01562 820279 Email: shop@woolwise.co.uk, www.woolwise.co.uk

Malvern – The Knitting Parlour, 4A Graham Road, WR1 2HN. Tel: 01684 892079, www.theknittingparlour.co.uk, Mail Order

NORTH YORKSHIRE

Filey – Beachcomber, 35 Bellevue St, YO14 9HV. Tel: 01723 514434

KNARESBOROUGH – ROWAN AT Sheepish, 2 Market Place, HG5 9AG. Tel: 01423 864390 Mail Order, Knitting up service available

NR SKIPTON – ROWAN AT Embsay Crafts, Embsay Mills, Embsay, BD23 6QF. Tel/Fax: 01756 700946 Mail Order E-mail: enquiries@embsaycrafts.com www.embsaycrafts.com

WHITBY – ROWAN AT Bobbins, Wesley Hall, Church Street., YO22 4DE. Tel/Fax: 01947 600585 Email: bobbins@globalnet.co.uk, www.bobbins.co.uk Mail Order

YORK – ROWAN AT Craft Basics, 9 Gillygate, YO31 7EA Tel: 01904 652840 Mail Order

YORK – ROWAN AT Sheepish, 46 The Shambles, YO1 7LX. Tel: 01904 627595 Knitting up service available Mail Order

SOUTH YORKSHIRE

SHEFFIELD – ROWAN AT John Lewis, Barkers Pool, S1 1EP. Tel: 0114 2768511 Mail Order

WEST YORKSHIRE

Castleford – Bromley & Vairy, 5 Vickers Street, WF10 4AA. Tel: 01977 603069

HEBDEN BRIDGE – ROWAN AT Attica, 3 Garden Street, HX7 3AQ. Tel: 01422 844327 Email: info@attica-yarns.co.uk, www.attica-yarns.co.uk Mail Order

HOLMFIRTH – ROWAN AT Up Country, 78 Huddersfield Road, HD9 3AZ. Tel/Fax: 01484 687803, Email: info@upcountry.co.uk, www.upcountry.co.uk Mail Order

Leeds – The Wool Shop, Whingate Junction, Tong Road, LS12 4NQ. Tel: 0113 263 8383

THE WIRRAL

BRIMSTAGE – ROWAN AT Voirrey Embroidery Centre, Brimstage Hall, CH63 6JA. Tel: 0151 342 3514, Fax: 0151 342 5161

WALES

Aberystwyth – Clare's, 13 Great Darkgate Street, SY23 1DE. Tel: 01970 617786 Mail Order, Knitting up service available

Anglesey – Copperfield, Four Mile Bridge Road, Valley, LL65 4HB. Tel: 01407 740982 Mail Order

Conwy – Ar-y-Gweill, 8 Heol Yr Orsaf, Llanrwst, LL26 0EP. Tel: 01492 641149 Mail Order, Knitting up service available

Fishguard – Jane's of Fishguard, 14 High Street, SA65 9AR. Tel: 01348 874443 Mail Order, Knitting up service available

Monmouth – (see sep. county heading Monmouthshire for stockist details)

Penarth – Yarn & Yarns, 22 Cornerswell Road, CF64 2UZ. Tel: 02920 712097

SWANSEA – ROWAN AT Mrs Mac's, 2 Woodville Road, Mumbles, SA3 4AD. Tel: 01792 369820 Mail Order, Knitting up service

WHITLAND – ROWAN AT Colourway, Market St, SA34 0AJ. Tel: 01994 241333 Email: shop@colourway.co.uk, www.colourway.co.uk Mail Order

SCOTLAND

Aberdeen – John Lewis, George Street, AB9 1BT. Tel: 01224 625000 Mail Order

ALFORD – ROWAN AT The Wool Shed, Alford Heritage Centre, Mart Road, AB33 8BZ. Tel: 01975 562906 Mail Order Knitting up service available

Castle Douglas – Art 2 Go, 130-132 King Street, DG7 1LU. Tel: 01556 504923

EDINBURGH – ROWAN AT John Lewis, St James Centre, EH1 3SP. Tel: 0131 556 9121 Mail Order

EDINBURGH – ROWAN AT Jenners, 48 Princes Street., EH2 2YJ. Tel: 0131 225 2442 Mail Order

EDINBURGH – ROWAN AT HK handknit.co.uk, 83 Bruntsfield Place, EH10 4HG. Tel: 0131 228 1551 Email: julie@handknit.co.uk, www.handknit.co.uk Mail Order

GLASGOW – ROWAN AT John Lewis, Buchanan Galleries, G4 0BZ. Tel: 0141 353 6677 Mail Order

Hamilton – Stitching Time, 14 Haddon Street, ML3 7HX. Tel: 01698 424025 Mail Order

Isle of Arran – Trareoch Craft Shop, Balmichael Visitors Centre, Shiskine, KA27 8DP. Tel: 01770 860515

Kelso – Woolly Ewe, 7 Abbey Court, TD5 7JA. Tel: 01573 225889

Lanark – Strands, 8 Bloomgate, ML11 9ET. Tel: 01555 665757 Mail Order

Newburgh – Twist Fibre Craft Studio, 88 High Street, Fife, KY14 6AQ. Tel: 01337 842843 Email: enquiries@twistfibrecraft.co.uk, www.twistfibrecraft.co.uk Mail Order

ST ANDREWS – ROWAN AT Di Gilpin @ The Wool Merchants, Burghers Close, 141 South St, KY16 9UN. Tel: 01334 476193, Email: di@handknitwear.com, www.handknitwear.com

STIRLING – ROWAN AT McAree Bros Ltd., 55-59 King St, FK8 1DN. Tel: 01786 465646 Fax: 01786 464759 www.mcadirect.com, Mail Order

Troon – Fankle Wools & Needlecrafts, 25b Portland St, KA10 6AA. Tel: 01292 318873 Email: enquiries@fankle.co.uk, www.fankle.co.uk

Ullapool – Unlimited Colour Company, 2A Latheron Centre. Tel/Fax: 01854 612844 Email: polly@ucolour.co.uk, Mail Order

Rowan Internet Stockists

All Rowan Internet stockists offer secure online shopping facilities of a wide selection of Rowan products.
* denotes retail store and internet

AUSTRALIA
www.sunspun.com.au*
www.woolshack.com*

DENMARK
www.tribsen.com

GERMANY
www.wolleundesign.de*

JAPAN
www.rowan-jaeger.com

KOREA
www.myknit.com*

SWEDEN
www.wincentgarner.se*

UK
www.colourway.co.uk*
www.cucumberpatch.com*
www.englishyarns.co.uk*
www.mcadirect.com*
www.upcountry.co.uk*
www.celticove.com*
www.kangaroo.uk.com
www.laughinghens.com
www.angelyarns.com
www.getknitted.com
www.coolwoolz.co.uk

USA
www.colorful-stitches.com*
www.handworksgallery.com*
www.jimmybeanswools.com*
www.theknittinggarden.com
www.royalyarns.com
www.yarnmarket.com

ROWAN YARNS, GREEN LANE MILL, HOLMFIRTH, WEST YORKSHIRE, ENGLAND TEL: +44 (0)1484 681881

AUTUMN
WINTER
2006/07

CONTENTS